Advocacy Organizations

Advocacy organizations are viewed as actors motivated primarily by principled beliefs. This volume outlines a new agenda for the study of advocacy organizations, proposing a model of NGOs as collective actors that seek to fulfill normative concerns and instrumental incentives, face collective action problems, and compete as well as collaborate with other advocacy actors. The analogy of the firm is a useful way of studying advocacy actors because individuals, via advocacy NGOs, make choices which are analytically similar to those that shareholders make in the context of firms. The authors view advocacy NGOs as special types of firms that make strategic choices in policy markets which, along with creating public goods, support organizational survival, visibility, and growth. Advocacy NGOs' strategy can therefore be understood as a response to opportunities to supply distinct advocacy products to well-defined constituencies, as well as a response to normative or principled concerns.

ASEEM PRAKASH is Professor of Political Science and the Walker Family Professor for the Arts and Sciences at the University of Washington, Seattle.

MARY KAY GUGERTY is Associate Professor in the Daniel J. Evans School of Public Affairs at the University of Washington, Seattle.

Advocacy Organizations and Collective Action

Edited by

Aseem Prakash

and

Mary Kay Gugerty

CAMBRIDGE
UNIVERSITY PRESS

CAMBRIDGE UNIVERSITY PRESS
Cambridge, New York, Melbourne, Madrid, Cape Town, Singapore,
São Paulo, Delhi, Dubai, Tokyo, Mexico City

Cambridge University Press
The Edinburgh Building, Cambridge CB2 8RU, UK

Published in the United States of America by Cambridge University Press,
New York

www.cambridge.org
Information on this title: www.cambridge.org/9780521139670

First published 2010

Printed in the United Kingdom at the University Press, Cambridge

A catalogue record for this publication is available from the British Library

Library of Congress Cataloguing in Publication data
Advocacy organizations and collective action / edited by Aseem Prakash,
Mary Kay Gugerty.
    p. cm.
ISBN 978-0-521-19838-7 (hardback) – ISBN 978-0-521-13967-0 (paperback)
1. Pressure groups. 2. Social advocacy. I. Prakash, Aseem. II. Gugerty,
Mary Kay. III. Title.
JF529.A38 2010
322.4–dc22
                                                            2010031214

ISBN 978-0-521-19838-7 Hardback
ISBN 978-0-521-13967-0 Paperback

To Mummy and Papa – Aseem
To Mom and Dad – Mary Kay

Contents

Figures and tables

Figures

Tables

Contributors

MARYANN BARAKSO earned her PhD at MIT and is currently Assistant Professor in the Department of Political Science at the University of Massachusetts Amherst. Her research and publications explore the factors influencing the strategic and tactical choices of interest groups and the political and civic implications of those choices. She also considers the conditions under which interest groups facilitate membership representation and participation in the polity. She is the author of *Governing NOW: Grassroots Activism in the National Organization for Women* (Cambridge University Press, 2004). Her published articles include a forthcoming piece that examines the factors contributing to interest group density across American communities (*British Journal of Politics*); an analysis of the levels of democracy in women's membership associations (*Politics and Gender*, 2007); and an article explaining variation in levels of organizational democracy in advocacy groups (*American Politics Research*, 2008). She is president-elect of the Women and Politics Research Section of the American Political Science Association.

ELIZABETH A. BLOODGOOD is Assistant Professor in the Department of Political Science at Concordia University. She is currently working on a book entitled *Information and Influence: NGO Advocacy and Foreign Policy in the United States and the United Kingdom*. Her research ranges from the politics of expertise and the formation of epistemic communities to the use of the complex adaptive systems approach to understand networking, lobbying, and the survival of international non-governmental organizations in the international system. She has received grants from the Fonds de recherche sur la société et la culture (FQRSC) of Quebec, the Canadian Department of National Defence, the Centre d'étude des politiques étrangères et de sécurité (CEPES), and the Social Science Research Council. Prior to coming to Concordia University, Beth taught at the University of Pennsylvania and Dartmouth College.

CLIFFORD BOB is Associate Professor in Duquesne University's Political Science Department. He is the author of *The Marketing of Rebellion: Insurgents, Media, and International Activism* (Cambridge University Press, 2005) which won the 2007 International Studies Association Best Book Award, co-won the 2007 North Central Sociological Association Scholarly Achievement Award, and was named a "Top Book of 2006" by *The Globalist*. His edited volume *The International Struggle for New Human Rights* was published in 2009, and he has published widely in sociology, political science, law, and policy journals including *International Politics*, *American Journal of International Law*, *Foreign Policy*, *Human Rights Quarterly*, and *Social Problems*. His research has been supported by the American Council of Learned Societies, the Social Science Research Council, the United States Institute of Peace, the Smith Richardson Foundation, the Carr Center for Human Rights (Harvard University), and the Albert Einstein Institution. He holds a PhD from MIT, a JD from NYU, and a BA *magna cum laude* from Harvard.

ALEXANDER COOLEY is Associate Professor of Political Science at Barnard College, Columbia University. His research examines the organizational and sovereign politics of international contracts and transnational contracting actors, with a regional focus on the Caucasus and Central Asia. He is the author of three books, including *Contracting States: Sovereign Transfers in International Relations* (2009, co-authored with Hendrik Spruyt). His research has been supported by the the Open Society Institute, the German Marshall Fund, the Carnegie Corporation, the Smith Richardson Foundation, and the Social Science Research Council.

ANTHONY J. GILL earned his PhD at UCLA and currently is Professor of Political Science at the University of Washington. He specializes in the political economy of religion and has written two books on the topic: *Rendering unto Caesar: The Catholic Church and the State in Latin America* (1998) and *The Political Origins of Religious Liberty* (Cambridge University Press, 2007). Professor Gill is currently studying contemporary challenges to religious liberty in the United States, including how property rights are manipulated by local governments to prohibit the construction or expansion of churches.

MARY KAY GUGERTY is Associate Professor at the Daniel J. Evans School of Public Affairs at the University of Washington. Her research interests focus on governance and the emergence and design of collective action institutions among individuals and organizations, particularly in developing countries. She is the co-editor of *Voluntary Regulation of NGOs and Nonprofits: An Accountability Club Framework* (Cambridge University Press, 2010). Her research has been published in the *American Journal of Political Science*, *Economic Development and Cultural Change*, the *Journal of Public Economics*, and *Public Administration and Development*, among others. She earned her PhD in Political Economy and Government at Harvard University and holds a Masters in Public Administration from the John F. Kennedy School of Government at Harvard.

SARAH L. HENDERSON is Associate Professor of Political Science at Oregon State University. She is the author of *Building Democracy in Contemporary Russia: Western Support for Grassroots Organizations* (2003). She works in the areas of democratization and civil society in Russia and Central and Eastern Europe as well as on issues pertaining to gender and postcommunism. Her research has been funded by the National Council for East European and Eurasian Research, the US Department of State, University Affiliations Program, and the Smith Richardson Foundation. Professor Henderson received her BA in Politics from Oberlin College, and her MA and PhD in Political Science from the University of Colorado.

JESSE D. LECY is a PhD student in the Social Science program at the Maxwell School of Citizenship and Public Affairs, Syracuse University. Previously, he worked in the field of humanitarian relief prior to earning a Masters in Public Policy at Carnegie-Mellon. His research focuses on structural components of collective action problems in civil society and how incentive systems influence NGO behavior. He also works on empirical issues of poverty measurement and the modeling of development interventions in communities.

GEORGE E. MITCHELL is a PhD candidate in Political Science at the Maxwell School of Citizenship and Public Affairs, Syracuse University. He holds MAs in Economics and Political Science from Syracuse University and a BS in Economics from West Virginia University. He has been a research assistant with the Transnational NGO Initiative at the Moynihan Institute of Global Affairs and a consultant with the Center for a New American Security in Washington, DC. Prior to joining the Maxwell School he was a research analyst for Halliburton/ KBR in the Middle East.

STEVEN J. PFAFF is Associate Professor of Sociology at the University of Washington. He works in the areas of historical and comparative sociology, collective action, and the sociology of religion. His articles have appeared in the *American Journal of Sociology, Social Forces,* the *Journal for the Scientific Study of Religion, Theory and Society,* and *Comparative Political Studies.* A study of collective action in the revolutions of 1989, *Exit-Voice Dynamics and the Collapse of East Germany,* was published in 2006 and won the President's Award of the Social Science History Association.

ASEEM PRAKASH is Professor of Political Science and the Walker Family Professor for the Arts and Sciences at the University of Washington. He is the founding General Editor of the Cambridge University Press series on Business and Public Policy and the co-editor of the *Journal of Policy Analysis and Management.* He is the author of *Greening the Firm: The Politics of Corporate Environmentalism* (Cambridge University Press, 2000), the co-author of *The Voluntary Environmentalists: Green Clubs, ISO 14001, and Voluntary Environmental Regulations* (Cambridge University Press, 2006). His recent co-edited books include *Voluntary Regulation of NGOs and Nonprofits: An Accountability Club Framework* (Cambridge University Press, 2010) and *Voluntary Programs: A Club Theory Perspective* (2009).

SARAH B. PRALLE is Associate Professor of Political Science at the Maxwell School of Citizenship and Public Affairs, Syracuse University. She is the author of *Branching Out, Digging In: Environmental Advocacy and Agenda Setting* (2006), which examines advocacy group strategies in Canadian and US forestry politics. She researches and writes about the policy process, with a particular focus on environmental politics and policy. Her research has been published in *Political Science Quarterly,* the *Journal of Public Policy, Policy Studies Journal,* and other outlets. Her current research project examines state environmental litigation in the United States.

THOMAS RISSE is Professor of International Politics at the Otto Suhr Institute for Political Science, Freie Universität Berlin. He co-directs the collaborative research center "Governance in Areas of Limited Statehood" at the Freie Universität Berlin and the research college "The Transformative Power of Europe," both funded by the German Research Foundation. He has taught at the European University Institute, Florence and at the University of Konstanz, as well as at Harvard, Stanford, Yale, and Cornell Universities, and the University of Wyoming. His most recent publications include *A Community of Europeans? Transnational Identities and Public Spheres* (2010), *Governing without a State? Governance in Areas of Limited Statehood*

(2010), and *The End of the West. Crisis and Change in the Atlantic Order* (2008, co-edited with Jeffrey Anderson and G. John Ikenberry).

JAMES RON is Associate Professor in the Norman Paterson School of International Affairs at Carleton University, where he teaches human security, human rights, and qualitative research methods. His current research focuses on the sustainability of rights-based NGOs in the global South, drawing on a cross-regional survey and interviews. In years past, Ron published on political violence, international NGOs, human rights, and field research methods.

HANS PETER SCHMITZ is Associate Professor of Political Science at the Maxwell School of Citizenship and Public Affairs, Syracuse University. He is the author of *Transnational Mobilization and Domestic Regime Change: Africa in Comparative Perspective* (2006). His journal publications include articles in *Comparative Politics*, *International Studies Review*, *Human Rights Quarterly*, and *Zeitschrift für Internationale Beziehungen*. His current research focuses on the nature and effectiveness of transnational activism as well as emerging accountability mechanisms for non-state actors. He is a co-recipient of a National Science Foundation grant aimed at developing a baseline study of transnational non-governmental organizations active on issues of conflict resolution, environmental protection, human rights, humanitarian relief, and sustainable development.

McGEE YOUNG is Assistant Professor of Political Science at Marquette University. He received his PhD from Syracuse University in 2004. He is the author of *Developing Interests: Organizational Change and the Politics of Advocacy* (2010). His other publications include articles in *Polity* and *Studies in American Political Development*. Young was a Pre-Doctoral Fellow in the American Political Development Program at the Miller Center of Public Affairs of the University of Virginia in 2002–03.

Preface

This volume outlines a new agenda for the study of advocacy. We focus on particular advocacy actors, NGO advocacy organizations, involved in public advocacy. We begin with the premise that since advocacy is a collective endeavor, advocacy NGOs should be viewed as actors pursuing collective action. Collective action issues should therefore bear upon their emergence and strategies. We draw on the firm analogy, modeling advocacy NGOs as "firms" operating in competitive policy markets. The firm analogy is instructive because individuals via advocacy NGOs make analytically similar choices regarding the collective organization of their social, political, and economic activities.

The book makes three contributions to the study of advocacy. First, unlike the dominant NGO politics and social movement literatures that tend to focus on advocacy *campaigns*, our book focuses on advocacy *actors*, specifically their emergence and strategies. Second, we outline a new way of thinking about advocacy actors. While many advocacy NGOs are motivated by normative goals, they have instrumental objectives as well. They operate in competitive arenas for funds, media visibility, and support from well-defined constituencies. They pay attention to organization survival and growth. We systematically examine how *both* normative and instrumental concerns influence their emergence and strategies. Third, by employing the collective action perspective to study advocacy, this volume seeks to integrate the study of advocacy in the broader collective action research program. This should foster greater analytical clarity regarding advocacy NGOs' emergence and strategies, and support analytic comparisons across various types of NGO as well as comparisons of advocacy NGOs with other forms of collective action.

Acknowledgments

We began working on this project in the summer of 2007. We developed an introductory concept chapter and carefully identified scholars doing interesting work on NGO advocacy. Thanks to generous financial support from the Center for International Business Education Research (CIBER) and additional support from the Lindenberg Center and the West European Studies Center, all at the University of Washington, we organized a workshop for the authors at the University of Washington in May 2008. At this workshop, the contributors presented the first drafts of their chapters. They received valuable feedback from each other and from UW graduate students and faculty who served as discussants. These were: Stephan Hamberg, Joaquin Herranz, Christopher Heurlin, Erica Johnson, Sanjeev Khagram, Stephen Page, Robert Pekkanen, and Scott Radnitz. After the workshop, we provided detailed feedback on every chapter. The chapters were revised in the summer and early fall of 2008. The result is a series of very strong chapters which respond to the theoretical framework outlined in the introductory chapter and which cohere. We believe the empirical chapters together make the volume greater than the sum of its individual contributions.

Chapter 1 draws on material from "NGO Research Program: A Collective Action Perspective" by Erica Johnson and Aseem Prakash in *Policy Sciences*, 40(3): 221–240 (2007) and is published with kind permission from Springer Science + Business Media.

A portion of Chapter 2 is taken from *Developing Interests: Organizational Change and the Politics of Advocacy* by McGee Young and is published with the permission of the publisher. © 2010 University Press of Kansas.

Chapter 8 draws on material from "The NGO Scramble: Organizational Insecurity and the Political Economy of Transnational Action" by Alexander Cooley and James Ron in *International Security*, 17(1): 5–39 (2002) and is published with permission from MIT Press.

We express our gratitude to John Haslam, the commissioning editor, for his support for this project. Finally, we would like to acknowledge the support we have received from our families over the years. We gratefully dedicate this volume to our respective parents.

1   Advocacy organizations and collective action: an introduction

Aseem Prakash and Mary Kay Gugerty

The volume outlines a new agenda for the study of advocacy organizations, which are often known as non-governmental organizations (NGOs) and social movement organizations. Instead of viewing advocacy NGOs as actors that are primarily motivated by principled beliefs, immune from collective action challenges, and prone to collaborating with other advocacy actors, we suggest modeling NGOs as collective actors that seek to fulfill both normative concerns and instrumental incentives, face collective action problems, and compete as well as collaborate with other advocacy actors that function in the same issue area. Because advocacy NGOs and firms share important characteristics (notwithstanding their differences), the firm analogy, we suggest, is an analytically useful way of studying advocacy actors.

The collective action perspective provides a unifying analytical approach to the study of advocacy NGOs and firms (as well as governments) because it directs attention to the core challenges inherent in structuring and managing collective actors. This approach suggests the need to move beyond viewing NGOs as "saints" and firms as "sinners." Indeed, the study of how and why hierarchies, networks, and alliances arise and are maintained in the context of firms can illuminate issues such as how advocacy NGOs and their networks emerge, how they internally organize, and how they strategize. We agree with Thomas Risse (this volume) that scholars interested in examining the structures, policies, and strategies of firms and their networks can derive useful insights from studying advocacy NGOs.

The term "advocacy" suggests systematic efforts (as opposed to sporadic outbursts) by actors that seek to further specific policy goals. Advocacy is integral to politics and not restricted to any particular policy domain. It could pertain to environmental protection, labor issues, healthcare issues, religion, democracy, shareholders' rights, and so on. The targets

This chapter draws on Johnson and Prakash (2007) with kind permission from Springer Science + Business Media.

of advocacy, the actors against whom claims are made, could be governments, businesses, or other advocacy organizations. While advocacy NGOs tend to be prominent and visible in democratic societies that allow freedom of speech and association, advocacy takes place in less democratic settings as well, although the channels and the organizations behind advocacy might differ.

This volume focuses on collective actors involved in public advocacy. We agree with Olson (1965) that Truman's (1951) argument that organized groups emerge in response to shared grievances ignores the supply side of collective action. While the current tendency in the NGO literature to repose faith in shared norms (rather than shared grievances) to solve supply-side issues is problematic, we also argue that discussions about advocacy need to move beyond the traditional Olsonian concerns about selective benefits, group size, and privileged groups. If organizations emerge in response to either shared norms or shared grievances, under what conditions and via what mechanisms do they sustain themselves once these issues become less salient in public discourse? How do they organize internally? Why do they choose specific advocacy strategies? Why do they sometimes collaborate, sometimes compete with other advocates? How do they reinvent themselves to respond to "normal" politics? These are the sorts of questions we think the advocacy literature should systematically examine and we argue that systematic attention to problems of collective action and agency dilemmas can illuminate aspects of NGO behavior that are not well explained by the existing literature.

Most advocacy activity tends to be undertaken by organized actors. Hence, instead of focusing on advocacy campaigns or advocacy (social) movements, our unit of analysis is the advocacy organization.[1] These could be professional organizations consisting of salaried employees with established organizational infrastructures or volunteer organizations representing sustained collective action by non-salaried actors. The broader point is that advocacy needs to be recognized as a collective endeavor and advocacy NGOs viewed as collective actors.

We draw on the interest group literature that has examined the challenges in mobilizing individuals for collective action (Olson, 1965; Salisbury, 1969; Walker, 1983; Baumgartner and Leech, 1998; Kollman, 1998; Jordan, Halpin, and Maloney, 2004). This literature identifies several explanations for collective action in groups that are neither small nor

---

[1] We make a distinction between non-governmental organizations formed primarily for service delivery, which we term nonprofits, and advocacy NGOs which we conceive as being formed largely for the purposes of policy advocacy. This volume focuses on the latter only.

"privileged" in the Olsonian sense including the provision of purposive and solidarity benefits for members (Clark and Wilson, 1961), exchange theory focused on benefits derived by collective action entrepreneurs (Salisbury, 1969), and the tendency of individuals to overestimate the impact of their contributions (Moe, 1980). Baumgartner and Leech's (1998) excellent review notes that the majority of interest groups in the United States are in fact professional associations that formed originally for non-political purposes, provide "selective incentives" to members in exchange for resources, and then use excess capacity to engage in lobbying activities. While building on the contributions of the interest group literature, we pay more attention to advocacy strategies and how the broader institutional context, domestic as well as international, affects the demand for and the supply of advocacy. We focus on both cooperation and competition for resources and media visibility among groups with similar objectives.

We view advocacy NGOs as special types of firms which function in policy markets (see also Salisbury, 1969; Jordan and Maloney, 1997; Bosso, 2003). These markets vary in terms of entry and exit barriers, as well as levels of competition, all of which provide organizations with the opportunity to supply distinct products to well-defined constituencies (see Bloodgood and Bob, both in this volume). The structure of policy markets provides opportunities for competition and collaboration. Instead of lobbying alone to promote human rights, individuals might create, support, or join a human rights advocacy NGO. Or, instead of agitating by themselves against child labor, individuals might join or support an advocacy NGO agitating on this issue. Thus, the study of collective action via firms can be instructive because individuals, via advocacy NGOs, make choices which are analytically similar to the ones shareholders make in the context of firms regarding the collective organization of their social, political, and economic activities. If conceptualized in this way, interesting theoretical possibilities emerge that help us to systematically study both the demand for and the supply of advocacy. We believe this helps us to uncover new questions in the study of advocacy, and respond to existing questions in ways that are more compelling than (and, in some ways, complementary to, as Risse suggests in Chapter 11) what the extant NGO politics literature provides.

NGO politics is a well-studied topic in political science as well as in sociology through the study of social movements. These literatures have documented hundreds of cases where advocacy actors have successfully influenced public policy and, in some cases, business policies (McAdam, McCarthy, and Zald, 1996; Keck and Sikkink, 1998; Tarrow, 1998; Berry, 1999). By and large, these scholars have focused on advocacy *campaigns* rather than advocacy *organizations* – the point of departure for this book.[2] Consequently, this rich empirical material is less helpful in explaining variations in advocacy strategies, funding strategies, and organizational structures across advocacy NGOs, and within a given organization across its organizational life cycle.

Even in the context of advocacy campaigns, the existing NGO literature has the tendency to study small subsets of the NGO population and neglect collective action issues inherent in any collective endeavor. Consequently, this literature is less focused on theoretical questions that bear upon NGOs' emergence (why, where, and when), internal organization (agency and accountability), and organizational strategies (funding and advocacy), and the relationship between emergence, structure, and strategy. The focus on advocacy campaigns, rather than organizations, leads scholars away from examining the tradeoffs facing individual organizations on issues such as what types and quantities of resources they will contribute to particular campaigns and the conflicts in agreeing on inter-organizational structures for advocacy networks. In other words, existing literature tends to focus on harmony within networks based on the implicit assumption that common normative goals tend to dominate over the interests of individual organizations. We do not share this view of the world as being populated by either saints (with principled beliefs) or sinners (following instrumental concerns). We believe that while NGO actions are certainly informed by (liberal) normative concerns, NGOs also pay close attention to instrumental concerns that bear upon organizational survival and growth.[3] They deploy resources in strategic ways and compete and cooperate with other "firms" in the same industry.

Our perspective is novel because much of the existing NGO literature (especially in political science) finds few commonalities between firms and NGOs.[4] Keck and Sikkink (1998), probably *the* leading authority on

---

[2] Exceptions include Bosso (2003) and Grossman (2006), who study environmental advocacy organizations. Khagram (2004) differentiates advocacy organizations, coalitions, networks, and movements from campaigns. In the social movement tradition, some scholars study social movement organizations, as opposed to social movements *per se* (McCarthy and Zald, 1977; Soule and King, 2008).

[3] While some political scientists have sought to challenge Putnam's portrayal of the civil society (Berman, 1997; Chambers and Kopstein, 2001), following Keck and Sikkink (1998) much of the recent literature, especially in international relations, seems to study advocacy groups which profess "good" liberal concerns. In contrast, the social movement literature in sociology examines "bad" counter movements alongside "good" social movements (Lo, 1982). As a result, unlike political science NGO literature, "norms" tend not to do the heavy lifting in explaining the strategies and structures of social movement organizations.

[4] While social movement literature tends to follow the dominant narrative of "contentious politics" (Tarrow, 2001), some scholars recognize similarities between NGOs and firms (McCarthy and Zald, 1977; Soule and King, 2008).

NGO advocacy, assert that NGOs, or participants in transnational advocacy networks, are not like firms because of "the centrality of principled beliefs or values in motivating their formations" (1998: 1). Recall that David Truman (1951) has asserted the centrality of shared grievances in the formation of interest groups. While they do not employ the language of demand and supply, arguably, for Keck and Sikkink, principled beliefs explain both the demand side (Who demands collective action?) as well as the supply side of the story (Who is willing to incur the costs of supplying advocacy?). Further, very much like Olson, they do not provide any theory to explain variations in the organization of advocacy actors.

At a more fundamental level, the assertion that firms emerge in response to instrumental concerns while NGOs emerge as a consequence of principled beliefs is empirically problematic, simply because instrumental concerns also shape why NGOs emerge, what objectives they pursue, and what strategies they employ (Sell and Prakash, 2004). NGO scholars might counter that the objectives NGOs pursue translate into policies that create predominantly non-excludable benefits that accrue largely to non-members. Firms, in contrast, pursue policies that benefit their shareholders only. Hence, the instrumental objectives pursued by NGOs are qualitatively of a different type (they are more altruistic) than the ones pursued by firms.

On the face of it, this seems a reasonable statement. However, on probing deeper, one can identify its problematic assertions. While NGOs may not generate or distribute profits or surplus to their principals (the so-called non-distribution constraint), they often serve well-defined constituencies and create excludable benefits for them (Sell and Prakash, 2004). Consider the case of labor unions which are identified as NGOs (components of transnational networks) by Keck and Sikkink (1998). Unions agitate for excludable benefits for their members – their vociferous campaign for taxpayer-funded bailout for automobile companies is a recent example (www.uaw.org). On less visible issues, unions often oppose imports, outsourcing, and/or the use of non-union labor. Again, the objective is to protect the "rents" (compensation above the opportunity costs) accruing to their members. It is a stretch to claim that unions are guided by "principled beliefs" and not "instrumental concerns."

Even NGOs that do not explicitly pursue material goals often have well-defined constituencies that reap other types of excludable benefits (see Barakso, this volume). Broadly speaking, NGOs (and firms) can be viewed as seeking to secure three types of benefits for their constituents: material, purposive/expressive, and solidary (Clark and Wilson, 1961; Salisbury, 1969). Material benefits are the sort of instrumental benefits we identified above – profits, jobs, pensions, subsidies, etc. One can think of advocacy groups ranging from the American Association for Retired People to the American Medical Association pursuing such benefits.

Expressive benefits accrue when the organization champions the values of their constituents. Many individuals believe that their world-views are superior and want to shape the society in their preferred image. A problem arises when multiple individuals make assumptions about the superiority of their world-views and those views conflict. Hence, there are culture "wars." Advocating alone, these individuals might find it difficult to influence public policy and might consider collective action via advocacy organizations to be more effective. Or, they may want their views to shape public policy but would rather have somebody else do the heavy lifting. So, they outsource their work to professional advocates and become passive members of the group. Advocacy groups such as the Family Research Council and the Sierra Club seek to create expressive benefits for their constituents; and these are the sort of benefits which these constituents working alone would find it difficult to produce efficiently.

Solidary benefits accrue to group constituents by associating with the organization or its mission. These include socialization, status, and identification. These often have the characteristics of excludable club goods which are non-rival among members but excludable to outsiders. Rotary Clubs and the Veterans of Foreign Wars are illustrative examples of groups seeking to create solidarity benefits.

All of this suggests that the variety of organizations subsumed under the term advocacy organization are motivated by multiple agendas and concerns, some of them ideological and some more instrumental. We therefore contend that advocacy NGOs and firms share more commonalities at the level of organizational motivations and strategies than the existing NGO literature recognizes. The neoclassical economics version of the theory of the firm is based upon a specific understanding of collective action and the conditions under which individuals might cooperate to pursue common goals. Individuals pursue collective action because they believe that by pooling resources and coordinating strategies with like-minded actors they can achieve certain goals more efficiently. Advocacy organizations, like firms, are institutions that embody a set of contracts between principals and agents whose interactions are governed by a system of consolidated control rather than decentralized exchange. While firms and advocacy organizations are non-governmental actors with many analytical similarities, we recognize that they differ in important ways. Unlike firms, advocacy organizations do not have owners with a claim to the residual earnings of the organization. In fact, they often have multiple principals and suffer from the multiple-principal problem.

Furthermore, to align managerial incentives with the organizational objectives, the numerous principals cannot promise a part of the residual to NGO managers, even though NGOs (particularly those involved in service-delivery as well as advocacy) may generate profits. The absence of a common metric to evaluate the performance of NGOs, and the absence of a market for mergers and acquisitions, further compound agency problems in NGOs (Johnson and Prakash, 2007). Yet, with varying levels of success, advocacy NGOs have found ways to curb agency abuse and mobilize their internal competencies to pursue advocacy objectives. While norms and common ideals can bring together and motivate individuals for collective purposes in NGOs, there is an inadequate appreciation in the literature of the role that individual-level benefits might play in such endeavors.

This book recognizes that advocacy organizations (1) function in competitive policy markets and therefore adopt firm-like characteristics because of structural imperatives (2) like firms, are guided by normative and instrumental concerns, and (3) are committed to organizational survival and growth. As the above discussion suggests, a careful appreciation of the similarities and differences between NGOs and firms can help scholars to employ insights from neoclassical theories of firms to explore the organization and functioning of advocacy NGOs and inform knotty management and policy concerns on NGO accountability, evaluation, and governance.

Institutional emergence and boundaries

Why do advocacy organizations arise? Why do we see varying populations in different sectors? What factors influence varying organizational size in terms of the membership, employees, and budgets of advocacy NGOs? One might argue that advocacy NGOs can arise in response to market and government failures, an explanation that is offered in the context of service delivery NGOs (Hansmann, 1980; Weisbrod, 1991). Since the time of Pigou (1960), scholars have suggested that governmental interventions can correct market failures. Because profit-seeking actors have incentives to externalize costs, governmental intervention may be necessary to compel these actors to internalize such costs (but see Coase, 1960; Ostrom, 1990). However, like firms, governments are also subject to failures for a variety of reasons (Wolf, 1979), including a lack of information about the policy problem, lack of appropriate policy instruments to correct the problem, bureaucratic incompetence, etc. Politicians and bureaucrats also have specific personal objectives and may use governmental instrumentalities to fulfill their own objectives instead of pursuing the broader public interest. Government capture by interest groups, including advocacy organizations, can accentuate governmental failures. Pluralists might suggest that advocacy groups may then arise in order to pressure or persuade governments to fulfill their public obligations.

Advocacy may also arise in response to preference heterogeneities among citizens that impede governments from satisfying every interest, even where governments are acting in the broader public interest. Citizens may therefore try to pressure governments via exit or by exercising voice via advocacy organizations. This also suggests that advocacy for one objective can potentially crowd out the advocacy claims put forth for some other issue area. Advocacy NGOs compete with actors that oppose their claims, with actors that advocate other claims, and with organizations that stake out the same territory and compete directly for the attention of policymakers, publics and donors.

The above explanations highlight the demand side of advocacy. The supply aspects are equally important. After all, even where the motivation for advocacy is clear, individuals must still find ways to organize themselves for the supply of collective advocacy. Collective action is the study of the conditions under which individuals might cooperate to pursue common goals. Individuals pursue collective action because they believe that pooling resources and coordinating strategies with like-minded actors can achieve certain goals more efficiently. Since Olson's (1965) seminal work, it is well recognized that free riding, among other things, impedes the supply of collective action when actors want to reap the benefit of collective action without bearing the costs.

As an institution, a firm exemplifies conscious and voluntary decisions by actors regarding the rule structures that will govern collective economic activity. Neoclassical theories of the firm provide a clear exposition of the challenges in the supply of collective action. As an institutional response to market failures, the firm replaces decentralized, anonymous market exchanges with structured, hierarchical exchanges (Coase, 1937; Williamson, 1985). Moreover, theories of the firm have provided valuable insights into principal–agency issues (Berle and Means, 1932) and the institutional arrangements that might mitigate them. Indeed, very much like firms, advocacy NGOs can be modeled as agents working on behalf of specific principals to accomplish specific economic, political, and social goals. As we discuss later, agency issues can also be expected to influence the organizational structures as well as organizational strategies of advocacy NGOs.

Coase (1937) introduced the notion of transaction costs and argued that firms would arise under conditions of complexity and uncertainty, when the transaction costs of developing multiple market contracts could be reduced by vertical integration of the means of production under one owner. Williamson (1985) provided more clarity on why firms (as hierarchies) arise and how they are organized. He linked the emergence of transaction costs in decentralized exchanges to asset specificity under conditions of bounded rationality and opportunism. Given the difficulties of writing contracts to cover all contingencies, he hypothesized that the "make or buy" decision – a firm's dilemma about whether to make its own inputs or to outsource the production to another firm – is contingent on the level of specificity entailed in a transaction: the greater the asset specificity and resulting level of necessary investment, the greater is the likelihood that the transaction would be undertaken within the firm's internal hierarchy. Williamson's logic provided a falsifiable hypothesis to predict the boundary of any firm and why make–buy decisions vary across firms and industries.[5] Scholars have used this logic to study the structure of the firm and membership in business alliances and networks (Dyer, 1996).

The issue of subcontracting-induced opportunism (the so-called "hold-up" problem) is less relevant for the study of advocacy NGOs than for firms. However, the broader issue of opportunism is quite relevant to organizational structure and strategies in formal advocacy organizations. The literature on nonprofit organizations (as opposed to advocacy NGOs) has long recognized that nonprofits are subject to collective action dilemmas of their own (Prakash and Gugerty, 2010). The non-distribution constraint may not fully prevent opportunistic behavior since it provides only a "negative" protection against potential malfeasance, rather than providing positive incentives for managerial performance (Ben-Nur and Gui, 2003; Gugerty and Prakash, 2010). In the case of advocacy organizations, we might hypothesize that formal advocacy organizations with employees are more likely to arise in complicated issue areas that require investments to develop substantial expertise, or on issues that are transnational in nature, where high levels of uncertainty and information asymmetry make it difficult to create contracts covering all contingencies.

While the dominant, neoclassical perspective on the emergence of firms focuses on transaction cost issues, some scholars suggest a transaction-cost-based efficiency considerations alone provide under-specified explanations. While firms might emerge to economize on costs of labor's opportunism, it is not clear how hierarchies (as opposed to arm's length contracting) suffice to mitigate managers' opportunism versus labor,

---

[5] For a recent survey of empirical research on transaction cost economics, see Macher and Richman (2008).

hierarchical failure as Miller (1992) puts it.[6] These scholars suggest that firms should not be viewed as emerging simply to mitigate market failures; leaders play a crucial role in their emergence and policies (Barnard, 1938; Prakash, 2000),[7] a theme also emphasized in organizational theory (Luthans, 1995). The argument is that leaders can build a shared vision and consensus, thereby reducing the costs of organizing collective action. Indeed, the literature on political entrepreneurship suggests the crucial role of leaders in organizing collective action in political arenas (Schneider and Teske, 1992). Thus, in addition to transaction cost issues, this volume urges careful attention to the role of leaders in the emergence and sustenance of advocacy organizations (Salisbury, 1969; Young, this volume).

Organizational structures

It is critical to appreciate that while NGOs are "institutions" in the sense of being rule systems, they also constitute "organizations" in terms of being physical entities with personnel, budgets, and offices. To coordinate the activities of their advocacy work-force, most established advocacy NGOs tend to have formal structures with clear job descriptions, similar to the ones displayed by multidivisional firms. A quick look at Amnesty International's website (web.amnesty.org/jobs) reveals the "job opportunities" available at this organization. As of October 6, 2007, Amnesty was recruiting for an "Adviser on International Organizations" for the International Law and Organizations, a researcher for the Middle East and North Africa Program, a consultant for developing a system to record information on individuals, and so on. Thus, the preeminent human rights advocacy NGO seems to be organized like other bureaucracies (and hierarchies), in which individuals have job descriptions, are located in specific divisions, and are subjected to rules and regulations of the organization.[8] How do such bureaucracies identify what to advocate and then organize advocacy campaigns? Can the study of for-profit bureaucracies illuminate our understanding of NGO advocacy bureaucracies?

---

[6] Miller (1992) suggests that to manage hierarchical failure, firms try to homogenize preferences and instill common organizational cultures.

[7] Oliver Williamson (1990) has edited a very interesting volume which examines Barnard's seminal contributions to organizational theory.

[8] While the compensation offered by Amnesty might seem low relative to that offered by firms, one must remember that most firms tend to operate on a small scale and do not compensate their employees well. Further, before comparing compensation in large NGOs and large firms, one needs to account for self-selection issues: the compensation of a typical employee is often linked to factors such as her educational attainment and prior experience.

Organizational structures are important because they bear upon organizational strategies and vice versa. Advocacy NGOs can be expected to strategize carefully about the issues for which they want to agitate, the tactics they wish to employ, and the organizational structures to achieve these goals. If they cannot effectively pursue a policy goal alone, they might create or join networks or alliances and pool resources with like-minded NGOs. Even when working in networks with like-minded actors, however, NGO activists are unlikely to be oblivious to the imperatives of organizational survival. As in the case of firms, cooperation and competition will go hand in hand. NGOs will seek to protect their interests, especially to take credit if their efforts succeed; after all, publicity is the oxygen for advocacy organizational survival. Furthermore, if membership in a network compels them to invest resources that are not fungible (say, resources that cannot be transferred from one advocacy campaign to another), they might be wary of committing such resources lest a competing NGO assume a leadership position and corner the fame and publicity. It follows that for NGO networks to function smoothly and not be consumed by internal bickering, rules are required to match investments and benefits for each network member. As these suggestions imply, employing insights from the theories of firms generates falsifiable hypotheses that carefully investigate NGOs' strategies.

In sum, NGOs are not spontaneous institutions in Hayekian terms. There is often agency involved to ensure that advocates will come together and seek to coordinate and sustain collective action. Oftentimes, NGOs will rely on implicit or explicit structures or organizational rules to address collective action issues. Studying these structures and rule systems provides a means for understanding and systematically explaining the strategic choices made by NGOs.

Agency conflicts and accountability

An agent is an actor who "acts for" a principal (Mitnick, 1982). Agency conflicts arise when agents do not act according to the wishes of the principals. Instead, they act in response to their own preferences, which do not necessarily cohere with those of the principals (Berle and Means, 1932; for a review, Shapiro, 2005). As managerial theories of the firm (Marris, 1964) and the budget-maximizing model of public bureaucracies (Niskanen, 1971) suggest, managers seek power and prestige by increasing the departmental headcount and budgets at the cost of the organizational missions. We believe advocacy NGOs are also vulnerable to such agency conflicts.

Why agency conflicts? Information asymmetries are often identified as the key culprit responsible for agency conflicts (Prakash and Gugerty,

2010). There are other causes as well. Principals may not adequately define and communicate their preferences to agents, leaving the agents with discretion on how to interpret principals' desires. Agency conflicts are inevitable when agents work for multiple principals with conflicting preferences – and nonprofits are particularly vulnerable to this situation.

Advocacy NGOs can be viewed as agents charged by (multiple) principals to advocate specific issues (Cooley and Ron, this volume). Principals have resources to fund activities that they cherish but cannot undertake themselves. Some actors organized as advocacy NGOs have the capacities or the inclinations to undertake these activities but do not have resources to do so, or at least on the scale that they would like. This creates an opportunity for an exchange (Salisbury, 1969): principals can provide resources to agents on the assumption that agents will undertake specific activities in certain ways. Advocacy is outsourced by concerned individuals to actors who have the organizational capacities and willingness to do it.

These principals could include individual members as well as private donors. Arguably, the publics on behalf of which advocacy NGOs agitate are *de facto* principals as well – as the burgeoning accountability literature points out. While the fund providers expect NGOs to utilize their funds judiciously and agitate about issues that are salient to them, they often do not have the capacities adequately to monitor NGOs' day-to-day operations, or judge their effectiveness.

In firms, shareholders create institutions to mitigate agency conflict. Within the firm, the board of directors is expected to serve as the shareholders' watchdog. Externally, regulators acting on the shareholders' behalf create rules to constrain managerial abuses. Further, executive compensation may be tied to profitability, and the market for mergers and takeovers empowers shareholders *vis-à-vis* managers (Manne, 1965). Because agency conflict is a neglected issue in the NGO literature, scholars tend to ignore how NGOs might (or ought to) establish internal institutions to mitigate it and how this, in turn, influences organizational strategy and performance. In some ways, this omission is emblematic of a normative bias in the NGO scholarship that has led to (1) the modeling of NGOs as non-instrumental actors seeking to serve public purposes and implicitly assuming that individuals work for NGOs for non-instrumental reasons, and (2) a focus only on successful cases of NGO advocacy to the neglect of failed endeavors (Price, 2003) – failures in which agency conflicts may be a contributing cause.

Recent work on NGOs (the second-generation or revisionist scholarship as one might label it), however, has made progress in addressing this normative bias by analyzing the impact of agency conflict on NGO action

(Henderson, 2002; Wapner, 2002; Cooley and Ron, this volume). For example, the body of work on post-Soviet civil society development finds that NGOs are often "ghettoized" and are more responsive to their foreign donors than the communities and individuals they were created to serve (Henderson, 2002; Mendelson and Glenn, 2002). Moreover in their cross-regional case studies, Cooley and Ron (this volume) suggest modeling the relations between donors, contractors, and recipients as a double set of "principal–agent" problems. Likewise, nonprofit research finds that nonprofit actors claim multiple levels of accountability and are more driven by upward accountability to managers, donors, trustees, and boards of governors, rather than by downward accountability to those whose interests the organizations claim to promote (Christensen and Ebrahim, 2006; Gugerty and Prakash, 2010). In addition, the mechanisms for enforcing upward or external accountability to donors lead NGOs and funders to focus on short-term accountability at the expense of longer-term strategic processes which are necessary for long-term social and political changes (Ebrahim, 2003).

NGOs make claims about legitimacy and differentiate themselves from instrumental actors such as firms with the assertion that they serve the public interest. Revisionists, nevertheless, suggest that NGOs also pursue very parochial interests and often have no clear internal democratic characteristics to counter agency loss (Edwards and Hulme, 1996). Compounding these problems, NGOs mostly have appointed, rather than elected, leaders and those who are elected are generally chosen by a small group of like-minded advisors or directors. While NGOs claim to represent the public interest, their accountability does not arise from the same democratic bases as some parties and governments (Grant and Keohane, 2005: 37–38).

Wapner (2002) also argues that organizational structures and goals complicate NGO transparency and responsiveness to various principals. Rather than being free to act on their own, NGOs must advance the concerns of their principals and, while these individuals usually share similar ideological stances, they are rarely homogeneous. In addition, NGOs must cooperate, coordinate, and compromise with other NGOs to advance their causes in networks; they must adjust their strategies, goals, and relationships to appear attractive to states in order to influence policy or state behavior; and, finally, to the extent that they work to influence international governmental organizations, NGOs must demonstrate deference toward international NGOs and associated international regimes. Moreover, in several countries NGOs are subject to more stringent reporting about their finances and activities because of their tax-exempt status. All these examples add layers of accountability to NGO activities and, to the degree that they fail to exhibit responsiveness, NGOs risk their very survival (Meyer, 1999; Wapner, 2002).

Wapner correctly points out different types of accountability to which NGOs might be subject,[9] but he fails to address the issue of agency conflict (accentuated by the multiple-principal issue), which is likely to cause accountability problems. These problems are compounded because, without benchmarking, which allows comparisons of firms with their peers based on similar Standard Industrial Classification (SIC), it is difficult to assess an NGO's performance relative to its competitors. Spar and Dail (2002) propose a classification system similar to the SIC composed of ten broad categories in which NGOs operate. Such a classification might make it easier for potential members and donors to assess how NGOs are "performing" in a given industry.[10]

While measuring the performance of a service-delivery nonprofit might be possible – for example, an industry benchmark might be based on firms and government agencies working in the same industry – how would one benchmark the performance of advocacy NGOs (Covey, 1995; Edwards and Hulme, 1996; Fowler, 1997)? Would my membership dollars have more impact on public policy via Greenpeace or via Friends of the Earth? What types of proxy might a potential member employ? Further, even if such information were available, in the absence of a stock market where shares are listed and performance scrutinized by "reputational intermediaries" (thereby forcing managers to pay attention to profits) and in the absence of a market for mergers and acquisitions (which allow shareholders to remove non-performing managers), how would external institutions enforce accountability? While NGOs might have many conceptual similarities with firms, they are not embedded in an institutional environment that creates incentives for their managers to behave responsibly. In other words, *the potential for agency abuse is far greater in NGOs than in business firms.* Anticipating this, the adverse selection problem in recruiting managers (agents) is likely to be more accentuated in NGOs than in firms. Hence, the institutional design to mitigate agency abuse needs *more attention, not less* in the NGO literature.

Resource acquisition strategies Organizations require scarce resources to survive and they acquire such resources from the external

---

[9] For different types of accountability, see Grant and Keohane (2005: 35–37) and Rubenstein (2007).

[10] Such rating systems by watchdog organizations have been established for service delivery nonprofits. See, for example, Charity Navigator (www.charitynavigator.org). To the best of our knowledge, no such systems exist for rating the use of funds by, or performance of, advocacy NGOs.

environment. Salaries have to be paid, research must be done, and plac-
ards and banners for protests supplied. Advocacy NGO scholars, however, have not paid much attention to how NGOs acquire material
resources to sustain their activities. Implicitly, they suggest that non-
material, value-oriented motivations suffice to sustain collective action.
While early social movement scholars acknowledged that the quantity
and type of resources affect organizations' strategies and structures
(Gamson, 1975; McCarthy and Zald, 1977), subsequent work has under-
emphasized the resource mobilization theory in favor of issues of political
opportunity structures, framing, and organizational infrastructures
(McAdam, McCarthy, and Zald, 1996). In doing so, these scholars have
not adequately explored how resource acquisition influences NGO advocacy strategies, and how the pursuit of resources can move NGOs away
from their stated objectives and normative orientations. In fact, the imperatives for resource acquisition might be a primary motivator of the agency
conflicts discussed above that make advocacy NGOs less responsive to the
objectives of members and/or constituencies, the presumed principals, and
more attentive to the requirements of the donors (Christensen and
Ebrahim, 2006).

Recent NGO scholarship has begun to acknowledge this important
omission. This new line of research examines how reconciling material
pressures and normative motivations produces outcomes at odds with the
expectations of the NGO literature (Henderson, 2002; Cooley and Ron,
this volume). The alleged value-orientations and "good" intentions of
NGOs do not necessarily lead either to desired policy outcomes or induce
cooperation among NGOs that have similar normative motivations (Bob,
2005; Bob, this volume). Similarly, this alleged value orientation does not
lead NGOs to focus on most egregious violations;[11] indeed they choose
their advocacy issues strategically and as a result, the less egregious but
more media-appealing issues become salient on the international agenda.
Worse still, anticipating such strategic behavior by the gatekeeper transi-
tional advocacy networks, local NGOs often repackage their grievances to
make themselves appealing to such gatekeepers.

Issue selection is also influenced by politics within NGO networks, a
topic that tends to be glossed over in the NGO literature. Carpenter
(2007) challenges an important claim put forth by Keck and Sikkink
(1998) regarding the effect of network density on advocacy. Her study
of the non-adoption of the issue of children born of wartime rape suggests

---

[11] Nicolas De Torrente, the executive director of Doctors Without Borders, famously noted:
"We find out where conditions are the worst – the places where others are not going – and
that's where we want to be." (www.letterstofriends.com/links.html)

some egregious abuses fail to get attention of advocacy networks, not only because of problems with the issue itself, its visibility, or shaky legal precedent. Rather, she lays the blame at the doorstep of inter-network politics.

There is a further problem. An important claim in the NGO literature is that the values or norms these actors propound are universal norms. There is little discussion of an alternative argument: global advocacy by well-resourced Northern advocacy groups is another manifestation of hegemony (Bob, this volume). It may be a projection of US norms and reproduce global inequities. Some scholars point to the crucial role of foundations in creating organizational fields within which such advocacy groups function (Bartley, 2007). This is highly problematic for some scholars. Vogel (2007) suggests that, given that most of these foundations are American and their class interests cohere with that of the US state, they are likely to fund those advocacy organizations that articulate the interests of the US state.

This situation, of course, raises a host of new questions. If competition is an attribute of instrumental actors seeking private gains, cooperation should be easy among principled, non-instrumental actors seeking to supply public or private goods with widespread positive externalities. Why then do we see presumably non-selfish, principled actors competing for material resources in ways similar to profit-seeking firms competing for market share?

These revisionist NGO scholars make important progress in this regard, but go only half-way in recognizing that NGOs can be expected to compete like firms for resources. From the perspective of individual NGOs, membership and foundation dollars acquire the characteristics of rival goods – if I have them, you don't (Bob, this volume; Cooley and Ron, this volume). While the salience of these resources is likely to vary across NGOs, external funders provide a significant percentage of resources for NGO activities, typically much higher than the average service-delivery nonprofit. This resource-scarce environment creates conditions for NGOs not merely to compete with one another but also to prioritize resource acquisition over their real objectives, including faithfully working toward principals' (members') goals.

Indeed, NGOs do look and behave like firms, facing similar constraints regarding resource mobilization, organizational dynamics, and competition for market share. Exploring the relationship between foreign aid and the development of civil society organizations in post-Soviet Russia, Henderson (2002) finds that in order to safeguard their own funding, these groups do not share their grant ideas. Cooley and Ron (this volume) also emphasize that the increasing marketization of NGO activities, as demonstrated by the use of competitive tenders and renewable contracting, "generates incentives that produce dysfunctional outcomes."

While this emerging literature makes important inroads, it blames the environment in which NGOs function for inducing these firm-like behaviors and does not recognize that such behavior is inherent to any organization. Let us assume that the competitive environment is indeed at fault. Imagine a perfect world in which a monopolist NGO occupied every sector and donors did not invite multiple NGOs to compete for the same pool of funds. If revisionists are correct, NGOs would not compete and would stick to their principled objectives. It follows, therefore, and somewhat ironically, that the democracy and pluralism championed by NGO advocates undermine the normative basis of their existence.

Advocacy strategies Explanations for advocacy strategies are among the most advanced topics in the advocacy NGO scholarship. Among political scientists, Keck and Sikkink's (1998) model of transnational advocacy networks (TANs) develops an understanding of the "boomerang effect" to identify how domestic groups draw on international linkages to mobilize external pressure for changing a state's domestic policies. But Keck and Sikkink do not address how different TANs are created and structured, how resources affect the ability of various actors to sustain their efforts, or what principal–agent problems arise when foreign assistance is introduced into domestic politics and to the actors in the network. They also leave unexplored the extent to which domestic advocacy groups modify their agendas to fit with the agendas of international NGOs and how this change affects the strategies they employ and their ability to mobilize domestic constituencies.

Similarly, the social movement literature examines how social movement organizations make strategic use of political opportunity structures (POS) – the degree to which groups are likely to gain access to power and to manipulate the political system, to accomplish their goals (McAdam, McCarthy, and Zald, 1996). Political opportunities are measured in terms of (1) the relative openness of the institutionalized political system (2) the stability of elite alignments (3) the presence of elite allies, and (4) the state's capacity and propensity for repression (McAdam, 1996: 27). The POS concept is used loosely to identify the conditions that facilitate the emergence of social movements *and* the strategies they use in different contexts. In addition, the POS approach (as opposed to the resource mobilization perspective in the social movement literature) offers little explanation for social movement resource mobilization and agency problems.

While some social movement scholars recognize that successful NGOs adopt a variety of strategies that promote their causes, most tend to focus on contentious politics (Tarrow, 2001) as the key organizational strategy. In this view, advocacy NGOs represent new issue demands and political values that are in conflict with the status quo (Rohrschneider and Dalton, 2002; Dalton, Recchia, and Rohrschneider, 2003). The desire to influence policy means that NGOs must choose between the tactics of protesting the political status quo or working within conventional channels to implement new policies. By and large, political science and social movement research expects NGOs to be loosely structured and to engage in "alternative" action repertoires, especially protest activities (Lipsky, 1968; McAdam, 1997). It is argued that unconventional action draws attention to NGOs' causes that would not occur through normal political processes. Again, there is seldom a discussion about resources, organizational structures, or agency problems. Nor can this literature explain how and when NGOs decide to use "insider" versus "outsider" strategies, or the decisions of some NGOs (Oxfam America is one such example) to make explicit decisions to reorient their strategies toward advocacy. The revisionist literature has begun to address these deficits. For example, Ron, Ramos, and Rodgers (2005) examine alternative explanations for the choices made by Amnesty International about the type of campaigns they will pursue. They find that while Amnesty is motivated in part by the severity of human rights violations, considerations of efficacy and visibility play an important role in the choice of campaign. The source and type of funding received by advocacy NGOs may also affect their strategies. As research on the "resource curse" (Ross 2001) and foreign aid (Remmer, 2004) suggests, governments that do not rely on citizens for taxes, become less responsive to them. We might expect that advocacy NGOs that rely on external support from foundations, international financial institutions, and bilateral aid may be more responsive to those constituencies and that this may affect their choice of strategy.

In any issue area (or industry), one can find several NGOs advocating similar policies. Why should citizen A support NGO X over NGO Y? And knowing that members have a choice, how would NGOs respond to make themselves more attractive to potential members? Let us examine how firms respond to such situations. In industries with undifferentiated products (such as generic pharmaceuticals or gasoline distribution), firms expect consumers to prioritize price over other product attributes; hence they seek to be cost leaders. If a firm does not want to play the price game, it seeks to differentiate its product, often via advertising and marketing to artificially set apart its products. In doing so, the firm hopes that consumers will not benchmark its products against lower-priced competitors.

We expect NGOs to behave similarly (see Barakso; Pralle, both in this volume). While the price game (e.g. membership fees) may make less sense in the NGO context (religious organizations may be an exception; see Gill and Pfaff, this volume), the differentiation game is important. NGOs are likely to differentiate themselves either via their "products" or via the strategies employed to supply these products. Thus, competition for membership dollars leads NGOs to exploit preference heterogeneities among potential members and donors.

Some firms differentiate themselves not so much by the product they offer but by the processes employed to supply it. Dolphin-safe tuna may taste no different from other tuna in a blind taste test, yet consumers might pay a premium for the former because they support the fishing process that firms have adopted. Analogously, NGOs might differentiate themselves not by the product they offer but by the processes through which they supply it. Supplying the generic product of environmental protection, Greenpeace differentiates itself via its aggressive advocacy tactics while the Natural Resource Defense Council's distinctiveness lies in legal advocacy skills (Young, this volume). Given these similar responses to competition for market share, theories of the firm offer important lessons for understanding NGO structures and strategies. Indeed, drawing on theories of firms, future research on advocacy should seek to examine how attributes of the sector affect NGOs' incentives to differentiate and brand.

Book outline   Our key claims are (1) NGOs should be viewed as collective actors prone to collective action problems (2) advocacy NGOs are motivated by principled beliefs as well as instrumental concerns, and (3) the collective action approach and the firm analogy can help uncover and explain anomalies that the extant advocacy NGO literature has had difficulty in explaining, such as why some advocacy groups do not collaborate, why they pursue instrumental objectives, and why some focus on lesser problems while ignoring the most egregious abuses. Furthermore, the firm analogy can help explain the emergence and tactics of both "good" NGOs pursing policies that arguably are in the public interest and "bad" NGOs pursuing illegal or ethically questionable ends.

The book provides nine empirical chapters to examine the usefulness of the collective action approach for the study of advocacy NGOs. In addition to this introduction and the concluding chapter that lay out the key theoretical ideas, we have included a dissenting chapter by Thomas Risse, a prominent scholar of the moral or normative advocacy tradition. With the inclusion of this essay, we provide two different perspectives in the same volume. We hope this will encourage a conversation between the moral and the collective action traditions, and help the reader to recognize the strengths and weaknesses of both perspectives.

Following this introductory chapter, the book is organized in four parts. The first part, "The institutional environment and advocacy organizations," examines issues pertaining to the emergence and structure of advocacy NGOs. Chapter 2, "The price of advocacy: mobilization and maintenance in advocacy organizations," is by McGee Young. This chapter examines the emergence of a leading environmental advocacy organization, the Natural Resources Defense Council (NRDC). This organization is distinguished by its focus on employing legal strategies to enforce environmental law through court and administrative law proceedings. By carefully examining the NRDC case, Young illustrates how the political environment, coupled with the material and normative motives of advocacy organization entrepreneurs, influences the supply of advocacy. The chapter examines the formation of NRDC, the development of its organizational structure, and its relationship with other similar environmental organizations. It shows how scholars can begin to appreciate the processes of organizational differentiation and political development that occur among advocacy organizations by considering advocacy organizations as entrepreneurial undertakings, public goods as marketable products, and other organizations as potential competitors. Young outlines how advocacy organizations respond to external stimuli in ways that reflect the fit between their organizational structures and the direction of new political opportunities.

Chapter 3, "Acting in good faith: an economic approach to religious organizations as advocacy groups," is by Anthony Gill and Steven Pfaff. Much of the NGO literature has considered secular advocacy groups or religious groups advocating secular causes. Gill and Pfaff make a forceful argument that scholars need to carefully study religious groups as advocates for religious causes. In doing so, they introduce a new literature to the study of advocacy: the "religious economies" school which draws on microeconomic theory to understand how churches organize and function in a variety of environmental settings. Gill and Pfaff argue that the scholarship on how religious leaders solve collective action problems is especially instructive for researchers studying advocacy groups. The key collective action problem faced by churches is to induce members to contribute voluntarily to the provision of public, club and credence goods. The problem is accentuated because religions are seeking contributions to the production and distribution of unverifiable promises of future benefit (salvation) to a wide range of individuals, in a similar way to secular advocacy groups that seek to promote a better future for humanity or a specific group of constituents. Collective action for churches takes the form of financial support of the church and/or volunteering for activities ranging from providing daycare or crisis counseling to serving as a missionary in a foreign land. The authors illustrate their argument with the help of two examples: the rise of Christianity in the first three centuries of its existence and efforts by Protestant missionaries to establish a presence in Latin America during the last century.

Chapter 4, "Institutional environment and the organization of advocacy NGOs in the OECD," is by Elizabeth Bloodgood. This chapter examines how national legislation within the Organization for Economic Cooperation and Development (OECD) countries has influenced the emergence of advocacy NGOs. From a collective action perspective, national legislation shapes the costs of organization, the incentives available to attract members and financing, barriers to entry in the political marketplace, the organizational forms and legal identities available, and the strategies for advocacy. This chapter investigates the scope and the specificity of national legislation regarding advocacy NGOs within the OECD using a new dataset containing national legislation on rules regarding the legal identity, rights, responsibilities, available resources, and political freedoms for advocacy NGOs among OECD members. The chapter tests two hypotheses. First, given the incomplete convergence in regulations regarding advocacy NGOs, the population of advocacy NGOs is expected to look different across OECD countries as NGOs strategically select where and how to operate. Second, the content of national regulations on access to government decision-making, economic resources, and legal identity is expected to be more concrete, specific, and formal than regulations on speech, protest, or publication. This is because national regulations seek to raise barriers to entry to advocacy NGOs within a country in order to allow decision-makers to select NGOs that are credible sources of information with which they can form constructive partnerships. Thus, decision-makers are expected to carefully regulate access using specific markers of reputation and credibility.

Part 2 of the volume presents empirical studies on advocacy tactics and strategies. Chapter 5, "The market for human rights," is by Clifford Bob. This chapter challenges the dominant perspective, the "moral theory," in NGO politics which views advocacy organizations as "principled" actors. While "moral theory" suggests that international human rights advocates will select causes for support based primarily on the seriousness of the abuses they find, Bob finds these actors selecting causes to support based on instrumental factors. Consequently, the worst-off groups frequently do *not* receive the most support. For him, advocacy groups are not just moral actors but are also organizations committed to their own survival and growth. Thus, like firms, advocacy organizations depend on income (often in the form of donations and grants) and customers (members, foundations, donors, or governments). Bob conceives of the human rights field as a marketplace in which aggrieved local groups "supply" a "product" (information about their grievances), while advocacy organizations "demand" this product and pay for it by providing various forms of support. This market is closely linked to a second market in which the advocacy organizations repackage the aggrieved groups' information and distribute it to international audiences of citizens, media, and foundations, in exchange for donations and grants. Bob's chapter examines the advocacy choices of Amnesty International and shows how demand-side factors, such as the demands of key constituents and supporters, play a critical role in the choice of advocacy targets.

Chapter 6, "Brand identity and the tactical repertoires of advocacy organizations," is by Maryann Barakso. She begins with the assumption that to survive and thrive in politics, advocacy groups must satisfy an internal constituency (their current members and donors) as well as external constituencies (potential members, funders, and policymakers). This chapter examines the extent to which advocacy groups accomplish these imperatives by creating, advertising, and maintaining what we might usefully characterize as their "brand." Like firms, advocacy groups compete with other groups for members, funding, and other crucial resources (such as attention from news media and policymakers). One way an advocacy group might differentiate itself from others in its policy sector is by clearly defining its core identity (signaled via a "brand"), maintaining its integrity, and by advertising it. The chapter considers why some advocacy groups use this strategy more than others, showing how more policy competition increases the use of branding and how the choice of organizational governance affects the likelihood of branding.

Chapter 7, "Shopping around: environmental organizations and the search for policy venues," is by Sarah Pralle. This chapter focuses on how advocates make strategic choices about the venues for their political action. She notes that a collective action perspective assumes that advocacy organizations are acting rationally to achieve goals in a competitive environment. To survive and prosper, they must find ways to distinguish themselves from other organizations that may compete with them for prestige, members, resources, and the like. As such, advocacy organizations may target particular strategic niches and policy venues to distinguish themselves from others. Thus, Pralle expects that different advocacy organizations will display different patterns of venue shopping. She attributes this to variations in internal organizational beliefs and values, organizational resources, the preferences and expertise of leaders, and the nature of an organization's goals. Furthermore, she notes that while most advocacy organizations tend to respond to significant changes in external opportunities and constraints by shifting their strategies and tactics, smaller shifts may not produce dramatic venue shifts if a group has a long-term view of policy change, works within a crowded interest-group environment, and has considerable expertise in a particular venue or arena.

Part 3, "International advocacy and market structures," focuses on advocacy in the international context. Chapter 8, "The political economy of transnational action among international NGOs" by Alexander Cooley and James Ron, shows how increasing marketization of the aid economy and the resulting incentives embedded in the operating environment of NGOs condition their strategies and responses. They examine international NGOs engaged in relief activities after the Rwandan genocide and show how the pressure to obtain contracts and remain active participants in relief activities stifled principled concerns that NGO operations were enabling the continued operation of genocide perpetrators. Similarly in Bosnia, Cooley and Ron document how humanitarian agencies engaged in competition rather than cooperation in prisoner-of-war monitoring. When a number of agencies vied for the first chance at prison inspections, Bosnian prison commanders were able to play one agency off against another, subverting the prisoner protection agenda and actually threatening the welfare of prisoners. In both cases, material incentives such as the concerns about future funding and organizational reputation tended to trump normative concerns. International NGOs, like any other organization, must respond to the challenge of organizational survival.

Chapter 9, "Advocacy organizations, networks, and the firm analogy" is by Jesse Lecy, George Mitchell, and Hans Peter Schmitz. Drawing on an interview study of 182 transnational NGOs, selected on the basis of size, financial efficiency and capacity, and main area of activity (conflict resolution, human rights, humanitarian relief, environmental activism, and sustainable development), this chapter explores how transnational NGO leaders define advocacy and understand the role of partnerships and collaborations in advancing their goals. By understanding how leaders perceive their advocacy efforts as part of transnational networks, Lecy et al. seek to provide a fresh look, illuminating the organizational and strategic choices within the TNGO sector. The chapter reports that the leaders of those NGOs that most clearly define themselves as advocacy organizations view their organizations more as nodes in unbounded social networks than as bounded institutions with clear hierarchies and hard distinctions between "internal" and "external" actors. While advocacy organizations may appear to the outside world as bounded hierarchical organizations with official headquarters, professionalized staff, and unitary objectives, this chapter suggests that this formality is primarily sustained for tax and legal purposes and may be less relevant when describing organizational activity.

Chapter 10, "Shaping civic advocacy: international and domestic policies towards Russia's NGO sector," is by Sarah Henderson. Since the 1990s, scholars have noted the comparative weakness of the Russian third sector, and by extension, civil society. In response to this weakness, a variety of Western organizations have supplied grants and technical assistance to Russian nonprofit organizations in the hope that such assistance would help create a vibrant civil society, capable of organizing citizen interests and lobbying those interests to the state. Despite foreign donors' aspirations, however, their funding strategies often created perverse incentives, orienting NGOs away from local constituencies and toward funders and international agencies. From 2004, President Putin publicly questioned the purpose of such foreign assistance, and the Duma passed a variety of policies with the potential to dramatically reshape the activities and structure of Russia's nonprofit sector. This chapter illustrates the ways in which both international and domestic policies toward Russia's NGO sector constrain and facilitate NGO advocacy. Each set of policies presents a competing view of the nature, purpose, and hoped-for outcome of organized citizen activism. Each approach privileges some organizations and behaviors over others, and facilitates alternative visions of civic advocacy rather than the presence or absence of civic advocacy. However, both approaches will create perverse incentives, just in separate ways.

Part 4, "Toward a new research program," consists of two chapters: Chapter 11, "Rethinking advocacy organizations? A critical comment" by Thomas Risse, and Chapter 12, "Conclusions and future research: rethinking advocacy organizations" by Mary Kay Gugerty and Aseem Prakash. In his dissenting chapter, Risse suggests that, while the collective action perspective provides new insights on established empirical and theoretical questions, it should be viewed as complementing rather than challenging the original advocacy network literature. Further, Risse cautions scholars regarding the limits of employing the firm analogy because advocacy NGOs and firms differ in fundamental ways. He also argues that moral authority and knowledge are the distinctive products that advocacy actors are producing, and that the "market for human rights" therefore functions differently than the "market for automobiles," with reputational concerns playing the disciplinary role that the profit motive plays for firms. Finally, Risse wonders how insights from the advocacy network literature might illuminate questions (such as corporate social responsibility) that scholars studying firms are grappling with.

In the concluding chapter, Gugerty and Prakash pull together the empirical and theoretical findings of the various empirical chapters. In doing so, the chapter highlights both the weaknesses and the strengths of the collective action perspective as an approach for examining the emergence, structure, and strategies of advocacy organizations. They also address the key issues raised by Risse in his chapter. Finally, Gugerty and Prakash identify areas for further research.

References

Barnard, C. 1938. *The Functions of the Executive*. Cambridge, MA: Harvard University Press.

Bartley, T. 2007. How Foundations Shape Social Movements. *Social Problems*, 54(3): 229–255.

Baumgartner, F. R. and B. L. Leech. 1998. *Basic Interests*. Princeton University Press.

Ben-Nur, A. and B. Gui. 2003. The Theory of Nonprofit Organizations Revisited. In H. Anheier and A. Ben-Nur (eds.), *The Study of Nonprofit Enterprise*. New York: Kluwer Academic Publishers.

Berle, A. A. and G. C. Means. 1932. *The Modern Corporation and Private Property*. New York: Harcourt, Brace & World.

Berman, S. 1997. Civil Society and the Collapse of the Weimar Republic. *World Politics* 49(3): 401–429.

Berry, J. 1999. *The New Liberalism*. Washington, DC: Brookings Institution.

Bob, C. 2005. *The Marketing of Rebellion: Insurgents, Media, and International Activism*. Cambridge University Press.

Bosso, C. 2003. Rethinking the Concept of Membership in Nature Advocacy Organizations. *Policy Studies Journal*, 31(3): 397–411.

Carpenter, R. C. 2007. Setting the Advocacy Agenda. *International Studies Quarterly*, 51(1): 99–120.

Chambers, S. and J. Kopstein. 2001. Bad Civil Society. *Political Theory*, 29(6): 837–865.

Christensen, R. A. and A. Ebrahim. 2006. How Does Accountability Affect Mission? *Nonprofit Management and Leadership*, 17(2): 195–209.

Clark, P. B. and J. Q. Wilson 1961. Incentive System: A Theory of Organization. *Administrative Science Quarterly*, 6 (September): 129–166.

Coase, R. H. 1937. The Nature of the Firm. *Economica*, 4: 386–405.
   1960. The Problem of Social Cost. *Journal of Law and Economics*, 3: 1–44.

Covey, J. G. 1995. *Accountability and Effectiveness of NGO Policy Alliance*. IDR Reports, 11(8). Boston: Institute for Development Research.

Dalton, T., S. Recchia, and R. Rohrschneider. 2003. The Environmental Movement and the Modes of Political Action. *Comparative Political Studies*, 36(7): 743–771.

Dyer, J. H. 1996. Does Governance Matter? Keiretsu Alliances and Asset Specificity as Sources of Japanese Competitive Advantage. *Organization Science*, 7(6): 649–666.

Ebrahim, A. 2003. Making Sense of Accountability: Conceptual Perspectives for Northern and Southern Nonprofits. *Nonprofit Management and Leadership*, 14: 191–212.

Edwards, M. and D. Hulme. 1996. Too Close for Comfort? The Impact of Official Aid on Nongovernmental Organizations. *World Development*, 24(6): 961–973.

Fowler, A. 1997. *Striking a Balance*. London: Earthscan.

Gamson, W. A. 1975. *The Strategy of Political Protest*. Homewood, IL: Dorsey.

Grant, R. and R. Keohane. 2005. Accountability and Abuses of Power in World Politics. *American Political Science Review*, 99(1): 29–43.

Grossman, M. 2006. Environmental Advocacy in Washington. *Environmental Politics*, 15(4): 628–638.

Gugerty, M. K. and A. Prakash. 2010. *Voluntary Regulation of NGOs and Nonprofits: An Accountability Club Framework*. Cambridge University Press.

Hansmann, H. 1980. The Role of Nonprofit Enterprise. *Yale Law Review* 89: 835–898.

Henderson, S. 2002. Selling Civil Society: Western Aid and the Nongovernmental Organization Sector in Russia. *Comparative Political Studies*, 35(2): 139–167.

Johnson, E. and A. Prakash. 2007. NGO Research Program: A Collective Action Perspective. *Policy Sciences*, 40(3): 221–240.

Jordan, G. and W. Maloney. 1997. *The Protest Business?* Manchester University Press.

Jordan, G., D. Halpin, and W. Maloney. 2004. Defining Interests. *British Journal of Politics and International Relations*, 6: 195–212.

Keck, M. and K. Sikkink. 1998. *Activists Beyond Borders: Advocacy Networks in International Politics*. Ithaca, NY: Cornell University Press.

Khagram, S. 2004. *Dams and Development*. Ithaca, NY: Cornell University Press.

Kollman, K. 1998. *Outside Lobbying*. Princeton University Press.

Lipsky, M. 1968. Protest as a Political Resource. *American Political Science Review*, 62: 114–158.

Lo, C. Y. H. 1982. Counter Movements and Conservative Movements in the Contemporary U.S. *Annual Review of Sociology*, 8: 107–134.

Luthans, F. 1995. *Organizational Behavior*. New York: McGraw-Hill.

Macher, J. T. and B. D. Richman. 2008. Transaction Cost Economics: An Assessment of Empirical Research in the Social Sciences. *Business and Politics*, 10(1): Article 1.

Manne, H. 1965. Mergers and the Market for Corporate Control. *Journal of Political Economy* 73(2): 110–120.

Marris, R. L. 1964. *The Economic Theory of 'Managerial' Capitalism*. London: Free Press of Glencoe.

McAdam, D. 1996. Conceptual Origin, Current Problems, Future Directions. In D. McAdam, J. D. McCarthy, and M. N. Zald (eds.), *Comparative Perspectives on Social Movements*. Cambridge University Press.

    1997. Tactical Innovation and the Pace of Insurgency. In D. McAdam and D. Snow (eds.), *Social Movements: Readings on Their Emergence, Mobilization and Dynamics*. Los Angeles: Roxbury.

McAdam, D., J. D. McCarthy, and M. N. Zald (eds.). 1996. *Comparative Perspectives on Social Movements*. Cambridge University Press.

McCarthy, J. D. and M. Zald. 1977. Resource Mobilization and Social Movements. *American Journal of Sociology*, 82: 1212–1241.

Mendelson, S. E. and John K. Glenn (eds.). 2002. *The Power and Limits of NGOs.* New York: Columbia University Press.

Meyer, C. A. 1999. *The Economics and Politics of NGOs in Latin America.* Westport, CT: Praeger.

Miller, G. 1992. *Managerial Dilemmas.* Cambridge University Press.

Mitnick, B. 1982. Regulation and the Theory of Agency. *Policy Studies Review,* 1(3): 442–453.

Moe, T. 1980. *The Organization of Interests.* University of Chicago Press.

Niskanen, W. 1971. *Bureaucracy and Representative Government.* Chicago: Aldine-Atherton.

Olson, M. 1965. *The Logic of Collective Action.* Cambridge, MA: Harvard University Press.

Ostrom, E. 1990. *Governing the Commons.* Cambridge University Press.

Pigou, A. 1960 [1920]. *The Economics of Welfare.* London: Macmillan.

Prakash, A. 2000. *Greening the Firm: The Politics of Corporate Environmentalism.* Cambridge University Press.

Prakash, A. and M. K. Gugerty. 2010. Trust but Verify? Voluntary Regulation Programs in the Nonprofit Sector. *Regulation and Governance,* 4(1): 22–47.

Price, R. 2003. Transnational Civil Society and Advocacy in World Politics. *World Politics,* 55: 579–606.

Remmer, K. 2004. Does Foreign Aid Promote the Expansion of Government? *American Journal of Political Science,* 48(1): 77–92.

Rohrschnieder, R. and T. Dalton. 2002. A Global Network? *Journal of Politics,* 54 (2): 510–533.

Ron, J., H. Ramos and K. Rodgers. 2005. Transnational Information Politics: NGO Human Rights Reporting, 1986–2000. *International Studies Quarterly,* 49(3): 557–587.

Ross, M. 2001. Does Oil Hinder Democracy? *World Politics,* 53(3): 325–361.

Rubenstein, J. 2007. Accountability in an Unequal World. *Journal of Politics,* 69 (3): 616–632.

Salisbury, R. H. 1969. An Exchange Theory of Interest Groups. *Midwest Journal of Political Science,* 13(1): 1–32.

Schneider, M. and P. Teske. 1992. Toward a Theory of the Political Entrepreneur. *American Political Science Review,* 86(3): 737–747.

Sell, S. K. and A. Prakash. 2004. Using Ideas Strategically. *International Studies Quarterly,* 48(1): 143–175.

Shapiro, S. P. 2005. Agency Theory. *Annual Review of Sociology,* 31(1): 263–284.

Soule, S. and B. King. 2008. Competition and Resource Partitioning in Three Social Movement Industries. *American Journal of Sociology,* 113(6): 1568–1610.

Spar, D. and J. Dail. 2002. Of Measurement and Mission: Accounting for Performance in Non-Governmental Organizations. *Chicago Journal of International Law,* 3(1): 171–182.

Tarrow, S. G. (ed.). 1998. *Power in Movement: Social Movements and Contentious Politics,* 2nd edn. Cambridge University Press.

  2001. Transnational Politics: Contention and Institutions in International Politics. *Annual Review of Political Science,* 4: 1–20.

Truman, D. 1951. *The Governmental Process.* New York: Alfred Knopf.

Vogel, A. 2007. Who's Making Global Civil Society: Philanthropy and US Empire in World Society. *British Journal of Sociology*, **57**(4): 635–655.

Walker. J. 1983. The Origins and Maintenance of Interest Groups in America. *American Political Science Review*, **77**(2): 390–406.

Wapner, P. 2002. Defending Accountability Mechanisms in NGOs. *Chicago Journal of International Law*, **3**(1): 191–205.

Weisbrod, B. A. 1991. *The Nonprofit Economy*. Cambridge, MA: Harvard University Press.

Williamson, O. 1985. *The Economic Institutions of Capitalism*. New York: Free Press.

Williamson, O. (ed.). 1990. *Organization Theory: From Chester Barnard to the Present and Beyond*. Oxford University Press.

Wolf, C. 1979. Theory of Nonmarket Failure: Framework for Implementation Analysis. *Journal of Law and Economics*, **22**(April): 107–139.

Part 1

The institutional environment and advocacy
organizations

2   The price of advocacy: mobilization and
    maintenance in advocacy organizations

McGee Young

In the late 1960s, growing awareness of environmental issues spurred the
creation of scores of new environmental organizations. In the subsequent
decade, these groups took part in writing or rewriting nearly all of the
United States' environmental statutes. The leading advocacy organizations took different approaches to environmental advocacy: Earth Action
organized students on college campuses; the Sierra Club led conservation
lobbying efforts in Washington, DC; and local groups formed coalitions
of citizens to clean up their towns and neighborhoods (Hays, 1987). Some
local groups, such as the Environmental Defense Fund, grew beyond their
particular issue to become active on wide-ranging national environmental
issues.

One particularly influential advocacy organization was the Natural
Resources Defense Council (NRDC), an organization consisting mainly
of attorneys and dedicated primarily toward the enforcement of environmental law through court and administrative law proceedings. Of all the
groups that emerged out of the environmental fervor of the late 1960s,
none surpassed the NRDC in scope, effectiveness, or importance in
establishing guidelines for environmental protection. Soon after being
founded in 1970, the NRDC established itself as the leading environmental litigation organization in the country and its lawsuits both clarified
and expanded the regulatory scope of federal authority. In short, the
NRDC provides a window into one of the central questions of this
volume: how does a group's political environment, coupled with the
material and normative motives of advocacy organization entrepreneurs,
influence the supply of advocacy?

This chapter examines the formation of the NRDC, the development
of its organizational structure, and the advantages it gained by moving
quickly to capitalize on new opportunities. In pursuing an alternative

A portion of this chapter is taken from *Developing Interests: Organizational Change and the
Politics of Advocacy* by McGee Young and is published with the permission of the publisher.
© 2010 University Press of Kansas.

31

theoretical formulation of the collective action problem facing advocacy organizations, this chapter demonstrates the value of borrowing constructs from theories of firm behavior to advance our understanding of advocacy organizations. When we adopt an analytical perspective that considers advocacy organizations as entrepreneurial undertakings, public goods as marketable products, and other organizations as potential competitors, we begin to see with greater clarity the processes of organizational differentiation and political development that occur among advocacy organizations. Much like we observe firms and industries changing over time as markets evolve, advocacy organizations respond to external stimuli in ways that reflect the fit between existing organizational structures and the direction of new political opportunities. In following the development of the NRDC, this chapter shows how one of the leading environmental organizations in the United States came to inhabit a particular political identity and appropriate a particular set of advocacy tools for achieving its goals. This perspective should be a useful way to understand the development of a wide variety of advocacy organizations, even across different types of polities.

Briefly, the development of the NRDC occurred as follows. The organization was conceived in the late 1960s, when there was great demand for environmental protection and new opportunities for novel approaches to environmental advocacy. The NRDC's founders were lawyers who were inspired to create a "NAACP Legal Defense Fund for the environment." They found a receptive institutional environment in the courts and sustained early political advocacy with a mixture of private and foundation support. To the extent that "collective action" occurred, it was made possible by external actors, primarily the Ford Foundation, which – to use the terminology that I develop later in this chapter – "purchased" the NRDC's collective goods by providing the NRDC with a large grant. Also important was a non-competitive environment in which rival organizations like the Sierra Club Legal Defense Fund impinged neither on the availability of legal resources nor on the number of new cases to litigate. As a first-mover in a sparse field, the NRDC enjoyed the advantage of crafting an advocacy strategy that best fitted the political opportunities of the time rather than one designed to ward off potential competitors. Finally, as political entrepreneurs, the NRDC's founders enjoyed the benefits of policy influence and eventually fame and notoriety that accompanied the growing clout of the organization. When we assemble these pieces – entrepreneurial activity, institutional receptivity, market demand for advocacy products, and limited competition – the advocacy organization begins to more closely resemble the firm, and as we assess the effects of the interactions between these pieces we can shed new light on questions of organizational formation and development.

Collective action and advocacy organizations

The collective action approach provides an opportunity to address questions central to our understanding of political advocacy: what motivates entrepreneurs to form advocacy organizations, and why do some groups pursue different advocacy strategies than others? As Prakash and Gugerty explain in the introductory chapter to this volume, Olson's discussion of collective action deeply influenced our understanding of advocacy organization formation, but on these critical questions the Olsonian approach is quiet (Olson, 1965). Olson explains incidents of successful organization by pointing to the ability of groups to supply members with inducements to participate. Latent groups – those for whom the calculus of membership suggests that they would otherwise not be able to supply themselves with a collective good – will successfully recruit members in two cases: when they can make membership compulsory, as is the case with some labor unions and professional associations, or when they can provide selective benefits to members as an inducement to join (Olson, 1965: 133). Olson calls this a "byproduct" theory of lobbying because, for these large groups, the provision of selective benefits is the primary purpose of the organization. Lobbying can only occur once sufficient resources have been accumulated in the exchange of selective benefits.

While Olson's insights into the problems of collective action are the specific point of departure for this chapter, the collective action approach spelled out in the introductory chapter of this volume allows us to move beyond Olson by addressing not just the limiting effects of collective action problems, but also the emergence and structure of advocacy organizations as entrepreneurial undertakings. We posit that the institutional context of advocacy integrally shapes the formation of organizational identities and the development of political strategies and tactics. For example, as Barakso shows in her chapter, the institutional environment of an advocacy organization both influences organizational branding and lends stability to organizational identities over time. As the NRDC case demonstrates, organizational structure reflects the imperatives of the group's founders, the perception that the chosen institutional access point will be fruitful, and the availability of resources to fund group operations. Our perspective yields insight into the relationships among advocacy organization emergence, the structure of advocacy organizations, and the strategies and tactics that form their repertoires of action, by focusing on advocacy organizations rather than particular advocacy campaigns.

Advocacy organization formation

In seeking to understand the NRDC's emergence as a central actor in the environmental policymaking arena, I engage with two key theoretical questions. First, why do new advocacy organizations emerge? Second, how do the conditions under which advocacy organizations form affect their development? Borrowing from classic theories of firm behavior, we can suggest that formation occurs because formal organization reduces transactions costs by internalizing routine interactions (Coase, 1937; Williamson, 1985). Individuals are much less efficient political actors when acting alone than as part of a group. Indeed, the sorts of collective action problem identified by Olson plague any efforts at political action that require the continued voluntary participation of individuals outside of a formal organization. Consequently, it is important to remember that advocacy organizations represent solutions to the collective action problem rather than manifestations of it.[1] When a group is established, it reflects an effort to consolidate resources and reduce the challenges of voluntary coordinated political participation.

Sustained advocacy efforts require organization, but advocacy groups offer a variety of organizational structures. Some encourage member participation in advocacy efforts and formal decision-making processes, while others restrict participation so that members are primarily sources of revenue for the group (Skocpol, 2003). With the rise of modern advocacy organizations, which typically rely on a professional staff and little participation from members, theories of firm behavior are increasingly relevant to our understanding of their emergence and development. In these latter types of organization managerial hierarchies separate lobbying and political advocacy from organizational maintenance responsibilities, which for a group like the NRDC means that advocacy is not simply a consequence of voluntary association, but rather a product developed and produced by the organization and then marketed and sold to members.[2]

As policy advocates, organizations promise to represent a particular set of interests and, in a variety of different contexts, to pursue a range of tangible benefits for members and/or the broader public. As Olson notes,

---

[1] To be sure, ideological commitments and social pressures are present in most voluntary organizations and may even motivate individuals to participate.
[2] Other selective incentives are typically included, but their value is often tied to the lobbying that provides the organization with its political identity.

these goods are often obtained in forms that are non-rivalrous and non-excludable – they are public goods. However, because of the ambiguity inherent in the policymaking process, such as the difficulty associated with identifying successes and failures or tracing responsibility for outcomes, it is difficult to guarantee particular policy benefits or outcomes to members (Arnold, 1992). Rather, it is the act of lobbying (or political representation) that advocacy organizations can promise to their supporters. Of course, good lobbyists will still claim credit and put a positive spin on outcomes, even those that are suboptimal. But the same type of collective good problem that in the Olsonian paradigm bedevils strictly voluntary associations also challenges formally organized advocacy associations which provide lobbying benefits. That is, the core product that an advocacy organization must market to potential consumers is also a collective good.

If an advocacy organization must sell a product that is freely available to those who might benefit from it regardless of whether or not they choose to purchase a share of it, questions of organizational maintenance become critical to the survival of the association (Salisbury, 1969; Walker, 1991). Absent sufficient customers an advocacy organization will simply go out of business. In contrast to a strictly voluntary association, where the impetus for providing the collective good comes from the share of the collective good that a contributing member might receive, formally organized advocacy organizations decouple the collective good from spillover benefits that accrue within the managerial hierarchy. For example, a manager within the NRDC might share the same collective benefits as a member, but the manager will also enjoy the ability to influence policymaking, develop a set of transferrable career skills, and to a greater or lesser extent earn a living. In effect, formal advocacy organizations are able to bypass internal collective action problems but still face challenges stemming from the fact that they have to try to sell a product that most people would be able to otherwise obtain for free (Nownes and Neeley, 1996: 124).

To be clear here, this claim, that advocacy organizations market collective goods to potential buyers, lies in tension with a key tenet of Olsonian interest group theory. Olson conceived of the collective action problem as a coordination problem among individuals who each stood to benefit from the provision of a collective good.[3] In order to convince the potential recipients to contribute to the costs of providing the public good, Olson suggested that the group would have to provide selective incentives to each of its members. The reason why Olson's perspective is problematic is

---

[3] For a discussion of different problems of coordination and collaboration, see Stein (1982).

that he gave no explanatory mechanism for how the group would provide either the collective good or the selected incentives (Frohlich, Oppenheimer, and Young, 1971; Elster, 1989). As one early critic put it, "[a]ny mechanism designed to insure ... the supply of the good would be a costly collective good itself, benefiting the same individuals who were scheduled to receive the original collective good" (Frohlich, Oppenheimer, and Young, 1971: 18). Thus, what I offer here is a way around this core theoretical problem.

If we further differentiate between the purchase of collective goods and the supply of collective goods, the firm analogy at the heart of this volume becomes more tractable in the context of advocacy organizations. First, the purchase of collective goods need not come from members *per se*; advocacy patrons may also provide the necessary resources for the provision of collective goods. As Walker notes, roughly a third of the advocacy organizations in the United States are made up of representatives of non-profit institutions and much of the funding for these groups comes from federal and state governments (Walker, 1991: 60). Citizens' groups comprise another 20 percent of advocacy organizations; the vast majority of these groups receive at least partial funding from foundations and other sources of private philanthropy. Rather than relying on members (if the organization even has members) to purchase shares of the collective good, these groups operate in a marketplace of large institutional purchasers of their products. Thus, there are multiple categories of buyers to which an advocacy organization may market its advocacy products, including individuals, foundations, business firms, and other associations.

Second, in making this distinction, it is no longer necessary to rest the supply of collective goods on an ambiguous notion that group members put aside their differences and self-interest to create a political organization. Instead, we treat advocacy organization founders much like we would treat business entrepreneurs. The founders of an advocacy organization provide collective goods in order to enjoy spillover benefits from their efforts, apart from any portion of the collective good they might also receive. Just as business entrepreneurs enjoy profits that accompany the sale of a product, advocacy organization entrepreneurs enjoy greater access to policymakers, greater influence over policy decisions, and greater peer recognition as key political players.

The origins of the NRDC illustrate these basic dynamics and demonstrate the utility of analyzing advocacy organizations from this perspective. The political entrepreneurs who founded the NRDC found great value in coordinating what had previously been *ad hoc* advocacy efforts. While convincing large numbers of people to support their efforts by joining as members was initially out of the question, the NRDC's leaders found that the Ford Foundation was receptive to the idea of funding a public interest law firm. In essence, the Ford Foundation agreed to purchase the NRDC's advocacy product until other sources of revenue could be located. With what amounted to a guaranteed market for its advocacy product, the NRDC could focus its attention on mastering the important skills to succeed in its policy domain.

Advocacy organization development

As noted, the problem of organizational maintenance looms large for advocacy organizations that produce and sell public goods. How does an organization stay afloat when its product can be enjoyed irrespective of contributions to the cause? The work of Olson notwithstanding, there is general agreement among interest group scholars that organizational entrepreneurs and patrons play a central role in defraying the expenses associated with organizational maintenance and political advocacy (Salisbury, 1969; Frohlich, Oppenheimer, and Young, 1971; Wilson, 1974; Berry, 1978; Walker, 1991; Imig and Berry, 1996; Nownes and Neeley, 1996; Sheingate, 2003).[4] While patrons provide funding, organizational entrepreneurs forge a political identity that galvanizes support while distinguishing the group's work from that of other similar organizations.

In general terms, organizational maintenance is best achieved when organizations are protected from competition over scarce resources. This can happen in one of two ways. An advocacy organization can be a first-mover and use the strength of its initial position to ward off potential competitors. If a group can quickly establish dominance, for example through strategic branding, rivals may find it difficult to challenge for members or attention from policymakers. For example, once the AARP established itself as the dominant advocacy organization for the elderly, rival organizations could only carve out niche positions on the periphery. Second, if demand is inelastic for an advocacy product, competing groups may occupy the same market niche, but maintain a selling price that supports the fixed costs of multiple organizations. Demand inelasticity makes organizational maintenance possible by expanding the producer surplus associated with the sale of a product. If organizations can create advocacy products that are imperfect substitutes (i.e. it means something different to purchase advocacy from NRDC than it does from the Sierra Club), they can sustain their operations in a market characterized by

---

[4] See also Barnard (1968) and Miller (1992).

monopolistic competition. When citizens, foundations, and private phi-lanthropists are consistently willing to pay above market rates for environ-mental advocacy,[5] organizations can survive without engaging in destructive competition. Absent these conditions, a race to the bottom results and organizations are unable to produce advocacy products at a price high enough to sustain production.[6]

The notion that monopolistic competition supports the production of collective goods originates in efforts by economists to explain private technological development. Technological innovations are typically col-lective goods, and economists have explained their development in terms of spillover effects. In the course of pursuing profits, firms that are pro-tected by monopolistic competition can invest in technological develop-ment without worrying about losing market share (Romer, 1990). In addition to specifying the conditions that make possible the production of knowledge, economists have also recognized that side benefits, pro-duced as part of the production of knowledge, will inherently be *partially excludable*.[7] The producer of a collective good will reap rewards from the process that are not shared with others who receive the collective good. While the excludable portion of benefits is insufficient by itself to justify the production of the collective good, hence the specification of monop-olistic competition, it can be sufficient to *motivate* the production of a collective good.[8]

In the context of advocacy organization development, the availability of excludable benefits is critical because it explains the motivation of political entrepreneurs.[9] The excludable benefits available to advocacy

---

[5] As compared to the equilibrium price where price elasticity is neutral.

[6] For an example of this type of process, see Young (2010: 38–57).

[7] The production of knowledge is a complicated phenomenon because knowledge can be constituted in more than one form. On the one hand, knowledge comprises what we might consider "textbook knowledge," or the gradual accretion of collective understanding about the way the world works. This is knowledge in its collective form available to anyone who possesses the requisite training and skills to comprehend it. On the other hand, every individual holds a particular type of knowledge in the form of what we can call human capital. Human capital of this sort is completely excludable, meaning that whatever improvements are made on it return solely to the individual. The most common types of human capital improvements would include the acquisition of new skills, the adaptability that is learned from engaging with a variety of challenges, and the wisdom that one acquires from a lifetime of experience. See Arrow (1962), Griliches (1992), Mankiw (1995).

[8] The open-source movement serves as an illustrative example of this phenomenon in a market setting. See von Hippel and von Krogh (2003).

[9] There is an extensive discussion in Salisbury (1969) with respect to the motivation of the entrepreneur, in which the decision to organize a group is determined by the potential profitability of the undertaking. Salisbury imagines peripatetic entrepreneurs restlessly searching for the best opportunities to invest capital into new groups. In principle, this notion is consistent with the argument presented here, as Salisbury defines profit very

organization entrepreneurs come in two forms. First, advocacy organization entrepreneurs receive temporary rewards for developing new pressure tactics that provide a strategic advantage in the form of political influence (Vogel, 1989). The rollout of a new strategy may recast the current conflicts of a group in more favorable terms. Second, advocacy organizations enjoy returns on human capital investments.[10] The more a group invests in a strategy, the better the group becomes at implementing that strategy. For example, as NRDC hired more lawyers to implement its strategy of becoming a law firm, the experience of litigating cases created unparalleled expertise among NRDC lawyers. The greater NRDC's expertise, the more effective it became at litigating environmental cases. One important implication of this phenomenon is that choices by advocacy organizations with respect to strategies and tactics are path-dependent. The decision to invest in a particular technique or approach is tantamount to investing in human capital that cannot be transferred to another person or another approach. *The greater the investment of human capital, the more difficult is the decision to reverse course.*

In explaining the necessary conditions to sustain organizational maintenance, we find a theoretical starting point to consider how internal dynamics drive the development of advocacy organizations. When advocacy organizations invest in particular strategies or tactics, they make commitments of resources that are difficult to reverse. Because these investments provide partially excludable benefits, they are central to the motivation of entrepreneurial activity. For example, when a particular strategy or tactic succeeds, the entrepreneur receives accolades and legitimacy as a "true" representative of a set of interests. At a deeper level, authority claims are linked to the organizational identity established early in a group's existence. The more firmly established the organizational identity, the more credible the authority claims that can be made on its behalf. In short, this approach encourages us to examine the way decisions

---

loosely. However, the notion of excludable benefits avoids the connotation of the term *profit* in its strict economic sense and allows for greater nuance in examining the developmental impact of investment decisions.

[10] Lobbyists who stalk the corridors of power also trade in a form of human capital, earned through years of experience in navigating the intricacies of policymaking processes. For the novice lobbyist there is a general knowledge available with respect to the various jurisdictions of power, avenues of authority, and circles of influence. The more seasoned veteran knows which bottle of wine to order at dinner, or, even better, introduces her lobbying target to a new favorite bottle of wine. The more time spent cultivating relationships and honing strategic appeals for support, the more effective the lobbyist will be. Like the computer programmer, the lobbyist generates a collective knowledge about how to exert influence during the policymaking process. At the same time, lobbyists develop distinctive sets of skills, relationships, and experiences that allow them to pursue their targets with ever-greater effectiveness. See Birnbaum (1992) and Nownes (2006).

about organizational form and purpose generate feedback for the way group leaders engage with the political world around them.

Having explored the tenets of organized interest development, I now turn to the case of the NRDC. Using the theoretical tools outlined above, we can identify the important internal and external forces that guided the political development of the NRDC and in turn shaped environmental politics in the United States. Finally, we can address some of the central questions raised in this volume: how do the conditions under which advocacy organizations form affect their subsequent political development? If entrepreneurs are the motive force of advocacy organization formation, what causes groups to adopt particular organizational forms and characteristics?

Scenic Hudson and the origins of the NRDC

In the late 1950s, Consolidated Edison (Con Ed), the huge New York electric company, began to develop plans to build a massive new power plant at the base of Storm King Mountain, located along the Hudson River approximately sixty miles north of New York City. The New York City area faced a skyrocketing demand for electricity as new appliances flooded into the homes of the city's 5 million residents and ever-expanding suburbs. To meet that demand, Con Ed sought to build an additional nuclear reactor at Indian Point and a hydroelectric facility at Storm King Mountain. The plant at Storm King, which became the locus of conflict, would not include a dam, as was common with most hydroelectric facilities. Rather, the Storm King facility would utilize pumped storage. Using electricity generated elsewhere, the plant would pump millions of gallons of water from the Hudson River up to a reservoir behind Storm King Mountain. Then, during periods of high demand for electricity, Con Ed would release water from the reservoir, which would flow through turbines at the base of the mountain, generating additional energy to meet the peak-level demand. If completed, the Storm King Mountain plant would have been the largest of its kind in the world. Although it would use three kilowatts of electricity to pump the water up the mountain for every two kilowatts of electricity generated by the plant, Con Ed stood to reap hefty revenues by pumping water up the mountain during periods of slack demand (when electricity was cheap) and releasing it during periods of high demand (when they could charge significantly more) (Talbot, 1972).

The Federal Power Commission (FPC) considered Storm King relatively straightforward. There was a clear need for the electricity; alternatives were scarce; Con Ed had the wherewithal to build and operate the plant; it would be profitable; and the environmental effects appeared to be benign. Most significantly, the plant would provide power without exacerbating the air pollution problems of the region. But it was exactly the environmental effects that aroused the ire of local residents. Not only was Storm King Mountain itself important, but the Hudson River, despite its considerable pollution, was a vital breeding ground for fish populations. The new plant would substantially impair both the mountain and the river and threaten the beauty of a region that possessed enormous cultural history.

Led by Wall Street lawyer Stephen Duggan, a group of about twelve concerned citizens formed an organization called the Scenic Hudson Preservation Conference to coordinate opposition to the project. Despite an army of volunteers and a substantial public relations campaign on the part of Scenic Hudson, the FPC approved plans to build the plant in 1963. The FPC's criteria for approval were strictly technical. Questions of natural beauty had no relevance to FPC decisions. So Duggan and his partner, Whitney North Seymour, Jr., along with David Sive, filed suit in federal court, arguing that decisions made by the FPC were required by Congressional statute to take into full account the public's interest (*Scenic Hudson Conference* v. *Federal Power Commission*, 1965). Since the FPC had clearly disregarded an important aspect of the public interest by not considering the effect of the power plant on the natural beauty of the area, the court should overturn the permit.

The question that the court grappled with was whether a citizens' group, such as Scenic Hudson, should be granted standing in such a case. The FPC argued that Scenic Hudson had no standing in the case because they did not have an economic stake in the outcome. The court demurred, however, and, in a critical move with far-reaching effects, granted standing to Scenic Hudson on the grounds that a recreational interest is as legitimate as an economic interest in such a case (Sax, 1970). Moreover, the court reprehended the FPC for acting like an "umpire blandly calling balls and strikes" instead of seeking out as much evidence as possible and attempting to find the best possible outcome that would protect natural resources. In this dramatic turnabout, the court substantially curtailed the considerable administrative autonomy enjoyed by the FPC – and the implications were substantial. Although the case lingered in the courts for two decades, the initial decision to grant standing to Scenic Hudson paved the way for future administrative challenges by public interest groups, and environmental groups in particular. More broadly, the decision by the court to grant standing to a public interest group in an administrative procedure case was a pivotal moment in the development of environmental politics. The rationale behind the court's decision would eventually find its way into statutes like the National Environmental Policy Act (NEPA) and the Clean Air Act, as Congress created formal procedures for challenging executive agency decisions.

The three lawyers who initiated the case on behalf of Scenic Hudson – Duggan, Seymour, and Sive – soon realized that the battle they had started was merely an initial skirmish in a conflict that would soon grow much wider. As the case dragged through the courts, the three began discussions about forming a law firm for strictly environmental issues (NRDC, 1995b). As Duggan recalled, "[i]n the fall of 1969, Mike Seymour and I became aware that we were amateurs: we weren't sure if this was a hit-or-miss, one-shot deal of a particular interest. But if we wanted to do anything nationally, we needed a national organization, and to employ lawyers and scientists" (NRDC, 1995a). The three decided to approach the Ford Foundation for the funds that would be necessary to commence operations of the awkwardly named Natural Resources Defense Council (NRDC).

The origins of NRDC, thus, lay in a particular set of efforts to halt the construction of a hydroelectric facility. It is in this context that collective action problems of the sort identified by Olson were overcome. A large number of citizens stood to benefit from the efforts of the Scenic Hudson Preservation Conference, but only a small fraction of the beneficiaries participated in the group. As Olson predicted, the lawyers and scientists immediately connected with the project effectively subsidized the collective good on behalf of all the rest who stood to benefit from their litigation battle. Yet, even if the immediate collective action problems were addressed, the Scenic Hudson participants recognized that they would need to move beyond collective action, and beyond the scope of their initial engagement, in order to advocate effectively on behalf of the environment. The real challenge lay in building an organization that could fulfill the vision of the founders. How would one effectively coordinate the efforts of lawyers and scientists? On what basis would the organization contest public policy? Who would provide the necessary resources for organizational maintenance and growth?

Finding common ground

As environmental pressures grew in the late 1960s – the accumulation of a string of mishaps, exposés, and unchecked economic expansion – so did social pressures, and nowhere more so than on college campuses. The rising tide of protest against the Vietnam War fueled an unprecedented political activism among students, led in part by Students for a Democratic Society. Environmental awareness and student activism coalesced in the spring of 1970, when Earth Day events commenced on campuses across the country. Earth Day brought the simmering frustration of students to bear on emerging concerns about the health of the environment and the long-term consequences of environmental degradation. Denis Hayes' Environmental Action organized some 22,000 students in the wake of Earth Day, and even Richard Nixon agreed that the 1970s would become the "environmental decade" (Flippen, 2000; Christofferson, 2004).

Even before campus environmentalism reached its zenith in 1970, efforts were afoot to engage in some sort of constructive behavior on behalf of environmental issues. In the fall of 1968 at Yale Law School, a group of students hatched a scheme to create a public interest law firm that would litigate solely on environmental issues. Led by James Gustave "Gus" Speth, these students formed an organization that they called the Environmental Legal Defense Fund (ELDF) (Martin, 2006: 32). ELDF represented an alternative to the stereotypical career path in the corporate world. The organizational template upon which the students hoped to build the ELDF was the Legal Defense Fund of the NAACP.[11] One of the students who participated, Richard Ayers, recalled the process that led to the ELDF's formation:

During my last year in law school at Yale, a group of us felt we wanted to make a contribution to society in some way when we finished our studies. Eventually, we landed upon the idea of starting an environmental law firm. All of us thought that it would be exciting to be in on the ground floor of something like this, and we all agreed that there would be a need for such a thing. But after we had talked through what a wonderful project this would be, we came to a moment of pause, when somebody said, "Who's going to pay for this?" One person in the group, who was a little more sophisticated than the rest of us about the foundation world, said, "There's only one thing to do. We have to put together a proposal for the largest amount we can imagine, and we have to take it to the biggest foundation around," and that was the Ford Foundation, of course (NRDC, 1995a).

When the Ford Foundation received the ELDF's request for funding, it was initially skeptical. For starters, Congress had recently investigated Ford for questionable funding practices related to members of the Kennedy family, and it felt gun-shy about the appearance of a partisan agenda. More fundamentally, the idea of a legal organization for environmental protection had no existing template. Federal courts had only just

---

[11] NRDC co-founder Gus Speth was inspired by an article in the *New York Times* about the NAACP Legal Defense Fund. According to Speth, "[i]t just occurred to me that there really should be an NAACP Legal Defense Fund for the environment" (Shabecoff, 2003: 117).

begun to recognize the legitimacy of environmental litigation. While some green groups, like the Sierra Club, had begun to litigate as part of a broader strategy of advocacy, the ELDF would have been the first group organized primarily for the purposes of environmental litigation.

The Yale students envisioned an autonomous organization with minimal oversight from a board of trustees that would use the tools of litigation as a way to influence public policy development. The group would litigate on behalf of the public interest, as well as join with local groups to provide expertise and other forms of assistance. In keeping with the traditions of the Bar, the group would provide free legal assistance where possible, in addition to acting as a central clearing-house linking environmentalists across the country. Yet, the Ford Foundation envisioned a group that would be research-oriented, a resource for local groups rather than a litigator in its own right. The Yale students expected to see a considerable amount of courtroom time; the Ford Foundation wanted them in the law library. And the Ford Foundation wanted a strong board of directors to keep an eye on the students' activities, whereas the ELDF had envisioned something more along the lines of a board of advisors (Martin, 2006: 33–35). With neither side willing to compromise, Ford delayed its decision on funding the ELDF until some of these basic differences were resolved.

Before the differences were resolved between the Yale law students and the Ford Foundation, Duggan, Seymour, and Sive had gone ahead with their efforts to build the NRDC. Yet they had few resources with which to build an organization and professional commitments that kept them from staffing the NRDC themselves. When they approached the Ford Foundation for funding, the Yale ELDF group had already been enmeshed in negotiations that were heading toward an impasse. Gordon Harrison of the Ford Foundation decided that the best chance for a new environmental law group would come if the New York-based NRDC and the ELDF could be merged into one new organization. Having been frozen out of funding for a year at this point, the Yale group was more willing to entertain a merger and more willing to accept supervision from a board of directors.

In the meantime, the NRDC solicited for an executive director, meekly promising to the prospective candidates future remuneration, future support staff, and a borrowed office in a New York City law firm until funding could be secured to pay for a permanent location. Their first choice was David Brower, who had just recently ended his relationship with the Sierra Club. But Brower had already formed Friends of the Earth and wanted to build that organization (Martin, 2006: 26). With Brower out of the running, the New York group settled on a lawyer who had been working as an Assistant US Attorney for the Southern District of New York, named

John Adams (NRDC, 1990: 10). Adams struck a chord with the NRDC trustees, who described him as having "boundless energy and dedication" (NRDC, 1995a).

Adams had three priorities when he arrived at the NRDC: find salary money, find permanent office space for the organization, and figure out what the NRDC was going to do (NRDC, 1995a). An additional, non-trivial task was to meet with the Yale law students to work out an accommodation. After several rounds of negotiations, Adams convinced the Yale students that he shared their goals for environmental advocacy, and together they developed a rough structure that would allow for a mutually acceptable balance of autonomy and oversight (Martin, 2006: 39).

Still, even with Adams and the Yale group finding common ground, the New York group had imagined a much narrower focus for the organization, and had to be convinced that a Washington, DC office was even necessary. As these issues were being resolved, a $10,000 grant procured by William Beinecke allowed the NRDC to host a founding conference at Princeton University in March 1970, pulling together environmentalists from across the country (NRDC, 1995a). With luminaries like David Brower and Congressman Richard Ottinger (D-NY) in attendance, and an infectious spirit of optimism for new environmental ventures motivating the two sides, the NRDC and the ELDF began to reach a consensus. By May, the lure of Ford Foundation money had convinced the two sides to agree on the final points of contention – representation for the Yale law students on the board of directors, and a Washington, DC office – and the new staff began to move into its temporary headquarters (Martin, 2006: 41).

The NRDC's structure thus emerged out of the experiences of the New York group, the aspirations of the Yale group, and the willingness of the Ford Foundation to purchase the advocacy product from this type of organization. Each faction received partially excludable benefits for their efforts in forming the advocacy organization. The New York group earned public accolades and seats on the board of directors of NRDC. The Yale lawyers were provided with an unparalleled opportunity to litigate environmental law cases with significant resources at their disposal. As one of the Yale students recalled, "[l]itigation gave us real power, at least initially. It was a heady thing, at barely thirty years of age, to be litigating cases that had a major impact on the shape of environmental law and also sometimes forced industries to spend billions of dollars, frustrated cabinet-level decisions, or were covered on network news" (Schoenbrod, 1989: 357–358). The Ford Foundation furthered its mission of progressive policy change, which it accomplished through the actions of its client organizations. Moreover, while the entrepreneurs who founded the NRDC received selective benefits for their efforts, the particular organizational forms that they adopted and the strategies and tactics they pursued provided additional returns for the organization as its growing capacity for litigation attracted additional support.

Building an organization

Shortly after procuring a $410,000 grant from the Ford Foundation in 1970, John Adams received word that the Internal Revenue Service (IRS) would not agree to confer nonprofit charitable status on the NRDC. Instead, a waiver had to be obtained for each legal action the organization took. In effect, the IRS would have to sign off on all NRDC legal activities. The Ford Foundation, facing scrutiny of its own, refused to release the grant money to the NRDC until it had received full approval from the IRS.

The prominent Wall Street lawyers who had participated in the NRDC's founding were well positioned politically to exert pressure on the Nixon administration to rule in their favor. Not only was the IRS threatening the NRDC, it was also looking for opportunities to harass the Ford Foundation (Andrew, 2002). However, the IRS handed the NRDC a significant political weapon by ruling that not only would it scrutinize the NRDC's legal actions, but also all public interest law would be scrutinized for potential violations of tax rules. The NRDC quickly capitalized by calling on other environmental and public interest groups to help pressure the IRS to protect what the agency had started calling public interest law as a legitimate charitable function (Shanahan, 1970: 1).

The NRDC's allies, including several prominent Republicans, lobbied Nixon's top advisors, arguing that by denying the NRDC its tax exemption, Nixon would be pilloried as anti-environmental. The Yale contingent went to work on Capitol Hill looking for sympathetic listeners and met an unexpectedly spectacular reception. As one of them explained:

Suddenly it was very easy to get Members of Congress to make speeches to attack the IRS . . .. It was kind of like shooting fish in a barrel. For a lobbyist, when you're going up to see a Senator, you are not asking him to introduce a bill, you are not asking him to take a position on a pending bill. All you're asking him to do is make a speech attacking the IRS. And they loved it. I mean everybody loved it: we had people from Roman Hruska and Karl Mundt on the very right wing . . . through Jac Javits to Ted Kennedy to folks on the progressive end. Everybody was willing to say "these people are entitled to tax exemption. And the IRS is once again standing in the way of Americans doing their duty" (Martin 2006: 51).

The Nixon Administration, ever fearful of a 1972 presidential challenge from Senator Ed Muskie, acquiesced. The IRS announced several weeks later, in late November 1970, that public interest litigation organizations, like the NRDC, would be granted tax-exempt status (Anon., 1970; Webster, 1970; Dowie 1995: 35–36).

Once the question of tax status had been resolved, the Ford Foundation released the rest of its grant to the NRDC and the organization was able to set out to define what an environmental public interest law firm would look like in practice. With substantial professional autonomy afforded by the structure of the NRDC, staff lawyers began to take on cases in which they had personal interest or expertise. Collectively, the staff focused its efforts on core issues of air and water pollution, but as individuals, staff members were able to develop their own areas of specialization. One of the founding staff members, David Hawkins, described his experience as entailing a steep learning curve. The lawyers tried to press issues where Congress had written citizen intervention language into the statute. Said Hawkins:

My early cases were involved in local air pollution and DES [an anabolic steroid used for weight gain] in cattle feed. Also in 1971 I worked on a citizen lawsuit to challenge EPA's failure to adopt a proper test procedure for motor vehicle air pollution. It probably was the first citizen test suit under the 1970 Clean Air Act – and the first one that the citizens lost. But we went on from there to do other cases at which we were more successful. The challenge that we faced was our relative inexperience in this type of litigation. We were learning by the seat of our pants. We'd have to make a lot of phone calls every time a new type of motion was required. It was pretty humorous, in retrospect; we'd anxiously sit around saying, "Has anyone ever seen a paper like this before?" But we picked it up pretty quickly (NRDC, 1995a).

The unique organizational structure of the NRDC contributed to the fairly broad set of cases that staff lawyers initiated. The staff organized as a sort of collective, much like partners in a law firm, rather than hierarchically, as would be found in traditional organizational settings. Likewise, the ballooning number of environmental issues created plentiful opportunities for the NRDC to become involved. As one NRDC lawyer noted, "[t]here were far more opportunities for winning lawsuits than NRDC could possibly bring" (Schoenbrod, 1989: 3). Provisions for citizen suits written into laws such as the Clean Air Act, and the availability of legal recourse under the National Environmental Policy Act provided the NRDC and other environmental groups with plenty to litigate. "There was a sense of freedom that we all felt about our ability to do the things that needed to be done," recalled Gus Speth about the early days of the organization. "Our program started out with pollution, and then grew into energy, and agricultural issues, and deforestation" (NRDC, 1995a).

The insights that are uncovered by this case emerge when we consider the origins of the NRDC from the perspective of business firm theory.

Utilizing this perspective allows us to better explain the motivations of the founders – as both ideologically and instrumentally motivated – as well as to understand the development of the group in the context of the politics of the early 1970s. Three further insights demonstrate the value of rethinking advocacy organizations in this way. First, the NRDC's expansion in the early 1970s followed from a lack of direct competition for resources within this advocacy niche and a guaranteed market for its advocacy product. Second, the specialties and expertise generated in the process of developing an organization made the NRDC the immediate authority among environmentalists in the nascent field of environmental law. Finally, the success enjoyed by the NRDC (and other groups) encouraged a proliferation of environmental lawsuits in the 1970s, as well as new organizations, law school specialties, and think-tanks designed to further the practice of environmental law.

Litigation and the environment

While in certain respects the organizational hurdles that the NRDC was forced to overcome helped to define the character of the organization – i.e. the negotiations between the New York branch and the Yale group, the intervention of the Ford Foundation, and the battle with the IRS – the NRDC's organizational identity did not crystallize until after it had commenced operations. All involved had agreed that the NRDC would pursue legal means for protecting the environment, but what would that mean in the practice of an organization? What issues would be addressed? What strategies and tactics would be developed?

Litigation was considered the most important strategy for several reasons. First, environmentalists were at less of a resource disadvantage in courtrooms than in other political venues. This lower-cost option was important for a group like the NRDC that did not enjoy the resources that would stem from a large membership base. Second, the power of precedent allowed for victories in one area of environmental law to be applied to other cases. The NRDC enjoyed economies of scale as it redeployed its advocacy tools in multiple iterations of the same basic approach. Third, litigation could change environmental policy more quickly and efficiently than a program of public education. Finally, the NRDC considered the practice of environmental law an agent of stronger democracy (NRDC, 1972; Stoel, 1974). For John Adams, the litigation strategy was a key to achieving broader social changes, which were achieved in part by garnering publicity for the group's efforts – a formula with which environmental groups in the past had found success (Young, 2008). "I think there is no more dramatic way to bring public attention to an issue than a well-chosen, well prepared lawsuit ... The legal system is one of the best avenues for social change – most changes have occurred after the issues have been fought out in the courts" (Webster, 1972).

In its first two years, the NRDC engaged a wide variety of environmental issues. Its activities included enforcing Clean Air Act emission deadlines, upholding sulphur oxide standards, challenging stream channelization efforts, retaining water flow in the American River, preventing fish kills at the Indian Point nuclear plant on the Hudson River, banning poison as a means of predator control, increasing recycling, and banning the hormone DES in feed for cattle and sheep (NRDC, 1972: 2–3).

By far the most important statutory resource for the early efforts of the NRDC was the National Environmental Policy Act (NEPA) (Lindstrom and Smith, 2001). Signed by Richard Nixon on January 1, 1970, NEPA established environmental protection as an official policy of the federal government. The NRDC called NEPA, in particular section 102(2)(C), which required federal agencies to issue environmental impact statements for significant projects, a "sleeper" among environmental statutes (NRDC, 1975: 3). As interpreted by the Council on Environmental Quality, the purpose of section 102(2)(C) was to "build into the agency decision making process an appropriate and careful consideration of the environmental aspects of proposed action" (Federal Register, 1971). NRDC lawyers initiated litigation on several fronts to require federal agencies to issue environmental impact statements that both fully addressed the environmental issues at stake and explored alternatives that would minimize environmental damage.

The stipulations of NEPA were an important weapon for the NRDC in its efforts to contravene administrative agency decisions. One of the first major cases decided by the federal courts under NEPA was *Calvert Cliffs' Coordinating Committee, Inc.* v. *United States Atomic Energy Commission* (1971), which pitted the autonomy of the Atomic Energy Commission to regulate nuclear power against the legislative mandate of Congress to force consideration of environmental issues. In what the court saw as the "beginning of what promises to become a flood of new litigation," NEPA was interpreted as requiring consideration of environmental effects when deciding whether or not to proceed with an action. The court declared that NEPA provided it with the power to review agency decisions when environmental issues were at stake. Quoting an earlier decision from a lower court, the majority declared: "It is hard to imagine a clearer or stronger mandate to the Courts."[12] Moreover,

---

[12] Quoted in *Calvert Cliffs* from *Texas Committee on Natural Resources* v. *United States* (1970).

Section 102 of NEPA mandates a particular sort of careful and informed decision making process and creates judicially enforced duties. The reviewing courts probably cannot reverse a substantive decision on its merits ... unless it be shown that the actual balance of costs and benefits that was struck was arbitrary or clearly gave insufficient weight to environmental values. But if the decision was reached procedurally without individualized consideration and balancing of environmental factors – conducted fully and in good faith – it is the responsibility of the courts to reverse.[13]

Fueled by its success in *Calvert Cliffs*, the NRDC attempted to harness NEPA to achieve a wide variety of environmental reforms. This effort, however, met with decidedly mixed results. In one effort to reduce strip mining in the Appalachian Mountains, the NRDC filed suit against the Tennessee Valley Authority (TVA) claiming that it failed to conduct an environmental impact assessment of the coal that it was purchasing (*Natural Resources Defense Council, Inc.* v. *Tennessee Valley Authority*, 1972). However, the court threw out this lawsuit on the grounds that the NRDC, based in New York, was too far removed from the Alabama-based TVA to warrant standing in the case.

In a friendlier outcome, *Natural Resources Defense Council, Inc.* v. *Morton* (1972) proved NEPA a valuable resource for challenging certain types of agency decision. The NRDC utilized NEPA's environmental impact assessment requirement to challenge the leasing of gas and oil tracts located off the coast of New Orleans. Secretary of the Interior Rogers Morton had proposed a sale of tracts on the Outer Continental Shelf in response to President Nixon's initiative to increase domestic energy production. The environmental impact statement circulated by Bureau of Land Management director Burton Silcock did not contain an assessment of the possible alternatives to the proposed drilling. The NRDC argued that the Department of the Interior should have considered alternatives such as eliminating oil import quotas, which also would have addressed energy needs. Even though the Interior Department lacked the authority to enact such an alternative policy, the spirit of NEPA required the agency to at least consider that as an alternative.

Other environmental statutes soon joined NEPA in providing the NRDC with grounds to engage in litigation. When the NRDC was launched, major revisions to the Clean Air Act were wending their way through the Congressional policymaking labyrinth. Nixon signed the Clean Air Act amendments at the same time that the NRDC was assembling its

---

[13] Note that this expansive interpretation of NEPA was eventually curtailed by a series of Supreme Court decisions beginning with *Vermont Yankee Nuclear Power Corp.* v. *Natural Resources Defense Council, Inc.* (1978) in which Justice Rehnquist declared that NEPA's "mandate to the agencies is essentially procedural."

staff and setting its agenda. In January 1971, the NRDC launched its first major Project on Clean Air to insure that citizens would be empowered to monitor the implementation of the Act. The Clean Air Act amendments stipulated that each state hold public hearings to solicit input into state implementation plans. The NRDC published a citizen's manual to help guide citizens in their assessment of state implementation plans. In concert with approximately 400 state and local civic and environmental groups across the country, the NRDC participated extensively at the public hearings and in their aftermath. At the same time, staff lawyers filed suit against the EPA for setting hydrocarbon emission standards below what the Clean Air Act mandated. The NRDC also initiated litigation against twenty-two state plans that failed to meet the standards of the Act. Finally, NRDC lawyers pressured EPA administrator William Ruckelshaus to reject a request from automobile companies to delay the implementation of air pollution standards set to begin in 1975 (NRDC, 1975: 4).

As Congress began to address the issue of water pollution, the NRDC launched a Project on Clean Water modeled on the successful air pollution program. The organization emphasized that *citizens* were instrumental in reversing deteriorating water quality. Again, NRDC staffers created a citizen's handbook to assist individuals and organizations in efforts to reduce pollution in local bodies of water (NRDC, 1975: 5).

While riding high on their initial success, NRDC lawyers found that other issues beyond water and air were beginning to compete for attention. The NRDC was prompted to begin work on energy issues by a $75,000 grant from the Ford Foundation. Ford requested an investigation into the way in which energy policy was made at the national level. In addition to the work done at the behest of Ford, NRDC also took it upon itself to establish a "public interest presence" in the field of energy policy. They justified this program in two ways. First, energy issues were directly related to pressing environmental issues, and thus worthy of attention from the NRDC. Second, the NRDC considered their energy program "a channel for citizens throughout the country to participate in the public policy formation and implementation process on energy issues" (NRDC, 1975: 6).

Finally, in addition to the citizen mobilization aspect of energy policy, the NRDC engaged in litigation opposing the development of fast-breeder nuclear reactors. Representing the Scientists' Institute for Public Information against the Atomic Energy Commission (AEC), the NRDC utilized provisions in NEPA to argue for a temporary cessation of the development of the breeder reactor. Because the AEC had not completed an environmental impact assessment on the hazards of radiation contamination, the NRDC argued, the project should be put on hold (and hopefully disbanded altogether) (NRDC, 1975: 7).

In sum, the NRDC experienced a great organizational expansion in the early 1970s as it mastered the domain of environmental litigation. By the time of the Carter presidency, NRDC's top lawyers like Gus Speth and David Hawkins were leaving the organization to take high-ranking positions within the administration. With widespread name recognition, support from important patrons like the Ford Foundation, and a growing roster of members, the NRDC had successfully ensconced itself as the leading environmental litigation organization in the country. In response to Ronald Reagan's election to the White House in 1980, the leading national environmental organizations began to collaborate formally under the auspices of the Group of Ten (later renamed the Green Group) (Gottlieb, 2005: 168–173). The NRDC's John Adams assumed a leadership role in the Green Group and steered environmentalists toward a direct conflict with the Reagan administration. The public outrage that followed Reagan's attacks on environmentalists proved a boon for the NRDC and its fellow environmental organizations as memberships and revenues soared. However, in recent years, the NRDC has come under fire from fellow environmentalists for being too preoccupied with national politics and too willing to compromise with polluting industries (Dowie, 1995). Others have criticized the NRDC for ignoring local environmentalists, or worse, appropriating their conflicts only to surrender to the forces of compromise (Gottlieb and Ingram, 1988: 14–15). In 2004, Michael Shellenberger and Ted Nordhaus penned an essay called "The death of environmentalism" that suggested groups like the NRDC and the approaches that they followed were outdated and unable to confront modern challenges like global warming.[14] These criticisms stem from the fact that the advocacy strategy pursued by the NRDC deeply impacted the way environmental politics is contested in the United States. However, given the difficulties inherent in fundamentally changing the direction of well-established organizations, realizing changes may be more difficult than critics anticipate. Until the generation of environmentalists that came of age in the 1960s and 1970s steps aside, the current state of environmental politics is likely to continue.

Conclusion

This chapter has utilized the case of the NRDC to explore an alternative perspective on the development of advocacy associations. Traditional collective action approaches tell us little about the organizational

---

[14] The authors have followed up on that essay with a book that raises many of the same concerns. See Nordhaus and Shellenberger (2007).

development of advocacy groups, mostly because they approach the problem from the perspective of individual beneficiaries of collective goods. It is clear that organizational entrepreneurs do the bulk of the heavy lifting, aided, of course, by patrons who defray costs and provide big-picture guidance. To achieve a clearer perspective on the motivations of entrepreneurs, I show that under certain conditions collective goods can be provided in a market context. The case of the NRDC reflects the importance of spillover effects, which, for advocacy organizations, are the selective benefits afforded to entrepreneurs in the process of supplying a collective good. In the early 1970s, the NRDC achieved notoriety and prominence within the environmental community. Its lawyers developed skills that led to executive branch appointments, and, most importantly to those involved in the organization, it was able to influence public policy at a time when environmental consciousness was arguably at its peak. As the NRDC became more involved in the new environmental politics of the 1970s, the distinct set of organizational capacities that had been somewhat idiosyncratically developed became defining organizational characteristics. Most importantly, because the NRDC formed in a merger between the leaders of the Scenic Hudson Preservation Conference and the group of Yale law students, the group could assign staff lawyers to challenge agency decisions under the various provisions of the new environmental legislation. If the merger had never come about, if instead the Scenic Hudson group had forged ahead on its own, it would have lacked the capacity to engage in this type of litigation. In all likelihood, the group would have been confined to an advisory role in aiding other local litigants. Instead, with an eager staff that enjoyed considerable autonomy, the NRDC developed the expertise needed to litigate complex environmental cases and placed environmentalists on a relatively equal footing with industry and agency experts.

The findings in this chapter engage the broader theoretical framework of this volume in two ways. First, Prakash and Gugerty reassess the way that we consider advocacy organization formation. "Why do advocacy organizations arise?" they ask. Theories of the firm suggest that market disequilibria commonly motivate entrepreneurial activity. Likewise, I submit that the formation of advocacy organizations – as evidenced by the case of the NRDC – occurs when political entrepreneurs sense a market for a particular advocacy product. Because organizations face potential competition from similar rivals, these efforts are most successful when they can establish a first-mover advantage or when demand is great enough that multiple providers of similar products can coexist. In the 1970s, the demand for environmental advocacy was so great (with giant subsidies from large institutions like the Ford Foundation) that the NRDC could expand its operations without fearing competition from similar organizations.

The formation of advocacy organizations is linked to another set of concerns raised by Prakash and Gugerty. Why do organizational structures look the way they do? Again, theories of the firm suggest that reducing transaction costs is a primary function of organizational structures. However, organizational structures also reflect internal and external constraints on organizational entrepreneurs. NRDC's organizational resources consisted largely of a few lawyers and some office space. While in certain respects litigation was the purpose of the organization, it was also the only option available. Reliant on foundation money and lacking members, the litigation strategy could not be substituted. Moreover, the immediate success of the litigation strategy meant that if the organization were to grow it would be in the direction of more litigation.

What, then, are the takeaway lessons for the study of advocacy organizations more broadly? What pathways does this perspective provide to address enduring questions about the formation and development of advocacy associations? I would like to highlight three potential areas of research that would profit from the insights of this model. First, advocacy organization formation and development have been conceived in terms of individual collective action. That is, when collective action occurs it is a consequence of autonomous individuals seeking to supply a collective good for themselves. The shadow of Olson is longest here, and as Baumgartner and Leech (1998) point out, few new advances have been made on this front in recent decades. Even the stipulation that entrepreneurs advance the fortunes of groups in the initial stages has been limited by an effort to fit that insight into the Olsonian collective action framework. Even though the collective goods problem remains a salient concern, this chapter suggests that it should be understood in the context of the organizational development of associations rather than the participation of individual members. How do advocacy organizations develop, and what constraints are placed on them by the political environment and competition from other groups?

Second, the growth and development of advocacy organizations has long been an exercise in comparative statics that has measured the aggregate number of groups over time (see, e.g., Walker, 1991). The approach here suggests that we should instead be looking at the development of advocacy organizations *through* time, as dynamic participants in the broad processes of political development (Bosso, 2004). Advocacy organization development is fundamentally a historical process because the formation and development of advocacy organizations is fundamentally interactive: existing political institutions shape opportunities for advocacy organization formation, and competition among advocacy organizations for distinctive identities allows selective benefits to be retained.

Finally, the significance of monopolistic competition deserves greater scrutiny in the context of advocacy organization communities. The work of Gray and Lowery (1995) and Browne (1990) has suggested that advocacy organizations tend to organize themselves into niches that protect core identities. The economic notion of monopolistic competition suggests a similar insight: advocacy organizations do poorly when they face direct competition for their advocacy efforts. The ecology of an advocacy organization system might vary quite widely given different institutional arrangements; it is less clear whether or not a protected niche is a universal requirement for successful advocacy.

References

Andrew, J. A. 2002. *Power to Destroy: The Political Uses of the IRS from Kennedy to Nixon.* Chicago: Ivan R. Dee.

Anon. 1970. Tax Report. *Wall Street Journal*, November 18, 1970.

Arnold, R. D. 1992. *The Logic of Congressional Action.* New Haven, CT: Yale University Press.

Arrow, K. J. 1962. The Economic Implications of Learning by Doing. *Review of Economic Studies*, **29**(3): 155–173.

Barnard, C. I. 1968. *The Functions of the Executive.* Cambridge, MA: Harvard University Press.

Baumgartner, F. and B. Leech. 1998. *Basic Interests.* Princeton University Press.

Berry, J. 1978. On the Origins of Public Interest Groups: A Test of Two Theories. *Polity*, **10**(3): 379–397.

Birnbaum, J. 1992. *The Lobbyists: How Influence Peddlers Get Their Way in Washington.* New York: Times Books.

Bosso, C. 2004. *Environment Inc.: From Grassroots to Beltway.* Lawrence: University Press of Kansas.

Browne, W. P. 1990. Organized Interests and their Issue Niches. *Journal of Politics*, **52**: 477–509.

Calvert Cliffs' Coordinating Committee, Inc. v. United States Atomic Energy Commission. 146 F.33 (1971).

Christofferson, B. 2004. *The Man From Clear Lake: Earth Day Founder Senator Gaylord Nelson.* Madison: University of Wisconsin Press.

Coase, R. 1937. The Nature of the Firm. *Economica*, **4**(16): 386–405.

Dowie, M. 1995. *Losing Ground: American Environmentalism at the Close of the Twentieth Century.* Cambridge, MA: MIT Press.

Elster, J. 1989. Social Norms and Economic Theory. *Journal of Economic Perspectives*, **3**(4): 99–117.

Federal Register (1971) 36, 7724 (April 23).

Flippen, J. B. 2000. *Nixon and the Environment*. Albuquerque: University of New Mexico Press.

Frohlich, N., J. A. Oppenheimer, and O. R. Young. 1971. *Political Leadership and Collective Goods*. Princeton University Press.

Gottlieb, R. 2005. *Forcing the Spring: The Transformation of the American Environmental Movement*, 2nd edn. New York: Island Press.

Gottlieb, R. and H. Ingram. 1988. The New Environmentalists. *The Progressive*, **52**(8): 14–15.

Gray, V. and D. Lowery. 1995. The Population Ecology of Gucci Gulch. *American Journal of Political Science*, **39**(1): 1–29.

Griliches, Z. 1992. The Search for R&D Spillovers. *Scandinavian Journal of Economics*, **94**: S29–S47.

Hays, S. 1987. *Beauty, Health, and Permanence: Environmental Politics in the United States, 1955–1985*. Cambridge University Press.

Imig, D. R. and J. M. Berry. 1996. Patrons and Entrepreneurs: A Response to "Public Interest Group Entrepreneurship and Theories of Group Mobilization." *Political Research Quarterly*, **49**(1): 147–154.

Lindstrom, M. J. and Z. A. Smith. 2001. *The National Environmental Policy Act: Judicial Misconstruction, Legislative Indifference and Executive Neglect*. College Station: Texas A&M University Press.

Mankiw, N. G. 1995. The Growth of Nations. *Brookings Papers on Economic Activity*, **25**(1): 275–310.

Martin, J. A. 2006. "Do They Practice Law in Washington?": The Founding of the Natural Resources Defense Council. Unpublished MA thesis, University of Wisconsin.

Miller, G. J. 1992. *Managerial Dilemmas: The Political Economy of Hierarchy*. Cambridge University Press.

Natural Resources Defense Council (NRDC). 1972. *NRDC – The First Two Years*. New York: Natural Resources Defense Council.

　1975. *Five Year Report*. New York: Natural Resources Defense Council.

　1990. *Twenty Years Defending the Environment*. New York: Natural Resources Defense Council.

　1995a. *A Force of Nature: NRDC – 25 Years on Earth*. New York: Natural Resources Defense Council.

　1995b. *Twenty-Five Years Defending the Environment: NRDC, 1970–1995*. New York: Natural Resources Defense Council.

Natural Resources Defense Council, Inc. v. *Morton*. 148 F.5 (1972).

Natural Resources Defense Council, Inc. v. *Tennessee Valley Authority*. 459 F.255 (1972).

Nordhaus, T. and M. Shellenberger. 2007. *Break Through: From the Death of Environmentalism to the Politics of Possibility*. New York: Houghton Mifflin.

Nownes, A. 2006. *Total Lobbying: What Lobbyists Want (And How They Try to Get It)*. Cambridge University Press.

Nownes, A. J. and G. Neeley. 1996. Public Interest Group Entrepreneurship and Theories of Group Mobilization. *Political Research Quarterly*, **49**(1): 119–146.

Olson, M. 1965. *The Logic of Collective Action: Public Goods and the Theory of Groups*. Cambridge, MA: Harvard University Press.

Romer, P. M. 1990. Endogenous Technological Change. *Journal of Political Economy*, **98**(5): S71–S102.

Salisbury, R. 1969. An Exchange Theory of Interest Groups. *Midwest Journal of Political Science*, **13**(1): 1–32.

Sax, J. L. 1970. *Defending the Environment: A Strategy for Citizen Action*. New York: Alfred A. Knopf.

Scenic Hudson Conference v. *Federal Power Commission*. 354 U.S. 608 (1965).

Schoenbrod, D. 1989. Environmental Law and Growing Up. *Yale Journal on Regulation*, **6**: 357–358.

Shabecoff, P. 2003. *A Fierce Green Fire: The American Environmental Movement*. New York: Island Press.

Shanahan, E. 1970. I.R.S. to Restudy Tax-Exempt Units: Those Engaging in Litigation Could Lose Exemptions. *New York Times*, October 9, 1970.

Sheingate, A. D. 2003. Political Entrepreneurship, Institutional Change, and American Political Development. *Studies in American Political Development*, **17**(2): 185–203.

Skocpol, T. 2003. *Diminished Democracy*. Norman: University of Oklahoma Press.

Stein, A. 1982. Coordination and Collaboration: Regimes in an Anarchic World. *International Organization*, **36**(2): 299–324.

Stoel, T. B., Jr. 1974. Environmental Litigation from the Viewpoint of the Environmentalist. *Natural Resources Lawyer* 7(3): 547–554.

Talbot, A. R. 1972. *Power Along the Hudson: The Storm King Case and the Birth of Environmentalism*. New York: Dutton.

Texas Committee on Natural Resources v. *United States*. 1303 F.1304 (W.D. Tex. 1970).

Vermout Yankee Nuclear Power Corp. v. *Natural Resources Defense Council, Inc.* 435 U.S. 519 (1978).

Vogel, D. 1989. *Fluctuating Fortunes: The Power of Business in America*. New York: Basic Books.

von Hippel, E. and G. von Krogh. 2003. Open Source Software and the Private-Collective Innovation Model: Issues for Organization Science. *Organization Science*, **14**(2): 209–223.

Walker, J., Jr. 1991. *Mobilizing Interest Groups in America*. Ann Arbor: University of Michigan Press.

Webster, B. 1970. I.R.S. Move Stays Ford Fund Grant. *New York Times*, November 9, 1970.

1972. Grant Enables Ecology Agency to Expand to Coast. *New York Times*, June 17, 1972.

Williamson, O. 1985. *The Economic Institutions of Capitalism*. New York: The Free Press.

Wilson, J. Q. 1974. *Political Organizations*. New York: Basic Books.

Young, M. 2008. From Advocacy to Environment: The Sierra Club and the Organizational Politics of Change. *Studies in American Political Development*, **22**(2): 183–203.

2010. *Developing Interests: Organizational Change and the Politics of Advocacy*. Lawrence: University Press of Kansas.

3   Acting in good faith: an economic approach to religious organizations as advocacy groups

Anthony J. Gill and Steven J. Pfaff

Advocacy groups are all the rage! Over the past two decades, a new cottage industry has erupted in academia examining the seemingly explosive growth in new social movements, advocacy groups and non-governmental organizations (NGOs) that has occurred in Western industrialized nations and several developing nations as well. Many of these movements and NGOs have crossed international boundaries, feeding the notion that globalization is eroding boundaries between people all around the world. This literature certainly has added to our knowledge of how advocacy groups originate and operate. But curiously missing from these recent studies has been any discussion of what amounts to the world's most common, oldest, and largest advocacy bodies – religious organizations.

Consider the following question: what is the world's oldest formal, hierarchical institution that is still in existence today? If you answered the Roman Catholic Church,[1] go to the head of the class. Depending on how one defines the hierarchical origins of the Roman Catholic Church, that institution has been around between 1,700 and 2,000 years.[2] Even with the lower estimate, the Catholic Church has existed far longer than any contemporary state or historical dynasty and has done so even in the most turbulent of times. Further consider that the Catholic Church possesses roughly 1 billion members around the globe, with a presence in nearly every country. What other formal organization can boast of such

---

[1] Credit will also be given if you answered the Eastern Orthodox Church.

[2] It is somewhat difficult to date when the Catholic Church became a formal hierarchy. Christianity has been around since his first followers proclaimed the Resurrection of Jesus Christ in 33 CE and there certainly were efforts made to provide organization in the movement at least by 50 CE (cf. the Council of Jerusalem mentioned in Acts 15). Thus, an estimate of roughly 2,000 years seems reasonable. The other common dates associated with the creation of a hierarchical Church are 313 CE, when Constantine declared Christianity to be one of the official religions of the Roman Empire, and 325 CE, the First Council of Nicea, wherein Church leaders set about defining a unified Christian canon. However, even prior to the Edict of Milan (313), the Church did have well-defined leaders who had authority over territory and who interacted with one another.

tremendous size and international scope? One would imagine that social scientists interested in organizational emergence, preservation and collective action would want to know what makes this organization tick. But we should not just stop there. Protestantism, Judaism, Islam, Hinduism, and a variety of other religious traditions have existed for hundreds or thousands of years, often without the benefit of a centralized organization like the Catholic Church.

Can these religious traditions be considered advocacy groups? Most certainly! At a bare minimum, they are advocating for the acceptance of their spiritual ideas to be adopted by as many people as possible – something known as evangelization or proselytization.[3] Like secular advocacy groups, they seek to increase membership and financial donations from their adherents. Even in the realm of public policy, churches behave similarly to secular NGOs; religious leaders frequently find it necessary to lobby for government policies that serve their organizational ideals or needs (cf. Fetzer and Soper, 2005). These policies may include issues related to moral ideals (e.g. traditional marriage, assisting orphans) and/or organizational interests (e.g. property rights for churches). Promoting religious freedom has been a major advocacy cause for Protestant missionary groups worldwide. On the flipside of that coin, some national churches have become advocates for policies that limit the freedoms of religious minorities that are seen as a threat to their own spiritual hegemony, often asking governments to ban missionary activity or make it difficult for a religious group to get a building permit (Gill, 2007). Beyond promoting their own interests in evangelizing, religious organizations have long been influential actors in social and political advocacy movements, many of which have influenced government policies across a wide swathe of nations. The abolitionist movement in the eighteenth and nineteenth centuries, wherein leaders from a number of different Christian denominations pressured for the end of the international slave trade in the West, immediately comes to mind (Stark, 2003: 291–365). From the 1960s through the 1980s, the Roman Catholic Church, joined by the World Council of Churches, in countries such as Chile, Brazil, and Nicaragua became highly vocal opponents of the authoritarian regimes that were ruling over their respective nations and in other parts of the region (Gill, 1998). In contemporary times, an uncountable number of Christian missionary groups have been active throughout the world providing relief following natural disasters, engaging in community

---

[3] This is certainly true of Christianity and Islam. Contemporary Judaism probably could not be considered an aggressively proselytizing religion. Some Hindu sects and Buddhist organizations also actively proselytize.

improvement projects, and providing education to children. Indeed, when we think of secular international NGOs at work in various parts of the developing world, we often forget that they are frequently outnumbered by religious missionaries or indigenous members of international churches who perform similar tasks, often more efficiently and based upon purely volunteer labor. Surely anybody interested in studying advocacy organizations would want to rethink (or just *start* to think about) the role and historical success of religious groups.

The primary purpose of this chapter is to issue a clarion call to researchers studying advocacy groups to consider the role of religious organizations as advocacy groups. Second, while we understand that asking a group of scholars embedded in one field of research to immerse themselves in an entirely new literature is difficult and costly, we will present some of the basic findings about religious organizations associated with a newly emerging "religious economies" school. This theoretical perspective borrows heavily from microeconomic (or rational choice) theory to understand how churches organize and function in a variety of environmental settings. In particular, we will argue that scholarship on how religious leaders solve collective action problems is especially instructive for researchers studying advocacy groups. The primary collective action problem faced by churches, and one relevant to the collective action approach highlighted in this volume, relates to how religious institutions can induce members to contribute voluntarily to the provision of public, club, and credence goods.[4] In essence, religions excel at getting people to contribute to the production and distribution of unverifiable promises of future benefit to a wide range of individuals, similar to secular advocacy groups that seek to promote a better future for humanity or a specific group of constituents. Collective action for churches comes in the form of contributing to the financial support of the church and/or volunteering for a variety of activities ranging from providing daycare or crisis counseling to serving as a missionary in a foreign land. Secular advocacy groups also require voluntary financial contributions and labor.

Our final section will present two brief empirical discussions in differing environmental contexts – the rise of Christianity in the first three centuries of its existence and efforts by Protestant missionaries to establish a presence in Latin America during the last century. In conjunction with the themes of this book, our emphasis throughout will be upon the emergence and structure of religious (advocacy) organizations. We believe that the key contribution of an examination of religious groups for the study of

---

[4] These different types of good will be defined below.

secular advocacy groups lies in understanding how religions can success-fully obtain voluntary compliance from their membership even when the benefits that they provide to those members are essentially promises of greater things to come. These promises, known in the literature as "cre-dence goods," present unique and difficult problems for organizing vol-untary compliance, yet religious groups have been more historically successful than secular groups.

The economics of religion

Scholars studying advocacy groups can be forgiven for long neglecting the role of religious institutions.[5] For most of the past century, scholarship around religion was informed by secularization theory – i.e. the general notion that as societies modernized religious practice and/or belief would become less prevalent in society, if not become extinct (cf. Bruce, 2002; Norris and Inglehart, 2004). If the very experts who studied religion thought their subject of inquiry was becoming less relevant, why would any other scholar consider the topic important? But by the last few decades of the twentieth century, a giant problem emerged for secualiza-tion theory – the data did not match the predictions. Not only was the world's most modernized country – the United States – seemingly immune from secularization, but there also seemed to be a "global resur-gence" in religiosity, particularly of the fundamentalist or evangelical variety (Berger, 1999; Jenkins, 2002). A variety of terrorist attacks by Islamic militants certainly drew attention to the ongoing religious fervor of populations in the Middle East, and Central and South Asia. Slightly less noticed but equally amazing was the "rapid" spread of evangelical Protestantism and Pentecostalism in Latin America (Stoll, 1990),[6] prompting the Catholic Church to "reevangelize" the region and increase active participation in their faith (Gill, 1998).

    In response to the empirical problems faced by secularization theory, a small number of sociologists, economists, and political scientists began exploring new theoretical models that explained both the persistence and

---

[5] What is a paper on religion without a little grace after all? If you are one of the scholars who has ignored religion, we shall turn the other cheek, so long as you keep turning the pages here.

[6] Protestantism seemed to "explode" out of nowhere in Latin America in the 1980s and 1990s, giving the impression that it was all based upon rapid mass conversions. However, Protestants had been missionizing in the region several decades before academics really took note of the phenomenon. The "explosion" of Protestantism was no more miraculous than the typical growth curve of most historical religions that rely upon simple geometric expansion to seemingly burst forth from nowhere.

growth of religion in some areas of the world (namely the United States and the developing world) and its apparent decline in other parts (most notably Europe). Relying upon "rational choice theory," these scholars formed what would become known as the "religious economies school."[7] The basic idea behind their theories was simple. Religiously motivated people tend to respond to cost-benefit incentives just as much as people operating in non-religious spheres of life (e.g. in secular businesses). The religious economies school tends to place a high level of explanatory emphasis on the "supply side" of religion, explaining differences in religious practice on the basis of how efficiently religious firms (churches) meet the underlying demand for religious goods in society (cf. Stark and Iannaccone, 1994). This is in contrast to traditional secularization theorists who saw cross-national differences in religiosity as a function of consumer demand – religious practice falls simply because people stop believing in God. Interestingly, Grace Davie's (1994) path-breaking survey of religion in Britain (since extended to Europe) found that even in areas of low church attendance, there were high rates of belief in God and even private expressions of faith such as daily prayer. This certainly indicates that European churches, which face low attendance rates, do a poor job at securing collective participation (action) of their latent membership whereas US churches are much more successful at this task.

For present purposes, two central findings from the religious economies school are important for those studying the relative success and failure of advocacy groups in organizing collective action: (1) over time, strict churches that impose sacrifices and stigmas on their members tend to be more efficient and successful than churches that are less strict; and (2) religious groups (and religiosity in general) tend to flourish in countries where the religious marketplace is deregulated – i.e. where there is extensive religious freedom. These two findings are somewhat interconnected: state churches that are highly regulated and subsidized tend to lose their "strict" nature and desire to cultivate their flock whereas unregulated churches that are not subsidized by the government tend to work harder at solving the collective action problems (i.e. securing voluntary attendance, financial support, and labor) that they face. Before detailing these findings, it is first necessary to understand the collective action problem facing religious organizations, a problem that is similar to that

---

[7] See Stark and Finke (2000) and Iannaccone (1995) for good summaries of this perspective. The scholars who were associated with the early development of this perspective include Rodney Stark, William Sims Bainbridge, Roger Finke, and Laurence Iannaccone. Stathis Kalyvas, Carolyn Warner, and Anthony Gill were the first political scientists to adopt this perspective.

faced by secular advocacy groups promising to improve life circumstances for some group of people.

Religions as successful collective actors

The provision and survival of religion can be viewed largely as a collective action problem. Like other collective actors (e.g. labor unions), religious groups face difficulties not only in recruiting and retaining members, but also in getting their members to pay for the provision of the goods and services that churches offer, especially considering that there are strong incentives to free ride and shirk. Before discussing how religious organizations have successfully (and unsuccessfully) solved their collective action problems, it is first necessary to conceptualize what religious collective action is actually trying to achieve. In other words, what are the collective goods and services that churches provide? We will argue that religions provide both public and club goods.[8] Moreover, religious goods also tend to be something economists call "credence goods." This aspect exacerbates the collective action problem faced by religions, but also points to how churches solve their collective action dilemmas.

The most fundamental goods (or services) that religions produce are philosophical answers to the "big questions" of life. Why are we here? Is death really an end to life? Is there meaning or purpose to life? What are the moral codes that can help guide me to a better life and/or salvation in the afterlife? The success of Rick Warren's *The Purpose-Driven Life: What On Earth Am I Here For?* – which has sold over 30 million copies worldwide – provides strong evidence that there is a demand for this type of good. Of course, the Bible has sold innumerable copies throughout history, but Warren's book demonstrates that the search for meaning in life remains an attractive goal for people in contemporary times, and that they are willing to pay for it. Like classic public goods, these fundamental religious goods have the qualities of non-excludability and non-rivaledness associated with them. In other words, my understanding of the purpose of life in no way takes away from your understanding (non-rivaled) and once the message is out it is difficult to keep people from

---

[8] Religious organizations also provide private goods (that is, goods which are divisible and can become unique possessions of adherents, e.g. salvation or a blessing) and religious organizations can also be private goods in that possession of one excludes possession of another (you cannot be member in good standing of the Roman Catholic Church and the Church of Latter Day Saints at the same time). However, to the extent that they are interested in the production and distribution of publicly available creeds, charitable services, and the like, most religious organizations focus on providing public goods (cf. Ekelund, Hébert, and Tollison, 2006).

enjoying that knowledge (non-excludability). Just like a digital song, I could borrow a copy of Rick Warren's book from a friend without having to pay for it and "download" (read) all of the information provided therein. It is similar with Sunday sermons. I could listen to a sermon and not contribute to the salary of the pastor or the rent of the church building when the collection plate is passed around. Churches could obviously charge admission before you hear the sermon, but it would be just as easy for the general message of that sermon to be disseminated to others by attenders. What amazes even further is that most churches in the United States only ask for voluntary contributions (i.e. no required admission or membership fee) and an increasing number are putting their sermons online for free access. Given this, why would anybody attend or contribute financially to a church service?

Part of the explanation to the above question lies in the fact that churches often provide more than just classic collective goods – i.e. "fundamental answers" to life's great mysteries. They provide fellowship with like-minded people, educational services, emotional support, and opportunities to sing publicly outside of karaoke bars. These additional services have the qualities of club goods. Club goods are goods that are non-rivaled yet excludable, meaning that their quality is often enhanced the greater the number of people that consume them. While one could certainly get the fundamental answers to life by reading Rick Warren's book or the Bible, you can only obtain fellowship, education, emotional support, and singing by belonging to and participating in the group.[9] Eternal salvation could also be conceived of as an excludable club good to the extent that public participation in a religious group is a requirement of receiving grace; if you do not go to church regularly, St. Peter will not open the Pearly Gates. Religious rites such as baptism, confirmation, or repentance are common methods of preparing for salvation and can only be obtained through participation in a collective religious organization, often at a price. Interestingly, though, many Christian denominations conceive of salvation or grace as freely given by God, requiring only simple belief. In other words, salvation can be a club good or not depending upon the theological interpretation of a specific denomination. The effective provision of these club goods helps to attract people into the church and partially solves the collective action problem surrounding the provision of the more "public good-like" philosophic answers. Individuals only reap the benefits of many of these club goods so long as they participate in

---

[9] A large number of churches also maintain funds to help their members in times of financial need, very similar to insurance. Only members who are in good standing with the church are allowed access to these funds.

the group. In the process, their participation for the club goods helps to provide for the production and dissemination of the public goods. Of course, the ability of the group (church) to provide these services effectively will depend on how much members contribute either financially or via volunteer work. Pastors need to be paid, buildings rented, and Sunday schools staffed. Without this, there will be no fellowship, no spiritual succor, no baptisms, no confirmations and no chance of obtaining forgiveness. Churches still face the possibility of shirking, that is, tithing less than what is required or necessary of the group to flourish (Harris, 1993).

There is one final quality of religious goods that requires mention, and it is a quality that helps us understand how religious groups reduce free riding and shirking. The most fundamental religious "goods" fall under the rubric of what economists call "credence goods." A credence good is a good wherein a consumer cannot determine the quality of the good until some future date, often long after the point when it is purchased. Insurance is a classic example. A motorist buys car insurance under the expectation that when he is in an accident the insurer will pay to fix his car. However, it is only after having paid the premium and been in an accident that the purchaser can know if the company will follow through on its promise to pay. In essence, a consumer buys insurance on "faith." Religion, particularly one offering some afterlife salvation, represents the ultimate credence good; one "purchases" a religion in the present with the expectation that they will receive everlasting life or spiritual enlightenment at some point in the future. The credibility of the philosophical answers that churches provide are largely unverifiable and also need to be taken "on faith." It is reasonable to assert that churches face an uphill battle in convincing people to pay a significant price for something that they do not know they will receive, nor how accurate the answers are. Dying is the only way to verify the quality of salvation. And there are no refunds associated with religious goods; lemon laws do not apply.[10] That religious goods are a combination of public goods, club goods, and credence goods provides incentives for people to free ride or shirk their responsibility for paying for such goods.

In many ways, secular advocacy groups exhibit the same type of qualities with respect to the goods that they provide and also face similar collective action problems such as free riding and shirking. Most notably,

---

[10] Lemon laws were created to alleviate the credence good problem associated with the purchase of automobiles, particularly used cars. If a vehicle did not perform according to some minimal standard, the purchaser would be owed a full refund from the seller. The US court system does impose a "Lemon test" on government policies associated with the support of religion (see *Lemon* v. *Kurtzman*, 403 US 602 [1971]), but these are not the same as lemon laws.

many secular advocacy groups are involved in the production of public, club, and credence goods. For example, an environmental group such as the Sierra Club promises to work toward a cleaner environment. A cleaner environment is obviously a public good, but it is also a credence good in that there is no way of determining whether or not that promise is fulfilled until some point much later in the future. Potential contributors must trust in the promises of the Sierra Club. But the Sierra Club is also a club, as evidenced by its name, and members who contribute do get access to a variety of individual perks (e.g. discounted admissions to partner institutions, magazines and newsletters, a glossy calendar filled with cute animal pictures) and club goods, such as discounted prices on eco-tourism trips. Likewise, the National Rifle Association promises a defense of Second Amendment rights (a public and credence good) while simultaneously offering members special discounts on life insurance (club good),[11] as well as private goods (e.g. a glossy calendar of game animals).

Solving religious collective action problems

Given the public good and credence nature of religion, how are churches able to secure the collective support of their membership? Moreover, why are some denominations more successful at solving these problems than others? As noted above, the club aspect of religion provides a partial resolution to the problem of free riding. In order to obtain some of the club benefits, you have to be an active member of the club. To enjoy the fellowship of the club, you have to engage in fellowship yourself. Additionally, churches do provide some individual benefits that help attract participation such as free coffee and donuts on a Sunday morning. This leads us to the proposition that churches (advocacy groups) that provide club and/or private goods will be more successful than those that do not, *ceteris paribus*. Groups that ask people to contribute to "save the world" will not garner as much collective support as those that ask people to "save the world" and give them discounted insurance and baseball caps.

While these actions help to alleviate free riding to some degree, they certainly do not guarantee against shirking – contributing, but contributing less than what is necessary for the collective to flourish. A parishioner

---

[11] One might argue that discounts on eco-tourism packages and life insurance are actually private, selective benefits. However, both of these services require a bulk purchase of many people and all club members share in the lower prices of those services, which represents the non-rivaled nature of the club good – my ability to purchase discounted life insurance is not affected by your purchase.

can come and sing during Sunday services (enhancing fellowship) but not drop any cash in the collection plate. Those "free donuts" need to be paid for by someone, not to mention the pastor's salary and the church's mortgage. If people do not contribute substantially more than the bare minimum for entry into the club, the group probably will not survive. Likewise, Sierra Club or National Rifle Association members might be able to pay the basic membership fee, but neither group will likely succeed in their larger advocacy goals (beyond increasing membership) if some significant number of members do not contribute additional funds or labor. So how do religious groups solve the shirking problem?

The first general method of solving the shirking problem relates to investing in the credibility of the organization. As noted above, religious goods are credence goods and it is only natural that people will be reluctant to contribute large amounts of resources to an organization that cannot guarantee its product. For religious groups, this is difficult given that the quality of the fundamental goods produced by religions is nearly impossible to verify. Nonetheless, religious organizations have found a myriad of ways to invest in the credibility of their organization. Priests who take vows of poverty or chastity signal to the consumer that they are not pursuing their career for worldly gain or pleasure.[12] The public celebration of martyrs is another means of signaling the quality of a good. If someone is willing to die for their faith, it must be a pretty good product! Missionaries are often individuals who could have pursued lucrative careers in some other line of work, yet choose to give up creature comforts to pursue proselytization even under the most dangerous of conditions. Public testimonies (witnessing) of faith healing and of remarkable spiritual transformations serve to enhance a religion's credibility. Religious organizations also perform good deeds (i.e. charity). While this may relate to the heart of its moral mission, these good deeds often build trust among a population of non-believers who then eventually build an emotional attachment to the church. By providing food or shelter, a church may subtly signal that they are an altruistic organization, which in turn enhances the believability of the credence goods they are "selling."

---

[12] It is fascinating to consider the extravagant facilities and clothing that many televangelists (not to mention Roman Catholic prelates) maintain and we have thought that this would be an interesting research project (dissertation) in the sociology of religion. The lavish life styles of many televangelists would seem to send a signal that the religion they are peddling is less than credible. Financial scandals involving the likes of Jim Bakker certainly chip away at the credibility of other televangelists – at least this would seem a reasonable hypothesis. Nonetheless, televangelists appear to remain popular. Perhaps the grandeur of the televangelist life style indicates that God has blessed this particular ministry, much in the way that the Sistine Chapel signals the glorious achievement and divine favor enjoyed by the Catholic Church.

To the extent that people are more likely to contribute to the provision of credence goods when they have strong signals about the trustworthiness of the organization, churches that build credibility will be more successful than those that do not.[13] In short, advocacy groups that invest more heavily in establishing credibility will have greater success in obtaining voluntary compliance than groups that do not.

The other solution to solving free riding and shirking problems within religious organizations is to screen out any free riders or shirkers at the outset. One of the most intriguing findings in the religious economics literature is that the denominations that are the strictest (e.g. Mormons, Jehovah's Witnesses, Orthodox Jews) are the ones that tend to have the highest levels of participation and tithing (Iannaccone, 1994; Stark and Finke, 2000: 169–190). By strictness it is meant that these churches impose high behavioral standards and sacrifices upon their members. The Latter Day Saints (Mormons) prohibit members from consuming alcohol or caffeine, cutting down on the outside activities they can indulge in. Likewise, Witnesses are forbidden from drinking alcohol, are required to do significant amounts of "doorbelling" and are not permitted to pursue a college degree (significantly restricting their career opportunities). Pentecostals face similar restrictions on booze and engage in a variety of behaviors that set them apart from their neighbors (e.g. glossalia, faith healing). Orthodox Jews must observe strict dietary restrictions and cannot use electronic devices during the weekly Sabbath. Other denominations such as Pentecostals, Adventists, and Baptists impose similar restrictions on their members.

Iannaccone (1992) has argued that various sacrifices and stigmas associated with different religious groups serve to limit free riding in the organization. If being a member of a certain religious denomination entails wearing specific clothing (e.g. yarmulkes, turbans, hijabs), agreeing to different behavioral restrictions (e.g. no drinking, eating meat, or attending college), or making an extensive time commitment (e.g. doorbelling ten hours per month), those who are most likely to free ride on the tangible benefits of the religious group will not likely be the ones willing to pay those upfront costs. Sacrifice and stigma, in essence, screen out free riders and shirkers. The members who agree to these sacrifices and stigmas are more likely to be active in other areas of the church organization and add to the overall club benefits, be it singing louder during services, helping out with childcare or contributing financially. Iannaccone has shown that members of strict churches attend services at

---

[13] The flipside of this coin is that religious organizations are very vulnerable to scandals that eat away at trustworthiness.

a substantially higher rate and contribute a greater percentage of their income relative to less strict churches, even after controlling for various socio-economic factors (1992: 285–286). This implies that strict churches tend to be more efficient than their less strict counterparts when it comes to furthering collective action. In this situation, the overall club benefits will actually increase, thereby making membership in a strict religion a "good bargain" even when the high costs of sacrifice and stigma are considered.[14] The fact that many of these religious organizations appear so vibrant from the outside acts as an inducement for some people to consider joining them, and hence such strict religions often have high growth rates.[15]

Religious organizations that do a good job in screening out potential free riders also enhance their collective action potential in two other ways. When members of a church find it in their best interest to be active participants in that organization, they build up what Iannaccone (1990) has termed "religious human capital." Simply put, "religious capital" is the stockpile of knowledge one has about a theology, religious practices, and relationships within an organization. A certain "virtuous cycle" is at play here: the more one is active in a church, the more one builds up religious capital, and this makes one more willing to participate in the church. Successful experience with collective action begets more collective action. Additionally, greater participation in a religious group helps to build denser social networks among the people involved in that church. This has the effect of enhancing trust and trustworthiness among the group's members. Successful collective action often involves knowing the intentions of others within a group so as to prevent possible defection in a collective endeavor (Chwe, 2001). If I know that a person close to me is planning to cooperate in a potentially risky or costly endeavor, I am more willing to participate. Dennis Chong (1991) has shown that church social networks were immensely important in signaling trust among

---

[14] Iannaccone (1992) does note that strictness has its limits, though. Religious groups or cults that demand members turn over their worldly possessions to the group may be able to get a few followers, but they seldom grow to any significant size. Likewise, Amish and Mennonite communities show a remarkable ability to control free riding within their community, but they tend not to be attractive religions to join.

[15] There are still a large number of factors that influence an organization's effectiveness that have not been discussed here. One of the obvious questions left unanswered is that if strictness enhances the vibrancy and growth rates of a religious organization, why do all religions not follow suit and become stricter? And why do some previously strict churches such as the Congregationalists (now the United Church of Christ) and Methodists (namely the United Methodists) become much more "lax" in their behavioral codes? We would argue that much of this can be explained by the organizational structure and its effects on the incentives of clergy, but that is another topic for another time (cf. Finke and Stark, 2006).

participants of the Civil Rights Movement in the 1960s and formed a key element of the movement's success.

While the issues of requiring sacrifice and stigmas may not be of direct applicability to secular advocacy groups (after all, it would be silly for environmentalist groups to require all their members to wear Birkenstocks and maintain vegan diets), understanding why religious groups are so successful at collective action should be of interest to those studying advocacy groups. How important is a sense of collective identity that imposes behavioral requirements or mandates sacrifices by members for organizational success? What institutional mechanisms reduce free riding in groups? What organizational requirements enhance trustworthiness and build social capital within an advocacy group? Are there strategies and tactics that successful religious groups have employed that are transferable to secular NGOs? On a more normative front, to what extent can secular advocacy groups partner with (or piggyback on) the organizational strengths of religious groups, benefiting from their preexisting efforts to collectively mobilize?[16] As noted above, religious groups have had their fingerprints all over a number of very successful social movements throughout history, from the abolition of slavery to the Civil Rights Movement, not to mention women's suffrage, Prohibition, the Central American sanctuary movement and anti-abortion protests. And Christian missionaries currently can be found in all corners of the world providing medical care, education, and other social services to communities lacking in basic infrastructure. How these missionaries locate in these different areas is related to the next topic – religious freedom and pluralism.

Religious liberty, government subsidies and organizational vitality

In addition to noting that churches have been successful in collective action, the other major finding of the religious economies school has been that religious organizations tend to flourish in countries with a great deal of religious pluralism, which in turn is a function of the degree to which the religious marketplace is deregulated (Finke, 1990; Iannaccone, 1991). To state it a different way, where a government provides a substantial degree of religious liberty it is likely that a wide

---

[16] Froese and Pfaff (2001) note this tendency for secular advocates to find a home in religious organizations in Poland and East Germany under Communist rule. Not only did these activists benefit from the organizational structures of the Catholic and Lutheran churches, but also these denominations provided them with some "cover" from persecution as the Communists in these two nations were more reluctant to attack a traditional religious institution than a secular protest movement. Hewitt (1991) noted a similar phenomenon in Brazil during the bureaucratic authoritarian period in that country.

array of religious organizations will arise and will be free to pursue their mission via the means they best see fit. It is likely that these religious groups will find themselves in competition with one another. Where this happens, clergy have an incentive to find the best means of attracting converts and keeping them active in their church – i.e. solve collective action problems. In contrast, where there is a state-supported monopoly church, there is little incentive for the clergy to devote extensive energy to evangelization, particularly if their salaries and other organizational costs are paid for by the government (Stark and Iannaccone, 1994).

The religious economies school begins with the assumption that religious preferences within society are naturally pluralistic, varying by general theological approach or more mundane desires such as the presentation style of the pastor (Stark and Finke, 2000). From this assumption, it is argued that no one single church can completely satisfy all religious preferences. A "successful" religious monopoly requires government coercion to prevent upstart sects from entering the religious market and stealing away the dominant church's flock. Along with prohibitions on religious competitors, religious monopolies often receive official sanction and, perhaps more importantly, financial subsidies from the government. Noting that churches do face a collective action problem in providing intangible credence goods (see above), it is not surprising that religious officials may welcome government funding for their mission. Government subsidies are one way of solving the financial difficulties with the free riding and shirking problems in church, particularly with regards to suboptimal tithing on the part of the congregation. As Adam Smith observed long ago, this creates enormous incentives for religious organizations to seek state subsidies and protections. Indeed, recent cross-national research shows that, outside of the United States, nearly all religious economies are regulated to some degree (Fox, 2006). Moreover, even where formal religious freedom obtains, government efforts to favor some religious communities over others or to discriminate against undesirable religions is nearly ubiquitous (Grim and Finke, 2007).

However, research has shown that such favoritism comes at a substantial cost in terms of organizational energy. First, where competing denominations are essentially prohibited, clergy within the dominant faith have little incentive to constantly evangelize the population since their membership is essentially guaranteed (Gill, 1998).[17] If the clergy are

---

[17] This does not imply that clergy no longer care about the pastoral cultivation of their flock. What it does imply, though, is that with a "captured market," clergy with scarce time resources will feel less pressure to devote extensive amounts of time to getting people into the pews on Sunday, especially if government funding makes voluntary contributions less

guaranteed some level of funding from the state, they have less of an incentive to seek voluntary contributions from their members. Pleasing government officials who control budgetary matters becomes more important than enticing parishioners to tithe by providing interesting services that they may want or demand. Advocacy also suffers as religious leaders will likely discourage any clergy or parishioners from undertaking activities that may run counter to or compete with government interests.

In countries where the religious marketplace is deregulated and churches are "on their own" with respect to funding, it is totally predictable that the religious market would be more dynamic.[18] Without any government-imposed barriers to organization, different denominations are likely to arise and satisfy different market niches. Pluralism flourishes under conditions of religious freedom. These denominations will likely compete with one another for members. Such competition may have zero-sum qualities to it such that one denomination may draw members from another denomination.[19] But there may also be positive-sum qualities to religious diversity. Specifically, leaders of one church may learn how better to serve their own congregants by observing the successful techniques of other churches. Christian bookstores are filled with "self-help" books for pastors on how to build a successful church. Indeed, Rick Warren's first "purpose-driven" book was titled *The Purpose-Driven Church* indicating that he was more than happy to share the organizational secrets of his hugely successful Saddleback Church.

Religious pluralism and the lack of government subsidies have substantial consequences for the advocacy role of churches. First, given that the fundamental role of a religion is to spread the faith, there is an incentive to be as successful as the competing denomination down the road by seating as many people in the pews on Sunday. No minister would like to feel that his message is less appealing than another minister's, thus he will likely

necessary (cf. Smith, 1976 [1776]). Parishioners who are disgruntled with the services they receive have few remedial options given that their "exit" option to other denominations is essentially forbidden by government decree. Their only real option is not to attend services that they find boring or distasteful. While a monopoly church may see low levels of attendance, the inability of disgruntled consumers to move to a different denomination makes it appear as if the non-attenders still belong to the major faith but are just too lazy to come.

[18] Although the present authors find this assertion to be remarkably predictable, there are some who find it completely counterintuitive. Noted secularization theorist Steve Bruce, when confronted with the fact that the United States maintains high levels of religious freedom and is one of the most religiously dynamic Christian nations, claimed that US citizens were either lying about attending church or not practicing real religion at all (2002: 205–213).

[19] A recent Pew Foundation survey found that roughly 40 percent of all Christians in the United States, a country with a relatively free religious market, have switched denominations at some point in their life.

work hard to be at least as successful as others. This provides a strong incentive to find creative ways to solve the collective action problem faced by churches (as noted above). Second, in working hard to attract and activate lay members of their congregation, clergy in a pluralistic religious market will actually be laying the groundwork for future advocacy activities. Keeping people engaged in their faith often means providing them small leadership roles in the congregation, which in turn provide those members with organizational skills (and religious capital) that can be used for other activities, whether it be overseas missionary work, providing social services in the local community (e.g. clothing drives for the poor) or mobilizing politically for specific causes (e.g. advocating prayer in public school, lobbying politicians for tougher abortion laws).[20] In short, the success of religious groups in solving collective action problems provides a unique source of organizational skills for other advocacy groups to piggyback on. In many ways, this explains why religious groups have had their fingerprints on some of the great social movements of the past several centuries – from abolitionism to women's suffrage to civil rights (Chong, 1991; Smith, 1996; Stark, 2003).

The important lesson here for scholars of advocacy groups is that when organizations are forced to compete independently for the attention and resources of members, they will tend to devote more time toward solving the inherent collective action problems associated with bringing together such groups. Should such groups become beholden to government funding or protection from competing organizations, they are less likely to cultivate the needed voluntary human resources that can make an organization dynamic. This assertion could be tested empirically by determining whether voluntary-funded advocacy groups are more efficient in accomplishing their tasks than government-funded ones. I will leave this task to others.[21]

---

[20] There has been research showing that members who are active in a religious community are more likely, to volunteer and contribute financially to secular causes (Gill, 2004; Brooks, 2006).

[21] Our casual impression is that private charities tend to have much lower deadweight costs associated with their activities than government agencies performing similar tasks. Of course, a government agency is fully funded by the government. The more appropriate comparison would be with a private advocacy group that gets a portion of its funding from government grants. The recent Faith-Based Initiative of the Bush administration offers a perfect test case. One of that program's intentions was to allow private religious charities to obtain government grants for their work. Not all religious charities signed on to this program. The empirical prediction, if we are correct, is that those religious charities participating in getting government grants would have higher deadweight (administrative) costs than those that continue to rely upon private contributions, controlling for such things as the nature of the charitable work, the size of organization, etc.

Empirical illustrations

With the above theoretical groundwork laid, we now turn our attention to two brief illustrations of the insights provided by the religious economies perspective – the rise of Christianity and the spread of Protestantism in Latin America. These examples are not meant to be rigorous empirical tests, but rather serve only to highlight some of the points above and possibly inspire thought among others.[22]

The rise of Christianity

It can be reasonably said that Christianity is one of the world's most successful social movements, transcending national, racial, and ethnic boundaries. With an initial goal of spreading to the four corners of the earth, a small handful of disciples following the crucifixion of Jesus Christ has expanded to encompass nearly 2 billion adherents today (Barrett, Kurian, and Johnson, 2001). The success of Christianity was in no way guaranteed. For the first three hundred years of its existence, the Church received virtually no state support and instead had to suffer at least three major persecutions (Johnson, 1976: 3–63). Indeed, the Jesus movement that began in the first century (Common Era) would appear to have faced insurmountable obstacles: it arose in Palestine, on the periphery of the Greco-Roman world amongst a rebellious and widely distrusted ethnic group (the Jews); it faced official rejection by the state and periods of bloody repression; and its doctrines rejected the key values and achievements of pagan civilization. Christian doctrines and morals were hostile to many of the cherished values of Greco-Roman paganism, among them the virtues of nobility, worldliness, and mastery. And the elite were offended by Christian denunciation of Roman glory as sinful.

In addition to official disfavor, Christianity was not the only novel religion spreading in the Empire. The Jesus movement faced stiff *competition* from other new religions that were also spreading. These included not only Judaism but also the cults of Isis and Mithras. These "mystery cults," as they were called, also promised wisdom and consolation in this world and salvation in the next. Relying on nothing but voluntary labor and financial support, Christianity managed to grow to roughly 10 percent of the Roman Empire by the year 300 (Stark 1996: 7). How was such an amazing feat possible given the technological conditions of the time?[23]

---

[22] There have been numerous empirical tests of the religious economies school to date. For a comprehensive introduction to these, consult Stark and Finke (2000).

[23] Believers do not rule out divine providence in the Church's early expansion. Nonetheless, social science provides important insights that may be generalizable to other like cases. It

Given that Christianity was a new religion at the time, albeit one based upon Judaic tenets, Christian missionaries – as an advocacy group for their faith – faced a huge credibility problem. Why should a pagan or Jew switch religions, particularly one that for pagans demanded devotion to one divinity[24] or that for Jews required a break from tribal traditions that might leave them ostracized in their own community? Why was Christianity a better, more credible option than paganism or any other preexisting faith?

The initial answer to the credibility question relates to the receptivity of the first converts. Rodney Stark (1996) asserts that a large portion of early Christian converts were probably recruited among Hellenized Jews – i.e. Jews living outside of Palestine who retained a weak connection to their ethnic and religious heritage and were becoming increasingly attracted to the perquisites of Gentile life. It must be remembered that Jews were not a popular ethnic group in the Roman Empire at the time. The message of early Christians may have been especially appealing to those Hellenized Jews who wanted to be closer to their Gentile neighbors without abandoning their Judaic heritage. The message of early Christianity was credible in that it fit within the Judaic tradition; Christianity did not require a wholesale change in theology, but rather only an "updated" version. Moreover, abandoning the more outward expressions of their Jewish heritage (e.g. dietary restrictions) made it easier for Hellenized Jews to become integrated into Roman and Gentile culture.

Second, whereas Christianity provided a means whereby Jews could integrate more easily into their Gentile surroundings, early Christian proselytes faced disgrace, ostracism, torture, and even death for promoting their faith. Prominent individuals who bore witness to the glories of Christianity while simultaneously facing intense persecution greatly enhanced confidence in the message of salvation (credence good) promoted by Christianity. To illustrate the point, consider the most important Christian missionary, Saul of Tarsus, later known as the apostle Paul (c. CE 10–67). Born a Jew in Asia Minor and trained as a Pharisee, he was a credible witness among Hellenized Jews, who appear to have been the principal focus of his mission. Paul himself was an excellent symbol of conversion; as a pious Jew he had initially rejected the Gospel and had taken part in the persecution of Christians in Palestine (Crossan and

is interesting to note that Stark (1996, 7) calculated that the rate of Christianity's expansion in its first three centuries roughly mirrors the growth rate of Mormons over the past century and a half – approximately 40 percent per decade.

[24] The decision to leave paganism was a rationally difficult decision to make if one considers that paganism functioned as a "diversified portfolio" religion wherein you had many deities. Switching to a monotheistic religion would be like moving from a mutual fund and putting all your retirement savings into one security.

Reed, 2004; Gorman, 2004). Not surprisingly, Paul has been championed throughout the ages as a major symbol of Christian commitment and conversion. If Paul, who had no economic or social interest in converting and enduring persecution, could tolerate imprisonment and execution, then the "product" of Christianity must be good value at any lower price.

Paul was not the only martyr. Many early Christians bore the brunt of social discrimination, local riots, and lynch mobs. While the repression was more episodic than consistent, it did come with great cruelty. And yet many early adherents willingly chose to suffer through such harsh treatment. Indeed, many Christians brought to trial in the Roman Empire were given the option of absolution if they chose to recant their faith; but many did not and became lion food. Consistent with the religious economies model, such willing martyrdom boosted the credibility of the movement. As per the Christian teacher Tertullian: "By the blood of the martyr the Church is refreshed." As per modern economics of religion, the public payment of high costs to belong to an organization by a small group of zealots enhances the overall credibility of the good when the validity of the product being offered might be in doubt. Admittedly, Tertullian said it better.

Amidst a highly competitive religious market populated by numerous pagan cults, the organizational structure of Christianity enhanced its ability to recruit and retain members. Religious pluralism provided strong incentives for early proselytizers to create an appealing product, one based not only on theological public goods, but also on an attractive set of club goods available to members. Christianity expanded because it opened club membership to all: Gentile and Jew, citizen and slave, man and woman. But membership required a set of behavioral changes. One could no longer participate in the rather bacchanalian pagan festivals and many Christians changed their names (as Saul of Tarsus did). Like Mormons or Jehovah's Witnesses who cannot drink, these behavioral traits served to bind the members to the group as they tended to limit outside activities. This in turn enhanced the club goods. Christians were admired for sticking together. In a society of profound inequality and injustice they offered fellowship and social assistance. This became obvious in the creation of charities to feed the destitute, assist widows and orphans, redeem prostitutes, and nurse the sick and abandoned, especially during plagues (Stark, 1996: 73–94). While many of these "good deeds" were offered to non-Christians, thereby enhancing the credibility of the organization in the eyes of non-members, it also became readily apparent that belonging to this Christian "club" provided benefits well beyond the behavioral costs. Pagan groups with open commitments and low entry costs created huge free riding and shirking problems and eventually found that they could not effectively compete with the club benefits offered by Christianity (Stark, 1996: 196–208).[25]

Christianity did not bring about a Kingdom of God on Earth, as so many of Jesus' followers desired. But Christianity does seem to have helped restabilize Roman society and improve social conditions. It achieved this in two ways that are tremendously relevant to the work of NGOs in contemporary societies. First, the Church created a network of charitable institutions and provided social assistance to the destitute. Urban conditions improved. Christianity also seems to have improved the status of women, suppressed sexual commerce, regulated the treatment of slaves, and encouraged charity. Second, Christianity provided a vehicle by which newcomers could be integrated into the imperial society. Through its missions to Hellenized Jews, to the barbarians on the Roman borderlands, and among recently arrived immigrants, Christianity spread literate culture and Greco-Roman civilization to the peoples of Europe.

But Christianity was not left unchanged in the process. Under the motto "One Emperor, One Empire, One Church," Constantine's conversion began the evolution of a religious movement into a *state church* based on a single set of Orthodox doctrines, state patronage, and the power to persecute "heretics" and deviants. Bishops became, in effect, princes of the Church. The established Church went from being a dynamic activist group championing simple people and humility, to one fully invested in the majesty of the imperial state. In part, this was beneficial to officials of the Church as they received guaranteed funding and protection from the state, which collected tithes from people forcibly. Unfortunately, though, the Church lost its collective dynamism. With an end to voluntary membership and tithing, shirking became a major problem. Efforts to overcome this problem and "reform" the Church of its corruption continued by devoted adherents and zealots for centuries until Martin Luther led a successful revolt that reintroduced organizational pluralism into Christianity and reinvigorated its parishioner base (Stark, 2003: 15–119). Leaving the European story to be told by others, we now turn to another tale of religious advocacy that succeeded centuries later and a half a world away.

Protestant advocacy in Latin America

From the time of the Conquest in the early sixteenth century, Latin America has always been thought of as a Catholic continent. The

---

[25] The upkeep of pagan temples and the provision of pagan festivals were not shared widely among adherents, but rather these costs were borne by only a few wealthy patrons (MacMullen, 1981: 112).

Roman Church maintained a strict monopoly over the provision of religious goods and services throughout the colonial era with the assistance of the Spanish and Portuguese crowns. Following independence from Iberia in the early nineteenth century, Catholicism remained the most prominent faith in the region despite a series of successful attempts by republican governments to weaken its organizational structure, largely by the confiscation of Church wealth. However, by the last two decades of the twentieth century, scholars were surprised by the "sudden" appearance of a substantial number of evangelical Protestants and Pentecostals in a number of countries, including Brazil, Chile, Nicaragua, and Guatemala (Martin, 1990; Stoll, 1990). Estimates of their penetration in these four countries by the end of the century ranged from 15 to 25 percent (Barrett, Kurian, and Johnson 2001). Protestant growth in the other countries in the region was occurring as well (Chesnut, 2003). If one considers Protestant missions and indigenous churches to be advocacy groups pushing their "brand" of Christianity, the success of these advocates in "Catholic-dominated" territory is nothing short of astonishing. How were Protestants able to get a toehold in the region?

The answer to the above question, not surprisingly, fits well with the religious economies perspective and mirrors the reasons for early Christian success. Some things never change. Protestants succeeded in Latin America by exploiting both a growing environment of religious freedom in the early 1900s and the organizational weakness of the Catholic Church. Being "strangers in a strange land," their success also depended upon the ability to convince potential converts that their message was credible. This was accomplished by enduring persecution, doing good deeds and indigenizing the movement. Finally, just like early Christians, Latin American Protestants grew with organizations that provided an attractive set of club goods for those who were willing to abide by a strict set of behavioral standards. In the process of making inroads into the continent, Protestant competition provided a strong incentive for the Catholic Church to reinvigorate itself, becoming a much more effective "advocate" for its own parishioners.

The first step in becoming a successful religious advocate group is having the freedom to champion your ideas. The turbulence that followed Latin American independence in the 1800s created small cracks in the regulatory policies that favored the Catholic Church. While Catholicism was still the preferred religion, a number of governments – particularly those wishing to establish trade relations with the United States and Europe – grew more tolerant of visiting Protestants (Gill, 2007: 136–138). This first allowed the establishment of "ethnic" Protestant churches to serve the needs of foreigners but eventually some missionary groups began getting a foothold in the region. While the Catholic Church was irritated by these developments, national governments generally (with a few exceptions) considered missionaries harmless and allowed them to go about their lives with minimal interference.[26] Local persecution did occur as will be detailed below, but religious freedom tended to expand at the national level in most countries as the twentieth century wore on (Gill, 2007). A big shift in attention by missionaries occurred in the 1930s when Asian mission fields became too dangerous because of Japanese military expansion. Missionaries typically went to places where earlier missions had proved successful and in the 1930s and 1940s the expansion of evangelical Protestantism took wing.

The success of Protestantism was first conditioned by the general weakness of the Catholic Church. Having relied upon government assistance to ensure their dominance for centuries, the Church lacked a strong connection to its parishioners. While guaranteed funding was cut during the 1800s for several national churches, bishops tended to devote their scarce personnel to serving the upper classes in the cities, since that was where the most money was. As such, the Church tended to rely upon a small handful of donors to fund an organization that ostensibly was meant to serve the entire population. Since the majority of the population was poor and the Church did not seek actively to engage them in participation (in large part because of a significant shortage of clergy), most of the population became free riders on Catholic theology by default. They received the overall blessings and spiritual message of the Church, but did not have to contribute financially or actively attend Mass. When missionaries entered the region, they found the easiest pickings among those who were least connected to the Church – the rural and urban poor. Although the Protestants demanded attendance, financial contributions, and voluntary labor to support their new churches, they also provided an opportunity for fellowship and other club goods that the Catholic Church had failed to provide for so long. We shall discuss these club goods momentarily.

One of the biggest problems faced by these foreign missionaries was the problem of credibility. Why would an indigenous Latin American want to join a church run by some "gringo" speaking in broken Spanish? Like early Christians in the Roman Empire, Protestant missionaries had to find ways to invest in the trustworthiness of their organizations so as to

---

[26] There were a number of instances where the national government did prosecute and/or evict Protestant missionaries, particularly in Argentina and Colombia. Most government persecution of missionaries occurred at the local level at the behest of a parish priest or bishop. See Gill (1998) for a discussion of this persecution.

convince potential members that their "credence goods" were worth purchasing. And like early Christians this was accomplished through strong witness in the face of persecution and by performing good deeds. While national governments were less willing to persecute Protestants for proselytizing, local governments or communities would often be whipped up into a persecuting frenzy against missionaries, who would have their houses ransacked, their possessions seized, and their families harassed. A number of missionaries even suffered physical aggression (Goff, 1968; Gill, 1998: 93–94). But like St. Paul, these missionaries demonstrated a no quit attitude that sent the signal to potential adherents that the goods they were peddling were worth the price.

Another creative method of enhancing credibility came in the form of indigenizing the movement. Blonde-haired, blue-eyed missionaries would always be treated with a bit more mistrust than somebody from the local town. Where missionary movements were able to recruit local residents to staff their churches, membership soared. Credibility comes with familiarity, and evangelical Christians used this to great advantage whereas the Catholic Church relied heavily on imported priests from the United States and Europe (Gill, 1998: 86).[27] Beyond this, Protestants excelled at doing good deeds to build trust. Foreign missionaries and indigenous pastors would help with community works projects such as digging wells or irrigation ditches. They would care for the sick and provide free immunizations. And oft-times they would provide education to children and adults in towns where such opportunities were limited. Indeed, it could be easily argued that evangelical Protestants had a "preferential option for the poor" long before their Latin American Catholic counterparts did (Cook, 1985).

In addition to building credibility to win converts, evangelicals excelled at providing a number of attractive club and private goods for members, thereby making their groups more attractive than Catholic parishes. These club goods included social insurance for economic losses: members of the evangelical community would pool their resources if one of their spiritual brothers or sisters was in need. Members were also provided with self-help groups, available only to members, aimed at reducing drinking, gambling, and other sorts of destructive behavior (Brusco, 1995). Simple fellowship

---

[27] One significant advantage that evangelicals, and particularly Pentecostals, have over Catholics is the time and cost it take to train clergy and put them in the field. Becoming a Catholic priest largely requires a high-school degree and an additional five to seven years of seminary training. Pentecostal ministers are generally trained via informal apprenticeship while attending services, need not be formally educated, and can be sent out to plant their own church within a year or two of being identified as a congregational leader (Chesnut, 2003: 56–59).

was also largely attractive. Catholicism tends to be a more priest-centric religion where the congregants take a secondary role. And until the mid 1960s, Catholic Mass was still widely recited in Latin, a language only understood by the clergy (and then not by all of them). This created a sense of formalism and isolation within the parish. Evangelical and Pentecostal services, by contrast, heavily involved the laity and included communal confessions and enlivening music. The lay involvement in religious services provided many individuals with valuable leadership skills that directly translated into the working world, yet another attractive club good (Chesnut, 1997).

These club goods did not come free, however. Membership in evangelical and Pentecostal congregations generally required significant behavioral modifications that would set an individual apart from their Catholic neighbors, hence increasing the costs of ostracism and sometimes even exposing them to physical attack. In southern Mexico, Protestants who opted out of mandatory payments for Catholic fiestas became the target of violent assaults on property and person (Isáis, 1998). Like behavioral and dress codes for Orthodox Jews, Jehovah's Witnesses, and Mormons, these restrictions had the effect of limiting a member's outside social activities. As per Iannaccone's (1992) prediction, these sacrifices and stigmas filtered out any potential free riders at the outset. This, in turn, meant that the members of the church would be more likely to participate in collective activities, thereby enhancing the quality of the public goods provided. When outsiders viewed the huge benefits that members received, they were more apt to pay those initial behavioral costs and join the group. The movement grew exponentially and continues to be remarkably vibrant today.

It was not only the Protestants that benefited directly from their own work. These advocates for a new religious tradition in Latin America spurred the old tradition to consider new techniques. The competitive pressure from evangelicals that arose in religiously deregulated markets forced the Catholic Church to pay closer attention to its own adherents lest they lose them to their competitors (Gill, 1998). While Catholic bishops initially tried to get governments simply to ban Protestants in the mid twentieth century, this strategy proved impractical as governments were naturally reluctant to punish good citizens. By the 1960s, though, the Catholic Church began adopting many of the practices of Protestant missionaries and Pentecostal communities. They bolstered their offerings of club goods such as literacy groups designed after Protestant missions. They even began offering greater opportunities for lay leadership and fellowship. The charismatic Catholic movement in Latin America is an effort by the Church specifically to imitate the pastoral techniques of Pentecostals – and it is working (Chesnut, 2003: 64–100). It quickly became apparent that the Catholic Church was a more vibrant organization after it found methods of involving the laity in the production of these club goods and relied less upon the support of the government for their funding. Finally, Catholic Church officials began reinvesting in the credibility of their own organizations by creating programs designed to show greater pastoral care for the poor whom they had long neglected.

Muslim advocacy in the United States

The same competitive factors that explain religious vitality historically and comparatively can help to explain why religion can serve the most important vehicle for immigrant integration into a new society and polity. This general statement applies not only to religions common to the sending and receiving country, but to "newcomer" religions as well. The case of Islam in the United States offers something close to a "natural experiment" in how religious deregulation promotes both religious vitality and the development of advocacy organizations that promote immigrant interests.

The Muslim population of the USA grew substantially with changes in immigration law after 1965, leading to more than 1 million Muslim immigrants, chiefly from Arab countries and the Middle East, South Asia, Iran, Sub-Saharan Africa, and Southeast Asia (in that order), entering the country between 1965 and 1997 (Nimer, 2002: 25; Pew, 2007). There are more than 2 million Muslims in the United States (Smith, 2002; Pew, 2007). This pattern of migration has given the country the most ethnically diverse Muslim population in the world (Read, 2008). This ethnic diversity, combined with the fact that religious life is heavily regulated in all majority Muslim societies but deregulated in the USA, has led to a flourishing of Islamic diversity. The result is substantial competition for influence and support among Muslim clergymen and leaders that sprawls across various liberal, traditionalist, reformist, and Islamist positions.

The resulting pluralism within American Islam has promoted innovation and openness to discovery that has allowed intellectuals and theologians to address the compatibility of Islam with democracy, Muslim respect for human rights, and the toleration of diversity (Esposito, 2007). Leonard (2003: 159) reports an Indian American Muslim scientist declaring that "internally, it [the USA] is the most Islamic state that has been operational in the last three hundred years ... the existence of a Muslim pubic sphere where Muslims can think freely to revive and practice Islam is a gift to Muslims." Similarly, the former president of the Association of Pakistani Physicians in North America declared: "In this country, Muslims have the opportunity to practice Islam as it should be practiced because there is no government edict to restrict religion, nor is there sectarian control over belief" (159). Nimer sums up the opinion of moderate Muslim leaders that, despite the fallout from the 9/11 attacks, "America is the land of promise for Muslims."

In the United States, Muslim immigration is primarily driven by educational and economic opportunities, especially in the fields of healthcare, science, and engineering (about 50% migrated for these opportunities), as well as the seeking of refuge from persecution and conflict (20%) (Pew, 2007). This means that Muslim immigration is drawn disproportionately from resourceful sections of the society of origin (Nimer, 2002: 36–37). Muslim immigrants and their offspring generally enjoy relatively high income and educational levels; the share of Muslim adults identifying as White or Asian (65% of all Muslim adults) who were college graduates in 2001 was 52% – 19% above the US average. More than 40% of American Muslims rate their financial situation as "excellent or good" and about 70% believe that people who work hard get ahead in the USA (Pew, 2007).

Unlike the situation that obtains in much of Europe, American Muslims are not highly concentrated into urban ghettos. American Muslims of Arab and Middle Eastern origins are largely suburban residents living in mixed districts in the New York, Washington, Detroit, San Francisco, and Los Angeles metro areas (Nimer, 2002: 36–37). And while African-American Muslims and African-born Muslims are relatively disadvantaged, about two-thirds of Muslims in the USA can be considered prosperous suburbanites. Like culturally distinctive immigrant groups before them, in America Muslims and their offspring have built their communities around religious associations that provide a link with the "homeland" and a basis for group advocacy in the new country (Breton, 1964; Hirschman, 2004). And, much like other fairly prosperous suburbanites in the USA, American Muslims have been especially drawn to religiously conservative, congregationally organized religion as a vehicle for their public identities and interests.

In other words, neither the predominant forms of Muslim organization nor the conservatism of many of the leading religious organizations stands out as distinctive in the USA. More than three-fourths of Americans identify with a religious group and nearly 60% belong to a religious organization. Kosmin and Mayer (2001) have found that about 60% of Muslim Americans report belonging to a mosque, which is about the same as the share of American Christians that report church membership. And just over a fifth

(20.6%) of Muslims report mosque attendance at least once a week, substantially below the level of reported weekly church attendance in the USA (*c.* 45%). While there are differences in beliefs and values between Muslims and adherents of other faiths, the religiosity of American Muslims is not particularly noteworthy in the USA.

Recent organizational surveys estimate that there are about 1,200 mosques and prayer rooms in the USA (Kosmin and Mayer, 2001; Nimer, 2002). Most have been established by Muslim nonprofit organizations that, in addition to establishing mosques and places of worship, also offer language instruction, charitable assistance, cultural outreach, academic parochial schools, and religious training. In the USA the usual form of governance in mosques is congregational and locally oriented. As Nimer (2002: 47) reports, while some mosques are registered as places of worship, others are chartered under laws regulating the operation of nonprofit organizations. As private entities, these centers answer to their own boards. Local community leadership typically includes boards of directors or trustees, usually including the founding members, executive officers and imams. In addition to the directors and hired staff most activities in the Islamic centers are planned and supervised through volunteer committees, whose level of commitment usually determines the vibrancy of mosque life.

In many cases, American Muslim congregations are "not very large and usually do not have full-time imams; some hire part-time employees for the job" while others "assign these duties to the most learned mosque member willing to volunteer his time" (Nimer, 2002: 47–48). Most American Muslim congregations were established by members of particular ethnic groups and remain primarily associated with that ethnicity; nevertheless, few (10%) report being ethnically exclusive (Nimer, 2002: 49).

Nimer's description of organized American Muslim religious life is virtually indistinguishable from that of other congregationally organized religious groups in the United States and bears a close resemblance to the experience of other immigrant groups. In fact, the description of the local governance and widely varying attitudes toward professionalized clergy is comparable to American Protestantism, which ranges from mainline denominations staffed by seminary graduates through non-denominational churches with lay clergy. Likewise, the provision of parochial schooling is a classic feature of America's immigrant religious organizations and, in establishing a growing sector of religious schools of their own, Muslims have followed on the ground trod by Roman Catholics, Jews, and Missouri-Synod Lutherans, among others. In 2001, Nimer (2002: 54–55) already identified more than seventy full-time Muslim private schools enrolling up to 30,000 students in the range from Kindergarten to Level 12.

Many Muslim organizations in the United States aspire to fill the role described by Breton's (1964) classic depiction of a self-organizing immigrant community, with a church, synagogue or mosque serving as a ubiquitous feature of the immigrant experience in the USA. The immigrant center of New York City with about 400,000 Muslim residents has more than seventy registered mosques and prayer rooms and at least fifty Muslim advocacy organizations. These have a variety of issue focuses in areas such as education (15 organizations), ethnic affairs (13), media (7), college student associations (7), religious liberties (4), and social services (2) (Nimer, 2002: 255–266). The Imam Al-Khoei Foundation located in the Jamaica section of Queens is an example of the variety of roles that Muslim advocacy organizations play. This Shiite organization offers a diverse range of services to adherents that includes prayer rooms, a conference center, a medical clinic, a parochial school, a Saturday school for religious and Arabic language instruction, a library, a monthly newsletter, prayer timetables and moon sightings, marriage counseling, family dispute resolution, the coordination of charitable giving, Islamic funeral services, and a question-and-answer service for the faithful (www. al-khoei.org).

Nimer (2002: ix–x) identifies about two dozen Islamic organizations operating at the national level, ranging across the ethnic, theological, and political spectrums. Many of these are organized as national peak, or umbrella, organizations based on a federation of local congregations and cultural centers. Some of the most prominent include the Islamic Society of North America, the largest umbrella group, a multiethnic association of Muslim professional and youth groups that grew out of the largely Arabic Muslim Students' Association; the Islamic Circle of North America, largely composed of South Asian groups concerned with education, public affairs, and lobbying; the Muslim American Society, a federation of mosques focused on education and cultural affairs with an agenda said to be strongly influenced by foreign Islamism; and the Nation of Islam – W. D. Mohammed, the Sunni branch of the African-American Muslim community (Nimer, 2002: 71; Leonard, 2003: 151).

In addition, American Muslims have founded nationwide political lobbying organizations, including the predominantly South Asian American Muslim Alliance, the Muslim Public Affairs Council, the American Muslim Council, the Council on American-Islamic Relations, and the American Muslim Political Coordinating Council (AMPCC) umbrella group (Leonard, 2003: 151). Prior to 9/11, some Muslim political leaders were responding to the agenda of the Republican Party, particularly the emphasis on business ownership, family values, and faith-based initiatives. Indeed, in the 2000 election, AMPCC, the largest political organization of American Muslims, endorsed George W. Bush's presidential candidacy (153). Nimer (2002: 173) considered this indicative of political maturity and willingness to integrate into American institutions: "Muslim leading organizations are increasingly expressing views based on their own strategic interests as American Muslim citizens who earn a living in North America." Nevertheless, this endorsement was neither repeated nor courted in the 2004 national election.

In general, American Muslim advocacy organizations at the national level engage in a range of initiatives including religious liberties, Muslim civil rights, international relief, domestic charities and social services, refugee assistance, health and welfare services, education and outreach, and press and media affairs. Most American Muslim congregations are not closely associated with a particular school of Islamic thought and, beginning in the 1990s, some Muslim leaders intentionally distanced themselves from foreign sponsors. Rather, many prominent voices in Muslim advocacy call for the elaboration of a specifically American Islam and are making "conspicuous efforts to bring Muslims into US public life" (Leonard, 2003: 153).

Daniel Olson (2007: 10) summarizes much of the recent literature on religious diversity and congregational life aptly: "In America, people are free to belong to an unusual religion without being considered un-American. In these religious spaces, people are free to construct their own unique subcultural identities, interact with others like themselves, and even speak their own language without pressure from others to conform." In the United States, Islam takes on the characteristic organizational forms and theological diversity previously observed in other American immigrant religions (Casanova, 2007; Esposito, 2007). For the most part, Muslims have taken up their place in a diverse religious landscape as have other religious newcomers; indeed, surveys indicate that, even after 9/11, Americans have the greatest contempt not for "foreign" religious minorities but for those that reject religion altogether (Edgell, Gerteis, and Hartman 2006). In short, organized Islam has been an important voice for asserting the interests and identities of Muslims and has certainly eased their integration into American polity and society.

Conclusion: Lessons from the economics of religion

No one could expect secular advocacy groups to mimic the success of early Christians by feeding some of their organizational leaders to the lions. Nor would prohibiting members of these same groups from drinking be a smart policy to implement. In some ways, the organizational methods used by successful spiritual denominations are unique to religious organizations. Nonetheless, the techniques employed by churches to attract and retain members, and to limit free riding and shirking, do indicate some general points to think about in the study of advocacy groups. Successful religious groups historically have excelled in generating committed memberships that share a common philosophical (or theological) goal that is not always achievable in the short run. Given that advocacy groups by their very nature are advocating some sort of improvement for humanity at large or their constituents specifically, the issue of the credibility of the group's message takes on central importance. Members will not join, nor will they contribute wholeheartedly, if they do not believe the promise they are hearing from the advocacy group. Enhancing such credibility will involve behaviors and signals by the leadership that they can be trusted with donations, and that they will not abuse the volunteer labor that they request. Credibility may also include showing short-term successes in areas not necessarily related to the greater cause, something akin to doing "good deeds" by churchgoers.

And while many advocacy groups such as the Sierra Club and the National Rifle Association are involved in producing public goods for a large constituency (nature lovers or gun owners), they also need to be aware of the nature of the club goods that they provide. Advocacy groups can provide not only a basket of private goods (e.g. nifty calendars) for members, but also some club goods that give an incentive for greater participation among members. Those groups that tend to provide a mixture of private, club, and public goods will be more successful in the long run than those that merely focus exclusively on either the public or private goods they provide. Indeed, an exclusive focus on ideologically generated public goods without some attention to private goods will result in anemic participation over time (cf. Gill and Lundsgaarde, 2004). Finally, it needs to be recognized by scholars that advocacy groups will be most effective when they are able to secure the voluntary collective participation of their membership in terms of monetary contributions or donated time. Advocacy groups that rely upon the coercive force of a government to help them meet their financial obligations may meet their goals in the short term, but will invariably lose the organizational connection to the people that they need the most – the ones that believe in their cause. Acting in good faith will always motivate faithful acts. Amen.[28]

---

[28] QED for the secular readers.

References

Barrett, D. B., G. T. Kurian, and T. M. Johnson. 2001. *World Christian Encyclopedia*, 2 vols. Oxford University Press.

Berger, P. L. (ed.). 1999. *The Desecularization of the World: Resurgent Religion and World Politics*. Grand Rapids, MI: Eerdmans.

Breton, R. 1964. Institutional Completeness of Ethnic Communities and the Personal Relationships of Immigrants. *American Journal of Sociology*, **70**: 193–205.

Brooks, A. C. 2006. *Who Really Cares: The Surprising Truth about Compassionate Conservativism*. New York: Basic Books.

Bruce, S. 2002. *God Is Dead: Secularization in the West*. London: Blackwell.

Brusco, E. 1995. *The Reformation of Machismo: Evangelical Conversion and Gender in Colombia*. Austin: University of Texas Press.

Casanova, J. 2007. Immigration and the New Religious Pluralism: A European Union/United States Comparison. In T. Banchoff (ed.), *Democracy and the New Religious Pluralism*. Oxford University Press.

Chesnut, R. A. 1997. *Born Again in Brazil*. New Brunswick, NJ: Rutgers University Press.

2003. *Competitive Spirits: Latin America's New Religious Economy*. Oxford University Press.

Chong, D. 1991. *Collective Action and the Civil Rights Movement*. University of Chicago Press.

Chwe, M. S.-Y. 2001. *Rational Ritual: Culture, Coordination and Common Knowledge*. Princeton University Press.

Cook, G. 1985. *The Expectation of the Poor: Latin American Base Ecclesial Communities in Protestant Perspective*. Maryknoll, NY: Orbis Books.

Crossan, D. and J. Reed. 2004. *In Search of Paul*. New York: HarperCollins.

Davie, G. 1994. *Religion in Britain since 1945: Believing without Belonging*. Oxford: Wiley-Blackwell.

Edgell, P., J. Gerteis, and D. Hartmann. 2006. Atheists as "Other": Moral Boundaries and Cultural Membership in American Society. *American Sociological Review*, 71(2): 211–234.

Ekelund, R., R. Hébert, and R. Tollison. 2006. *The Marketplace of Christianity*. Cambridge, MA: MIT Press.

Esposito, J. 2007. America's Muslims: Issues of Identity, Religious Diversity, and Pluralism. In T. Banchoff (ed.), *Democracy and the New Religious Pluralism*. Oxford University Press.

Fetzer, J. S. and J. C. Soper. 2005. *Muslims and the State in Britain, France and Germany*. Cambridge University Press.

Finke, R. 1990. Religious Deregulation: Origins and Consequences. *Journal of Church and State*, 32(3): 609–626.

Finke, R. and R. Stark. 2006. *The Churching of America, 1776–2005: Winners and Losers in Our Religious Economy*. New Brunswick, NJ: Rutgers University Press.

Fox, J. 2006. World Separation of Religion and State into the 21st Century. *Comparative Political Studies*, 39(5): 537–569.

Froese, P. and S. Pfaff. 2001. Replete and Desolate Markets: Poland, East Germany and the New Religious Paradigm. *Social Forces*, 80(2): 481–508.

Gill, A. 1998. *Rendering Unto Caesar: The Catholic Church and the State in Latin America*. University of Chicago Press.

2004. Weber in Latin America: Is Protestant Growth Enabling the Consolidation of Democratic Capitalism? *Democratization*, **11**(4): 42–65.

2007. *The Political Origins of Religious Liberty*. Cambridge University Press.

Gill, A. and E. Lundsgaarde. 2004. State Welfare Spending and Religious Participation: A Cross-National Analysis. *Rationality and Society*, **16**(4): 399–436.

Goff, J. E. 1968. *The Persecution of Protestant Christians in Colombia, 1948–1958*. Cuernavaca, Mexico: CIDOC.

Gorman, M. J. 2004. *Apostle of the Crucified Lord*. Grand Rapids, MI: Eerdmans.

Grim, B. and R. Finke. 2007. Religious Persecution in Cross-National Contexts: Clashing Civilizations or Regulated Religious Economies. *American Sociological Review*, **72**(4): 633–658.

Harris, J. C. 1993. Pennies for Heaven: Catholic Underachievers. *Commonweal*, **9**(April): 8–9.

Hewitt, W. E. 1991. *Base Communities and Social Change in Brazil*. Lincoln: University of Nebraska Press.

Hirschman, C. 2004. The Role of Religion in the Origins and Adaptation of Immigrant Groups in the United States. *International Migration Review*, **38**(3): 1206–1223.

Iannaccone, L. R. 1990. Religious Practice: A Human Capital Approach. *Journal for the Scientific Study of Religion*, **29**(3): 297–314.

1991. The Consequences of Religious Market Structure: Adam Smith and the Economics of Religion. *Rationality and Society*, **3**(2): 156–177.

1992. Sacrifice and Stigma: Reducing Free-Riding in Cults, Communes and Other Collectives. *Journal of Political Economy*, **100**(2): 271–291.

1994. Why Strict Churches Are Strong. *American Journal of Sociology*, **99**(5): 1180–1211.

1995. Voodoo Economics? Reviewing the Rational Choice Approach to Religion. *Journal for the Scientific Study of Religion*, **34**: 76–88.

Isáis, J. M. 1998. Mexico: Out of the Salt Shaker. *Christianity Today* (November 16): 72–73.

Jenkins, P. 2002. *The Next Christendom: The Coming of Global Christianity*. Oxford University Press.

Johnson, P. 1976. *A History of Christianity*. New York: Atheneum.

Kosmin, B. and E. Mayer. 2001. Profile of the U.S. Muslim Population: American Religious Identification Survey (ARIS), Report No. 2. New York: Graduate Center, City University of New York.

Leonard, K. 2003. American Muslim Politics: Discourses and Practices. *Ethnicities*, **3**(2): 147–181.

MacMullen, R. 1981. *Paganism in the Roman Empire*. New Haven, CT: Yale University Press.

Martin, D. 1990. *Tongues of Fire: The Explosion of Protestantism in Latin America*. Cambridge, MA: Basil Blackwell.

Nimer, M. 2002. *The North American Muslim Resource Guide: Muslim Community Life in the United States and Canada*. London: Routledge.

Norris, P. and R. Inglehart. 2004. *Sacred and Secular: Religion and Politics Worldwide*. Cambridge University Press.

Olson, D. 2007. American Religion: Will it Heal or Divide the Nation? *Contemporary Sociology*, **36**(1): 8–11.

Pew. 2007. *Muslim Americans: Middle-Class and Mostly Mainstream*. Washington, DC: Pew Research Center.

Read, J. 2008. Muslims in America. *Contexts* (Fall): 39–43.

Smith, A. 1976 [1776]. *An Inquiry into the Nature and Causes of the Wealth of Nations*, vol. II. Indianapolis: The Liberty Fund.

Smith, C. (ed.). 1996. *Disruptive Religion: The Force of Faith in Social Movement Activism*. New York: Routledge.

Smith, T. 2002. The Muslim Population of the United States: The Methodology of Estimates. *Public Opinion Quarterly*, **66**(3): 404–417.

Stark, R. 1996. *The Rise of Christianity: A Sociologist Reconsiders History*. New York: HarperCollins.

2003. *For the Glory of God: How Monotheism Led to the Reformations, Science, Witch-Hunts, and the End of Slavery*. Princeton University Press.

Stark, R. and R. Finke. 2000. *Acts of Faith: Explaining the Human Side of Religion*. Berkeley: University of California Press.

Stark, R. and L. R. Iannaccone. 1994. A Supply-Side Reinterpretation of the "Secularization" of Europe. *Journal for the Scientific Study of Religion*, **33**(3): 230–252.

Stoll, D. 1990. *Is Latin America Turning Protestant?* Berkeley: University of California Press.

4 Institutional environment and the organization of advocacy NGOs in the OECD

Elizabeth A. Bloodgood

Research on international advocacy organizations has generally focused on the agency of organizations and their ability to organize campaigns, gather resources, and contact decision-makers to shape foreign policy and international regimes. This is the approach taken in contributions to this volume by Maryann Barakso and McGee Young. In this chapter, I take a slightly different approach and examine the political institutions which frame advocacy. I examine national regulation within OECD countries to gauge variations in the opportunities and costs imposed on international advocacy organizations in different countries. Existing literature sees states and international organizations as targets of advocacy organizations, but governments also make the rules within which domestic and international advocacy organizations operate. In the collective action approach presented in this volume, national regulation determines the costs of organizing, the incentives available to attract members and financing, and available legal identities, thus raising or lowering barriers for international advocacy organizations considering entry. The opportunities and constraints written into national legislation thus shape the choice of locations for international advocacy organizations as they decide where to establish national branches.

This chapter investigates the scope and specifics of national regulation regarding advocacy NGOs within the Organization for Economic Cooperation and Development (OECD). By scope I mean the number and types of regulatory instruments applicable to advocacy organizations in a particular country. I also examine the specific details of regulations, in particular the ability of advocacy organizations in a given country to engage in political and/or economic activities and the process by which organizations gain legal identity and the ability to operate. I address two questions in particular: how do governments approach the regulation of international advocacy organizations and how do regulations vary across OECD members? Governments select among a number of different approaches to regulating international and domestic advocacy organizations, including the use of civil codes, laws specific to associations, and tax codes; prescriptive versus proscriptive rules on behavior; and different levels of specificity producing regulations of very different complexity and stringency. The severity of regulations varies with the number of distinct provisions advocacy operations must follow, while the overall complexity depends on the total length of regulations of which advocacy organizations must be aware. At the end of this chapter, I also assess the relationship between the regulatory approach of governments, including the scope, severity, and complexity of regulation, and the location of international advocacy organizations within the OECD.

A collective action approach to international advocacy organizations which focuses on the incentives and constraints presented by national regulations not only helps to examine variations in the locations and operations of advocacy organizations, but also differences in national regulations. The gaps in our understanding of international advocacy organizations are exacerbated by an empirical problem. We lack a systematic record of national regulations regarding advocacy organizations' organizational structures, legal identity, resources, and allowable operations. This chapter uses a new dataset containing national regulation on rules regarding the legal identity, rights, responsibilities, available resources, and political freedoms for advocacy organizations in the members of the Organization for Economic Cooperation and Development. This dataset contains information taken from national legal codes, national legislation, and explanatory publications for twenty-nine countries as well as economic and political indicators from the World Bank, the OECD, Polity IV, the CIA, and Smith and Weist (2005).

Different countries take different approaches to regulating the operations of international advocacy organizations in their jurisdictions. Governments such as those of Norway and Sweden see nongovernmental organizations, including international advocacy organizations, in a positive light, as groups working toward the common interest, and thus national regulations on the creation and operation of advocacy organizations are quite friendly and impose few burdens. In countries such as Switzerland and Luxembourg, NGOs are seen primarily as economic entities and thus the majority of legislation concerning international advocacy organizations concerns taxation and accounting standards. In countries such as Hungary and Poland, civil society organizations, including international advocacy organizations, have their own legal codes and are generally nurtured and protected. The cross-sectional analysis of regulations regarding international advocacy organizations within the OECD in this chapter complements the detailed case of

Russia by Sarah Henderson (this volume). The tradeoffs governments face in selecting how to regulate international advocacy organizations – the scope and specifics of regulation as well as whether regulation is generally proscriptive or prescriptive – and the impact of national regulations on advocacy organizations in these countries can be seen in more detail in this case study.

To the extent that national regulations make it more difficult for advocacy organizations to operate in a particular country, they raise barriers to entry for international advocacy organizations that might seek to locate there. In most countries, the resources legally required to operate an advocacy organization are minimal. But a government's requirements to account for resources, register activities, and file regular reports all impose costs on international advocacy organizations operating within its borders. Governments have a motivation to regulate advocacy organizations in their countries, as the existence of rules forces the organizations to reveal specific markers of their reputation and credibility. Registration and accounting rules allow governments to track the leadership, resources, activities, and contacts of international advocacy organizations and ensure that they behave in a responsible fashion. Proscribing behavior and explicitly describing procedures for dissolution provide a means to quickly and credibly punish undesirable behavior. But such rules may have the unintended consequence of raising the costs of collective action and cause international advocacy organizations to locate in other countries. National regulations are not universally negative or costly for advocacy organizations, as some governments use regulations to lower the costs of organizing and subsidize operations rather than instituting barriers. I find considerable variation in the scope (total amount and number of different types of regulation) and severity (number of separate requirements organizations must meet) of national regulations as well as in the extent to which government funding is a significant resource for nonprofit organizations, including advocacy organizations, and in the size of the international advocacy organization population in each country. Governments in the future might seize upon a clearer link between national regulation and the costs of collective action to manipulate regulations to set appropriate institutional conditions for international advocacy organizations to locate and operate within their borders given their desired relations with these organizations.

The institutional affinities of advocacy organizations

The literature on nonprofit, non-governmental organizations in international relations as well as in economics and public administration agrees that not all geographic locations are equally agreeable for the operation of international advocacy organizations. While the location of their operations may be dictated in part by their issue focus – for example, local groups advocating change in local legislation will have to work locally – theories of collective action and the new economics of organization assert that external institutions can have a strong effect on the ability of organizations to function in certain contexts, and thus on their interest in these locations.

Academics in international relations argue that organizations focus their advocacy campaigns in liberal democratic countries while treading lightly (if at all) within authoritarian and repressive regimes, even when it is the policies of these countries they most often want to change. Risse, Ropp, and Sikkink's boomerang model and Finnemore and Sikkink's norm cascade are classic examples. Activism by international advocacy organizations in key Western states creates domestic pressure within liberal democracies which can then put diplomatic pressure on closed regimes for norm-based policy change (Finnemore and Sikkink, 1998; Keck and Sikkink, 1998; Risse, Ropp, and Sikkink, 1999). Within sociology, collected volumes on global civil society and nonprofits (the third sector) focus upon OECD countries. In Salamon *et al.*'s *Global Civil Society* (1999, 2004), eighteen of twenty-three chapters concern OECD countries. Only in volume II, published in 2004, do they begin looking in earnest at non-OECD countries. Anheier and Seibel's *The Third Sector* (1990) has only one chapter devoted explicitly to non-OECD countries.

International advocacy organizations' geographic preferences are related to the issues they pursue, the availability of financing, and the nature of domestic political institutions. The expectation that most international advocacy organizations will be located in Western liberal democracies originates from the freedoms, rights, and access civil society organizations are guaranteed within national constitutions and the availability of funding from wealthy foundations and governments (Lipschutz, 1992: 409–413; Reimann, 2006). Keck and Sikkink (1998) and Risse, Ropp, and Sikkink (1999) reiterate the expectation that advocacy organizations, given the choice, will locate in places in which they have access to the policymaking process, which depends upon the institutional environment and principles and priorities of government. Often Middle Power liberal democratic states provide the most fodder for state partnerships. Quantitative studies of the activities of international NGOs from 1963 through 2000 find that most international NGOs are headquartered and financed within OECD countries (Skjelsbaek, 1971; Feld, 1972; Boli and Thomas, 1999; Smith and Weist, 2005). Only from the 1960s and 1970s have significant numbers of international NGOs built memberships and located offices in first Latin America and then Asia and Africa followed by

Central and Eastern Europe (Boli and Thomas, 1999: 32–34; Mendelson and Glenn, 2002: 1–5; Reimann, 2006: 51–54). As globalization enables dense network linkages on a global scale, we see an increasing number of international advocacy organizations active in an increasing number of locations, although with a strong preference for democracy and stability.

While the number of international advocacy organizations grows as global civil society and the third sector expand, international advocacy organizations are not spread evenly around the world and they take many different forms (Salamon *et al.*, 2004: 15–20). Social movement research within sociology takes two different approaches to explaining the conditions under which social movements are likely to prosper – political opportunity structure and resource mobilization (McAdam, McCarthy, and Zald, 1996; Staggenborg, 2008). While international advocacy organizations differ significantly from social movements in terms of their goals and internal structure, they too must be cognizant of the political institutions and resource constraints under which they operate. The awareness that political, institutional, and material constraints and opportunities can deter or facilitate international advocacy organizations is less useful than specific understandings of how institutional and material factors shape operations by international advocacy organizations. The collective action approach to advocacy organizations links insights from both political opportunity structure and resource mobilization theories in terms of effects on advocacy organizations' ability to form and operate and clarifies key concerns for international advocacy organizations which impact where they choose to locate.

National legislation and international advocacy organizations' collective action problem

The collective action perspective on advocacy organizations presented in this book (Prakash and Gugerty, this volume) proposes that advocacy organizations exist in a competitive policy market which is likely to have a significant impact on their structures and operations as these organizations seek to influence policy, survive, and grow. Advocacy organizations are thus guided by instrumental concerns as well as normative principles, and must overcome the challenges presented by diverse actors within the organization seeking to use the organization to pursue their self-interest while seeking common goals and the provision of public goods. While the collective action approach focuses on internal factors which affect the organization and operation of groups, external institutions matter to the extent that they affect the calculations of members of a potential group or organization (Moe, 1980; Yarbrough and Yarbrough, 1990;

Baumgartner and Leech, 1998). This chapter examines the effect of different types and combinations of national regulations on the ability of international advocacy organizations to overcome collective action problems in different places and thus the likelihood that international advocacy organizations will locate in a particular institutional context. I build from the central realization by Olson that not all possible groups have an equal likelihood of participating in politics. Group size, the interests at stake, and the ability to offer selective incentives (or to restrict the benefits of advocacy to members of the group) all affect the ability of an advocacy organization to operate effectively (Olson, 1965). Olson concludes that private interest groups are likely to out-organize and out-perform public interest groups, but gives few insights into variations among advocacy organizations, the vast majority of which seek to produce a public good. The lack of a theory of organization within Olson's work on the collective action problem is discussed in more detail by McGee Young in this volume, but there are several useful insights for understanding advocacy organizations here. Advocacy organizations are more likely to operate when they can avail themselves of incentives for membership, if they can bound their membership, and if they can increase members' stake/interest in the outcomes of advocacy such that members benefit directly when the organization benefits.

I argue in this chapter that there is a second set of factors which are important in determining international advocacy organizations' ability to operate in a particular country and thus their location decisions. Reflexive, self-interested decision-makers (the targets of advocacy organizations) are aware of the collective action problem advocacy organizations face. Decision-makers can and do use national institutions to impose barriers to entry and ameliorate or exacerbate certain of the organizational challenges that advocacy organizations face. National regulations can thus be used to select for certain types of groups and the representation of certain interests over others according to the preferences of key decision-makers. The more difficult and costly it is to operate an advocacy organization legally in a given institutional environment, the less likely an international advocacy organization is to choose this location to organize and operate such an organization (Ben-Ner and Van Hoomissen, 1993; Salamon and Toepler, 2000).

Governments have mixed interests regarding relationships with, and thus the regulation of, advocacy organizations both domestic and international. Advocacy organizations provide policymakers with the following: information about domestic and international issues, including the preferences of others on these issues; policy recommendations and expert advice on alternatives; help in lobbying to form winning coalitions for policy votes; orderly interest representation; a sense of public opinion on an issue; and a means to educate the public and mobilization tools which can be used by decision-makers to help sell a policy to the public. But domestic and international advocacy organizations have their own distinctive interests (instrumental and principled) and a strong desire to use their relationship with government for their own ends. Any given advocacy organization is likely to have opponents as well as supporters in government, depending on the side of the policy or issue they fall. Advocacy organizations as a category are likely to pose decision-makers a problem of mixed interests. Decision-makers anticipate benefits from some advocacy organizations, when these organizations provide information as well as supporters to help sway opinion toward their shared policy goals, but expect to face challenges by other organizations opposed to their policies.

As Salamon and Toepler explain, this is a variation of the common principal–agent problem which complicates relations between governments and advocacy organizations (Salamon and Toepler, 2000; see also Moe, 1984: 756; Williamson, 1991). Advocacy organizations want to sway policy to their own ideal point, rather than to negotiate or help to win support for a more moderate policy that might be preferred by policymakers. Advocacy organizations thus have strong incentives to use favorable relations with government (in terms of access for lobbying or economic resources) to push their interests (both policy and organizational) over the desires of the decision-makers (principals) in their dealings with their constituents, policymakers, donors, and other advocacy organizations. Decision-makers are also concerned that advocacy organizations can quickly become vocal critics and challenge government policy (particularly when blaming and shaming) in ways that may threaten policy objectives, especially in times of crisis. Advocacy organizations have a well-known incentive to exaggerate information and the urgency of issues, even going so far as to misinform decision-makers in order to get their own way. The public education they provide tends to be biased toward their own principles and priorities rather than be objective. Advocacy organizations also seek government funding for their organizational development (to grow the capacity of the organization) and inflated overhead may help guarantee organizational longevity at the cost of issue success.

The incentives of international advocacy organizations are similar to domestic advocacy organizations, although in comparison with international groups domestic groups may have different sources of power as their primary support (local constituency versus network which provides more resources and a claim to a larger international membership). Generally governments regulate international and domestic advocacy organizations in the same way. This is largely because most countries require that international advocacy organizations establish local (national) organizations with a national address, national funding, and/or national membership. Establishing a national branch is also in the interest of many international advocacy organizations as national presence provides legal protections, a local constituency, and access to national pools of resources. International advocacy organizations with national branches in a country may provide better information, more public opinion support, and stronger normative pressure for change on international issues than fully domestic advocacy organizations. Government decision-makers are more likely to form relationships with national branches of international advocacy organizations as they are better able to regulate these groups.

Government regulation can be used to limit advocacy organization independence, increase the ability of decision-makers to monitor organizations' activities and results, and force advocacy organizations to reveal their preferences and goals. Accounting rules and strict limitations on certain kinds of behavior (excessive politicization) as well as harsh punishments to deter cheating and lying (at the extreme, organizational dissolution as well as legal derecognition and fines) all help government decision-makers as principals control advocacy organizations as agents, while still benefiting from their information, expertise, and connections to the public (Moe, 1984; Yarbrough and Yarbrough, 1990).

Government regulation of nonprofits within any one OECD country is not entirely independent of regulations in other countries. Historic styles of law, primarily civil and common law traditions, have affected the way that nonprofits are regulated as has the length of time that advocacy organizations have been active in a country. While the UK (1872), Ireland (1875), and France (1901) have longstanding relationships with advocacy organizations, and thus older regulations, the Czech Republic (1990), Poland (1989), the Slovak Republic (1990), and South Korea (1975) are newer democracies with much newer legislation regulating newer populations of advocacy organizations. While nonprofit laws have been updated and amended over time, in most cases the initial laws still constitute the core of the regulations regarding advocacy organizations. As can be seen in Table 4.1, many countries use similar types of regulation to control advocacy organizations, albeit in different combinations. That said, the actual content of nonprofit law within the OECD is quite varied.[1] With the exception of small clusters within the OECD, particularly among Nordic countries and Eastern European countries, there is relatively little

---

[1] Data are available at http://alcor.concordia.ca/~eabloodg.

Table 4.1. *Popularity of alternative regulation types in the OECD*

Type of regulation	Use of regulation type
Taxation	100% (29/29)
Accounting	86% (25/29)
Registration	86% (25/29)
Campaign contributions	62% (18/29)
Lobbying	31% (9/29)
Demonstrations/direct action	17% (5/29)
Countries which use five or more types	17% (5/29)
Countries which use four types	48% (14/29)
Countries which use three types	31% (9/29)
Countries which use two or fewer types	4% (1/29)

isomorphism among advocacy organization regulations even for similar governments within the OECD (Bloodgood and Tremblay-Boire, 2008).

The collective action approach to advocacy organizations suggests several key leverage points for government decision-makers in their effort to use national regulation as a means of selecting certain types and structures of advocacy organization. Regulations limiting the range of organizational forms which will be given legal identity; raising the costs of organization by instituting more reporting requirements or hurdles to incorporation; increasing the ability of the government to punish organizations for unwanted behavior; and providing selective incentives and opportunities for financial support are the primary tools decision-makers possess to control and direct advocacy organizations' organizational forms and operations.

Barriers to entry

National decision-makers serve as gatekeepers not only to the policymaking process, but also to the legal system and the domestic populace of a country (Busby, 2007). As gatekeepers, decision-makers can raise several different types of barriers to entry to keep international advocacy organizations from entering (establishing a local branch in) their country. According to the collective action perspective, barriers to entry for an advocacy organization include the available legal forms a group can take and the requirements for legal personality; the necessity for legal personality to operate; allowable activities given the organizational form; and geographic limitations on operations.

Almost all countries make a distinction between public and private benefit organizations, and between associations, foundations, corporations, partisan political organizations and social benefit groups (often called charities or public benefit organizations (PBOs)). The extent to which advocacy organizations are able to cross boundaries and adopt multiple forms (or hybrid forms) of organization, and the range of activities and benefits allowed different forms, can vary dramatically across countries. The primary organizational forms available for advocacy organizations are nonprofit association or corporation; however, in practice, a larger set of organization types engage in substantial amounts of advocacy, and so even charities or public benefit organizations can be advocacy organizations. The legal line commonly drawn between nonprofit associations and public benefit organizations/charities concerns the extent to which the organization can engage in political advocacy. While formally and officially charities and PBOs are prohibited from partisan political activities, including giving campaign contributions, and political activity which is not central to their primary mission, this leaves plenty of room for political advocacy on the primary issues of concern to the organization. For example, according to Canadian regulations,

> where an organization devotes substantially all of its resources to charitable activities carried on by it and (a) it devotes part of its resources to political activities, (b) those political activities are ancillary and incidental to its charitable activities, and (c) those political activities do not include the direct or indirect support of, or opposition to, any political party or candidate for public office, the organization shall be considered to be devoting that part of its resources to charitable activities carried on by it. (1985 Income Tax Act, art. 149.1(6.1, 6.2))

The permissible economic activities also vary by organizational type, particularly between nonprofit corporations, associations/CSOs, and charities/PBOs. States differ primarily on whether nonprofit organizations can engage in commercial activities of any kind, whether the proceeds of commercial activities in line with the central mission of the organization are tax-deductible, and the range of money-making activities which are permissible. For example, in France,

[n]othing goes against the possibility of a declared association making profits, as long as it does not distribute them to its members. Among the economic activities that an association can undertake, some are commercial activities which can have various consequences depending on their type. Acts of commerce that are occasional and ancillary to the main activity cannot be dissociated from the nonprofit goal pursued by the association (organization of a ball, a carnival/kermesse, exploitation of a bar, selling of postcards, etc.). Acts of commerce that are habitual are the object of certain rules of commercial law (selling of books, etc.). (http://vosdroits.service-public.fr/particuliers/)

Alternatively, in Japan,

[a] specified nonprofit corporation may engage in operations other than those relating to specified nonprofit activities (referred to hereafter as "other operations"), to the extent that said other operations do not interfere with operations relating to specified nonprofit activities. Revenue generated from said other operations, if any, must be used in the specified nonprofit activities. (1998 SNPC Law, art. 5(1))

While nonprofit income can clearly not be distributed to members as direct gain and generally the income must be used toward the larger public interest goals of the organization, often the type of commercial activity is flexible, including contracts for services (e.g. consulting contracts), fundraisers, and even rental income and membership fees. National regulations vary widely on how this income is treated for tax purposes. In the Czech Republic,

the following kinds of income shall not be subject to the tax: (a) income from activities following from their mission provided that costs (expenses) spent according to this Act in connection with execution of these activities are higher; activities that are considered [within the] mission of these taxpayers are defined by special regulations, statutes, by-laws, establishment or foundation documents; (b) income from subsidies and other forms of state support and support given from municipal and regional budgets if this support is granted according to a special regulation; (c) income from interest from deposit on current account. (Act No. 586/1992, Income Tax Law, art. 20(4), Tax on Donations)

In Luxembourg, on the other hand, all associations and public benefit organizations pay tax on industrial and commercial activities (1967 Income Tax Act, art. 161(1)), while in the Slovak Republic and the United States organizations only pay tax on non-statutory economic activities (2003 Income Tax Act, § 13(1)(a), § 13(2)(b)). In Switzerland, Spain, and Portugal nonprofits pay tax, while public benefit organizations do not (1990 Income Tax Law, art. 71; Law 27/1984, of July 26, art. 22; 1988 Corporate Income Tax Code, art. 11), but in Sweden even public benefit organizations pay tax on operating expenses and property (Skatteverket, "Ideella föreningar – skatterättsliga regler").

The number of possible organization forms varies from country to country (from two to eight) as does the specificity with which categories are defined and the strength of the constraints imposed on the activities of different kinds of organization. For example, in England and Wales almost anything can be an association, but there are very strict organizational and operational constraints upon the creation and operation of charities. A charity must do one of the following:

(a) the prevention or relief of poverty; (b) the advancement of education; (c) the advancement of religion; (d) the advancement of health or the saving of lives; (e) the advancement of citizenship or community development; (f) the advancement of the arts, culture, heritage or science; (g) the advancement of amateur sport; (h) the advancement of human rights, conflict resolution or reconciliation or the promotion of religious or racial harmony or equality and diversity; (i) the advancement of environmental protection or improvement; (j) the relief of those in need by reason of youth, age, ill-health, disability, financial hardship or other disadvantage; (k) the advancement of animal welfare; (l) the promotion of the efficiency of the armed forces of the Crown, or of the efficiency of the police, fire and rescue services or ambulance services. (Charities Act 2006, part 1, sections 1–2)

In other countries, such as Hungary or Norway, organizations can belong to multiple categories at the same time. In Hungary,

[t]he following organizations, registered in Hungary, may be qualified as public benefit organizations: (a) civil society organizations, except insurance associations, political parties and interest groups of employers or employees, (b) foundations, (c) public foundations, (d) public benefit companies, (e) public chambers, if allowed by the act regulating their establishment. (1997. évi CLVI. törvény, 5(26. §)(c))

The meaning of public benefit for the purpose of organization is also much broader in Hungary, including environmental matters, societal matters, health, education, human rights, European relations, scientific activities, sports, public order, and consumer protection.

In countries in which advocacy organizations are able to adopt a greater range of organizational forms (or incorporate elements of several different legal identities), they may be better able to increase their freedom of movement and the types and amounts of political and economic resources available to them. For example, in Japan, advocacy organizations, like all associations, can only be specified public interest corporations (1998 SNPC Law, art. 15), while in Sweden advocacy organizations can be associations, foundations, non-investment funds, not-for-profit organizations providing publicly beneficial services (NPOs), religious organizations, political parties, political movements, trade unions, and professional associations. Choices regarding organizational form may cut in both directions, however, as in France all nonprofit organizations are considered associations and nonprofits since, in French, nonprofit organization and association are translated as "association sans but lucrative" and thus all are able to gain legal personality as associations, engage in advocacy, and sell goods and services to raise funds (although not to advance the economic interests of the board or individual members of the association) (Loi du 1er Juillet 1901).

The process by which an organization seeks legal identity can be as important as the criteria for being a particular entity. The number and complexity of steps necessary for status can increase costs and impose a barrier for some groups. In France, legal personality is acquired by all associations immediately upon issuing a declaration of the establishment of the organization (Loi du 1er Juillet 1901, art. 5), while in Poland advocacy organizations can get legal identity as incorporated associations but need not in order to undertake some tasks (1989 LOA, art. 40(1)), and in Denmark and Finland, in order to operate within these countries, associations must register with the appropriate body to become legal entities (2007 Tax Assessment Manual, A.F.5.2; 1989 Associations Act, art. 6). The need for formal government approval as opposed to simple publication of rules of conduct also increases the power of government to select for certain kinds of organization. In Japan, government ministries are tasked with approving the establishment of organizations, including advocacy organizations (Civil Code, art. 34), while in Hungary associations need court approval (1989. évi II. törvény, 1(4. §)(1)), and in the United States, the UK, and Canada, advocacy organizations seek approval for certain organizational forms from tax authorities (US Code, title 26, subtitle A, chapter 1, subchapter F, part 1, section 501(c)(3); Charities Act 2006, part 1, sections 1–2; Income Tax Act, chapter 148 of the Revised Statutes of Canada, 1952).

When it comes to the allowable activities of different categories of organization, countries vary on whether they prescribe allowable activities (leaving prohibited activities implicit) or explicitly prohibit certain activities but otherwise leave the field open. Differences in the legal approach to groups – whether the government regulates the purposes and objectives, as is the approach of common law countries, or the structure of the organization, as is done in civil law countries – matter here (Charities Definition Inquiry, 2001).[2]

Most common law and civil law countries distinguish between political activities (such as supporting or opposing candidates for public office or providing financial

---

[2] Data are available at http://alcor.concordia.ca/~eabloodg.

support to political parties) and advocacy activities (such as lobbying for causes or working for legislative reform). Civil law countries tend not to restrict legislative activities, while common law countries tend to follow historical practices of restricting both political and legislative activities. (Garland, 1999)

While a number of observers have commented on the affinity between civil and common law countries and proscriptive versus prescriptive approaches, there is little theoretical reasoning for why this might be the case. More comprehensive, systematic codes are found in civil code countries in which there are explicit bodies of association laws, while common law countries tend to provide broad rights and regulate against abuses or potential abuses (e.g. accounting, tax fraud, or partisanship) by advocacy organizations on an *ad hoc* basis, although charities/public benefit organizations often have more complete codes than nonprofits. Differences in regulatory approaches may also be cultural residuals, reflecting for example French stress on associational life, Japanese corporatism, and American freedom of association and activity.

National treatment of advocacy organizations (and other nonprofit organizations) is not the predominant rule, unlike with multinational corporations in economic transactions. In general, the registration requirements, reporting requirements, and limits on behavior are more stringent for foreign organizations than for domestic. For example, in Belgium, organizations can have either domestic or international status.

Organizations open to Belgian nationals as well as foreigners, with their headquarters in Belgium, and which pursue international nonprofit goals, as long as they do not disturb the public order, can be given *personnalité juridique* by the king. Only those international nonprofit organizations that have been created in accordance with the present law or the law of October 25, 1919, which gives personnalite civile to international organizations pursuing a philanthropic, religious, scientific, artistic, or educational goal, can be given the title "international non-profit organizations. (27 juin 1921, art. 3.47.2)

Luxembourg and Mexico represent the extremes. In Luxembourg, foreign organizations may operate as long as they respect national laws and do not pose a threat to domestic peace and stability (1928 Associations Law, art. 26(1)), while in Mexico "[t]he civil society organizations that constitute the national chapters of international organizations which fulfill the conditions established in article 3 can enjoy the rights established therein, if and when their organs of administration and representation are composed in their majority of Mexican citizens" (Ley Federal de Fomento, capitulo 1, art. 4).

Often governments reserve the right to allow a foreign organization to operate (or not), even if a right for nationals to assemble and associate is included within the national constitution. For example, "[t]he promotion and constitution of international associations in Portugal depends on authorization from the Government" (1974 Decree 594, art. 14) while all citizens enjoy the right to form associations (1966 Civil Code, art. 168). National bias in advocacy organizations can likely be explained by decision-makers' preferences for services and goods from local advocacy organizations, including local information and local interest representation rather than international opinion and pressure. National advocacy organizations also have increased legitimacy to participate in the policy-making process. Nelson and Dorsey (2007) argue that increasingly advocacy organizations find more common ground with their home governments than with international advocacy organizations which seem to threaten local norms and interests. National branches of international advocacy organizations may want to reinforce this bias if they feel that their position in a global network might be weak compared to more affluent and better connected foreign organizations (Jordan and Van Tuijl 2000). While this dynamic may be more obvious in developing countries, there are still large degrees of divergence among OECD countries and their advocacy organizations, particularly established advocacy organizations from the USA and UK versus organizations in South Korea, Mexico, Turkey, or Eastern European states. In Turkey, "foreign associations may operate or establish cooperation in Turkey, or open representations or branches, or form associations or supreme organizations or may join already founded associations or supreme organizations with the permission of the Ministry of Interior subject to the opinion of the Ministry of Foreign Affairs" (2004 Associations Law, art. 5). Such legislation, like that in Mexico, helps to discourage competition from international organizations and requires local presence. This home bias provides incentives for international advocacy organizations to use national branches for a coordinated international campaign, even if national legislation might impose tight constraints on the formation and operation of an organization.

Costs to organize and operate

The collective action approach to advocacy organizations points to a second concern regarding advocacy organizations' operations. Even in places in which there are few regulatory barriers to the creation and operation of an organization, there are still significant costs to the mobilization and maintenance of such a body. These costs may be sufficient to deter the creation of an advocacy organization, particularly in cases in which activities take on the character of a public good, as is often the case with advocacy (Moe, 1980; Tarrow, 1988; Meyer, 1997). Successful advocacy for policy change often benefits a large audience, but one that has limited incentives to participate actively. National regulations can intentionally and unintentionally manipulate the costs of organization and thus provide a second mechanism to screen and select for certain types of NGOs.

As Olson argues, the smaller the group, the easier the collective action problem is to solve. Each member feels the lack of contribution of any other more sharply and is better able to identify free riders (Olson, 1965). National legislation can thus set standards for the minimum size of an NGO which increase the size of the group and make collective action more difficult. National legislation can also set the minimum financial endowment necessary to obtain legal personality as a means to deter groups lacking well-endowed individuals or the capacity to obtain necessary government funding. Within the OECD, minimum size regulations range from twenty members in Greece to fifteen members in Poland, ten in Japan and Hungary, and two in Austria and France. Financing requirements range from no minimum (most countries) to 50,000 euros in Germany. Foundations more often have minimum requirements than nonprofits and relatively few advocacy organizations take this form as a result.

Regulation can impose costs of three other types on advocacy organizations: the costs of knowing the rules, following changes in the rules, and complying with regular accounting and reporting obligations. The first costs come in the form of the necessary knowledge and expertise to identify, understand, and comply with all of the rules which apply to nonprofit, non-governmental organizations. The more legislation (and the more types of legislation) that exist, the harder it is to stay abreast, to determine which parts do and do not apply, and to fully comply. National regulations regarding nonprofit, non-governmental organizations vary between three types of laws and sixteen requirements written in 4,076 characters (Switzerland) to five kinds of regulation written in 38,794 characters with sixty-seven requirements to fulfill (United States). In all cases character counts are based on English translations of laws to standardize linguistic differences. While not an exact match, character count as a measure of complexity is analogous to measures of complexity used in computer, cognitive, and complexity sciences. More bits of information, or more characters in a computer program, indicate a more complex task or phenomenon requiring greater processing abilities, either human or computer (Lloyd, n.d.; Lovasz, n.d.).

The second cost of organizing comes from having to comply with regulations. The more specific and detailed the regulation, and the more requirements there are, the higher the costs. Earlier examples of regulation from Japan as opposed to Luxembourg demonstrate a vast difference in terms of the specificity of the requirements that advocacy organizations must know and follow. The third cost written into national regulation comes in the form of registration and accounting rules. Registration and accounting may require paying fees to file forms, filing annual reports, and verifying income resources and expenditures as well as hiring an external auditor. The more detailed the information that NGOs have to report, and the more often that reports need to be filed or status renewed, the higher the costs and the fewer organizations that can form. For example, Austria requires larger organizations to hire chartered accountants (2002 Associations Act, art. 5(5)), while Poland only requires that organizations publish information in a way which is accessible to anyone interested (2003 PBO Law, art. 10(1)). Portugal allows one joint accounting according to organizational standards, while Poland requires different kinds of accounting practices and reporting for different kinds of income within an organization (1977 Decree 460, art. 12(a); 1997 PBO Law, art. 33–34).

Ability of advocacy organizations to offer selective incentives to attract members and financing

While the small size and clear private benefits of a group can help it overcome the collective action problem, this is unlikely to be very helpful for most public interest advocacy organizations which naturally serve large populations. Olson points to a second category of solutions to the collective action problem in the form of selective incentives to encourage members to contribute to the group. National legislation can be used to provide groups with selective incentives for their members, and can help advocacy organizations with their finances. Tax laws can provide tax deductions for individuals and corporations who contribute to approved advocacy organizations. The ability to deduct donations may encourage some members to contribute more than they might otherwise. While in Austria and Belgium individuals can deduct up to 10% of their previous year's earnings (Austrian Tax Book 2007, 49; CIR 92 Exercice d'imposition 2008, arts. 221–223), in Hungary and the Slovak Republic taxpayers do not receive a tax benefit but can directly apply part of the taxes they pay to a designated organization (1996. évi LXXXI. törvény, schedule 6(A); 2003 Income Tax Act, §13(1)(a), §13(2)(b)), while in Finland and Sweden individuals get no tax advantages from donations (109/1930 Foundations Act; Skatteverket, "Ideella föreningar – skatterättsliga regler"). France, Japan, and Spain provide the most generous tax deductions for individuals at 20%, 25%, and 30% of income respectively, while

Finland and Sweden provide the least. In terms of corporate deductions, Poland (10% taxable income), Hungary (20% pre-tax income), and Switzerland (20% net income) provide the most generous provisions, while Portugal (0.8% of turnover), France (0.5% of turnover), and Sweden (nothing) provide the least.

Tax laws may also contain tax exemptions for nonprofits of certain types, conducting certain activities (public interest rather than private interest, and charitable rather than economic or political) in certain issue areas. In general, public benefit organizations are tax-exempt while other nonprofit organizations (including advocacy organizations) are only tax-exempt if they fulfill certain conditions, and income from economic activities is taxable, except if it is from an indispensable economic activity of a charity (Austria, art. 35 (1) BAO). The greatest variety of organizations have the highest value exemptions in the United States, the UK, the Czech Republic, and Hungary. In the United Kingdom, for example, registered charities are exempt from income tax on grants, donations, and commercial activities below a certain threshold; charities can claim 80% relief on property taxes, with local authorities able to grant an additional 20% relief; certain goods and services are zero-rated (exempt from VAT) for charities; and charities and NGOs making less than £64,000 a year on goods and services are VAT-exempt (Income and Corporation Taxes Act 1988, part 12, chapter 6, section 505(1)). Italy, Sweden, and Switzerland represent the opposite end of the range, as nonprofit associations are not exempt and charities only have tax exemptions on income directly related to public benefit purposes (Switzerland, 1990 Income Tax Law, art. 56(g)).

National regulations can also limit the financial resources of groups, making it more difficult to obtain the necessary funds to maintain some kinds of NGO. Regulations generally specify the kind of financing NGOs can attract, in what amounts, and what they can and cannot do with the money. The ability of an organization to sell goods and services or collect fees in order to raise money may determine whether the advocacy organization can afford to continue and the willingness of members to continue to contribute.

Variations in the extent to which governments can and do fund associations and other kinds of nonprofits also affect location decisions. National regulations which provide funding for nonprofit organizations in the form of grants as well as contracts are likely to have a strong national bias, but attract advocacy organizations willing to establish local branches. For example, "[a] relevant Minister may give financial assistance to any charitable, benevolent or philanthropic institution in respect of any of the institution's activities which directly or indirectly benefit the whole or any part of England" (Charities Act 2006, part 3, chapter 3, art. 70). National regulations on grants are also strict as to the amount of money, if any, which can be spent on overhead. In the Slovak Republic, for example,

[s]ubsidies from the state budget, the state fund budget, or the community budget may also be provided to the nonprofit organization ... A nonprofit organization may receive state budget or state fund subsidies for the same services from only one source usually from that source which has some relation to the predominant activity of the nonprofit organization. The subsidy from the state budget, the state fund budget, or the community budget may not be used to cover the expenditure (costs) of the administration of the nonprofit organization. (1997 PBO Law, §29(3–4))

Direct funding of organizations enables government to encourage advocacy organizations to reveal large amounts of information about their organization and purposes, to limit their use of monies for organizational rather than policy goals, and privilege national over international organizations in ways that help the government as principal tighten control over advocacy organizations as agents. Within the OECD, government funding for the nonprofit sector as a whole, including advocacy organizations in their different forms, ranges from 9% in New Zealand and 24% in Korea to 77% in Belgium and Ireland (Salamon *et al.*, 2004).

Governments' regulatory incentives

Governments can use regulations to impose varying costs on the national organization and operation of international advocacy organizations by strictly regulating the types of legal identity permitted and the political and economic activities different organization forms can conduct, and by delimiting selective incentives available to entice members. National regulations make it more difficult for some organizations to form than others, thus effectively enabling key government decision-makers to favor the operation of certain organizations and influencing advocacy organizations' choice of legal identity, activities, and geographic location. There are three main choices for legal identity for advocacy organizations in most countries, although not all organizations may be legally recognized nor need legal personality to operate. Charities or public benefit organizations primarily provide services for those in need in cases for which the state cannot provide sufficient to meet demands, including welfare provision, education, health, and development assistance. But charities in many countries are also allowed to be advocacy organizations, although their advocacy cannot be partisan nor their primary activity nor can it be on issues unrelated to the core mandate of the organization. Affective and interest associations work for the benefit of their members, either by making them feel good or by providing enjoyable activities, such as through sports or cultural clubs, or private benefits, in the case of interest groups which work for the private benefit of their members by lobbying for policy change. While many associations are more concerned with entertainment, leisure, or affinity activities, others, including labor and trade organizations, take explicitly political positions and work to change government or social policies or practices. Civil society organizations work to build democracy and promote participation in democracy, and may include lobbying for public benefit, political education activities, fostering local community groups, and increasing the capacity of others to participate economically and politically at home or abroad.

Different groups need different amounts of resources and thus have distinct thresholds for organization and maintenance. Service organizations need high levels of resources to provide good-quality public services in sufficient amounts. These are also likely to be the most compatible with government needs and interests. Governments may be more willing to give these organizations the freedom to act most efficiently and innovatively as well as access to financial resources, as long as they comply with strict standards on political activity and accounting. Advocacy organizations require fewer resources, but are also the most politically uncertain, given that the interests and preferences of government decision-makers are often likely to diverge from those of the advocacy group. Thus many governments formally endow associations with rights to assembly and free speech, but limit access to economic resources and potential political power, such that these advocacy organizations cannot become strong bases for political opposition or electoral machines capable of removing and replacing the government in power.

Advocacy organizations' institutional environment in the OECD

The second half of this chapter examines patterns in the national regulations regarding advocacy organizations in the Organization for Economic Cooperation and Development (OECD) in order to assess variations in the regulatory approach, scope, and specificity of regulations as well as the effect of variations on the location of international advocacy organizations. Have variations in national legislation regarding NGOs actually affected the populations of advocacy NGOs that result in these countries?

This research centers on national regulations regarding the identity, rights, access, resources, and responsibilities of an NGO. The dataset contains information on all countries in the OECD with the exception of

Iceland, for which there is no English-language information ($n= 29$). There is also no coverage of Iceland in other works on national nonprofit regulations, including publications by the US International Grantmaking Project, the Council on Foundations, the European Foundation Center, the Johns Hopkins Center for Civil Society Studies, and the International Center of Not-for-Profit Law. Information on national legislation comes from national codes and reports as well as the International Center of Not-for-Profit Law and the US Library of Congress' website (www.loc.gov/law/guide/nations.html). Missing indicators were completed with information from the US International Grantmaking Project surveys of nonprofit legislation for ten members of the OECD (www.usig.org/countryinfo.asp).

Control variables concerning national economic indicators, level of democracy, and memberships in inter-governmental organizations come from the OECD, the World Bank, the CIA Factbook, and the Polity IV database. Information on the number of international advocacy organizations found within each country is taken from Smith and Weist's study of transnational social movement organizations (Smith and Weist, 2005). The data collected by Smith and Weist include the national memberships of international non-governmental organizations with the stated goals of social or political change for 144 countries in the year 2000 as recorded in the Union of International Associations' Yearbook of International Associations (Smith and Weist, 2005). Transnational social movement organizations (TSMOs) as coded by Smith and Weist are "international non-governmental organizations that were explicitly formed to promote some social or political change goal" (2005: 628). While TSMOs as a category are not identical to advocacy organizations as defined in this volume, these data are better fit to my purposes than the other, limited options available. Smith and Weist (2005) exclude organizations that are focused exclusively on service provision or philanthropic giving to focus on organizations with the goal of political or social change; this definition corresponds roughly to that of advocacy organizations used in this volume. While international advocacy groups/TSMOs are not further differentiated, this is consistent with the examination of national regulations here, which also do not differentiate within political advocacy organizations by issue. Like Smith and Weist (2005) and Salamon et al. (1999, 2004), I exclude political parties, sports or cultural associations, and professional associations. The other available data source for cross-national statistics on national nonprofits, Johns Hopkins' Center for Civil Society Studies' Comparative Nonprofit Sector project, examines variations in the nonprofit sector as an aggregate rather than individual advocacy organizations. These data are used to gauge government financial support for nonprofits, including advocacy organizations, across the OECD (Salamon *et al.*, 2004).

The key variables to understand how governments regulate advocacy organizations and the primary factors that should affect where international advocacy organizations locate according to the collective action perspective[3] are: (1) the approach to regulation, including the available legal identities, whether laws are found in civil codes or common law and whether regulations proscribe or prescribe, and the allowable economic and political activities; (2) the scope of laws, including the number of types used and the total amount of law (complexity); and (3) the severity of laws, including the number of distinct requirements NGOs must meet, in particular government permission, to operate. For all variables, English translations of laws are used to calculate complexity (the number of characters in a regulation) and severity (the number of distinct requirements applied to nonprofit advocacy organizations), in order to standardize across languages. In the following sections, I examine first the relative use of different types of regulation across the OECD, followed by variations in regulatory approach, scope, and then severity in order to understand the nature of regulation across the OECD and the relationship between national regulatory differences and the location of international advocacy organizations.

Types of NGO regulation

When it comes to regulating advocacy organizations, governments have several options. They can formally regulate international advocacy organizations' legal identity/personality and activities; they can regulate their income sources and accounting; or they can regulate the ability of government actors to form relationships and interact with these organizations. All members of the OECD (with the possible exception of Iceland) have explicit regulation for the creation and operation of nonprofit, non-governmental organizations, including advocacy organizations. While countries may label and categorize advocacy organizations differently, all countries have some kind of regulations pertaining to associations/civil society organizations, foundations, and/or charities/public benefit organizations.

Advocacy organization regulations come in several different forms, including regulations on the legal identity and recognition of an

---

[3] The same factors and regulation are likely to have a strong impact on the emergence of local advocacy organizations as well as on the location decisions of international advocacy organizations, but reliable, complete cross-national data on local advocacy organizations do not exist to test this claim.

organization as being a charity, foundation, association, public benefit organization, civil society organization, political party, or special interest group (including labor unions). Governments also regulate the filing of taxes and tax exceptions, accounting practices, registration, lobbying and political campaigning, and the dissolution of organizations. Within the OECD, regulations relevant for advocacy organizations are primarily found in the constitution (rights and freedoms of association/assembly, speech, press, and religion),[4] the civil code (often in specific codes written on civil society organizations),[5] administrative rules regarding access to government,[6] and/or tax legislation.[7] Table 4.1 shows the relative use of regulation types across the OECD.

The most popular forms of advocacy organization regulation within the OECD are registration requirements (25 of 29 countries, or 86%), taxation regulations (29 of 29 countries, or 100%), and accounting requirements (25 of 29 countries, or 86%). Separate accounting requirements are applied to monies used for the basic operations of the organization and for monies used specifically for political activities such as campaign contributions and earned from commercial activities. Regulations on lobbying and explicit provisions regarding direct action as a tactic (as opposed to regulations on basic law and order) were the least common (less than 15% of OECD countries).

Countries vary in terms of the number of different types of regulation they apply to advocacy organizations. While countries like Canada apply all possible types of regulation, and the United States, the United Kingdom, and Japan apply five different types, countries such as Denmark, Finland, Sweden, and Switzerland only apply only three, and Greece only two.

Legal identity and operational limitations

Even among the relatively homogeneous countries of the OECD, non-profit, non-governmental organizations can take on a range of different

---

[4] For example, in the United States the First Amendment of the Constitution states "Congress shall make no law respecting an establishment of religion, or prohibiting the free exercise thereof; or abridging the freedom of speech, or of the press; or the right of the people peaceably to assemble, and to petition the Government for a redress of grievances."

[5] For example, Belgium, Poland, Hungary, and Luxembourg have specific civil codes for associations, public benefit organizations, and foundations.

[6] For example, in Austria the Rules of Procedure of the National Council (section 40, paragraph 1) and the Federal Council (section 33, paragraph 1) posit that experts representing interest groups may be invited to participate in deliberations on legislation (Malone 2004: 7).

[7] For example, in Canada the vast majority of regulation regarding charities is to be found in the tax code under the aegis of the Canadian Revenue Agency (Income Tax Act 1985, c. 1 (5th Supp.)).

legal identities, including association, foundation, corporation, public benefit organization, charity, and civil society organization. For the purposes of this volume, the most important variations occur in the range of issues and activities different organizational forms can undertake. In almost all countries, general form nonprofits and unincorporated associations can do just about anything that they want in any issue area, with the exception of activities for economic gain or the pursuit of activities or goals which violate national laws (for example, the glorification of Nazism within Germany or tax evasion more generally). "An association may be founded for the common realization of a nonprofit purpose. The purpose may not be contrary to law or proper behavior" (Finland, 1989 Associations Act, art. 1). Or in Luxembourg, "[t]he nonprofit organization is one which does not conduct industrial or commercial operations, or which does not attempt to procure material gains to its members" (1928 Associations Law, art. 1).

Even this general position varies, as some countries allow even nonprofits to undertake economic activities to raise funds to support the organization, although the members and managers of the organization cannot gain economically from the activities. For example, in Poland associations can engage in economic activities as long as they follow all related commercial codes, the benefits of the activities are not shared among its members, and economic activities are not the primary purpose of the association (LOA, art. 34). In Canada, advocacy organizations cannot make a profit, but they can engage in revenue-producing activities (USIG Canada, 7). While most countries limit the economic activities of organizations to a secondary role in support of other public benefit purposes, Mexico and the Czech Republic both adopt similar regulation to Poland, allowing economic activities in service of the primary organizational goals (1990 Czechoslovak LOA, art.12(3)). In Mexico, the civil codes do not prohibit civil associations from engaging in economic activities. However, the primary purpose of a civil association must not be of a predominantly economic character (Mexico, CC DF §2670). Hungarian, Norwegian, Japanese, and Korean regulation allows advocacy organizations official recognition as nonprofit corporations (Hungary, Company Law 2006; Norway, 1997 White Paper, section 3.4; Japan, 1998 SNPC Law, schedule 2; Korea, 1975 Nonprofit Act, art. 2), while in the United States and Canada nonprofits can be corporations and still receive tax deduction benefits as charities or 501(c)(3) organizations (www.irs.gov/pub/irs-pdf/; Canada Corporations Act, arts. 154(1)) and 155(1)).

Generally advocacy organizations need to limit their activities and purposes in order to be legally recognized as public benefit organizations, civil society organizations, and/or charities. For example, in France and

Germany associations are merely nonprofit organizations and may operate for the sole benefit of the members, while public utilities (France) or public welfare organizations (Germany) must be recognized officially as promoting a more limited set of public interest goals serving a large population of individuals.

This recognition, conferred by decree by the Conseil d'Etat, is attributed to organizations with a general interest or public utility purpose in the philanthropic, social, health, educational, scientific, cultural or regarding quality of life, environmental, protection of historical sites and monuments, and international solidarity fields. (http://service-public.fr, arts. 200 and 238bis, Tax Code of France)

In Hungary and Poland, the status of public benefit organization (PBO) can be added to an association, corporation, or even foundation to signify organizations that limit their activities in such a way. Australia, Canada, England, Ireland, and the United States recognize organizations that engage in these kinds of activities as a particular type of legal entity, the charity. While most organizations which select to become charities/public benefit organizations operate primarily as service organizations, many of these organizations do engage in advocacy as part of their basic operations, including public education and even lobbying for policies in their areas of expertise. In thirteen countries, charities/public benefit organizations are legally authorized to engage in advocacy in their areas of concern as long as this is not their primary purpose and they do not engage in partisan politics. In most cases, organizations which serve public benefit purposes (or charitable purposes) self-identify and register in order to receive tax benefits. This is the case in seventeen countries in the OECD.

The extent to which public benefit organizations and charities can engage in political activities and advocacy vary. In Hungary, public benefit organizations can even nominate candidates for local elections, although they cannot engage in direct political activity at the national level (Act CLV of 1997, section 26d). In France, only declared political associations established for limited periods of time may engage in direct political activity, although there is some debate about the extent to which public utility organizations may engage in political activities in support of their public interest activities (Opinion of the Conseil d'Etat of June 13, 1978, no. 322894). In the United States, 501(c)(3) organizations defined as "corporations, and any community chest, fund, or foundation, organized and operated exclusively for religious, charitable, scientific, testing for public safety, literary, or educational purposes" are prevented from having a "substantial" part of their activities devoted to "carrying on propaganda, or otherwise attempting, to influence legislation" as well as "interven[ing] in (including the publishing or distributing of statements) any political campaign on behalf of (or in opposition to) any candidate for public office." But,

[f]or purposes of this section, the term "influencing legislation," with respect to an organization, does not include – (A) making available the results of nonpartisan analysis, study, or research; (B) providing of technical advice or assistance (where such advice would otherwise constitute the influencing of legislation) to a governmental body or to a committee or other subdivision thereof in response to a written request by such body or subdivision, as the case may be; (C) appearances before, or communications to, any legislative body with respect to a possible decision of such body which might affect the existence of the organization, its powers and duties, tax-exempt status, or the deduction of contributions to the organization; (D) communications between the organization and its bona fide members with respect to legislation or proposed legislation of direct interest to the organization and such members ... (IRS, section 501(c)(3))

The new economics of institutions leads us to believe that the barriers to entry and the costs imposed on advocacy organizations by regulation would increase (while the economic benefits available decrease) with an increase in the private and/or political nature of the organization. Campaigning by political parties is more threatening to the existing government's policy agenda and electoral prospects than non-partisan advocacy by public interest organizations and thus likely to face more stringent regulation, registration, and reporting criteria. Public benefit organizations do more for the government by providing the public with services, including education and advocacy as well as interest representation and political participation, than mutual benefit clubs (for example, sporting associations) and thus are likely to receive more economic rewards (grants or tax benefits).

Of the twenty-nine of the thirty members of the OECD with data, all have a legal definition of either a nonprofit organization or a charity/public benefit organization (PBO). Of these twenty-nine, fifteen have distinct definitions which clearly delineate between these two organization types. Only two countries allow organizations to overlap the categories of association and public benefit organization (Hungary and Poland). Among OECD countries only nineteen explicitly allow nonprofit organizations to be politically engaged and only three, Poland, the Slovak Republic, and the Czech Republic, allow public benefit organizations to be as politically active as nonprofit associations. Another thirteen countries allow public interest organizations (charities or PBOs) to engage in advocacy at a lesser level. Civil society organizations, public benefit organizations, or charities may advocate in support of their primary public benefit activities, but are generally prohibited from engaging in partisan politics or politics on behalf of or in support of a particular party or government representative.

In terms of the price that governments exact in return for allowing advocacy, of the twenty-six states that give legal personality to nonprofit associations, twenty-four require organizations to register with the government and seventeen maintain the right to approve or reject the organization. For example, in Portugal,

[a]ssociations acquire legal personality by depositing, against receipt, a copy of the minutes of their constitution and their statutes with the civil government office in the area of their respective head office, after prior publication in the Diario do Governo [Diário da Républica] and in one daily newspaper, with wide coverage in the region of an excerpt, authenticated by a notary, of their constitutive title, which has to mention the name of the association, its headquarters, purpose, duration and conditions for admission, discharge, and exclusion of members. (1974 Decree 594, art. 4(1))

In Japan, on the other hand, "any association or foundation relating to any academic activities, art, charity, worship, religion, or other public interest which is not for profit may be established as a juridical person with the permission of the competent government agency" (Civil Code, art. 34). The number of requirements advocacy organizations must meet in order to be associations can range from four in Switzerland[8] to twenty-five in Japan. In order to register, which in most cases provides legal personality, organizations need to meet between one (Portugal) and fourteen (Hungary) additional steps. In not all countries must associations or advocacy organizations have legal personality (although, in the case of France, this is granted automatically), but in most cases organizations cannot obtain economic benefits or engage in economic or political activities without such legal personality. For example, in Finland,

[a]n association may obtain rights, make commitments and appear before a court or other authority as a party if it has been registered in accordance with the provisions of this Act. An association that is not entered in the register may not acquire rights or undertake obligations, nor sue or be sued in its own name. (1989 Associations Act, art. 58)

There is a statistically significant difference in the treatment of the political activities of nonprofit associations and public benefit organizations, as nineteen countries allow associations to be political compared to only thirteen that allow PBOs (a t-test for equivalence is rejected at $p = 0.0029$). Of the twenty-one countries which allow nonprofit associations to engage in political advocacy, sixteen require government approval for legal personality and thus to operate in the country. While government

---

[8] Statutes are in a written form and contain necessary dispositions on purpose, resources, and organization of the organization (1912 Civil Code, art. 60).

decision-makers may see benefits in the information, expertise, education, and mobilization abilities of advocacy organizations, they clearly want to keep a tight hand on these groups. The relationship between allowing associations to engage in political activities and advocacy and the need for government approval to operate in a country is positive and statistically significant (Pearson chi-square $(1) = 9.6878$, $p = 0.002$). There is a weakly negative relationship between the need for government registration and approval for an association to operate and the number of national branches of international advocacy organizations in a country, as would be expected, however ($r = -0.22$).

Proscribe or prescribe?

A country's approach to the regulation of associations/civil society organizations, charities/public benefit organizations, corporations, and foundations is likely to be related to its view of the purpose of such organizations and its perception of these organizations as complements or competitors to the state. A focus on nonprofit, non-governmental organizations as service providers tends to encourage a keen interest in controlling the accounting procedures used by the organization as well as registration or grant-making procedures which allow the government to track the performance of an organization. In the case of service organizations, the government has an interest in monitoring the quality of services being provided and the efficient use of government funds in order to guarantee accountability and responsibility to its constituents. But governments can have relatively limited concerns about service providers as political animals as long as they carefully prescribe the issues and activities of these organizations and limit them to apolitical areas such as healthcare and education. Those countries that focus on prescribing what nonprofits do should thus have more regulation (longer, more detailed, with more requirements) on registration, taxation, and accounting than on lobbying or campaigning ($r = 0.1467$).

Countries which tend to prescribe the behavior of advocacy organizations adopt legislation which explicitly lists the kinds of activities that organizations of a certain type *can* undertake. The regulation is stated in affirmative language. For example, in Mexico:

For the purpose of this law, the activities of civil society organizations which are subject to fomentation are the following: I. Social assistance, conforming to that established in the Law about the National Social Assistance and in the General Health Law; II. Support for popular food programs; III. Civics, focusing on promoting citizen participation in matters of public interest; IV. Juridical assistance; V. Support for the development of indigenous peoples and communities;

VI. Promotion of gender equality; VII. Contribution to services for groups with different capacities; VIII. Cooperation with community development; IX. Support for the defense and promotion of human rights; X. Promotion of sports; XI. Promotion of and contribution to services for health and sanitary matters; XII. Support in the use of natural resources, protection of the environment, flora and fauna, preservation and restoration of the ecological equilibrium, as well as promotion of sustainable development at the regional and communal levels, in urban and rural areas; XIII. Educational, cultural, artistic, scientific and technological promotion and fomentation; XIV. Foment actions for the improvement of the popular economy; XV. Participation in civil protection actions; XVI. Provision of support services for the creation and strengthening of the organizations that undertake activities affected by this law; and XVII. Those determined by other laws. (Ley Federal de Fomento, capitulo 2, art. 5)

Those countries that primarily see nonprofit, non-governmental organizations as advocacy organizations, including interest groups, labor unions, and political parties, or which view associations and public benefit organizations as containing diverse categories of organizations each with different purposes, are likely to take a proscriptive approach. By proscribing exactly what organizations cannot be, this approach leaves a wide range of space for innovation and flexibility in what an organization can be and do. Countries which take a proscriptive approach (or mix proscriptive and prescriptive regulation for different types of organization) are likely to have more regulation on campaigning and lobbying in order to select and control potentially challenging political organizations.

Countries which tend to proscribe the behavior of NGOs adopt legislation which explicitly *forbids* certain practices and behaviors but says little about allowable activities. The legislation is stated in the negative rather than in the positive. In Hungary, for example:

§2(2) The right of association shall not be exercised in such a way as to violate §2(3) of the Constitution to constitute a criminal offence or an invitation to commit such an offence, or to prejudice the rights and liberty of others. §2(3) A civil society organization may be founded for the purpose of carrying out any activity consistent with the Constitution and not prohibited by law. No civil society organization shall be established for the primary purpose of economic-entrepreneurial activities. No armed organization shall be created under the right of association. (1989. évi II. törvény, 2(6. §)(1–2))

Table 4.2 gives the coding on this variable for all the members of the OECD.[9]

---

[9] If the words "not" or "cannot" or "prohibit" were used, the legislation was classified as proscriptive. If there was no such term, then it was prescriptive. There were some exceptions in which the general feel of the passage was definitely more prescriptive than proscriptive, despite the use of negative language. These cases were coded prescriptive.

Table 4.2. *Regulatory approach to advocacy organizations in the OECD*

Country	Proscribe	Prescribe	Source of legislation	Common law	Civil law
Australia	NPO	Charity	Tax Act	✓	
Austria	NPO	Charity	Associations Law, Tax Act		✓
Belgium	✓		Civil Code		✓
Canada		✓	Corporations Act, Tax Act	✓	
Czech Republic	✓		Associations Law		✓
Denmark		Charity	Tax Law		✓
Finland	✓		Associations Law		✓
France	NPO	Charity	Civil Code		✓
Germany	NPO	Charity	Tax Act		✓
Greece	✓		Civil Code		✓
Hungary	✓		Civil Code, Associations Law		✓
Ireland		✓	Tax Law	✓	
Italy	Charity	NPO	Civil Code, Associations Law		✓
Japan		✓	Associations Law, Incorporation Act		✓
Korea		✓	Tax Act		✓
Luxembourg	✓		Associations Law		✓
Mexico		✓	Civil Code		✓
Netherlands	✓		Civil Code		✓
New Zealand	✓		Tax Act, Associations Law	✓	
Norway		✓	White Paper		✓
Poland	✓		Associations Law		✓
Portugal	NPO	Charity	Civil Code, Associations Law		✓
Slovak Republic	NPO	Charity	Associations Law		✓
Spain	✓		Civil Code, Associations Law		✓
Sweden		✓	Tax Agency		✓
Switzerland		Charity	Tax Act		✓
Turkey	✓		Associations Law		✓
United Kingdom		✓	Associations Law	✓	
United States		✓	Civil Code	✓	

Within the OECD, the prescriptive and proscriptive approaches are used about equally. Eleven states adopt a prescriptive approach to NGOs across the board, while another eleven adopt a proscriptive approach. Seven countries take a mixed approach, generally using prescriptions in laws regarding charities or public benefit organizations and using proscriptions in regards to nonprofit organizations and associations more generally, including many advocacy organizations. There is a positive correlation between the use of prescriptive regulations and the total length of the regulation in a country ($r = 0.1467$). In all of the countries which use proscription, registration with government authorities is required, while it is required in 90 percent of the countries which prescribe organizations' behavior (this difference is not statistically significant). In the eleven countries which take a prescriptive approach, there is an average of 357 advocacy organizations, while in the seven countries that take a mixed approach and prescribe PBOs/charities but proscribe associations there is an average of 389 advocacy organizations. In the eleven countries which take a proscriptive approach, there is an average of 326 advocacy organizations. Not only do proscriptive countries have fewer advocacy organizations on average, they also have a lower minimum and a lower maximum number of advocacy organizations than in prescriptive or mixed-approach countries (161 versus 182 and 183 and 495 versus 525 and 553).

In the past, scholars have linked a tendency toward a prescriptive approach to advocacy organizations and the use of a civil code to regulate associations, and have noted an affinity between common law countries and a more proscriptive approach. I find no statistically significant relationship, as a Pearson chi-square test for a link between type of law and a dummy variable for proscription of nonprofit organizations is rejected ($p = 0.158$). Of the six common law countries in the OECD, four take a proscriptive approach (66 percent), while of the twenty-three civil code countries, fifteen take a prescriptive approach (65 percent).

National bias

Foreign advocacy organizations do not receive the same treatment as national advocacy organizations in half of the countries of the OECD. Fourteen countries have explicit provisions in their regulations which privilege national organizations and thus encourage international advocacy organizations to establish a local presence. These regulations range from the requirement that advocacy organizations have local headquarters and register for legal personality in this locality (Poland, 1989 LOA, art. 5(1)) to the requirement that more than 50 percent of the members and management of an organization be of the local nationality (Mexico, Ley Federal de Fomento, capitulo 1, art. 4). There is a positive and relatively strong correlation between national bias regulation and the extent to which government funds nonprofits, including advocacy organizations, within a country ($r = 0.28$). There is little correlation, however, between national bias legislation and the location decisions of international advocacy organizations within particular jurisdictions ($r = 0.075$) and thus national bias may not deter organizations from establishing local branches, although they must establish local branches in many places.

Selective incentives and government funding

The question of national bias moves from discussion of national regulations as purely an institutional deterrent to advocacy organizations to the realization that national governments may use regulations to foster the operations of certain types of advocacy organization. There is significant variation in the amount of economic resources available to organizations for their organization, operation, and advocacy. In particular, countries vary in terms of the ability of organizations to reward their donors and members and of the government funding available compared to private funding from foundations or members. Most countries differentiate by organization type, and advocacy organizations which can make a credible claim to be public benefit organizations rather than political partisans can access more resources. There is a statistically significant difference between the ability of nonprofit organizations to engage in economic activities and that of charities (fifteen countries allow charities and nonprofit associations; fourteen allow only nonprofit associations; $t = 3.8389$). There is also a statistically significant difference between the extents to which tax exemptions are given to charities/public benefit organizations and nonprofit associations (sixteen countries give tax breaks only to charities or public benefit organizations; eleven give tax breaks to nonprofit organizations as well as public benefit organizations; $t = 6.1496$).

Governments are more lenient about the use of economic activities as a source of revenue for advocacy organizations than they are about the range of advocacy activities these organizations can conduct. Twenty-six countries allow nonprofits to engage in a range of economic activities, although these may not be the primary purpose of the organization nor can members of the board benefit directly, while fifteen allow charities to engage in commercial and money-making activities. There is a statistically significant difference between the propensity of governments to regulate the political activities of advocacy organizations as nonprofit associations compared to the economic activities ($t = 1.9831$, significant at the 95 percent level in a one-tailed test). In general, advocacy organizations have more freedom to fundraise than engage in explicitly political activities, although public education and some forms of advocacy are clearly acceptable. Interestingly, there is not a statistically significant difference between countries' propensity to regulate the economic and political activities of charities, as both are tightly controlled in most states ($t = 0.7009$)

The availability of resources within a country clearly matters to advocacy organizations in their decision where to locate. The correlation between government support for the nonprofit sector and the number of national branches of international advocacy organizations in a country is positive and strong ($r = 0.5793$).

National legislation and the location of advocacy NGOs

Do advocacy organizations tend to go to countries with the most sparse, and thus ostensibly least onerous, regulatory environment? Do we see more advocacy organizations in countries with fewer regulations of fewer kinds, with fewer requirements to meet, and fewer constraints on activities than in countries with more regulations of more types on more types of activities imposing more restrictions on behavior? In order to answer this question, I have coded the amount of regulation in each country in the OECD using the total number of requirements to be met as an indicator of the severity of regulation and the total number of characters in the regulations as an indicator of the complexity of regulation. I also factor in the number of types of regulation as an indicator of the ability of a government to impose barriers to entry, as increasing the number of types raises the costs of monitoring and meeting regulatory demands, and the need for NGOs to register or obtain government approval. As can be seen in Table 4.3, I find that Japan, the USA, Hungary, Australia, New Zealand, and the Slovak Republic have the most regulation, while Switzerland, Finland, Luxembourg, Turkey, and Ireland have the least, although it is difficult to rank these completely and consistently.[10]

Visually, the findings are clear, and surprising. The greatest numbers of advocacy organizations are not found in the countries with the least regulation, nor are the fewest advocacy organizations found in the countries with the most regulation. Indeed, in some cases the exact opposite is true, as Luxembourg and Turkey have some of the least regulation and the fewest advocacy organizations, while the USA has some of the most regulation and many organizations. While the countries with the most legislation do not have the most advocacy organizations and the countries with the least legislation do not have the fewest advocacy organizations, most advocacy organizations seem to locate in places with middling

---

[10] Rankings were found by sorting countries by the variables for complexity (character count), severity (requirement count), as well as the number of types of regulation (scope) and whether government approval was necessary to operate in a country.

Table 4.3. *Explaining advocacy organizations in the OECD*

Country	Most legislation	Least legislation	Most economic support	Least economic support	Most organizations	Fewest organizations
Australia	✓					
Austria						
Canada						
Denmark						
Finland		✓				
Greece						
Hungary	✓					
Ireland		✓	✓			
Japan	✓					
Norway						
Poland				✓		
Portugal						
Spain						
Sweden						
Switzerland		✓				
Luxembourg		✓				1
Turkey		✓				2
Korea				✓		3
Slovak Republic				✓		4
New Zealand	✓			✓		5
Czech Republic						6
Mexico				✓		7
France			✓		1	
Germany			✓		2	
United Kingdom					3	
Belgium			✓		4	
Netherlands			✓		5	
Italy					6	
United States	✓				7	

amounts of legislation. The correlation between the total number of requirements advocacy organizations must meet in a country and the number of organizations which locate there is in the expected direction but weak ($r = -0.1471$). The correlation between the total amount of regulation and the number of advocacy organizations is in the opposite direction (although very weak) at 0.0576.

The scope and severity of regulation do not determine the location of an advocacy organization without another important factor being taken into account. While the severity and scope of regulations impose costs on advocacy organizations, and thus raise barriers to operating in a particular location, these regulations may also bring economic benefits which enable the organization to overcome collective action problems more easily. Advocacy organizations consider not only the costs to their operations imposed by national legislation, but also the resources available within a country, from individuals, foundations, and the government, that might enable their operations. I find that Ireland, France, Germany, Belgium, and the Netherlands provide the most economically supportive environments, while the Slovak Republic, Poland, New Zealand, Mexico, and Korea provide the least support.[11]

Table 4.3 shows visually the relationship between economic support for advocacy organizations and their locations. Four of the countries with the greatest economic support have the most national branches of international advocacy organizations, while four of the countries with the least economic support have the fewest advocacy organizations. The correlation between the number of advocacy organizations within a country and the amount of economic support a government provides (using the percentage of total funding to the nonprofit sector which comes from the government as an indicator) is strong and positive ($r = 0.5639$). Relatively high levels of government regulation combined with limited economic support explain the relatively low numbers of advocacy organizations in New Zealand, Korea, and the Slovak Republic, while middling levels of government regulation in an economically supportive environment make Germany, France, and the United Kingdom popular locations.

Not all government regulations impose costs on the operation of an advocacy organization or are intended as barriers to entry. Regulations can also ensure regular access to policymaking and government grants and contracts or tax exemptions. While the relationship between the total number of requirements and the number of advocacy organizations in a country is negative, the relationship between the total length of the regulations and the number of advocacy organizations is positive.

To test the impact of government economic support alongside the complexity and severity of national regulations on the location of international advocacy organizations in a country, I run a classic regression. The number of international advocacy organizations in a country is the dependent variable against the number of requirements an organization must meet within a country, the total length of nonprofit regulations, the percentage of resources nonprofit organizations in the country receive

---

[11] Data are available at http://alcor.concordia.ca/~eabloodg.

Table 4.4. *Regression results*

Number of international advocacy organizations (ingocount)	Coefficient	Standard error	$p > \|t\|$ * Significant at 95% (** 99%) in one-tailed test	Standardized coefficients
Length of regulations (totalcharcount)	0.0044	0.002	0.085*	0.323
Number of requirements (totalreq)	−1.97	1.04	0.076*	−0.319
Percent funding from government	168.24	91.02	0.081*	0.260
IGO memberships (igocount)	10.6	1.988	0.000**	0.763
GDP per capita (2000)	−0.001	0.0017	0.427	−0.136
Polity IV score	−23.32	14.77	0.132	−0.205
	$R^2 = 0.7715$			

from government sources (averaged across the sector), and controls for GDP per capita, IGO memberships, and level of democracy (Polity IV score). Table 4.4 reports the results. The complexity and severity of national regulations and the degree of economic support from government all significantly affect the number of local branches of international advocacy organizations found in a country (significance is judged at the 95 percent level, using a one-tailed test). Using standardized coefficients, it is possible to see that the magnitude of the effect of each of these variables is about the same. The severity of national regulation has a negative effect on the number of advocacy organizations, serving as a barrier to entry, while the length of regulations and economic support both have positive effects. This likely reflects the fact that controlling for the number of requirements placed on advocacy organizations, more regulation means more guarantees to funding and political space for organizations to operate. These results are robust to variations in the international connectedness of the country (IGO memberships), level of economic development (GDP per capita), and state of democratization (Polity IV score). Of these control variables, only IGO membership is significant and has a strong effect on advocacy organization location decisions. This is likely to be a result of international advocacy organizations' interest in locating in countries in which they can exert their influence not only on domestic politics but in international relations as well via the boomerang effect posited by Keck and Sikkink (1998). Smith and Weist (2005) also find that the extent to which a country is tied into global networks increases its appeal for international advocacy organizations.

Conclusions

This chapter has clearly shown that all governments in the OECD regulate the creation, organizational form, and activities of nonprofit non-governmental organizations, including advocacy organizations. But how they regulate and the degree to which advocacy organizations are regulated varies markedly, even within the relatively homogeneous OECD. Empirically, international advocacy organizations do not flock to the countries with the lowest levels of regulation, measured in terms of the length of the regulation and the number of requirements imposed. But nor do they flock to countries with the highest levels of regulation. This finding likely indicates that it is not the raw amount of regulation, but the type of regulation, that shapes the costs and benefits of collective action in a particular country. Regulation can in fact help advocacy organizations to overcome collective action problems by lowering the costs of creation and operation for some organizations and by making available economic resources.

These findings provide strong support for the claim that international advocacy organizations' location decisions are linked to some of the key factors identified in the collective action approach, including barriers to entry and available economic resources for selective incentives to overcome the costs of organizing. There is even stronger evidence that advocacy organizations are responding not only to political institutions but also to economic incentives. Advocacy organizations may be inspired by normative goals and high principles, but they must also consider material factors and strategic concerns in their day-to-day operations (Prakash and Gugerty, this volume).

References

Anheier, H. and W. Seibel (eds.). 1990. *The Third Sector: Comparative Studies of Nonprofit Organizations*. Berlin: Walter de Gruyter.

Baumgartner, F. and B. Leech. 1998. *Basic Interests: The Importance of Groups in Politics and in Political Science*. Princeton University Press.

Ben-Ner, A. and T. Van Hoomissen. 1993. Nonprofit Organizations in the Mixed Economy: A Demand and Supply Analysis. In A. Ben-Ner and B. Gui (eds.), *The Nonprofit Sector in the Mixed Economy*. Ann Arbor: University of Michigan Press.

Bloodgood, E. and J. Tremblay-Boire. 2008. Race to the Bottom? NGO Policy Convergence and Divergence in the OECD. Paper presented at the 2008 Annual Meeting of the Association for Research on Nonprofit Organizations and Voluntary Action, Philadelphia.

Boli, J. and G. Thomas (eds.). 1999. *Constructing World Culture: International Non-Governmental Organizations Since 1875.* Stanford University Press.

Busby, J. 2007. Bono Made Jesse Helms Cry. *International Studies Quarterly,* **51**: 247–275.

Charities Definition Inquiry. 2001. Report of the Inquiry into the Definition of Charities and Related Organizations. Government of Australia. www.cdi. gov.an/html/report.htm.

Feld, W. J. 1972. *Nongovernmental Forces and World Politics.* New York: Praeger Publishers.

Finnemore, M. and K. Sikkink. 1998. International Norm Dynamics and Political Change. *International Organization,* **52** (4): 887–917.

Garland, J. 1999. Regulation of NGO Public Policy Activities. www.efc.be/cgi-bin/articlepublisher.pl?filename=HR-SE-10–99-23.html.

Jordan, L. and P. Van Tuijl. 2000. Political Responsibility in Transnational NGO Advocacy. *World Development,* **28**(12): 2051–2065.

Keck, M. and K. Sikkink. 1998. *Activists Beyond Borders.* Ithaca, NY: Cornell University Press.

Lipschutz, R. 1992. Reconstructing World Politics: The Emergence of Global Civil Society. *Millennium,* **21** (3): 389–420.

Lloyd, S. n.d. Measures of Complexity: A Nonexhaustive List. Unpublished paper. http://web.mit.edu/esd.83/www/notebook/complexity.pdf.

Lovasz, L. n.d. Information and Complexity (How to Measure Them?) Unpublished paper. www.cs.elte.hu/~lovasz/roma.pdf.

Malone, M. 2004. *Regulation of Lobbyists in Developed Countries: Current Rules and Practices.* Dublin: Institute of Public Administration.

McAdam, D., J. D. McCarthy, and M. Zald (eds.). 1996. *Comparative Perspectives on Social Movements: Political Opportunities, Mobilizing Structures and Cultural Framings.* Cambridge University Press.

Mendelson, S. and J. Glenn (eds.). 2002. *The Power and Limits of NGOs.* New York: Columbia University Press.

Meyer, C. 1997. The Political Economy of NGOs and Information Sharing. *World Development,* **25**(7): 1127–1140.

Moe, T. 1980. *The Organization of Interests: Incentives and the Internal Dynamics of Political Interest Groups.* University of Chicago Press.

    1984. The New Economics of Organizations. *American Journal of Political Science,* **28**: 739–777.

Nelson, P. and E. Dorsey. 2007. New Rights Advocacy in a Global Public Domain. *European Journal of International Relations,* **13**(2): 187–216.

Olson, M., Jr. 1965. *The Logic of Collective Action.* Cambridge, MA: Harvard University Press.

Reimann, K. 2006. A View from the Top: International Politics, Norms and the Worldwide Growth of NGOs. *International Studies Quarterly,* **50**: 45–67.

Risse, T., S. Ropp, and K. Sikkink. 1999. *The Power of Human Rights: International Norms and Domestic Change.* Cambridge University Press.

Salamon, L. M. and Stefan Toepler. 2000. The Influence of the Legal Environment on the Development of the Nonprofit Sector. Working Paper No. 17, Center for Civil Society Studies, Institute for Policy Studies, Johns Hopkins University.

Salamon, L. M., *et al.* (eds.). 1999. *Global Civil Society,* vol. I. Bloomfield, CT: Kumarian Press.

2004. *Global Civil Society,* vol. II. Bloomfield, CT: Kumarian Press.

Skjelsbaek, K. 1971. The Growth of International Non-Governmental Organizations in the Twentieth Century. *International Organizations,* **25** (3): 420–442.

Smith, J. and D. Weist. 2005. The Uneven Geography of Global Civil Society: National and Global Influences on Transnational Association. *Social Forces,* **84**: 621–652.

Staggenborg, S. 2008. *Social Movements.* Oxford University Press.

Tarrow, S. 1988. National Politics and Collective Action. *Annual Review of Sociology,* **14**: 421–440.

Yarbrough, B. V. and R. M. Yarbrough. 1990. International Institutions and the New Economics of Organization. *International Organization,* **44**: 235–259.

Williamson, O. E. 1991. Comparative Economic Organization: The Analysis of Discrete Structural Alternatives. *Administrative Science Quarterly,* **36**: 269–296.

Part 2

Advocacy tactics and strategies

5   The market for human rights

Clifford Bob

Over the past fifty years, international human rights organizations have grown in numbers and resources. Today, they play crucial roles in preventing and alleviating abuses. Acting singly or in loosely formed networks, such groups as Amnesty International, Human Rights Watch, the International Commission of Jurists, and the Fédération Internationale des Ligues des Droits de l'Homme undertake numerous tasks: they research and report on violations in other countries; they draw attention to abuses; they provide services and advice to threatened individuals; they apply pressure strategies such as sanctions and boycotts; and they lobby foreign governments to implement more forceful measures. More broadly, advocacy organizations and the human rights movement have proclaimed the universality, interdependence, and indivisibility of all rights (World Conference on Human Rights, 1993). But despite this ambitious agenda, there are myriad rights problems remaining in the world today, as the advocates themselves acknowledge. Why do some violations become the object of major international concern, while others do not? To what extent does the intensity of activism reflect the gravity of abuse?

In the burgeoning literature on transnational politics, a dominant theoretical perspective holds that advocacy organizations should be seen primarily as "principled" entities working to help "victims" of atrocities. This "moral theory," discussed in detail below, suggests that international advocates facing a world of human rights problems select particular causes for activism based primarily on the gravity of the abuses they find: all else equal, the more egregious the violation, the more likely that activists will exert pressure in an effort to end it. In this view, victims spark transnational activism either directly, by appealing for support overseas, or indirectly, as international activists, moved by their suffering, take action to

For important help with the ideas in this chapter, I thank Siddharth Chandra, Alexander Cooley, Mary Kay Gugerty, Aseem Prakash, James Ron, and Pavel Yakovlev. I alone am responsible for the chapter, however.

support them. The results are networks that grow organically, from the "bottom up," selflessly serving the needs of the abused.

A more recent, critical perspective challenges the foregoing view. Despite rights activism's many achievements, factors in addition to the needs of abused populations drive advocacy groups' selection processes. Among these are a conflict's preexisting recognition by the world media; the target state's reputation and standing; and the relative knowledge, resources, and contacts of the repressed group (Wolfsfeld, 1997; Smillie and Minear, 2004; Bob, 2005; Ron, Ramos, and Rodgers, 2005). The result is that activism tends to be spotty, inconsistent, and transitory, with the worst-off groups frequently *not* receiving the most support.

Notably, however, despite their differences, the moral theorists and their critics share a common focus on individual cases of activism (or non-activism). This chapter, by contrast, proposes a systemic explanation for the vagaries of human rights activism, based on the collective action perspective. I conceive of rights activism as a global marketplace in which the *supply* of abuses interacts with the *demand* for rights issues by donors, including foundations, governments, and individuals primarily based in affluent, rights-observing states. Because these two factors interact and because donor demand often does not correspond with an objective measure of need, the worst human rights abuses may not spark the most activism.

Advocacy organizations are key intermediaries in the market interactions posited here. On one hand, they create human rights "products," primarily information on violations, which they believe to respond to donor demand. More fundamentally, human rights advocates provide donors with psychic and reputational benefits gained from the belief that monetary and material contributions help reduce distant oppression. These donor contributions, received in exchange for advocacy groups' products, are the latter's lifeblood.

On the other hand, advocacy groups also construct their products from various "raw materials," primarily the conditions endured by aggrieved populations overseas. These conditions seldom speak for themselves, and often the populations involved are not able to make their voices heard on their own. In these cases, entering the human rights market requires various "inputs" from advocacy groups including fact-gathering, analysis, interpretation, writing, publication, and marketing. In this "manufacturing process," the aggrieved are not necessarily passive. Rather, they – or at least some of them – respond to advocacy group signals about the number and characteristics of causes for which there is donor demand, reshaping their grievances to make them more internationally appealing. Unfortunately, the most deprived or repressed will often have the least ability to respond in these ways.

In the human rights market, aggrieved populations receive various forms of support from advocacy groups, in a rough exchange for information about their problems. Such support may sometimes come directly, in the form of money or material goods, but more commonly it is indirect, involving advocacy groups lobbying their home governments to act against violators or pressuring the violators themselves. Whatever the exact dimensions of this support, it represents only a portion of the contributions given by donors, the rest going to support the organizational needs of the advocacy group.

A foundation of moral sympathy and good intentions clearly underlies these interactions. But from an analytic perspective, the selection of particular cases of local abuse for international activism is best understood in market terms. The supply of human rights issues is only one part of the explanation. The other part is demand by donors whose preferences often do not correspond with the gravity of oppression in various countries. Indeed, because donor funds are scarce relative to the number of aggrieved groups and the extent of their needs, many worthy causes will go unsupported. Moreover, the preferences of donors, rather than the needs of the aggrieved, will influence which groups, issues, or causes draw activism and in what amounts. In economic terms, the market's "structure" gives power to advocacy groups and donors, relative to those suffering violations.

The foregoing model cannot claim to explain every aspect of rights advocacy. But, as a systemic approach, it provides a useful lens for understanding powerful forces that influence activism. In this chapter, I elaborate the model, positing two intertwined markets for rights activism, one involving donors and advocacy groups, the other involving advocacy groups and aggrieved populations. In addition, I provide evidence to demonstrate the plausibility of the model and in particular its emphasis on demand factors as explaining rights activism. On this basis, I then suggest the application of certain economic tools, as a means of furthering understanding of the human rights market.

Caveats

Before proceeding, several caveats are in order. First, this chapter focuses on the understudied, demand-driven component of the human rights market, but this does not mean I deny that the supply of rights abuses plays a role in the market as well. In fact, a supply-driven logic similar to that posited by the moral theorists undoubtedly does influence the human rights market. But the structure of the market also gives power to donors (and, to a lesser extent, NGOs). As a result, the needs of populations suffering a variety of deprivations and oppressions are only one of many considerations leading to rights activism.

Second, I do not argue that local groups "produce" their own persecution or "manufacture" their own oppression. Powerful actors, particularly authoritarian states, mistreat and repress individuals and groups. In other cases, large populations suffer economic deprivation and social marginalization. What some aggrieved groups do, however, is to place their grievances in the human rights market, drawing attention to the abuses they suffer and making their causes appealing to advocacy groups and donors.

Third, in describing advocacy organizations as "intermediaries" in the human rights market, I do not argue that they thrive on other people's repression. International activism undoubtedly has helped alleviate some human rights problems (but see Hafner-Burton and Ron, 2009). Altruistic feelings also play a role in the human rights market. But to better understand the particulars of support, I emphasize organizational and economic factors. Notably, in their day-to-day operations, advocacy organizations place great importance on them as well, though this is primarily noticeable only to those who work within these groups (Cohen, 1995; Hopgood, 2006). Occasionally, however, advocacy groups' public statements reveal these concerns. As one example, Amnesty International-USA President William Schulz devotes a 2001 book to new ideas about how to "make the human rights 'sale' – to build a broader constituency for human rights, to convince larger numbers of people that human rights matter" (see, for example, Schulz, 2001: 7; AlertNet, 2005). More broadly, Amnesty, Human Rights Watch, and other NGOs view themselves as "brands," developing and using brand management and expansion techniques (Cohen, 1995; Amnesty International, 2004).

Finally, the importance of material factors does not negate the relevance of strategy and ideas. Just as a modern economy is built from myriad interactions in which marketing, branding, and numerous other tactics play important roles, so in the individual interactions composing the overall human rights marketplace similar factors are critical. However, in this chapter I largely omit these variables so as to illustrate more clearly the systemic processes at work. (I detail these strategic factors in Bob (2005).) More generally, this chapter is deliberately written in abstract terms, presenting the market approach as a heuristic device for understanding important, understudied aspects of human rights activism.

The market theory is obviously rooted in economic theory but also in this volume's collective action perspective. For one thing, the theory assumes that advocacy groups are not just moral actors but also, and fundamentally, organizations. Like firms, advocacy groups cannot be understood by focusing on their substantive goals alone. Whether those goals be profits, principles, or policies, both entities are simultaneously moved by organizational imperatives, to maintain themselves and to grow. Like firms, advocacy organizations depend on income (often in the form of donations and grants) and customers (members, foundations, and governments, which I call "donors"). In similar vein, the collective action perspective highlights the fact that advocacy organizations face sharp competition for critical resources. There are typically a number of advocacy groups in any particular issue area. Although they may sometimes cooperate (as firms sometimes do), the norm is competition for donor support (Ron, Ramos, and Rodgers, 2005; Berkovitch and Gordon, 2008; see also Barakso and Gill and Pfaff, both in this volume). Finally, the collective action approach is useful because it analytically disassembles what are often seen as cohesive coalitions, networks, or campaigns linking donors, international advocates, and local aggrieved groups. In fact, as the collective action approach suggests, these relationships often conceal important power differences and conflicting interests.

The moral theory

Many scholarly analysts have suggested a beneficent logic to international human rights activism. Individuals and groups repressed within their home states come to the attention of international rights advocates, sometimes by actively appealing for support, or in Keck and Sikkink's popular phrase, "throwing boomerangs" (Keck and Sikkink, 1998; Sikkink, 2005; Tarrow, 2005). The advocates are motivated by "causes, principled ideas, and norms ... that cannot be easily linked to a rationalist understanding of their 'interests'" (Keck and Sikkink, 1998: 9). As such, they are thought to differ fundamentally from other international actors such as power-hungry states and profit-driven multinational corporations. Moved instead by cosmopolitan altruism, advocacy groups leap into action when notified of oppression. Forming transnational networks, they act strategically to exert pressure against the victims' home states. This morally motivated foreign activism can help reduce state abuses in a kind of "boomerang" or "spiral" pattern (Keck and Sikkink, 1998; Risse, Ropp, and Sikkink, 1999).

Moral theorists have clearly advanced our understanding of transnational advocacy. Nor are they blind to the roles of power, conflict, and resources within the networks they study (Keck and Sikkink, 1998). However, they have spent little time analyzing these factors. Donors and their preferences have been similarly neglected. Rather, with their emphasis on the moral rather than material sources of transnational activism, these models suggest that advocacy organizations scour the globe, carefully identifying downtrodden groups and weighing their needs. In this view, the most likely cases to attract support are those involving the worst abuses: bodily harm to vulnerable groups; and overt, legalized discrimination, such as apartheid (Keck and Sikkink, 1998). In effect, there is a "meritocracy of suffering" in which the worst violations arouse the most human rights activism.

Anomalies

In a striking remark, Jan Egeland, United Nations Under-Secretary General for Humanitarian Affairs, has stated:

I don't know why one place gets attention and another not ... It's like a lottery, where there are 50 victimized groups always trying to get the winning ticket, and they play every night and they lose every night. I myself have said that the biggest race against the clock is Darfur, but in terms of numbers of people displaced, there are already more in Uganda and the eastern Congo. (Hoge, 2004)

On a more systematic basis, scholars have demonstrated that the level of repression within a state does not correlate fully with the amount of international human rights advocacy surrounding it. Rather, with regard to civil and political rights, countries with higher media profiles or greater linkages to key international actors spark greater activism (Smillie and Minear, 2004; Ron, Ramos, and Rodgers, 2005; cf. Saideman, 2002). More fundamentally, certain types of problems particularly civil and political violations, have attracted far more rights activism than economic and social rights issues, despite the latter accounting for higher levels of human suffering (Berkovitch and Gordon, 2008; Chong, 2009). Others have looked at similarly repressed groups within the same state and shown that international rights advocacy varies widely among them – but does not correspond to the levels of abuse they endure. For one thing, groups with superior resources, knowledge of media and NGO routines, and preexisting contacts with international actors attract the most international activism (Bob, 2002, 2005; cf. Wolfsfeld, 1997).

Following the collective action approach proposed in this volume, the foregoing research suggests that human rights organizations are not fundamentally different from other transnational political actors. While their motivations are in part political, they behave in much the same way as other organizations, albeit with different substantive goals (Willetts, 1982). For instance, Sell and Prakash (2004), examining NGO campaigns to expand global access to HIV/AIDS treatment drugs, show that advocacy organizations act much like businesses in their efforts to change government policies. Research in cognate disciplines such as nonprofit management and marketing reaches similar conclusions (Andreasen, 1995; Salamon, 1997). In the related areas of humanitarian relief, Cooley and Ron (2002) document fierce competition between advocacy organizations for contracts to support democracy-building efforts in Eastern Europe. More generally, advocacy organizations are closely related to and in some cases part of a vast nonprofit "industry" marked by sharp competition for scarce dollars and influence (Salamon, 1997).

All of this underlines a basic but often overlooked point. Advocacy organizations are like all organizations and firms in that they face the problem of economic scarcity. Having finite and often relatively small resources, their selection of particular issues on which to work limits or prevents their working on others. On a continual basis, they depend on donors, both institutional and individual, for much of their funds. And they are subject to many of the same financial fluctuations as other economic entities. Some of these hard material truths have been hidden by the general growth of donor monies devoted to human rights and other causes since the end of World War II (Smith, 1997). The largest such advocacy groups have also sought to increase their independence from donors by building their endowments or starting social enterprises. But the 2008–09 recession helped reveal the harsh realities, as nonprofits of many types, including premier human rights NGOs such as Amnesty International and Human Rights Watch, faced substantial cutbacks in personnel and operations. In sum, notwithstanding their altruistic principles, advocacy groups cannot escape economic fundamentals. To continue to exist as they are, they must at least break even or perhaps make a small "profit" which they presumably plow back into operations or support for other aggrieved groups.[1]

The human rights market

The foregoing suggests, at a minimum, that advocacy groups are moved by material as well as moral factors. It is therefore apt to conceive of two tightly related "markets" for human rights.[2] And, as I will show, this is more than just a metaphor, in addition providing useful insights into human rights activism.

---

[1] I thank Pavel Yakovlev for making this point.
[2] By hypothesis, development aid, humanitarian relief, and numerous other international and domestic issues could equally be modeled in market terms, as could the entire non-profit "industry" (Salamon, 1997).

In the first (Market 1), two players participate: "local" groups enduring situations, problems, or conditions that may be seen as rights abuses (aggrieved groups); and transnational advocacy organizations with resources available to help those groups. Thinking of this in market terms, the former supply human rights issues and the latter demand them. In some cases, aggrieved groups actively furnish information about their grievances to the market; in other cases, the oppressive conditions they suffer come to advocacy group attention without aggrieved groups affirmatively seeking this. In either case, there is a rough exchange in which the aggrieved receive support from the advocacy organization. Of course, it is true that those suffering abuses do not control information about their experiences in the way that suppliers of material goods usually do. Media and NGO reports about violations may be produced without the cooperation of the abused themselves. Nonetheless, core practices of rights NGOs – on-the-spot country missions, interviewing, and reporting – demonstrate that the cooperation of those suffering abuses is often critical to constructing a high-quality human rights "product."

As noted above, Market 1 is closely tied to a second one (Market 2) in which advocacy organizations in turn provide human rights products to donors primarily in wealthy democratic societies, in exchange for contributions. The advocacy groups assemble, analyze, repackage, and distribute information about aggrieved groups, in ways somewhat analogous to the ways in which multinational corporations manufacture finished goods from basic resources. With their addition of these critical "production factors," advocacy groups act as intermediaries between local suppliers and international donors. In Market 2, the latter "purchase" the resulting human rights products from the advocacy groups – sometimes with direct action on behalf of aggrieved groups (e.g. sending letters or emailing messages urging states to halt repression), more often with monetary donations to the advocacy groups (Skocpol, 2003). The advocates in turn pass back some of this income, in the form of support, to aggrieved groups in Market 1.

As in many markets, the "products" exchanged in the human rights market are intangible: in Market 1, between aggrieved and advocacy groups, information about human rights violations; and in Market 2, between advocacy groups and donors, information and, more fundamentally, benefits derived from helping reduce oppression – or at least from the belief that one is doing so. For individuals, these benefits are both internal (psychic gratification) and external (a reputation for doing good works). For institutions such as foundations, which play a major role in much human rights funding, the benefits are primarily external and reputational.

The market's scope is global, since exchanges are possible between aggrieved groups, advocacy organizations, and donors in any set of countries. Moreover, the range of products is potentially very broad, roughly defined by the expansive language of such major human rights instruments as the Universal Declaration of Human Rights, the International Covenant on Civil and Political Rights, and the International Covenant on Economic, Social and Cultural Rights. Finally, the total monetary value of the market, while difficult to measure, is large. The following figures give an admittedly partial and imperfect but nonetheless useful idea of its value. In 2001, two major donors, the Ford Foundation and the European Union, by themselves contributed $150 million and €105 million respectively to human rights related issues worldwide (Berkovitch and Gordon, 2008). In 2001 also, Amnesty International's budget was $34.84 million, up from $22.114 million in 1992 (Ron, Ramos, and Rodgers, 2005: 559).

Basis for exchange

What is the basis for exchange in the rights market? Notwithstanding the critiques of the moral theory noted above, morality and sympathy play some role. That is, donors and advocates are frequently inspired by ethical goals and care about those they aid. But, while these factors are often part of the human rights market, they are not sufficient to explain particular exchanges. More important, morality is not helpful as an analytic factor: one cannot use the constant of moral sympathy to explain the stark variations in transnational support among similarly needy aggrieved groups noted by Egeland and others.

From an analytic viewpoint, the exchange is more importantly based on mutual needs and complementary resources. Taking aggrieved groups first, their primary need is relief from their problems. In specific terms, this may mean removal of a repressive regime, change in an abusive policy, or lifting of an unjust condition. Advocacy organizations can help meet these goals because of their professional expertise, media contacts, and government access. Some of their resources (e.g. strategic and tactical expertise) can be transferred to aggrieved groups, directly helping them achieve their goals. In addition, using other resources, advocacy organizations can play an indirect but crucial role in galvanizing broader transnational advocacy campaigns that can exert pressure on a target.

For their part, advocacy organizations also have important needs, as the collective action perspective stresses. For one thing, they "need" human rights issues to provide themselves with a *raison d'être*, critical to attracting funds and members in Market 2. Aggrieved local populations can provide information about such issues using one of their few "resources," their own conditions, situations, and problems. More important, however, advocacy groups must concern themselves with their own survival and growth. For such vital organizational matters as personnel, equipment, and offices, they therefore need funding. Donor contributions and memberships are therefore critical to advocacy groups' very survival (Cohen, 1995). In this situation, it would not be surprising if donor and member preferences exert influence over advocacy groups' operations, including their choice of aggrieved groups on which to expend scarce resources.

Costs of support and the supply of causes

These mutual needs and complementary resources create incentives for interaction among donors, advocacy organizations, and aggrieved groups (cf. Gill and Pfaff, this volume). What is the character of these interactions? If support was costless and resources unlimited, a purely altruistic relationship might arise. But the reality is different. Indeed, it is very nearly the opposite. The number of aggrieved populations in the world is large, their needs are huge, and the costs of galvanizing advocacy group activism are substantial. By contrast, donor contributions are limited and can by no means provide advocacy organizations with sufficient resources to solve all human rights problems for all populations. Moreover, there are costs to support, most importantly opportunity costs. Given limited resources, aiding one group necessarily means doing less for some other. This point is central to the collective action perspective, and advocacy groups readily acknowledge it. As a Human Rights Watch (2002) World Report lamented, referring not only to itself but to the entire movement, "the scope of today's global human rights problems far exceeds the capacity of global institutions to address them."

These points have implications for both the supply and demand sides of the human rights market. On the supply side, the costs that aggrieved groups face may be considered "barriers to entry" to the human rights market. Among "factors of production" needed to overcome those barriers are time, money, and skill to amass information, transform it into cognizable form, and distribute it internationally. One should not exaggerate the height of these barriers. Some of them, such as the cost of distributing information, have undoubtedly fallen in recent decades. Nonetheless, although some aggrieved groups enter the human rights market on their own, many others do not have the basic economic or social capital to do so.

Thus, as a partial answer to this chapter's core question, one reason that the worst-off may not become objects of activism is that they do not have the minimal wherewithal to supply their causes to the rights marketplace (Bob, 2005). An example supporting this point concerns the "right to health," as recently noted by development economist William Easterly (2009). Long ignored except as a slogan, the right gained greater prominence in the 1990s, spurred primarily by mobilization among those suffering from HIV/AIDS in both the developed and developing worlds. In 2004 a major World Health Organization report emphasized the right, although it mentioned only one disease, HIV/AIDS. Bad as this disease has become in the developing world, however, its annual death toll is comparable to that of malaria and tuberculosis, with pneumonia, measles and diarrhoeal diseases also being major killers. Yet in the period 1997–2006, the World Bank, one of the world's largest donors, devoted 57% of its communicable disease funding to HIV/AIDS but only 3% to malaria, 2% to TB, and even less to the other diseases (World Bank, 2009). A likely reason is that HIV/AIDS "does not disproportionately affect the poor" but affects the middle and upper classes too (World Bank, 2009: 39). The latter are better able to make their voices heard in the human rights market, whereas most who die from the other diseases are poor.

Market structure and the demand for causes

Viewed from an economic standpoint, the disjuncture between enormous needs and limited donor resources also gives considerable market power to advocacy organizations relative to aggrieved groups in Market 1 and to donors relative to advocacy groups in Market 2. As a result, the preferences of donors in Market 2 can shift incentives for advocacy organizations as they operate in Market 1. Large institutional donors such as major foundations and governments, which provide substantial portions of advocacy organization budgets, exert particular sway. As Keck and Sikkink (1998) have noted, the Ford Foundation, with its large endowment and long interest in human rights, has helped fund and therefore build the human rights movement since the 1970s. Large donors also help steer the movement toward certain goals, rather than others. For instance, the Ford Foundation's recent emphasis on "bringing human rights home" to the United States has led to substantial growth in advocacy efforts to address social justice issues in the USA, using international principles, ideas, and institutions (Bob, 2008). In addition to shaping the development and direction of the movement, donors affect day-to-day operations. In recent years, for instance, donor concerns for "accountability" among recipients have led to an emphasis on grant-writing, tangible milestones, and reporting (Jenkins, 1998).

Advocacy organizations will implement their donor-influenced preferences at the local level in Market 1, favoring certain issues and approaches while slighting others. In some cases, donor preferences may correspond with the needs of the oppressed and the relative gravity of their problems. But this need not be the case because preferences among individual and institutional donors develop for a wide variety of idiosyncratic reasons – sometimes careful efforts to evaluate overseas needs, but also and probably more often donors' personal experiences, institutional histories, and ideological beliefs, to name only a few. Berkovitch and Gordon (2008) provide one example in the Middle East, showing that donor preferences have lead Israeli rights organizations to focus on lesser abuses in Israel proper (to the neglect of more serious violations in the Occupied Territories) and to deploy legalistic tactics (rather than mobilization and direct action). Blake *et al.* (2009) document analogous preferences with regard to economic and social rights in India. External donors, many of them wealthy overseas Indians, prefer to fund tangible capital projects such as schools and temples rather than broad policy initiatives that might provide greater benefits to more people – but would require high-level investment for long-term lobbying and campaigning (Blake *et al.*, 2009: 11; see also Dicklitch and Lwanga, 2003).

More generally, a careful study of Amnesty International's 1986–2000 human rights reporting shows that actual abuses in a country have a statistically significant effect on its work – but so do "factors other than human need" (Ron, Ramos, and Rodgers, 2005: 574). In particular, "considerations of efficacy and visibility" related to Amnesty's needs for external funding and long-term survival "force the group, like other transnational NGOs, to devote more attention to some areas than others" (Ron, Ramos, and Rodgers, 2005: 576).

On the other hand, it is undoubtedly true that advocacy groups sometimes shape donor preferences. Using claims to expertise and authority, the most powerful advocacy groups may influence donors to raise their contribution levels, support particular issues, or provide unrestricted funds. But advocacy groups are ultimately dependent on donor funds and must heed basic preferences among actual or potential donors even as they seek to affect them. Moreover, even if advocacy groups sway donors, there is no guarantee that the advocacy groups themselves will make the needs of aggrieved groups their top priority. Again, to the extent that advocates have freedom from donors to develop their programs, their preferences for activism may result from leaders' personal interests, institutional histories, or ideological proclivities.

For their part, the aggrieved may sometimes influence advocacy group preferences (and, in a more attenuated way, donor preferences). But because donor funds and advocacy resources are scarce relative to the needs of aggrieved groups, the latter will typically have little power in the interaction. Many of those seeking international activism will receive less than they desire – or none at all.

In sum, the structure of the human rights market means that the amount and type of activism will hinge not only on the needs of the aggrieved (supply) but also on donor and advocacy group preferences (demand).

Amnesty International and the demand for human rights

This section provides evidence to demonstrate the plausibility of the foregoing ideas, primarily derived from recent histories of Amnesty International (AI), one of the most important advocacy groups of the human rights movement (Buchanan, 2002; Hopgood, 2006). Admittedly, AI is somewhat unusual among human rights groups. It is a network of national organizations coordinated by an international head-quarters in London, rather than a purely national group. Like other such human rights groups, AI is run by a professional staff and supported by donors. Unlike most other groups, it also includes "members" some of whom play a minor role in the group's governance, both through annual meetings convening at least a small portion of the membership of national chapters and through biennial international meetings. Members also participate directly in a portion of the group's advocacy activities such as letter-writing campaigns and occasional protests (though other rights groups such as Human Rights Watch also urge their many individual donors to take similar actions). Finally, members probably make it possible for AI to rely somewhat more on individual support and somewhat less on institutional funding than other human rights groups. But precisely because AI is a hybrid, melding participatory and bureaucratic elements, studying it can provide important insights relevant to organizations that more closely hew to either model.[3]

AI began in 1961 – but not simply as a vehicle of solidarity or support to those facing persecution in repressive states. Rather, the organization's founder, Peter Benenson, viewed Amnesty as "primarily" a vehicle for fulfilling the politico-spiritual longings of its prospective membership in the United Kingdom and other countries with good human rights records.

---

[3] As the foregoing discussion suggests, many other human rights groups also blend participatory and bureaucratic characteristics.

As Benenson explained in a striking 1961 memorandum entitled "First Notes on Organisation,"

[t]he underlying purpose of this campaign – which I hope those who are closely connected with it will remember, but never publish – is to find a common base upon which the idealists of the world can cooperate. It is designed in particular to *absorb the latent enthusiasm* of great numbers of such idealists who have, since the eclipse of Socialism, become increasingly frustrated; similarly it is geared to appeal to the young searching for an ideal, and to women past the prime of their life who have been, unfortunately, unable to expend in full their maternal impulses. If this underlying aim is borne in mind, it will be seen that, à la longue, it matters more to harness the enthusiasm of the helpers than to bring people out of prison. With regard to the latter, as a friend pointed out to me, the real martyrs prefer to suffer, and, as I would add, the real saints are no worse off in prison than elsewhere on this earth, for they cannot be prevented by stone or bars from spiritual conversation . . . *Those whom the Amnesty Appeal primarily aims to free are the men and women imprisoned by cynicism, and doubt.* (Benenson, quoted in Buchanan, 2002: 593, emphasis added)

Benenson's style may seem quaint today. Nor is there doubt that he was moved both by deep sympathy for individuals suffering political repression and by firm belief that international activism might help them. But the memorandum, like other documents he wrote at the time, reveals that Benenson had another core reason for founding the group: his conviction that there was an unmet demand for activism among certain populations in the free world. Benenson hoped to harness this – but helping political prisoners was not the main goal. Rather, as the same memorandum states, the "principal aim (unpublished) is to get people of different opinions, class etc. to work together in the same direction, and to learn to cooperate. Thus, it does not matter so very much what they do, so long as they do something" (Benenson, quoted in Buchanan, 2002: 594).

Benenson was a good judge of his market.[4] The initial plea for support sparked considerable popular interest because it "offered to empower its volunteers, allowing ordinary men and women to feel that in a small but concrete way they were able to make a difference on an issue of international concern" (Buchanan, 2002: 596). In effect, the appeals turned latent into patent demand, first in the United Kingdom and later "among the idealists of the world." AI's foundation demonstrates also that, although advocacy organizations often are beholden to donors for

---

[4] In putting it this way, I do not mean to suggest that the appeal was a cynical ploy meant to enrich the new organization; it clearly was not. Rather, Benenson's deep moral commitments and political goals led him to make Amnesty's initial appeal. But, as we shall see, the group accommodated itself to its organizational needs.

funds, they may sometimes be able to influence (or even create) demand for their activities.

Beyond AI's establishment, demand-based considerations have guided the organization's agenda throughout its history. From its start in the Cold War era, the group announced that it would stand above ideology. In this period of sharp East–West tension, the founders hoped this approach would enhance its credibility and widen its appeal. Accordingly AI developed the "Groups of Three" concept, assigning its local members three cases to work on simultaneously, one each from the East (Warsaw Pact countries), the West (primarily southern Europe), and the developing world. This blanket policy arguably created "balance," at least among three rival political blocs of the era. But it is unlikely that it reflected the relative needs of those facing political repression or the relative levels of repression as between various countries.

As another example, consider the new advocacy group's policy toward abuses against people based on their religious practices. AI's founders had initially planned for an "international campaign to promote the free exchange of ideas and the free practice of religion" (Benenson, quoted in Buchanan, 2002: 591). At first as well, leaders of various religious organizations played a major role in the group. But, as Buchanan notes, "this special emphasis on religious persecution soon began to fade with religious issues subsumed in the generic concept of the 'Prisoner of Conscience,'" defined as "any person who is physically restrained (by imprisonment or otherwise) from expressing (in any form of words or symbols) any opinion which he honestly holds and which does not advocate or condone personal violence" (Buchanan, 2002: 591, 585). This shift toward broader political issues did not mean that Amnesty International ignored religiously based persecution. It remained a concern but only within the broader "prisoner of conscience" concept. Importantly, this change in the direction and focus of the group occurred because AI's core message, that human rights were "universal," won significant support "precisely because of [its] secularity" (Hopgood, 2006: 62). Maintaining religiously based persecution on a par with politically based persecution would have undercut an important basis on which the group gained early supporters, particularly in the United Kindgom and other countries of northern Europe. Thus, in this early case, AI appears to have bowed to the preferences of its supporters, notwithstanding the organization's original purposes.

More broadly, for much of AI's history – and that of another key advocacy organization, Human Rights Watch – religiously based persecution did not receive the attention that Benenson and other founders had initially envisioned. This does not appear to be due to a lack of such violations. Rather, as Allen Hertzke has argued, the "secular blinders" of the rights movement created a "powerful barrier" to highlighting religiously based persecution (Hertzke, 2004: 96). This changed only in the 1990s – but not, as the moral theorists might predict, because of an upsurge in religiously based abuses abroad. Instead, demand for activism around such violations increased with the rise of a "new constituency for human rights," politically powerful Christian conservatives based primarily in the United States (Goldberg, 1997; Hertzke, 2004: 127). In the 1990s, they succeeded in establishing new institutional bases for monitoring and reporting on religious persecution, including new advocacy organizations and a separate US State Department annual report on religious persecution. In response, AI and Human Rights Watch began to make religious issues a more explicit part of their missions.

Even as it downplayed religious persecution, AI's success in attracting a constituency and building its "brand" soon exerted pressure on its agenda. Beginning in the mid 1960s, the group's nerve center, the research office at the International Secretariat (IS) in London, placed cardinal importance on painstaking research to verify information about those whom it was considering as "prisoners of conscience," including whether they had engaged in violent activities (a factor that would exclude them from this status). This curbed the number of rights cases available for members to support. But as AI's membership in democratic states swelled, local chapters pressed for more prisoners to help. As Stephen Hopgood (2006) states, "researchers could not meet demand" (83). In response, the "IS tried to restrict the demand [for new cases] to meet the supply [of confirmed prisoners], arguing in May 1970 that a ceiling should be placed on new [local support] groups" (79).

Similarly, the NGO's narrowly defined early focus on "prisoners of conscience" kept it from speaking on broader rights issues, such as economic rights, discrimination against identity groups, or "cultural" issues (Hopgood, 2006: 151, 155). But this agenda too came under pressure for expansion – primarily again from activists in democratic states. As the organization's stature grew, particularly after winning the 1977 Nobel Peace Prize, "its moral authority – its moral capital – was a substantial resource, and it attracted those who wanted to fight more political battles" – over everything from poverty to gay rights (Hopgood, 2006: 106, 190). The group's powerful American chapter, Amnesty International USA, was particularly vocal in pushing enlargement. In addition, AI faced increasing competition for funding from other human rights NGOs, particularly Human Rights Watch which took a broader approach to rights issues and tactics (Hopgood, 2006: 76, 139). Debate raged for years at AI headquarters, and ultimately management widened its mission.

One example is AI's 1995 decision to include among its issues female genital cutting, a practice widespread among certain cultures in Africa and the Middle East. This had first been mooted as a possible rights violation at AI's 1981 International Council meeting, "in the wake of the interest aroused worldwide" by a 1979 World Health Organization meeting that discussed the issue (AI, 1997: section 2). AI opted not to take it up in 1981, however, because it did not fit with the group's definition of a rights abuse, which at the time covered only actions by states, not private actors. Later that decade, women's organizations based primarily (though not exclusively) in countries of Europe and North America, where the practice was almost non-existent, mobilized against cutting, now labeled female genital mutilation (FGM). In addition, some international legal scholars called for the public/private distinction in human rights law to be abandoned in part to deal with this issue. Several international treaty bodies also condemned the practice. AI therefore came under mounting pressure to change its stance. In early 1995, with the Fourth UN World Conference on Women scheduled in the fall, the pressure became acute. In this context, as the advocacy group itself acknowledged, "AI recognized the urgency of taking a position against this widespread form of violence against women prior to" the conference (AI, 1997: section 2). Notably, the urgency did not stem from any sudden or looming increase in cutting. Nor did it come primarily from "victims" of the practice, many of whom viewed it as acceptable, even honorable. Rather, AI's management appears to have believed that it could not remain out of step with a powerful constituency of actual or potential donors.

As another example, consider AI's shift toward monitoring the human rights practices of multinational businesses in the late 1990s. It seems unlikely that corporate practices were any worse in this period or immediately preceding years than they had been in the three decades after AI's founding. Certainly there were high-profile cases in the 1990s such as the Nigerian government's 1995 hanging of Ken Saro-Wiwa and eight other minority Ogoni activists on trumped-up murder charges. (The Ogoni had accused Royal Dutch/Shell of rights violations in the Niger Delta.) But similar cases of alleged corporate malfeasance, often involving far greater loss of life and more direct company involvement, had occurred for decades. What then explains the shift? The chairman of Amnesty International USA's Board of Directors, Morton Winston, flagged one important reason at the group's annual general meeting in 2003. As he noted, AI's members are primarily political progressives, especially progressive college students, many of whom had been stirred by the "anti-corporate globalization" movement of the late 1990s. In embracing the new business and human rights program, Winston said, Amnesty was "reading the trends in the world and riding them. We have adjusted our strategies to a changing world" (Winston, 2003).

In sum, these changes in Amnesty's agenda occurred not because of change in the incidence or intensity of events and incidents occurring among the populations experiencing them (supply), but because of shifting intellectual currents, legal argumentation, and political pressure among potential donors free of these incidents (demand). This is undoubtedly not the only reason for such shifts. AI and other rights organizations certainly pay attention to levels of abuse worldwide – and local aggrieved groups strive to bring their issues to AI's attention, with the hope of gaining support. Nor do these shifts suggest any devious or unprincipled motives. AI was acting in a fashion predictable for any organization that wishes to survive and continue its work in the future. What the foregoing cases suggest, however, is that demand-based factors play an important role in determining the size and scope of rights activism.

Demand reshaping supply

If that is the case, it seems likely that demand by donors and thence by advocacy organizations might also shape the amount and character of rights issues. Aggrieved groups at the local level, aware of advocacy group and donor preferences, may be able to adapt to tap international resources and support. As one example of this kind of phenomenon, consider the lead-up to Indonesia's 1999 democratic elections when international agencies flooded the archipelago with about $90 million for vote monitoring. The new-found money led to "needless proliferation of new monitoring groups – organizations with little experience and even less commitment" (Bjornlund, 2001: 22). Before the money became available, there was one such group; within a year, there were over ninety. The funds also "touched off a mad scramble," with these local groups "pouring their time and energy into grant proposals and budgets" at the time they should have been planning for the election (Bjornlund, 2001: 23). In the environmental field, Carrie Meyer has similarly documented the sudden growth of local ecology organizations in Ecuadorean villages when international actors made funds available for environmental issues (Meyer, 1995). More generally, the power of donor and advocacy group demand may encourage local groups with political agendas to publicize and reshape them to capture international resources and support.

There is one important caveat. Aggrieved groups will have varying capacity to note, understand, and respond to donor preference. It is likely that the most deprived or repressed groups will have the least ability to do so – another reason that the human rights market may not reflect the relative needs of the world's aggrieved populations.

Conclusion

In the foregoing pages, I have presented a market perspective on human rights activism. Although I have briefly illustrated it using secondary sources, the approach is highly abstract. As noted in the introduction to this chapter, the market perspective by no means reduces activism to an economic transaction. Nor does it negate the role of morality, sympathy, and strategy.

In fact, a market perspective based on the collective action approach provides new insights about key issues in human rights activism. Combining supply and demand factors, it underlines the agency not only of advocacy organizations but also of aggrieved groups. In the human rights literature, both the scholarly and policy accounts have often viewed "victims" primarily as objects of abuse, waiting passively for aid (Roldán, 2002). The word "victim" itself carries this connotation. Yet this is clearly a misconception. Those suffering abuses seldom go quietly into the night. Rather they and their representatives not only resist abuses directly, but also clamor for help from the outside world. Regarding the latter, they use a variety of strategies, from issuing rhetorical appeals to taking actions designed to attract the international media (Wolfsfeld, 1997; Kalyvas, 2003; Kuperman, 2004). Indeed, without some action by "victims," their plight will often not enter the human rights marketplace at all (Bob, 2005).

Moreover, as discussed, aggrieved groups' actions once in the marketplace strongly affect their ability to gain support. Keck and Sikkink's (1998) idea that local actors launch transnational appeal "boomerangs" calling for support therefore advances the literature. But it could also create a second misconception, that advocacy organizations wait to be struck by these "boomerangs" before intervening overseas. In fact in many cases, advocacy organizations actively seek local clients to serve as exemplars of new campaign issues, as "test cases" for novel claims, or simply as "poster children" for the organization's good works (Cohen, 1995). Thus, like buyers and sellers in commercial markets, both those suffering abuses and those offering succor must be seen as active participants in the transnational support market. Unfortunately, however, as this chapter has suggested, the most deprived groups are likely to have the most difficulty sparking international activism on their behalf.

More generally, however, the power of advocacy organizations (*vis-à-vis* aggrieved groups) in Market 1 and of major donors (*vis-à-vis* the advocacy groups) in Market 2 suggest that demand-side factors play a major role in the human rights market. That is, the preferences and requirements of donors in Market 2 shape the behavior and predilections of advocacy organizations, which in turn affect the behavior of aggrieved groups in Market 1 (Dicklitch and Lwanga, 2003; Berkovitch and Gordon, 2008). This demand-driven perspective stands in contrast to the conventional view that human rights activism grows organically from local grievances to international support. The latter view, which derives from the moral theory, can be integrated within the market perspective, as a supply-based conception of rights activism. Such supply-side mechanisms undoubtedly do occur, but given the structure of both Markets 1 and 2, they are likely to be weaker than demand-side processes. The result in many cases is that foreign rights NGOs and their donors will establish priorities that may not correspond to the real needs of populations facing various forms of rights violations. In addition, barriers to entering the human rights market, although relatively low, may prevent the worst-off from participating.

To conclude, the argument here is not that human rights activism can be reduced to economic principles alone. Even in commercial markets that is seldom the case, and it is certainly not the case among rights advocates. The claim here is more modest and analytic: thinking about human rights activism in market terms can open new insights about gaps between human rights rhetoric and reality.

References

AlertNet. 2005. Tip Sheet: How to "Sell" Forgotten Emergencies. Reuters Foundation. www.alertnet.org/thefacts/reliefresources/112849858584.htm.

Amnesty International (AI). 1997. Female Genital Mutilation: A Human Rights Information Pack. AI Index: ACT 77/05/97, London.

2004. Globalizing Justice! Amnesty International Integrated Strategic Plan 2004–2010. *Toolkit* 3. www.amnesty.org.nz/Publicdo.nsf/bf25ab0f47ba5 dd785256499006b15a4/fada703607576556cc256d080016acfa/$FILE/ISP. htm#_Toc30575023.

Andreasen, A. R. 1995. *Marketing Social Change: Changing Behavior to Promote Health, Social Development, and the Environment.* San Francisco: Jossey-Bass.

Benenson, P. 1961. *Persecution, 1961.* Baltimore: Penguin Books.

Berkovitch, N. and N. Gordon. 2008. The Political Economy of Transnational Regimes: The Case of Human Rights. *International Studies Quarterly,* **52**: 881–904.

Bjornlund, E. 2001. Democracy Inc. *Wilson Quarterly,* Summer: 18–24.

Blake, S., T. Chand, N. Dutta *et al.* 2009. Giving in India: A Guide for Funders and Charities. Copal Partners and New Philanthropy

Capital, http://www.philanthropycapital.org/research/research_reports/international/Giving_in_india.aspx

Bob, C. 2002. Merchants of Morality. *Foreign Policy*, **129**: 36–45.

2005. *The Marketing of Rebellion: Insurgents, Media, and International Activism.* Cambridge: Cambridge University Press.

2008. Promises and Pitfalls of Rights Strategies in American Social Justice Advocacy, *American Society of International Law Proceedings of the 101st Annual Meeting*, 22–24.

Buchanan, T. 2002. "The Truth Will Set You Free": The Making of Amnesty International. *Journal of Contemporary History*, **37**(4): 575–597.

Chong, D. 2009. Economic Rights and Extreme Poverty: Moving toward Subsistence. In C. Bob (ed.), *The International Struggle for New Human Rights*. Philadelphia: University of Pennsylvania Press.

Cohen, S. 1995. *The Impact of Information about Human Rights Violations: Denial and Acknowledgment.* Jerusalem: Centre for Human Rights, Hebrew University.

Cooley, A. and J. Ron. 2002. NGO Scramble: Transnational Action and Organizational Survival. *International Security*, **27**(1): 5–39.

Dicklitch, S. and D. Lwanga. 2003. The Politics of Being Non-Political: Human Rights Organizations and the Creation of a Positive Human Rights Culture in Uganda. *Human Rights Quarterly*, **25**(2): 482–509.

Easterly, W. 2009. Human Rights are the Wrong Basis for Healthcare. *Financial Times*, October 12. www.ft.com/cms/s/89bbbda2-b763–11de-9812–00144feab49a,%20Authorised=false.html?_i_location=http%3A%2F%2Fwww.ft.com%2Fcms%2Fs%2F0%2F89bbbda2-b763–11de-9812–00144feab49a.html&_i_referer=

Goldberg, J. 1997. Washington Discovers Christian Persecution. *New York Times Magazine*, December 21. www.nytimes.com/1997/12/21/magazine/washington-discovers-christian-persecution.html?pagewanted=all.

Hafner-Burton, E. and J. Ron. 2009. Seeing Double: Human Rights Impact through Qualitative and Quantitative Eyes. *World Politics*, **61**(2): 360–401.

Hertzke, A. 2004. *Freeing God's Children: The Unlikely Alliance for Global Human Rights.* Lanham, MD: Rowman & Littlefield.

Hoge, W. 2004. Rescuing Victims Worldwide "From the Depths of Hell". *New York Times*, July 10.

Hopgood, S. 2006. *Keepers of the Flame: Understanding Amnesty International.* Ithaca, NY: Cornell University Press.

Human Rights Watch. 2002. Introduction. In *Human Rights Watch World Report 2001*. www.hrw.org/wr2k1/intro/index.html.

Jenkins, J. C. 1998. Channeling Social Protest: Foundation Patronage of Contemporary Social Movements. In W. Powell and E. Clemens (eds.), *Private Action and the Public Good*, New Haven, CT: Yale University Press.

Kalyvas, S. N. 2003. The Ontology of "Political Violence": Action and Identity in Civil Wars. *Perspectives on Politics*, **1**(3): 475–494.

Keck, M. E. and K. Sikkink. 1998. *Activists beyond Borders: Advocacy Networks in International Politics*. Ithaca, NY: Cornell University Press.

Kuperman, A. J. 2004. Humanitarian Hazard: Revisiting Doctrines of Intervention. *Harvard International Review*, **26**: 64–68.

Meyer, C. A. 1995. Opportunism and NGOs: Entrepreneurship and Green North–South Transfers. *World Development*, **23**(8): 1277–1289.

Risse, T., S. C. Ropp, and K. Sikkink (eds.). 1999. *The Power of Human Rights: International Norms and Domestic Change*. Cambridge University Press.

Roldán, M. 2002. *La Violencia in Anioquia, Colombia, 1946–1953*. Durham, NC: Duke University Press.

Ron, J., H. Ramos, and Kathleen Rodgers. 2005. Transnational Information Politics: NGO Human Rights Reporting, 1986–2000, *International Studies Quarterly*, **49**(3): 557–587.

Saideman, S. M. 2002. Discrimination in International Relations: Analyzing External Support for Ethnic Groups. *Journal of Peace Research*, **39**(1): 27–50.

Salamon, L. M. 1997. *Defining the Nonprofit Sector: A Cross-National Analysis*. Manchester University Press.

Schulz, W. F. 2001. *In Our Own Best Interest: How Defending Human Rights Benefits Us All*. Boston: Beacon Press.

Sell, S. K. and A. Prakash. 2004. Using Ideas Strategically: The Contest between Business and NGO Networks in Intellectual Property Rights. *International Studies Quarterly*, **48**(1): 143–175.

Sikkink, K. 2005. Patterns of Dynamic Multilevel Governance and the Insider–Outsider Coalition. In D. della Porta and S. Tarrow (eds.), *Transnational Protest and Global Activism*. Lanham, MD: Rowman & Littlefield.

Skocpol, T. 2003. *Diminished Democracy: From Membership to Management in American Civic Life*. Norman: University of Oklahoma Press.

Smillie, I. and L. Minear. 2004. *The Charity of Nations: Humanitarian Action in a Calculating World*. Bloomfield, CT: Kumarian Press.

Smith, J. 1997. Characteristics of the Modern Transnational Social Movement Sector. In J. Smith, C. Chatfield, and R. Pagnucco (eds.), *Transnational Social Movements and Global Politics*. Syracuse University Press.

Tarrow, S. 2005. *The New Transnational Activism*. Cambridge University Press.

Willetts, P. (ed.). 1982. *Pressure Groups in the Global System: The Transnational Relations of Issue-Oriented Non-Governmental Organizations*. New York: St. Martin's Press.

Winston, M. 2003. Address to "Town Meeting", Amnesty International USA Annual General Meeting, Pittsburgh, April 4.

Wolfsfeld, G. 1997. *Media and Political Conflict: News from the Middle East*. Cambridge University Press.

World Bank. 2009. *Improving Effectiveness and Outcomes for the Poor in Health, Nutrition, and Population: An Evaluation of World Bank Group Support since 1997*. Washington, DC: World Bank.

World Conference on Human Rights. 1993. Vienna Declaration and Programme of Action. Vienna, June 14–25, 1993. UN Doc. A/CONF. 157/24, I.S.

6   Brand identity and the tactical repertoires of advocacy organizations

Maryann Barakso

In a recent study examining perceptions of nonprofit organizations, Venable *et al.* found that "across nonprofit classifications (health, environment/rights, and arts/humanities), there are distinct personality differences" (2005: 308). Respondents were able to discern differences among organizations with respect to qualities such as integrity, nurturance, sophistication, and ruggedness. For example, the perception of Greenpeace's integrity was low compared to other nonprofits studied (Venable *et al.*, 2005: 304). What factors drive respondents to such conclusions? In this chapter, I argue that how interest organizations go about their work – the tactical choices they make – represents an important component of their brand identity. Explaining public impressions of Greenpeace becomes more straightforward when we consider the organization's repertoires of contention. Arguably, Greenpeace's tactics, which tend to garner media attention, raise concerns among the public that the organization behaves unfairly with respect to its targets (Japanese whalers, for example). Nevertheless, while many may disapprove of Greenpeace's methods of operation, those techniques clearly appeal to its resource base. Furthermore, the group's distinct tactical repertoire also allows it to operate within its own niche in the environmental policy sector.

In her book *The Populist Paradox: Interest Group Influence and the Promise of Direct Legislation*, Elisabeth R. Gerber (1999) argues that the behavior of advocacy organizations is analogous to that of firms. Advocacy groups weigh the costs and benefits of proposed actions just as firms do. Both firms and groups seek to maintain themselves and to reap profits. For firms, profits are monetary, whereas for groups, profits take the form of policy successes. In this volume, several authors are guided by the firm analogy: McGee Young understands the organizational development of the Natural Resources Defense Council by grounding the group in a competitive market, for example. And as Clifford Bob notes in his analysis of human rights organizations, the policy choices human rights groups make are, like the choices of firms, a function of their particular niche in a larger "market."

Similarly, in this chapter I extend the concept of branding, typically associated with firms, to advocacy organizations. First, I suggest that like corporations, advocacy organizations develop distinctive brand identities as a means of differentiating themselves to internal and external audiences in a highly competitive market. For both firms and advocacy organizations, branding facilitates the attraction and retention of investors and customers. Successful branding also allows both firms and interest groups to reduce overhead: organizations with highly recognizable brands operate more cost effectively because their identity signals more efficiently to external audiences, for example. Moreover, by promoting loyalty, a familiar and trusted brand identity promotes the financial stability of both firms and advocacy groups.

Second, I consider the extent to which one important element of advocacy group practice – their tactical repertoires – constitutes a manifestation of organizations' brands. Tactical repertoires are "distinctive constellations of tactics and strategies developed over time and used ... to act collectively in order to make claims on individuals and groups" (Snow, Soule, and Kriesi, 2004: 265). Much of the literature on branding (whether in the context of firms or interest groups) defines a brand in the context of symbols (such as logos) and products (such as market or issue niches). One definition notes that a brand is "a name, term, sign, symbol or design, or combination of them, which is intended to define the goods and services of one seller or group of sellers and to differentiate them from those of competitors" (Kotler, 1991). Yet, an organization's brand identity can also be defined, at least in part, by the means it uses to pursue its goals. We can see this today as firms tout their environmentally friendly or "fair trade" products or their commitment to creating open-source software. For some firms, their "process," or the way they do business, is integral to their brand; for others, their process may be irrelevant. Advocacy organizations' processes, on the other hand, may or may not be an attribute that they choose to promote; nevertheless, how advocacy groups do business is likely to be central to the way they interact with the public and with policymakers. In fact, for some organizations, emphasizing their process as an integral element of their brand can be a significant differentiating device. For example, Anthony Gill and Steven Pfaff (this volume) link the successes of "high cost" religious denominations (such as the Latter-Day Saints) in part to practices like door-to-door evangelizing.

Above all, effective branding should prime expectations about what a firm or group stands for and what it does. Scholars frequently distinguish among advocacy groups' tactical repertoires according to whether an approach is dominated by an "insider" focus, such as lobbying or testifying before legislative bodies, or by an "outsider" orientation, which takes the form of petitioning, grassroots mobilization, and protest. If tactical repertoires are a manifestation of an organization's brand identity, we should find that groups' tactical orientations are identifiable: groups should choose a coherent set of tactics that reflect a particular orientation.

Second, we should find that a group's tactical orientation remains relatively stable over time. Advocacy organizations develop their practices using the skills, resources, and experiences of their members and staff. As such, repertoires do not typically shift dramatically, even in the face of social, economic, or political transitions, because such shifts engender substantial costs to organizations while also exposing them to increased risk (Barakso, 2004). Such costs would include, for example, the need to retrain members and staff. One possible risk for an organization that shifts its tactical orientation is that members and staff may oppose changes in its routines, in part because this necessitates changes in their own practice, but also because these individuals may be uncertain about the value of such changes. How do members and administrators know that the new tactics will be successful? Furthermore, tactical repertoires reflect an organization's identity: to the extent that tactical shifts upset the prior notions of members and staff about what the organization represents, group leaders face the strong possibility of resistance and internal conflict (Carmin and Balser, 2002).

One other factor contributing to the stability of tactical repertoires involves organizations' revenue streams. Advocacy organizations' funding sources play a role in stabilizing groups' tactical approaches (Jenkins and Perrow, 1977). "Preservationist" versus "ecocentric" environmental organizations, for example, rely on different funders. Preservationist groups depend on corporations, whereas environmental groups are typically supported by members, a distinction that influences their respective tactical repertoires (insider/conventional and outsider/contentious) (Carmin and Balser, 2002). Similarly, the ability of the humanitarian organization Médecins sans Frontières (Doctors Without Borders) to "strive for strict independence from all structures or powers, whether political, religious, economic or other" depends upon the fact that the majority of its funds are privately sourced (Médecins sans Frontières, 1995). In sum, then, we would not expect an advocacy organization whose dominant method of operation consists of insider strategies (such as legislative lobbying) to shift to outsider tactics (like organizing demonstrations) within the span of a few years.

Third, I examine the relationship between a group's tactical focus (the use of insider or outsider methods) and its propensity to participate in coalitions. Coalition work is a common tactic used by advocacy organizations, but one that may undermine or dilute an individual group's brand identity (Spruill, 2001). If the cultures, values, and goals of partici-pating organizations are incompatible, the repercussions can include coali-tion failure; lingering ill will among groups; and intra-organizational discord. Given that participating in coalitions can damage brand identity, what kinds of organization are most likely to enter into such alliances? It may be, for example, that organizations involved in policy areas linked to a social move-ment (such as environmental groups) are less likely to risk engaging in coalitions. Advocacy organizations with social movement ties may hold particularly strong ideological commitments, whereas scholars have found that groups with more inclusive perspectives are those most inclined to form such alliances (Rucht, 2004; McCarthy, 2005).

Employing data documenting the activities of highly influential interest groups (compiled by the CQ Press and the Foundation for Public Affairs), I analyze and compare the tactics employed by forty-seven advocacy groups in the environmental and political/governmental process sectors in 2001 and 2006. I examine whether the groups specialize in either outsider or insider tactical repertoires, and whether their reper-toires remain stable over time. I find that organizations are more likely to specialize in insider or outsider tactical repertoires in the environmental sector. The evidence also shows that organizations in both sectors exhibit substantial stability in tactical approach over time. I find that although groups in both sectors are likely to engage in coalition work, the organ-izations most likely to do so are those whose tactics are the least specialized.

The relationship between brands and tactics

Perhaps because of the explosion in the number of interest groups in the preceding decades, by the late 1990s advocacy groups began seriously applying concepts of corporate branding to their own organizations (Venable *et al.*, 2005). One observer wrote in the *Chronicle of Philanthropy* in 2001: "In recent years, nonprofit groups have embraced few ideas more zealously than one called branding, a marketing practice used widely in the for-profit world to build loyalty among customers and investors and one-up the competition" (Spruill, 2001).[1] Increases in the density of all forms of public interest organizations have heightened competition for dollars, members, and media – as well as for the attention of policymakers. In response, even nonprofit public purpose organizations that have enjoyed

---

[1] For example, the first mentions of branding in the *Nonprofit and Voluntary Sector Quarterly* occur in 1999.

high levels of public confidence and recognition have taken clear steps to "adopt a market culture." As Lester Salamon (2002: 4) notes,

[n]onprofit organizations are increasingly marketing their product, viewing their clients as customers, segmenting their markets, differentiating their output, identifying their market niche, formulating business plans, and generally incorporating the language, and the style, of business management into the operation of their agencies.

Furthermore, in an era of heightened distrust of "special interests," the confidence that a brand can inspire among the public is another benefit of this strategy (particularly considering that, unlike firms, advocacy organizations can rarely claim to have single-handedly produced any particular public goods) (Ritchie, Swami, and Weisburg, 1993: 33; Dixon, 1997; Berry, 2000). Today, the fact that nonprofit and advocacy organizations stand to benefit from developing, maintaining, and advertising a distinctive "brand" has become conventional wisdom (Ritchie, Swami, and Weisburg, 1993).

Typically, an advocacy or nonprofit organization's brand is equated with its logo, issue niche, and image (Heaney, 2006). A frequently significant yet overlooked component of an organization's brand identity is the means by which it pursues its goals – its practice. Groups may distinguish themselves by providing services to members (the AAUP offers counsel to university employees); by undertaking direct protests (PETA's campaign to embarrass those who wear fur); by recruiting and funding women candidates (EMILY's List); by lobbying legislators (AIPAC's efforts on behalf of US–Israel relations); and by disseminating information to the public (the Center for Responsive Politics' Open Secret project).

However, an organization's brand is not only its public face, but also a product of shared principles among group members. As such, the set of tactics that an organization chooses to employ (as well as those it disavows) may represent an important element of those shared principles (Carmin and Balser, 2002). Indeed, a group's identity is comprised of these principles as well as its norms, goals, structure, and preferred modes of operation. Discussions of the relationship between identity and an organization's tactical choices are most commonly found in literature examining the ways in which social movement organizations motivate members to act collectively. Polletta and Jasper (2001: 284) explain the relationship between tactics and group identity this way:

If people choose to participate because doing so accords with who they are, the forms of protest they choose are also influenced by collective identities. Models of strategic choice that had movement leaders selecting among strategies, tactics, and organizational forms by instrumentally assessing environmental opportunities and constraints missed the fact that strategic options may also be intrinsically appealing. They reflect what we believe, what we are comfortable with, what we like, who we are.[2]

As advocacy organizations define themselves, they "develop a shared cultural toolkit" which becomes their tactical repertoire (Robnett, 2002: 267).[3]

Tactical consistency

Repertoires of contention, then, can represent a central component of an organization's sense of itself. As such, the family of tactics a group draws upon most frequently to press its causes is typically narrow. Furthermore, while organizations certainly adopt new techniques in response to variations in resource availability or political and economic environments (Oberschall, 1973; McCarthy and Zald, 1977; McAdam, 1982), as a rule, groups' methods of operation remain highly stable (Tilly, 1978). Yet, as Holyoke (2003) notes, even when a particular tactic is unlikely to yield results, group leaders may persist in order to circumvent the dissatisfaction of a board of directors or membership that expects such action. In fact, the "stickiness" of a wide range of established intra-organizational routines and rituals is well documented and is at least in part a result of the close relationship between identity and practice (Stinchcombe, 1965; DiMaggio and Powell, 1983; see also Barakso, 2004).[4] By calling into question the continued correspondence between a group's values and individual supporters' values, radical changes in tactical choices (say, an inside lobbying group suddenly organizing a violent protest) are jarring to members, staff, volunteers, and donors (and sometimes to the public as well). Engaging in novel and discordant methods of operation can induce reactions from a group's constituency that range from disillusionment to abandonment (see, for example, accounts in Ferree and Martin, 2005).[5] Given the link between

[2] Polletta and Jasper refer here to social movement organizations, but the demarcation among nonprofits, advocacy organizations, social movement groups, and interest groups is exceptionally difficult to draw. As Costain and McFarland (1998: 43) note, "attempts to distinguish interest groups and SMOs [social movement organizations] on the basis of tactics do not work."
[3] Although Robnett is specifically speaking of social movement organizations, the principles are applicable to advocacy groups more generally speaking.
[4] For insights into the "stickiness" of institutional practices, even in the context of firms and international relations where the costs of lagging behind competitors are potentially quite high, see Szulanski (1996) and Ikenberry (1998).
[5] See, for example "Catastrophic Health Insurance for the Elderly." Kennedy School of Government, Harvard University, Case #1278.

organizational practice, organizational identity, and public image, I expect advocacy groups' methods will remain consistent across time.

Differentiation: insider versus outsider tactics

A strong brand allows an advocacy organization to distinguish itself among others operating within the same policy sector. The benefits of such differentiation are many, and include facilitating the ability to attract outside funding, volunteers, and members; attention from news media; and access to policymakers who associate the brand with valuable issue expertise (Browne, 1990; Heaney, 2004; Engel, 2007). As noted above, in a crowded sector, groups can and do seek out "niches" along a variety of dimensions to differentiate themselves (Wilson, 1973; Bosso, 1988; Browne, 1990; Gray and Lowery, 1996; Baumgartner and Leech, 2001; Heaney, 2006). In this view, interest groups may foster their brand and contrast their group with others in their larger issue sector (say, environmental policy) by establishing their expertise in a narrow subset of issues that they seek to be identified with (such as saving a particular endangered species).

Interest organizations may also distinguish themselves by their tactical choices. For example, Earth First!, an environmental organization formed in 1979, explicitly advertises the group's methods of operation as compared with those used by its "competitors" in that sector. The organization notes that it was formed

in response to a lethargic, compromising, and increasingly corporate environmental community. Earth First! takes a decidedly different tack towards environmental issues. We believe in using all the tools in the toolbox, ranging from grassroots organizing and involvement in the legal process to civil disobedience and monkeywrenching.[6]

Earth First!'s tactical orientation draws a robust distinction between insider and outsider methods of operation; it is clear that the group's repertoire of contention is central to its identity or brand. Yet, many interest organizations prior to Earth First!'s inception and since have used this dichotomy as a means of drawing attention to the ways in which they differ from other advocacy groups in their policy sector. Moreover, the practice of differentiating between these two broad categories of tactics – those that entail the use of conventional tools within political institutions and those seeking to pressure established power sources via extra-institutional means – is common within both the social

---

[6] "About Earth First!" (www.earthfirst.org/about.htm).

movement and interest group literatures, as I have noted above (see Berry, 1999).

Whether an organization relies predominantly on inside or outside tactics appears to depend upon a variety of factors, including a group's resource base, its size, and its level of professionalization (Gais and Walker, 1991; cf. Gormley, 1982).[7] Other important factors include an organization's internal culture and governance structure (Barakso, 2004) and its ideological orientation (Gormley, 1982; Spalter-Roth and Schreiber, 1995). Larger and more professionalized organizations as well as those more dependent on external funding all appear more likely to engage in institutionalized approaches (Gais and Walker, 1991). In this study, I examine whether groups appear to differentiate themselves with respect to tactical repertoire within their particular policy sector. For example, as noted above, groups associated with a social movement are more likely to engage in outsider tactics; as a result, I expect to find that organizations comprising the environmental sector will report a higher level of these tactics as compared to groups in other sectors. Within sectors, however, regardless of social movement association, I expect differentiation as groups seek to distinguish themselves from one another.

Coalitions: threats to the brand identity?

Joining coalitions imparts obvious benefits to participating groups, perhaps the chief being the fact that allying with the like-minded may dramatically extend an advocacy organization's reach and resources in addition to maximizing opportunities for policy success (Hyde, 1995; Hula, 1999; Sawyers and Meyer, 1999). Indeed, scholars have found that the practice has become increasingly central to many groups' tactical repertoires (Hojnacki, 1997; Nownes and Freeman, 1998; Berry, 1999). Furthermore, participation in coalitions is relatively stable: when groups choose to engage with other organizations in this way, they often do so repeatedly (Hojnacki, 1997).

Nevertheless, this course of action poses a dilemma for interest groups seeking to forge and maintain unique identities or brands. Presumably, the more an organization works in coalition with others in its sector,

---

[7] Tarrow (2005) suggests that transnational activism has somewhat diminished the validity of insider/outsider distinctions. Nevertheless, even among organizations whose tactical flexibility has been touted, such as the National Organization for Women (Tarrow, 1998), it is clear that shifts in practice developed slowly, required significant lobbying on the part of leaders to legitimize, and failed to replaced older forms of activism (Barakso, 2004).

the more challenging it is for that group to differentiate itself among others in that sector. For example, Médecins sans Frontières – a group that sees itself as a collection of "disobedient humanitarians" – has "declined participating in a humanitarian coalition promoting accountability among groups working in the field because it feared certain aspects of the plan would jeopardize its principles of neutrality and independence from the governments of recipient nations" (Tong, 2004: 180). In another example, on its website, the Family Research Council (a conservative Christian organization that seeks to influence public debate and policymaking in line with "family values") reveals how thorny the issue of coalition participation can be for an organization attempting to draw adherents to itself (www.frc.org/faqs#toggle3, emphasis added):

Q: Why don't more organizations combine efforts and resources? How do I know which organization to support?

A: Organizations such as Family Research Council, Focus on the Family, Concerned Women for America, Eagle Forum, etc. do keep in close contact with each other, perhaps even more so than our opposition. *Each organization fits a niche and fits it well.* When we have an opportunity to get together and discuss strategies, we do. Conservative "summits" do occur. Meanwhile, rest assured that the leaders of "the religious right" do converse frequently. *FRC is unique* in that we are a research and education organization in Washington, DC that focuses on public policy – issues that are specifically debated and voted on in Washington, DC.

In addition to diluting an advocacy group's brand identity, another drawback to coalition participation is that the tactic can ignite significant intra-organizational conflict (Hyde, 1995; Smith, 1995; Sawyers and Meyer, 1999; Barakso, 2004). A hastily convened coalition in which the values and governance structures of member groups are at odds can cause defection, the exposure of intra-coalition dissent, and intra-organizational conflict (Staggenborg, 1988; Ghosh, 2001; Gould, Lewis, and Roberts, 2004). Any of these outcomes may jeopardize the coalition's goals as well as the reputations, the brands, and the resources of all participating organizations. As a result, joining coalitions is not a tactical approach that organizations engage in lightly. Rather, groups typically consider the extent to which the values and goals of their partners correspond to their own, in addition to evaluating how willing they are to compromise (Hathaway and Meyer, 1997). In many cases, a substantial proportion of literature suggests, coalitions are formed primarily under conditions of clear political opportunity or when facing clear political threat (Hathaway and Meyer, 1997). Alliances are joined for narrowly defined purposes and typically disband once the coalition's *raison d'être* has been accomplished or once it becomes clear that the issue's political moment has passed.

The literature offers contradictory thoughts as far as the types of advocacy organization that may be particularly drawn to join coalitions.[8] Groups whose repertoires of contention emphasize outsider activities may be less likely to engage in coalitions. Such organizations are often characterized as being smaller, more responsive to individual members' viewpoints, more ideological, and less willing to compromise to work collaboratively with others. At the same time, those groups whose preference is to work extra-institutionally may also have the most to gain from joining forces with others, reaping the benefits of shared financial burdens and of the ability to project force in numbers. Additionally, Gais and Walker (1991) note that groups more dependent on external funding are more likely to join coalitions.

Organizations focusing on insider tactics, on the other hand, may be able to join coalitions with ease, but perhaps feel less urgency to do so – groups using insider strategies are typically thought to enjoy more stable finances, staff, and access to sources of power. Hojnacki's (1997) work suggests that such organizations may prefer to work alone, for example, a contention supported by Esterling's research on the decision to join coalitions: "a lobbying organization in general will compromise its direct interests in making a cooperative effort only if it needs to, and an organization with greater access to the government is less likely to need to make a joint lobbying effort to have its position taken into account in the policy making process" (1997: 5).

I expect both environmental and political process organizations will report that they participate in coalitions (Dalton, Recchia, and Rohrschneider, 2003). However, I hypothesize that because environmental groups are associated with a social movement, and may therefore focus more on outsider tactics, they will join coalitions to a lesser extent than those in the political process sector.

In the following section, I outline the data and methods I use to examine the extent to which advocacy organizations' tactical choices reflect the qualities that characterize a brand. I evaluate whether groups' tactical choices are consistent across time and whether groups' repertoires of contention serve to differentiate them from others within their policy sector. Finally, I examine whether group participation in coalition work, an activity that presents many potential challenges to groups' brand identities, varies according to tactical repertoires and policy sector.

---

[8] Hula (1999) found that both liberal and conservative organizations frequently worked in coalitions, suggesting that ideology is not necessarily a useful predictor of coalition participation.

Analyzing advocacy organization tactics

The groups included in this study are selected from Public Interest Profiles, 2006–2007 (*Public Interest Profiles*, 2006), which contain data compiled by the CQ Press and the Foundation for Public Affairs (FPA). This reference work provides information on 255 organizations. There are four primary criteria for inclusion: influence on national policy; frequency of inquiries about the group; news coverage; and "the representative nature of the group in its field of interest and activity" (*Public Interest Profiles*, 2001: xv). The sample of groups, then, represents well-established, national organizations.

Public Interest Profiles divides the profiled organizations into fourteen sectors, two of which are included in this analysis: Environmental and Political/Governmental Process (hereafter 'political process').[9] Among the primary concerns of groups in the political process sector is the efficacy, efficiency, and responsiveness of government. I selected these sectors because they differ in terms of how narrowly or broadly their purposes are defined, a distinction that may influence how strongly groups feel the need to differentiate themselves. The goals of the environmental sector are narrower and perhaps more easily defined than those of the political process sector. Environmental organizations may therefore find it more challenging – and yet more imperative – to differentiate themselves among their peers, since they are all "selling" essentially the same "product." The two sectors are comparable in terms of the number of organizations within the sector; both are among the largest of the fourteen sectors. Both sectors in this study are internally diverse with respect to issue focus. Together, the environmental and political process sectors comprise fifty-five organizations: twenty-eight environmental (including Greenpeace USA, the Natural Resources Defense Council, the Nature Conservancy, and Friends of the Earth) and twenty-seven political process groups (such as the Center for Public Integrity, the League of Women Voters of the United States, Project Vote Smart, and the American Conservative Union). See the appendix to this chapter for a complete list of organizations.

The two sectors also differ in that the environmental sector is strongly linked to a social movement, whereas the political process sector is not. This variation in terms of social movement association allows us to test

---

[9] These are: Animal/Wildlife; Business/Economic; Civil/Constitutional Rights; Community/ Grassroots Organizing; Consumer/Health; Corporate Accountability/Responsibility; Environmental; Families/Children; International Affairs; Media/Technology; Political/ Governmental Process; Public Interest Law; Religious; Research Institutes and Think Tanks.

whether groups associated with a social movement are impeded from joining coalitions (an activity that, as noted above, can be troublesome for a group working to maintain brand identity) in their tactical repertoires.

I coded both sectors according to several criteria; of central importance for this study was the coding of every tactic that each organization reported using. Data on these tactics (*Profiles* calls these "methods of operation") are drawn from a questionnaire sent by the FPA to each of 255 organizations. Each group was asked to specify which tactics they use from a standardized list; they were permitted to select as many tactics as they engaged in (the survey did not ask for a report of the frequency of use of each tactic). Groups in the environmental and political process sector reported using a total of forty different tactics, including campaign contributions, organizing conferences, maintaining information clearing-houses and issue libraries, engaging in international activities, media outreach, and voter registration. For this analysis I excluded tactics that were used by only one organization (land purchasing), those used by almost all groups (media outreach), membership communications (email alerts), grantmaking, and those whose target is indistinct (mediation).

Ultimately, I narrowed the list to eleven tactics. A factor analysis of these eleven revealed that they loaded on two separate dimensions that appear to capture insider and outsider approaches.[10] Insider tactics included those aimed at influencing government through institutionalized channels by participation in regulatory proceedings, lobbying, legislative/ regulatory monitoring, Congressional vote analysis, lobbying at the grassroots level, litigation, and grassroots organizing. Grassroots organizing also loaded on the second factor, which captured outsider tactics; also loading on this factor were direct action tactics, demonstrations, and boycotts. A list of these factor loadings can be found in Table 6.1. I used the factor analysis to generate factor scores for each group along these two

---

[10] Factor analysis is a statistical technique that takes a set of measures and attempts to discern the extent to which they may have a common underlying cause (or causes). For example, a researcher might have information about a student's SAT score, GPA, and hours spent studying each week. Factor analysis allows a researcher to detect whether these measures are interrelated because they are being generated by the same underlying concept. In this example, factor analysis might reveal that SAT scores and GPA are interrelated, presumably because both measures are affected by the student's intelligence. This would be one factor. GPA and time spent studying may also be interrelated because they both are influenced by the effort put forth by a student. Effort might constitute a second factor. Once factor analysis has identified these factors, the technique can be used to generate standardized scores for each factor. Thus, using SAT scores, GPA, and time spent studying, factor analysis can create a measure of intelligence and effort. In each case, the new measures would have a mean of 0 and a standard deviation of 1.

Table 6.1. *Factor loadings of tactics on two dimensions*

First factor: insider strategies	Factor loading	Second factor: outsider strategies	Factor loading
Congressional testimony	0.707	Boycotts	0.655
Congressional vote analysis	0.286	Demonstrations	0.770
Grassroots lobbying	0.667	Grassroots organizing	0.490
Grassroots organizing	0.524	Direct action	0.642
Legislation/regulation monitoring	0.486		
Litigation	0.632		
Lobbying	0.750		
Regulatory proceedings participation	0.627		
Eigenvalue = 3.165		*Eigenvalue = 1.572*	

Note: Variables only shown under a factor if they loaded at 0.25 or above.

dimensions. Each score is a standardized measure with a mean of 0 and a standard deviation of 1. Higher scores on these measures indicate that the group used more of the tactics loading on those factors. Finally, I also coded whether or not the group reported that it participated in coalitions.

To supplement the data for 2006–2007, I coded the same information for the groups reported in *Public Interest Profiles*, 2001–2002. Supplementing the data with information from 2001 allowed me to determine not only whether groups differentiate themselves with regard to tactics but also whether they maintain consistency over time in their tactical repertoires. (Groups were surveyed in 2000, prior to the election of President George W. Bush, and in 2005, during President Bush's second term.) Six groups were dropped because there was no information for them in the 2001 volume of *Profiles*; two additional groups were omitted because they did not report either a 501(c)(3) or 501(c)(4) tax status. This left forty-seven organizations in the analysis.

Findings

Consistency To capture whether groups maintained a consistent mix of insider and outsider tactics, I calculated the Euclidean distance between the groups' location on the two dimensions in 2006 compared that of 2001.[11] This information is presented in Table 6.2. Most organizations

---

[11] Euclidean distance is simply the length of a straight line drawn between two points. In other words, when plotting a group's position in each year on a two-dimensional scatterplot (such as the one in Figure 6.1), the Euclidean distance would be the separation between those two points.

Table 6.2. *Change in groups' tactical repertoires, 2001–2006*

Euclidean distance	Environmental groups	Political process groups
No difference	11 (42.3%)	8 (38.1%)
Between 0 and 0.5	5 (19.2%)	2 (9.5%)
Between 0.5 and 1	6 (23.1%)	8 (38.1%)
Over 1	4 (15.4%)	3 (14.3%)
Total	26 (100%)	21 (100%)

Note: Euclidean distance is the distance between the group's positions on the two dimensions in 2006 and 2001.

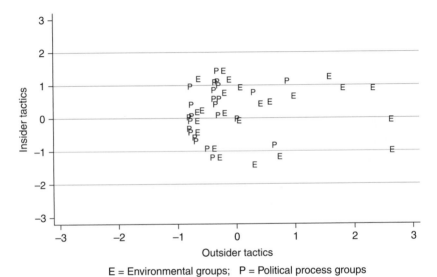

E = Environmental groups;   P = Political process groups

Figure 6.1. Tactics used by groups, 2006.

proved to be exceptionally consistent in terms of their tactical repertoires. Of the forty-seven groups, nineteen did not alter their tactical mix at all. Moreover, only seven organizations moved more than one standard deviation from their tactical repertoires in 2001. Four of those were environmental groups, three of whom increased their insider activity between 2001 and 2006.

Differentiation   Figure 6.1 plots each group according to the mix of outsider and insider tactics it uses. (Environmental organizations are represented by the letter E and political process groups are represented by the letter P.) Groups from both sectors appear dispersed along the insider dimension fairly similarly, with most organizations falling within a standard deviation of the mean. Older organizations, in both the environmental and political process sectors, are more likely to employ primarily insider tactics (average year of establishment in the environmental sector is 1967.5 and in the political process sector is 1965.6). This suggest that older organizations enjoy a comparative advantage in employing insider tactics, as well-established participants in the political sphere (Dalton, Recchia, and Rohrschneider, 2003).

However, environmental organizations show greater variance than political process groups in their propensity to use outsider tactics. In particular, environmental groups distinguishing themselves on the outsider dimension include Earth First!, Earth Island Institute, Friends of the Earth (FoE), Rainforest Action Network, and the Sierra Club. All of these organizations are more than one standard deviation above the mean in their use of outsider tactics.

Far fewer political process organizations distinguish themselves through outsider activities (those that do include the League of Women Voters, the National Women's Political Caucus, and US Term Limits) and even these are still far less likely to use outsider tactics than are environmental groups. It is important to note that, contrary to expectations, tactical choice was not correlated with the number of paid staff or the percentage of income derived from individuals for either sector in either dimension. As expected, groups in the environmental sector are more likely to differentiate themselves within their sector by tactical choice than those in the political process sector. Nevertheless, even political process groups seek to demonstrate that they operate distinctly from their peers, though in more muted ways. For example,

Project Vote Smart is known to adopt a somewhat more outsider stance with respect to political candidates than others who undertake similar activities, such as the League of Women Voters: they are more "aggressive" in the way that they "attempt to get candidates to be far more specific about their campaign stands . . . the group . . . criticizes candidates who don't fill out the questionnaire, saying they have "flunked." (Associated Press, 2007)

Coalitions Figure 6.2 illustrates coalition formation among groups in 2006 across the insider–outsider dimensions. (C represents a group that participated in a coalition; N represents a group that did not indicate that it engaged in any coalition work.) As expected, groups in both the environmental and political process sectors engage in coalitions. Contrary to my expectations, however, I found virtually no difference in rates of coalition participation between the environmental and political

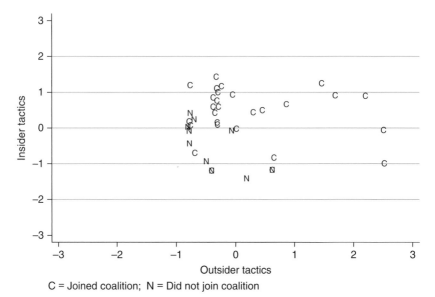

C = Joined coalition; N = Did not join coalition

Figure 6.2. Coalition formation among groups, 2006.

process sectors. In fact, the majority of groups in both sectors reported coalition work (69 percent of environmental organizations and 67 percent of political process groups). I found no income differences between organizations that participated in coalitions and those that did not; however, groups that received a higher percentage of their income from individuals (versus institutions) were more likely to join such alliances. This finding comports with those of Hula (1999) and others who emphasize the ubiquity of coalitions in legislative lobbying.

An important distinction between sectors did emerge, however: organizations that report engaging in *both* insider and outsider tactics at high levels are also more likely to participate in coalitions. The three groups that were among those reporting the highest number of both insider and outsider tactics all participated in coalitions and all are environmental organizations: the Sierra Club, Earth Island Institute, and Friends of the Earth. Each of these three groups reported engaging in an above average number of tactics compared to others in their sector. Overall, these findings suggest that the potentially deleterious impact of coalition participation on brand identity may be mitigated by the fact that groups joining such alliances typically engage in a large number and wide variety of tactics overall. One danger of joining coalitions is that an organization's brand could be undermined by its association with other groups with very different tactical preferences. Groups who forge tactically diverse repertoires, however, may be less vulnerable to protests of this nature (from funders or adherents, for example) because their brand identity is less contingent on sharp tactical distinctions. As a result, organizations that are highly active on both insider and outsider dimensions are granted more flexibility to join alliances.

Conclusion

Employing a collective action perspective that analogizes advocacy organization behavior with that of firms helps us begin to make sense of how they manage the inevitable competition with other actors in their sector (market) for resources like press attention (publicity), donations (investors), and policy goods (profits). The firm and market analogy permits us to draw upon a rich set of theories and concepts relating to organizational behavior in the fields of business and economics, such as the notion of brand identity. Furthermore, it corresponds well with the fact that increasingly, advocacy organizations see themselves in much the same terms.

In this chapter, I argue that a concept long associated with firms, that of brand identity, has useful applications when applied to understanding the activities of advocacy groups. I show that advocacy organizations are typically highly consistent in terms of the tactics they employ, and that some groups may differentiate themselves from others in their sector according to their tactical repertoire. Finally, the benefits of joining coalitions appear to outweigh the potential costs (such as the dilution of or damage to groups' identities) for the vast majority of advocacy organizations in this study. Nevertheless, even here we see differentiation based on tactical repertoires: environmental organizations that participate in coalitions are particularly likely to report engaging in higher than average numbers of both insider and outsider tactics. Importantly, these groups' diverse repertoires may inoculate them against the pitfalls of coalition work.

The tactical adaptation of both firms and advocacy organizations – even to take advantage of what appear to be significant economic or political opportunities – typically proceeds gradually, if at all. The underlying factors influencing organizational resistance to change apply to both firms and advocacy organizations, and include the fact that tactical alterations involve cost and uncertainty. In several important respects, however, firms and groups differ. First, firms commonly possess greater resources with which to (1) identify changes in political, social, and economic environments, and (2) carry out adaptations to those changes.

In addition to their superior access to financial resources, it is vital to underscore the fact that because firms do not employ volunteers, they are advantaged in terms of their ability to evolve tactically. In contrast, many advocacy organizations, including relatively high-profile groups, rely heavily on members, volunteers, and interns. Whereas firms can fire those who fail to adopt change as quickly as desired, advocacy organizations are often constrained in this respect. Advocacy group tactical repertoires are thus inherently more stable than those of firms. As a result, although some firms make their business practices central to their brands, for the most part tactical distinctions are likely to play a more central role in the brand identities of advocacy organizations.

The firm analogy is illuminating in another respect, again, even in areas in which firms and groups differ. Because advocacy organizations have inherently less to "sell," their methods of operation provide an important opportunity to differentiate themselves from others in their policy market. Because firms are producing a tangible good, in contrast, they can differentiate themselves from other producers in many ways besides their business practices.

This analysis suggests several areas for further research. First, while this chapter provides circumstantial evidence as to the potential links between brand and tactical repertoires, we need more qualitative evidence that would help us understand the extent to which such groups consciously craft their brand with their processes in mind. Furthermore, there is much to learn about the extent to which brand identity constrains tactical choice on the part of both firms and advocacy groups. For example, do publicly held firms that rely on process branding (say, a company that promotes its fair trade practices) operate under constraints similar to membership-based advocacy organizations?

Appendix: Organizations

Environmental	Political/governmental process
American Rivers	Advocacy Institute
Beyond Pesticides	American Conservative Union
Center for Health, Environment, and Justice	American Legislative Exchange Council
Conservation Fund	Americans for Democratic Action
Conservation International	Center for Public Integrity
Earth First!	Center for Responsive Politics
Earth Island Institute	Common Cause
Environmental and Energy Study Institute	Concord Coalition
Environmental Defense	Congressional Management Foundation

Environmental Law Institute
Environmental Working Group
Foundation on Economic Trends
Friends of the Earth
Greenpeace USA
Izaak Walton League of America
Keystone Center for Science and Public Policy
League of Conservation Voters
National Parks Conservation Association
National Trust for Historic Preservation
Natural Resources Defense Council
Nature Conservancy
Pesticide Action Network North America
Rainforest Action Network
Sierra Club
Wilderness Society
World Resources Institute

Council for Excellence in Government
Council of State Governments
League of Women Voters of the United States
National Governors Association
National League of Cities
National Women's Political Caucus
OMB Watch
Project Vote Smart
Public Citizen, Inc.
US Term Limits
United States Conference of Mayors
Women's Campaign Forum

References

Associated Press. 2007. Oregon Candidates Wary of Vote Smart Surveys. *Seattle Post Intelligencer*, July 17.

Barakso, M. 2004. *Governing NOW: Grassroots Activism in the National Organization for Women*. Ithaca, NY: Cornell University Press.

Baumgartner, F. and B. L. Leech. 2001. Interest Niches and Policy Bandwagons: Patterns of Interest Group Involvement in National Politics. *Journal of Politics*, **63**: 1191–1213.

Berry, J. 1999. *The New Liberalism: The Rising Power of Citizen Groups*. Washington, DC: Brookings Institution.

Berry, L. 2000. Cultivating Service Brand Equity. *Journal of the Academy of Marketing*, **39**: 32–39.

Bosso, C. J. 1988. *Pesticides and Politics: The Life Cycle of Public Issue*. University of Pittsburgh Press.

Browne, W. P. 1990. Organized Interests and their Issue Niches: A Search for Pluralism in a Policy Domain. *Journal of Politics*, **52**: 477–509.

Carmin, J. and D. Balser. 2002. Selecting Repertoires of Action in Environmental Movement Organizations: An Interpretive Approach. *Organization and Environment*, **5**: 365–388.

Costain, A. and A. McFarland (eds.). 1998. *Social Movements and American Political Institutions*. Boulder, CO: Rowman and Littlefield.

Dalton, R. J., S. Recchia, and R. Rohrschneider. 2003. The Environmental Movement and the Modes of Political Action. *Comparative Political Studies*, **36**: 743–771.

DiMaggio P. J. and W. W. Powell. 1983. The Iron Cage Revisited: Institutional Isomorphism and Collective Rationality in Organizational Fields. *American Sociological Review*, **48**: 147–160.

Dixon, M. 1997. Small and Medium Sized Charities Need a Strong Brand Too: Crisis Experience. *Journal of Nonprofit and Voluntary Sector Marketing*, **2**: 52–57.

Engel, S. M. 2007. Organizational Identity as a Constraint on Strategic Action: A Comparative Analysis of Gay and Lesbian Interest Groups. *Studies in American Political Development*, **21**: 66–91.

Esterling, K. 1997. Conflict, Information and Lobbying Coalitions. Paper delivered at the Annual Meeting of the American Political Science Association, Washington, DC.

Ferree, M. M. and P. Y. Martin (eds.). 1995. *Feminist Organizations: Harvest of the New Women's Movement*. Philadelphia: Temple University Press.

Gais, T. and J. L. Walker. 1991. Pathways to Influence in American Politics. In J. L. Walker, Jr. (ed.), *Mobilizing Interest Groups in America: Patrons, Professions, and Social Movements*. Ann Arbor: University of Michigan Press.

Gerber, E. 1999. *The Populist Paradox: Interest Group Influence and the Promise of Direct Legislation*. Princeton University Press.

Ghosh, M. 2001. Inside WTO Dissent: The Experiences of LELO and CCEJ. University of Washington History Project.

Gormley, W. 1982. Alternative Models of Regulator Process: Public Utility Regulation in the States. *Western Political Quarterly*, **35**: 297–317.

Gould, K., T. L. Lewis, and J. T. Roberts. 2004. Blue–Green Coalitions: Constraints and Possibilities in the Post 9–11 Political Environment. *Journal of World-Systems Research*, **10**: 91–118.

Gray, V. and D. Lowery. 1996. A Niche Theory of Interest Representation. *Journal of Politics*, **58**: 91–111.

Hathaway, W. and D. S. Meyer. 1997. Competition and Cooperation in Movement Coalitions: Lobbying for Peace in the 1980s. In T. R. Rochon and D. S. Meyer (eds.), *Coalitions and Political Movements*. Boulder, CO: Lynne Rienner Publishers.

Heaney, M. 2004. Issue Networks, Information, and Interest Group Alliances: The Case of Wisconsin Welfare Politics, 1993–1999. *State Politics and Policy Quarterly*, **4**: 237–270.

  2006. Identity Crisis: How Interest Groups Struggle to Define Themselves in Washington. Paper delivered at the Annual Meeting of the Midwest Political Science Association, Chicago.

Hojnacki, M. 1997. Interest Groups' Decisions to Join Alliances or Work Alone. *American Journal of Political Science*, **41**: 61–87.

Holyoke, T. 2003. Choosing Battlegrounds: Interest Group Lobbying across Multiple Venues. *Political Research Quarterly*, **3**: 325–336.

Hula, K. 1999. *Lobbying Together: Interest Group Coalitions in Legislative Politics*. Washington, DC: Georgetown University Press.

Hyde, C. 1995. Feminist Social Movement Organizations Survive the New Right. In M. M. Ferree and P. Y. Martin (eds.), *Feminist Organizations: Harvest of the New Women's Movement*. Philadelphia: Temple University Press.

Ikenberry, J. 1998. Institutions, Strategic Restraint, and the Persistence of American Postwar Order. *International Security*, **3**: 43–78.

Jenkins, C. and C. B. Perrow. 1977. Insurgency of the Powerless: Farm Worker Movements (1946–1972). *American Sociological Review*, **42**: 249–268.

Kotler, P. H. 1991. *Marketing Management: Analysis, Planning, and Control*, 8th edn. Englewood Cliffs, NJ: Prentice Hall.

McAdam, D. 1982. *Political Process and the Development of Black Insurgency: 1930–1970*. University of Chicago Press.

McCarthy, J. 2005. Velcro Triangles: Elite Mobilization of Local Antidrug Issue Coalitions. In D. S. Meyer, V. Jenness, and H. Ingram (eds.), *Routing the Opposition: Social Movements, Public Policy, and Democracy*. Minneapolis: University of Minnesota Press.

McCarthy, J. and M. N. Zald. 1977. Resource Mobilization and Social Movements: A Partial Theory. *American Journal of Sociology*, **82**: 1212–1241.

Médecins sans Frontières. 1995. Chantilly Document. Unpublished.

Nownes, A. and P. Freeman. 1998. Interest Group Activity in the States. *Journal of Politics*, **60**: 86–112.

Oberschall, A. 1973. *Social Conflict and Social Movements*. Englewood Cliffs, NJ: Prentice Hall.

Polletta, F. and J. M. Jasper. 2001. Collective Identity and Social Movements. *Annual Review of Sociology*, **27**: 283–305.

Public Interest Profiles. 2001. Washington, DC: CQ Press.
    2006. Washington, DC: CQ Press.

Ritchie, R., S. Swami, and C. B. Weisburg. 1993. A Brand New World for Nonprofits. *International Journal of Nonprofit and Voluntary Sector Marketing*, **4**: 26–42.

Robnett, B. 2002. External Political Change, Collective Identity, and Participation in Social Movement Organizations. In D. S. Meyer, N. Whittier, and B. Robnett (eds.), *Social Movements: Identity, Culture, and the State*. Oxford University Press.

Rucht, D. 2004. Movement Allies, Adversaries and Third Parties. In D. A. Snow, S. A. Soule, and H. Kriesi (eds.), *The Blackwell Companion to Social Movements*. Malden, MA: Blackwell.

Salamon, L. 2002. The Resilient Sector: The State of Nonprofit America. In *Snapshots: Research Highlights from the Nonprofit Sector Research Fund*, no. 25 (September/October).

Sawyers, T. and D. S. Meyer. 1999. Missed Opportunities: Social Movement Abeyance and Public Policy. *Social Problems*, **46**: 187–206.

Smith, R. 1995. Interest Group Influence in the U.S. Congress. *Legislative Studies Quarterly*, **20**: 89–139.

Snow, D., S. Soule, and H. Kriesi (eds.). 2004. *The Blackwell Companion to Social Movements*. Malden, MA: Wiley–Blackwell.

Spalter-Roth, R. and R. Schreiber. 1995. Outsider Issues and Insider Tactics: Strategic Tensions in the Women's Policy Network during the 1980s. In M. M. Ferree and P. Y. Martin (eds.), *Feminist Organizations: Harvest of the New Women's Movement*. Philadelphia: Temple University Press.

Spruill, V. 2001. Build Brand Identity for Causes, Not Groups. *Chronicle of Philanthropy*, **13**: 17.

Staggenborg, S. 1988. The Consequences of Professionalization and Formalization in the Pro-Choice Movement. *American Sociological Review*, **53**: 585–606.

Stinchcombe, A. 1965. Social Structure and Organizations. In J. G. March (ed.), *Handbook of Organizations*. Chicago: Rand McNally.

Szulanski, G. 1996. Exploring Internal Stickiness: Impediments to the Transfer of Best Practice Within the Firm. *Strategic Management,* **17**: 27–43.

Tarrow, S. *Power in Movement: Social Movements and Contentions Politics.* Cambridge University Press.

2005. *New Transactional Activism.* Cambridge University Press.

Tilly, C. 1978. *From Mobilization to Revolution.* Reading, MA: Addison-Wesley.

Tong, J. 2004. Questionable Accountability: MSF and Sphere in 2003. *Disasters,* **28**: 176–189.

Venable, B., G. Rose, V. Bush, and F. Gilbert. 2005. The Role of Brand Personality in Charitable Giving: An Assessment and Validation. *Journal of the Academy of Marketing Science,* **33**: 295–312.

Wilson, J. Q. 1973. *Political Organizations.* New York: Basic Books.

7 Shopping around: environmental organizations and the search for policy venues

Sarah B. Pralle

The Atlantic States Legal Foundation (ASLF), an environmental organization located in central New York State, was once the leading nongovernmental organization enforcing violations of the Clean Water Act (Atlantic States Legal Foundation, n.d.). Throughout the 1980s and 1990s, Atlantic States pursued a national litigation campaign, working with local environmental groups to sue industries that were out of compliance with their water pollution permits. In Indiana, during one six-week period alone, ASLF filed over one hundred lawsuits (Samuel Sage, personal interview, February 24, 2005). Today, the Atlantic States Legal Foundation uses the courts infrequently; rather, the organization spends most of its time providing technical assistance to groups and individuals with specific environmental concerns. Moreover, the group targets environmental problems beyond the local or even the national level. One of ASLF's more recent campaigns, for example, focuses on environmental issues in Eastern Europe, particularly pollution of the Black Sea watershed.

The organizational evolution of the Atlantic States Legal Foundation illustrates one of the key strategic questions faced by environmental organizations – and, in fact, by all advocacy organizations[1] – and that is where to press their policy claims. The US political system provides organized interests with a wide array of policy venues, from county councils, to state legislatures, to district courts, to federal agencies. And the increasingly international scope of environmental politics opens up an even wider set of policy arenas from which to choose. When public policymaking becomes a multilevel, multi-arena game, how do groups select one policy arena over another? Why do advocacy organizations occasionally abandon their chosen venue and move to an alternative

---

[1] I use the term "advocacy organizations" to refer to organized interests which promote public goods such as clean air and water, or which advocate for group-based rights. This analysis may also apply to interest groups which are organized around economic interests.

one? What, in other words, shapes the strategies of advocacy organizations when it comes to choosing a policy venue in which to exploit conflict?

The collective action approach adopted in this volume likens advocacy organizations to firms operating in a competitive marketplace. Shopping for a policy venue might be akin to a firm trying to decide what markets they would like to compete in. Such a decision would presumably require assessing the opportunities and challenges in each market, which may include a consideration of market size and scope, entry barriers, the number and strength of competitors, the rules governing the market, and other such factors. In short, firms must weigh the costs and benefits of competing in different markets, guided by the goal of securing a share of that market and earning a profit. While advocacy organizations are not profit-oriented, they rationally pursue policy goals, including getting their issue on agendas, reforming policy, and shaping a policy's implementation. And like markets, venues contain different properties that make them more or less attractive to advocacy organizations – properties conditioned, of course, by external circumstances. In general we can assume that advocacy organizations will search for venues that offer the greatest possibility of reaching their goals.

In addition, both firms and advocacy organizations adopt ancillary strategies as they struggle in competitive environments. As Maryann Barakso illuminates in this volume, firms and advocacy organizations will try to create and maintain a specific "brand" so as to distinguish themselves from their competitors and earn loyalty from customers and members. Such branding concerns also shape the venue choice of advocacy organizations. Organizations may try to distinguish themselves from other groups by adopting a particular strategy, such as litigation. In this case, a litigation strategy necessitates working within judicial venues. Other organizations may define themselves as Washington "insiders," thereby leading them to target Congress or bureaucratic agencies. In short, an advocacy organization's "brand" will shape its choice of strategies and venues.

This chapter examines venue-shopping because it has the potential to shape the direction of public policy. According to Baumgartner and Jones (1993), policy "punctuations" – dramatic changes in policy – are due in part to the successful movement of decision-making authority over policy from one venue to another. Often, a shift in venue can lead to new understandings of a policy problem and allow new participants to influence decision-making, leading to significant policy changes. For example, when the US Ninth Circuit Court of Appeals intervened in forest policy-making in the early 1990s, trumping the decisions of the US Forest Service and of Congress, forest policy in the US Pacific Northwest shifted in a more ecological direction (Hoberg, 1997). Advocacy organizations can influence such change dynamics by successfully "shopping" their issue to new venues and arenas. Their strategic behavior should therefore be of interest to scholars who want to understand advocacy organizations generally and the dynamics of policy change in particular.

This chapter has three goals. The first is to clarify the related concepts of policy venues, arenas, and jurisdictions in a way that advances our understanding of and theories about venue-shopping. A second goal is to stimulate our thinking about how advocacy organizations choose and change policy venues by offering abbreviated histories of two environmental advocacy organizations which display different patterns of venue-shopping. These case studies are not designed to test a theory of venue-shopping, but rather serve as preliminary illustrations of the theoretical claims made in the final section of the chapter. The third goal is to identify potential factors that influence the venue-shopping strategies of advocacy organizations. I identify three sets of factors: the internal organization and resources of a group, the set of external political opportunities and constraints, and the larger subsystem environment. These factors are then used as a basis for constructing propositions about interest group behavior in the area of venue-shopping.

Venues, arenas, and jurisdictions

Policy scholars are increasingly incorporating the notion of policy venues and arenas into their analyses of policy change (e.g. Baumgartner and Jones, 1993; Sabatier and Jenkins-Smith, 1993, 1999; Dudley and Richardson, 1998; Godwin and Schroedel, 2000; Hansen and Krejci, 2000; Timmermans, 2001; Burnett and Davis, 2002; Pralle, 2003). Like any relatively new and popular idea, however, the terms used are not always well defined and are often used interchangeably.[2] To lend some conceptual clarity to the literature, I distinguish among decision venues, policy arenas, and jurisdictions. The general term "targets" is used to refer to any and all institutions, processes, and actors that are the focus of advocacy group efforts.

The first distinction to make is between decision venues and policy arenas. *Decision venues* are governmental and quasi-governmental institutions where authoritative decisions about policy are made. As Timmermans (2001: 314) notes, *authoritative* means that "legal, political, or social sanctions are possible to prevent that decisions are ignored."

[2] Timmermans (2001) makes the most significant attempt to lend clarity to the related concept of "policy arenas" by identifying different types of arenas.

Because some institutions are quasi-authoritative in nature, it is perhaps best to think of decision venues as existing along a continuum representing different degrees of authoritativeness. *Policy arenas* differ from decision venues in that they are non-authoritative locations where policy debates and conflicts emerge and play out. Both venues and arenas are potential sites of competition over policy issues, but only venues issue authoritative decisions about specific policies.

Decision venues (hereafter referred to as "venues") exist at several levels of government: international, regional (as in the case of the European Union or the Great Lakes Commission), national, state, and local. Decision venues include legislatures, executive departments and agencies, and the courts. They also include semipublic bodies or special committees with autonomy and decision-making authority in a particular policy area. For example, in countries with a corporatist tradition, semi-public institutions often issue binding decisions on economic policy (Timmermans, 2001). I use the term *system venue* to refer to legislatures, executive agencies, and the courts, and *subsystem venue* to refer to "venues within venues." For example, the US Congress is a system venue while its various committees and subcommittees are subsystem venues. Similarly, the federal court system as a whole is a system venue, while specific appellate courts within the system are subsystem venues.

The actions and events in *policy arenas* (referred to also as "arenas") can shape policy decisions, but this influence is indirect. Since policy arenas do not issue authoritative decisions, substantive changes in policy must eventually be made in decision venues. Examples of policy arenas include the media, the public arena, the electoral arena, and the marketplace.[3] Arenas also exist at several levels, although not necessarily in a formal sense. For example, we might speak of a local media market versus a national media market, or local elections versus national elections. The "public" includes a mass public, a smaller "sympathetic" public, and an even more circumscribed "attentive" public (see Cobb and Elder, 1983).

Finally, *jurisdiction* refers to the issues, or aspects of issues, that decision venues have authority over at any particular time. The jurisdictions of decision venues can expand, contract, and/or grow more blurry over time. Sometimes institutions relinquish control over issues – either voluntarily or involuntarily – to another decision venue. At other times, the jurisdictions of decision venues expand – as when the courts began asserting jurisdiction over pesticides policy in the 1970s (Bosso, 1987). This

---

[3] The electoral arena can sometimes issue authoritative policy decisions, as when binding initiatives or referendums are held (Timmermans, 2001: 315). Outside of these cases, however, elections are usually understood to have an indirect effect on policy outcomes.

expansion is often accompanied by the blurring of jurisdictional boundaries, as other venues seek to maintain some decision-making authority over the policy in question.

The content and boundaries of a venue's jurisdiction are influenced by a number of factors, including Constitutional mandates and interpretations, institutional norms and rules, history, and custom (Baumgartner and Jones, 1993). Political actors – for example, legislators, judges, bureaucrats, and advocacy organizations – also play a large role in changing jurisdictional assignments and boundaries. King (1994), for example, describes the power of US House and Senate parliamentarians to shape committee jurisdictions in Congress through their power of referral. By referring a bill to one committee rather than another, "no matter how jurisdictionally ambiguous those bills may be," these unelected officials have a unique power to shape the jurisdictions of committees over time (King, 1994: 50). Advocacy organizations attempt to change jurisdictional assignments and boundaries when they shop for a new venue in which to press their policy claims. Jurisdictions, then, are the result of a complex of factors, some of a broad historical nature, and others which exist at the individual or group level.

We now turn to a discussion of two environmental advocacy organizations, the Atlantic States Legal Foundation and the Partnership for Onondaga Creek, to illustrate some of the dynamics of venue-shopping strategies.

The Atlantic States Legal Foundation: no longer "Atlantic" or "legal"[4]

Samuel Sage, president of the Atlantic States Legal Foundation, admits that his organization no longer lives up to its name. ASLF does not work solely, or even largely, in the mid-Atlantic region of the United States, nor does it pursue litigation as its main strategy. But the name has stuck, even if the organization has changed.[5] The history of Atlantic States suggests

---

[4] The organizational histories that follow are based on interviews with the leaders of the respective organizations and with secondary materials where available. Both the ASLF and the Partnership for Onondaga Creek are small organizations in which the leaders play a major role in shaping the direction of the organizations. Such organizations are useful for studying venue-shopping strategies, since the leaders are centrally involved in these decisions.

[5] The information presented in this section is taken from a personal interview with Samuel Sage on February 24, 2005 cited as "Sage, personal interview" hereafter. Some of the history of the ASLF was based on information found on the organization's website, www.aslf.org/ASLF/index.html (accessed February 22, 2005).

that venue-shopping strategies are shaped by both changes in external political opportunities and by factors internal to the organization.

Atlantic States was founded in 1982 after local citizens in the Hudson Valley of New York State successfully fought a large hotel development project along the Hudson River. Sage, who had participated in the fight against the project, was grateful for the victory but was dismayed at the substantial legal fees incurred by the local citizens group. The ASLF was created in part to respond to what Sage and others perceived as a need in the environmental movement: to provide inexpensive legal aid and technical assistance to grassroots environmental groups. Sage's background was as a scientist for the Sierra Club specializing in water pollution issues, while his co-founder was a lawyer. Their expertise helped the ASLF establish itself as an organization poised to assist local environmental organizations on technical and legal matters, and fill what they saw as a niche in the environmental movement.

While Atlantic States was a self-described "problem-solver," the organization rather quickly became involved in environmental enforcement through the courts. Sage was encouraged when the Sierra Club, his former employer, successfully sued industry using the citizen suit provision in the Clean Water Act. The Sierra Club, Sage claims, "wanted to show that this strategy worked," but the group "was not interested in doing this for a living" (Sage, personal interview). Since environmental organizations could recoup the legal fees associated with the lawsuits, critics might interpret the Sierra Club's actions as a crass way to raise money. For Atlantic States, however, the promise of recovering legal costs was a big draw. They therefore "picked up where the Sierra Club left off" and launched a national litigation strategy (Sage, personal interview). Through the late 1980s and into the 1990s, ASLF was the principal environmental organization filing citizen suits under the Clean Water Act (Atlantic States Legal Foundation, n.d.).[6]

Atlantic States had to ally with local citizens' organizations in order to attain standing in court, so in general, they went where they were invited. ASLF targeted relatively large corporations, such as Monsanto, who could easily pay the fines and legal fees in the event of an ASLF victory. Beginning in the 1990s, Atlantic States expanded their litigation strategy to include suits under the Emergency Planning and Community-Right-to-Know Act, a provision in the 1986 reauthorization of the "Superfund" legislation which requires companies to disclose the extent and volume of

[6] Lettie Wenner (1982) found that environmental organizations launched nearly three times as many Clean Water lawsuits against industry as Clean Air Act suits in the period between 1970 and 1979.

toxic materials stored at their facilities. In addition, they filed various suits under the Resource Conservation and Recovery Act and the Clean Air Act.

While Sage admits that using the courts to enforce environmental laws "sidetracked the organization from its original mission," he implies that opportunities in the courts at the time were too great for the group to bypass (Sage, personal interview). Sage even credits the Reagan administration for encouraging citizen suits as a way to shift the burden of enforcement from government to citizens. Edwin Meese, Sage claims, was relatively sympathetic to the idea of "private attorneys generals" because they represented an alternative to "big government" (Sage, personal interview).

In the latter half of the 1990s, the Atlantic States Legal Foundation gradually stopped filing lawsuits. Today, the organization spends most of its time providing scientific and technical assistance to environmental organizations and community groups. A number of factors help explain the shift away from the courts and toward other targets. First, Reagan's conservative judicial appointees rendered the judicial venue less sympathetic to the claims of environmentalists. Second, according to Sage, changes to the Freedom of Information Act made lawsuits more expensive and risky for lack of good, reliable information. It was difficult, Sage recalls, to find lawyers willing to take on cases. But the most important reason for abandoning the courts, Sage argued, had to do with industry mobilization and influence over the permit-writing process. In response to a flurry of lawsuits in the 1980s, industry became savvier about obtaining pollution discharge permits that "were written in such a way that the companies would not violate them" (Sage, personal interview). The ASLF dropped out of the enforcement game "rather precipitously," says Sage, because they could not find cases to press in the courts.

Much of the venue-shifting of the ASLF in the last two decades has been driven by shifts, both "real" and perceived, in external opportunities and constraints, but the group's choice of decision venues and policy arenas was also shaped by factors internal to the organization. First, the organization was founded as an alternative to the centralized environmental organizations in Washington, DC. Sage, while formerly in that world, did not agree that "all problems could be solved inside the Beltway" (Sage, personal interview). Such a view did not encourage direct contact and cooperation with the public, and it failed to grasp the difficultly involved in governing a large, diverse, and complicated country from the center. The more local, grassroots strategy embraced by Sage continues to shape the organization today; most of the group's targets are other local environmental organizations rather than governmental institutions.

A second organizational factor shaping the strategies of ASLF concerns the expertise and personal leadership style of the organization's founder and long-time president, Sam Sage. His scientific background in water pollution helped the group make the transition from a litigation group to an organization focused on providing environmental groups with technical information. And Sage's personal style – he admittedly "gets bored" doing the same thing – predisposes the organization to work on a variety of issues in a number of locations. Atlantic States currently works in Eastern Europe, in part because Sage and several members of the Board of Directors have personal ties to the area.[7]

This brief history of the Atlantic States Legal Foundation suggests one potential pattern of venue-shopping. Like Baumgartner and Jones' (1993) model of policy change, the strategic behavior of advocacy organizations can resemble a "punctuated equilibrium" model. That is, an advocacy group might work within one venue for a relatively long period of time, and then rather suddenly change venues or arenas as external opportunities shift. Subsequently, the group settles into another relatively stable pattern. The Atlantic States Legal Foundation is currently involved in a variety of campaigns in several locations, but the organization has gone through two distinct strategic phases. In the first, ASLF targeted the judicial venue; in the second, they adopted an indirect strategy by helping environmental organizations with scientific and technical matters. While involved in the policymaking process, their participation is less directly targeted at decision-making institutions and instead focuses on policy arenas. Their history contrasts quite notably with that of another group, the Partnership for Onondaga Creek.

The Partnership for Onondaga Creek: one issue, multiple targets

Unlike the Atlantic States Legal Foundation, the Partnership for Onondaga Creek (hereafter referred to as the Partnership, or POC) was formed for one, very specific reason: to oppose the construction of an above-ground sewage treatment plant in a poor, largely minority neighborhood in Syracuse, New York. For years, the POC campaigned for an alternative design, one that would minimize the environmental and aesthetic impacts of the facility on the creek and the neighborhood. Over the years, the group targeted the Mayor of Syracuse, the city council

---

[7] Of course, the opportunity to work in Eastern Europe opened up only after the fall of communism in the late 1980s. This example illustrates how both external political opportunities and internal organizational factors shape the choice of targets, venues, and arenas.

("Common Council"), the county government, state legislators, the New York State Department of Environmental Conservation (DEC), former New York State Attorney-General Elliot Spitzer, former New York Governor George Pataki, Representative James Walsh (R-NY), Senators Hillary Clinton (D-NY) and Charles Schumer (D-NY), and the Environmental Protection Agency. The Partnership targeted an increasing number of venues and arenas at higher levels of government, but they did not abandon other venues as much as expand their targets and shift their emphasis over time.[8] The POC epitomizes the pragmatic, rational venue-shopper so often characterized in the literature.

Opposition to the sewage treatment plant began soon after Onondaga County announced plans in March 1999 to build a Regional Treatment Facility (RTF or "Midland Avenue Facility") in a residential neighborhood on the south side of the city of Syracuse. The treatment plant was designed to decrease harmful sewage discharges into Onondaga Creek, a tributary to Onondaga Lake. The lake, located north of downtown Syracuse, is one of the most polluted lakes in the country;[9] its clean-up has been mandated since 1989 as a result of a lawsuit jointly filed by Atlantic States Legal Foundation, the New York State Attorney-General, and the New York Department of Environmental Conservation. The Partnership for Onondaga Creek, while supportive of the larger clean-up effort, disagreed with the location and design of the treatment facility. When it formed in 2000, the group initially targeted the city of Syracuse, specifically Republican mayor Matt Driscoll and the largely Republican Common Council, whose jurisdiction over the matter rested on the fact that the city owned the plant site. The county, which was the major promoter of the project, could only proceed with the construction once the city granted it an easement on the property. The Partnership's first victory was in March 2000, when the Syracuse Common Council voted 9–0 against the easement (Perreault, n.d.).

Aggie Lane, one of the founders and most active members of the Partnership, felt that they would have the most leverage over city officials who had been elected by both Republicans and Democrats. Moreover, according to Lane, the Mayor was experienced at "standing up to the

---

[8] Much of information presented in this section is from a personal interview with Aggie Lane, one of the founders of the Partnership for Onondaga Creek and its key spokesperson. The interview took place on March 7, 2005, and is cited as "Lane, personal interview" hereafter. This brief overview does not constitute a full recounting of the many strategies and tactics pursued by the POC; such a summary is outside the scope of the chapter.

[9] Onondaga Lake was placed on the federal Superfund's National Priorities List in 1994. See EPA's website at www.epa.gov/region02/water/lakes/onondaga.htm (accessed January 3, 2007).

county" (Lane, personal interview). The key issue for the Mayor revolved around the question of whether the county had a right to impose its solution on the city with minimal input from the city itself. These jurisdictional battles between the city and the county proved advantageous for the Partnership, who in the words of Lane, "played one off of the other" (Lane, personal interview).

While the Partnership targeted city officials throughout the conflict, their relationship with the city was alternately cooperative and contentious. The high point of cooperation between the Partnership and the city occurred when the city hired an engineer to evaluate alternative designs for the treatment facility plant. Lane claimed that the Partnership, which had felt "a bit lost" when they came up against the county's engineers who "threw numbers at them," was delighted with the city's decision and soon considered the engineer to be "theirs." As Meredith Perreault said at the time, "in terms of the power relations between the City and County, [the decision to hire a city engineer] has made a substantial difference. For the first time, the City is prepared to challenge the County engineers, and is better equipped to find an alternative" (Perreault, n.d.).[10] In meetings with the county, the city's engineer successfully disputed the county's arguments that an underground storage facility (the POC's preferred design) was not feasible (Lane, personal interview).

The Partnership did not always enjoy such close relations with and easy access to the city government, however. Lane admits that access was "up and down"; at times, the city seemed poised to negotiate "behind closed doors" with the county. Because of this, and because the city did not have ultimate authority over the project, the Partnership targeted multiple venues. Almost from the beginning, they sought out officials at the county level who were under pressure to meet Onondaga Lake clean-up deadlines and who had authority over the design of the treatment facility. The county, however, was much less receptive to the Parternship's claims and generally failed to provide them the access they desired. At one point in the conflict, Partnership members interrupted a county legislative session, claiming that county legislators were discussing the Midland Avenue Facility as though the design had already been finalized.

In general, the Partnership moved conflict into public arenas when they faced delays and obstacles in various decision venues. However, the POC was selective in its use of public arenas. Because the city was largely sympathetic to the group's claims and provided them with inside access

---

[10] Perreault is project scientist at the Onondaga Environmental Institute, another Syracuse-based environmental group that is working on the restoration of Onondaga Creek, a tributary to Onondaga Lake.

(the city even appointed a temporary liaison in the Mayor's office for the Midland Avenue issue), the Partnership rarely used public protests to target city officials. Rather, the POC conducted sit-ins and demonstrations when targeting venues where they had little access and influence. For example, the POC staged a sit-in at the office of (now former) state Senator Nancy Lorraine Hoffman in July 2004, vowing to stay until she met with them. According to Lane, state and federal officials only responded to the group under the threat of a "media mess" (Lane, personal interview).

By 2004, things looked bleak for the Partnership. Negotiations with the city and county, which the Partnership had successfully engineered, had broken down.[11] Moreover, nearly two years earlier, a federal judge had granted the county permission to seize the city land for the project. As the county began preparing the site for construction, the Partnership looked to a new venue. In April 2004, it filed a Title VI civil rights claim against Onondaga County and the New York State Department of Environmental Conservation with the Environmental Protection Agency, charging the defendants with environmental racism.[12] While the Partnership lacked the resources and expertise to file the lawsuit itself, Lane and others persuaded Syracuse University's public interest law clinic to take the case. In September 2004 the Environmental Protection Agency announced it would conduct a six-month investigation of the conflict to see whether environmental racism was a factor in the design of the facility. A year later, it found no evidence of discrimination based on race.[13] Meanwhile, the construction of the treatment facility was thoroughly underway and plans were in the works for two more treatment plants in other Syracuse neighborhoods. By summer 2008, the Midland plant was

---

[11] For an eight-month period, from December 2001 to August 2002, the Partnership participated in multi-stakeholder talks that culminated in two alternative design proposals for the facility, ones that the Partnership felt would have less adverse impact on the Midland Avenue neighborhood. According to Lane, "just as it looked like there might be consensus among the parties, the negotiations ended abruptly – in an impasse and in silence." See Lane (n.d.).

[12] While the EPA did not have the power to halt construction of the facility, Partnership members hoped that the suit would force the county and the New York Department of Environmental Conservation to negotiate with city residents (Johnson, 2004).

[13] In September 2006, the Inspector-General of the Environmental Protection Agency issued a report criticizing the EPA for failure to conduct environmental justice reviews of its programs and policies, despite being required to by law. A month later, the Partnership renewed its request for the EPA to consider the adverse impacts of the plant on the largely low-income, African-American community. See Environmental Protection Agency (2006). Midland Avenue activists claim that the EPA has only accepted thirty Title VI complaints over the last ten years and has not found civil rights violations in any of them.

nearly complete, but in a surprising turnaround, Onondaga County decided against building the other treatment plants, opting instead for "a combination of green technologies and underground storage" to address the sewage overflow problem (Mariani, 2008). Local environmental groups like the Atlantic States Legal Foundation considered this a victory. It is reasonable to conclude that the POC's tireless activism against the Midland plant helped pave the way for alternative solutions to the other two proposed plants.

Case discussion

The brief overview of the Atlantic States Legal Foundation and the Partnership for Onondaga Creek presented here is meant to illustrate some of the dynamics of venue-shopping strategies. A number of observations can be made. First, the two organizations represent rather distinct kinds of advocacy organizations. Atlantic States was founded with a general goal in mind, that of helping local environmental groups "solve problems." Such a broad mission did not predispose the group toward any particular target or set of issues, although Sage's background in water pollution and his co-founder's legal expertise positioned the group to work in the legal arena and on water-related issues. Because of the group's broad mission, we should expect it to engage in some venue-shopping, but it will look different than a group organized around a single, specific campaign or issue.

Atlantic State's pattern of venue-shopping, as noted, suggests long periods of relative stability (e.g. targeting one set of venues) punctuated by distinct changes as opportunities shift. Their initial choice of the courts was based on both normative and instrumental concerns. Specifically, the group turned to environmental enforcement in the courts because they perceived a broad opportunity to improve America's waterways and to get reimbursed in the process (thus maintaining their organization). Citizen suit provisions had opened the courts to environmental groups in ways that had not existed prior to the 1970s (see Wenner, 1982). Moreover, few environmental groups were taking advantage of this new venue; as a result, industry was initially caught off guard. The judicial venue was therefore a relatively untapped site to exploit conflict. Their opponents in industry were largely unorganized here, giving the ASLF a "honeymoon" period. When these opportunities diminished in the 1980s and 1990s, partly as a result of industry adjusting its strategy, Atlantic States largely withdrew from the courts and turned its sights elsewhere. The "where" was determined in part by Sage's own expertise and personal preferences.

The Partnership for Onondaga Creek, unlike Atlantic States, is a "one-shotter" advocacy group.[14] They were formed with one dominant goal in mind, and their definition of winning is tied directly to that goal. Consequently, they have been willing to try anything and everything. They have targeted every decision venue that has jurisdiction over the Regional Treatment Facility and have moved the conflict into policy arenas such as the media when they have experienced setbacks in decision venues. Two things have made this possible: first, decision-making authority over the building of the sewage treatment plant is extremely fragmented. The fragmentation is due in part to the original lawsuit that mandated the clean-up of Onondaga Lake and thus generated the building of the sewage treatment facility. Several government entities were parties to the suit and therefore have jurisdiction over the issue. Authority over the treatment facility is also shared between the city and county, and the federal government's interest stems from its authority over civil rights issues. For Aggie Lane, this fragmentation has been mostly beneficial, but it also complicates things. She admitted that sometimes there are "too many targets so that a lot is coming down at once."

The Partnership's impressive ability to negotiate this complicated landscape reveals another reason for their continued opposition. The leaders in the Partnership are highly dedicated and innovative policy entrepreneurs, willing to exploit any venue or arena that looks promising. When they did not have the resources to carry on the battle in a new venue, they sought outside help. Not only did they turn to the Syracuse University legal clinic for help in filing a Title VI claim, but they asked the Natural Resources Defense Council, the Sierra Club, and other national environmental organizations to help them when they expanded conflict to state and federal levels. Specifically, they enlisted these groups in sending mass mailings to state and federal officials, asking high-level state and national policymakers such as then Senator Hillary Clinton to intervene in the conflict. Put differently, the Partnership for Onondaga Creek looked for allies in order to target additional decision venues and policy arenas that appeared beyond their reach.

The two cases confirm models of venue-shopping found in the policy process literature. Both Atlantic States and the Partnership acted pragmatically, searching for vulnerabilities and openings in the system, and

---

[14] Marc Galanter (1974) made a distinction between one-shot and repeat players in the legal arena, defining "one-shotters" as those with only occasional access to the courts and repeat players as those frequently engaged in litigation. I am using the term more broadly, to distinguish between advocacy organizations who are involved in long-term and multiple campaigns, and those who organize around a single issue.

moving to new venues and arenas when perceived opportunities changed. But the analysis also supports the call for a more careful and nuanced analysis of how advocacy organizations choose strategies, including how they choose and change venues and arenas. Not all advocacy organizations will display the same propensities to venue-shop, nor have the same capacity to do so. Factors both internal and external to an organization impact its venue-shopping activities.

The next section outlines two broad models of venue-shopping – what I call the "static" and "dynamic" models – which can be gleaned from the interest group and public policy literatures. I then provide a more systematic analysis of the factors that influence venue-shopping, and offer some propositions that may serve as the basis for further empirical research.

Models of venue-shopping

To what extent do advocacy organizations engage in venue-shopping? The literature does not answer this question directly, but interest group theory and public policy models offer two contending theories. Several interest group scholars suggest that advocacy organizations choose a preferred strategy and stick with it, perhaps past the point where it is optimally effective. On the other hand, much of the recent public policy literature assumes that advocacy organizations frequently change their targets as opportunities in the political system shift. Because each perspective has merit, we must push our thinking beyond simple formulations to specify the factors that drive advocacy organizations to engage (or not) in venue-shopping. After reviewing these perspectives, I will identify what I believe are the most important factors.

The static model

An essential part of political advocacy involves deciding how to go about influencing the policy process. These choices as a whole are considered to be the "strategy" of an advocacy group.[15] Gais and Walker (1991: 3) suggest that advocacy organizations choose a strategy and then stick with it: "The choice between ... political strategies is a fundamental one made early in a group's history that orients the organization's tactical decisions throughout much of its life." Similarly, Kollman (1998: 34) notes the tendency of interest groups to "rely on tools they are familiar

---

[15] Choosing and/or changing policy venues are important aspects of an advocacy group's overall strategy for policy and political change, but do not constitute the entirety of its strategy.

with and that fit their organizational structure and culture." In this volume, Barakso points to the fundamental stability of an organization's "method of operation" and provides empirical evidence to show that groups are typically consistent in the repertoire of tactics that they use. In all, these authors suggest a rather static model of advocacy group behavior: strategies are decided on at the founding of an advocacy group, and shape its behaviors throughout its life.

Several arguments can be made in support of the idea that advocacy organizations do not vary their strategies greatly. First, leaders and individuals within an organization often develop strategic expertise concerning advocacy in a particular venue. This expertise is a valuable resource for an advocacy group, one that works against the rapid switch to new decision venues with different rules and norms. For example, if an environmental organization was founded by, and is led by, lawyers, it is unlikely that the group will abandon the judicial venue even when opportunities in the venue decline. Organizations not only cultivate expertise, but also contacts, leading to increased access to particular decision venues. It may take years for an advocacy group to develop close ties to legislators, for example, but once established, these ties become valuable resources for a group. Young (this volume) illustrates this process, noting that the Natural Resources Defense Council cultivated a cadre of skillful lawyers, leading to a type of strategic path-dependency because of their heavy investments in human capital.

A second argument in support of the static model concerns the public identity of an advocacy organization. As advocacy organizations develop strategic niches, potential supporters, allies, and the public may identify the organization with the strategy. Strategies and tactics, in other words, become part of how an advocacy organization brands itself, as Barakso explains in her chapter. This may lead to a certain amount of "stickiness" or inability to transition to a new "identity strategy" as Stephen Engel (2007: 74) argues. The environmental organization Greenpeace, for example, is frequently identified with "outsider" strategies, as it targets policy arenas such as the media, the public, and the marketplace. As Bosso (2005: 78) notes, Greenpeace has struggled to "outgrow its traditional niche," finding it difficult to move beyond its long-standing image as a confrontational direct-action group. More generally, as the introduction to this volume notes, interest groups often seek unoccupied niches, defined by strategies and tactics as well as by substantive issues (see also Gray and Lowery, 1996). Maintaining a consistent organizational identity can be an important fundraising and mobilization tool in a competitive interest group environment, helping groups distinguish themselves from others, just as firms attempt to do in the marketplace. In short, organizations appeal to members on the basis of a combination of substantive issues and strategic orientations. To the extent that an organization's appeal is based on its strategic identity, it has a greater incentive to employ the same or similar tactics as used in the past.

A third factor shaping an advocacy group's strategy is its ideological values and orientation. Organizations develop strategic niches not only for pragmatic reasons, but also because of fundamental beliefs about how political change is best pursued. Advocacy organizations may believe, or learn from experience, that long-term change requires the involvement of certain policy institutions or levels of government. In such situations, an advocacy group might look for policy problems or issues that fit their ideological commitments. This turns the usual way we think about venue-shopping on its head. Rather than choosing an issue and searching for the most appropriate venue, some groups might choose a venue first and then look for issues that are appropriate to advance within it. For example, some environmental organizations believe that problems must be solved locally; if their commitment to this kind of grassroots approach is strong enough, they might look for local issues and bypass opportunities at the state or federal level for advancing their causes. Engel (2007) illustrates this calculus in his study of gay and lesbian interest groups. The National Gay and Lesbian Task Force eschewed opportunities to work at the federal level on pro-gay legislation because it identified itself as working "outside" the mainstream political establishment, choosing instead to target state and local arenas.

These factors operate as barriers to fundamental changes in an advocacy group's strategy, and may work against the practice of venue-shopping more specifically. But we know from observation that venue-shopping occurs. As Bosso (1987) describes in his history of pesticide politics, environmental organizations alternately targeted judicial venues, Congressional committees, and the Environmental Protection Agency as opportunities and constraints within them changed. Several case studies have illustrated venue-shopping in the areas of federal forest policy, local and national gun control efforts, British transportation policy, military base closures, and anti-smoking policies (respectively, Burnett and Davis, 2002; Godwin and Schroedel, 2000; Dudley and Richardson, 1998; Hansen and Krejci, 2000; Shipan and Volden, 2006). Indeed, both empirical evidence and theoretical models suggest that venue-shopping is the norm, not the exception.

The dynamic model

The logic of the dynamic model is most clearly found in Baumgartner and Jones' (1993) punctuated equilibrium model of policy change. They note that one of the most effective political strategies involves changing the venue where decision-making over policy is made. One of the benefits of venue-switching is that advocacy organizations can effect policy change without necessarily mobilizing large numbers of people or without competing in the venues of their opponents, where they might be at a disadvantage on account of biased rules and unequal opportunities for access. Moreover, if an advocacy group repeatedly fails to enact change in one venue, it makes sense to look to other arenas and venues that offer a greater possibility of success. Dramatic policy changes can result when venue changes are combined with alterations in the definition of a policy issue (Baumgartner and Jones, 1993).

Not only do advocacy organizations have an incentive to shop for alternative policy arenas and decision venues, but the US political system in particular provides numerous opportunities to do so. We can expect that advocacy organizations will take advantage of the multiple levels of government, the shared jurisdictional authority among them, and the numerous venues by shopping for the most optimal target. As opportunities and constraints shift, we should expect advocacy organizations to leave arenas and venues that are less hospitable, and move to those where opportunities are growing. If we look at venue-shopping from a comparative perspective, we can expect that systems with more decision venues and blurred jurisdictional boundaries experience more venue-shopping than systems with a limited number of venues and distinct jurisdictional boundaries.

The dynamic model appears to discount the constraints identified by the static model. Advocacy organizations are assumed to freely and easily change their strategies, particularly when it comes to deciding where to press their policy claims. As Baumgartner and Jones (1993: 36) suggest, advocacy organizations or policymakers do not have strong preferences for one venue over another: "[T]here are many possible institutional agendas, and for the policymakers who seek that institutional niche where decisions would likely go in their favor, none is inherently better than another." Presumably, the constraints identified by the static model – expertise, resources, organizational identity, and ideological orientation – are not enough to prevent an advocacy group from shopping for an alternative venue when need be. A recent study by Charles Shipan and Craig Volden (2006: 840), for example, shows that US anti-smoking advocates have focused their efforts at the local level because it is here where "they find the least resistance from the tobacco industry." Similarly, Pralle (2006b) found that anti-pesticide activists in Canada targeted municipal governments for bans on lawn and garden pesticides after concluding that provincial and national venues afforded less access and were less sympathetic to their arguments.

Both the static and dynamic models make intuitive sense and are backed by logic and empirical evidence. The pertinent question, then, is when and under what conditions are advocacy organizations likely to respond in ways consistent with each? Put differently, what factors affect the practice of venue-shopping? I identify three sets of factors that are likely to have the largest impact on the pace and nature of venue-shopping: internal organizational factors, external opportunities and constraints, and subsystem characteristics.

Advocacy organizations and venue-shopping

Internal organizational factors

As the static model suggests, an advocacy organization's strategic orientation is shaped by several factors internal to the organization, including its ideology, its beliefs about how to achieve policy change, its perceived need to develop a strategic niche, and the preferences and expertise of group leaders. Taken together, these factors predispose an advocacy group to act in ways consistent with either the static or dynamic model described above. An advocacy group with strong ideological orientations and beliefs about how to impact policy change, which feels pressure to occupy a strategic niche, and whose leaders have highly specialized skills is more likely to act in ways consistent with the static model. Such groups may have been founded by charismatic leaders whose beliefs about policy and politics have shaped the organization for decades. Over time, an organization is so identified with a particular set of issues and strategic orientations that dramatic change in either is rare. It would take a rather large shock for the group to change course.

On the other hand, we can imagine advocacy organizations that do not conform to the above image. Such groups are true pragmatists; while they hold strong opinions about substantive policy issues, their organizational identity is not tied to any particular strategy. The leaders might be generalists, and the group does not feel undue pressure to identify with a unique set of strategies. Less competitive interest group environments can relieve the pressure on groups to distinguish themselves from others by occupying narrow issue niches and adopting specific strategies and tactics.

Two other organizational factors either reinforce or hamper an organization's tendency to conform to the static or dynamic model. First, an advocacy group's material and human resources affect its ability to change strategies, including switching policy venues. In general, greater material resources make it easier for an advocacy group to play the policy game at multiple levels, in numerous policy arenas, and in several decision venues if need be. A lack of material and human resources can prevent an organization from venue-shopping, even if they are prone to do so (see Miller, 2007). In such cases, groups may shop for allies who can carry on the battle in alternative venues and arenas, as the Partnership for Onondaga Creek did when they solicited the help of national environmental groups and high-profile politicians. This is an important, albeit overlooked incentive for forming coalitions and alliances. It could be that "one-shotter" groups initiate venue-shopping, but must solicit the support of repeat players to help them complete the job. These ideas can be stated in the form of a proposition:

Proposition #1: Other things being equal, advocacy organizations with greater resources have more ability to venue-shop. Advocacy organizations who are prone to venue-shop but who lack adequate material or human resources will form alliances with other groups so as to carry on the battle in multiple decision venues and policy arenas.

Second, whether an advocacy group is organized around specific or broad policy goals has a significant impact on its motivation to venue-shop. Advocacy organizations like the POC, which organize around one specific issue, are likely to target whatever venue holds the most promise for success, and are therefore prone to switch targets as political opportunities shift. Such groups form around a very tangible goal; their definition of winning is relatively narrow, as it is tied to the defeat or enactment of a specific policy proposal. Advocacy groups like the Atlantic States Legal Foundation, in contrast, organize around general goals or multiple aspects of an issue. Typically, these groups have a longer-term outlook and a broader understanding of success. While they too are motivated to win specific policy battles, their organizational mission is not so closely tied to victory in just one policy conflict. This leads to a second proposition:

Proposition #2: Single issue, "one-shotter" advocacy organizations are more likely to switch policy arenas and decision venues *in the short term* than advocacy organizations who are repeat players, have a longer-term outlook, and are organized around broad policy issues. These latter organizations may shift venues, but typically over longer periods of time.

External opportunities and constraints

Advocacy organizations do not operate in a vacuum, but work within political contexts where opportunities for policy change frequently shift. Successful groups are able to identify and perhaps even anticipate the opening and closing of policy windows (see Kingdon, 1984) and the shifting of political opportunities more generally. Access to decision venues can expand or contract; authority over a policy issue can become increasingly blurry or more sharply delineated; and the receptivity of decision venues to particular claims may increase or decrease as institutional actors and rules change (see, generally, Schattschneider, 1960; Baumgartner and Jones, 1993).

These shifts in external opportunities and constraints shape the strategies of advocacy organizations, including their propensity to shop for alternative decision venues and policy arenas. Even groups that are predisposed to stick with a familiar set of strategies and targets have an incentive to shop for an alternative venue when opportunities dramatically shift. As Sabatier and Jenkins-Smith (1999: 123) note, "changes in relevant socio-economic conditions and systemwide coalitions ... can dramatically alter the composition and resources of various coalitions." External conditions may "push" or "pull" groups to another venue. For example, increased opportunities in the judicial branch pulled the Atlantic States Legal Foundation to that arena. In contrast, environmental groups might find themselves with far less access to the administration, to government agencies, or to Congress after a national election, and thus may be pushed, if only temporarily, to other decision venues and policy arenas that afford more access and a better chance of success. As Engel (2007) shows in his study of gay and lesbian interest groups, the Human Rights Campaign eventually started working at the state level (after largely ignoring subnational arenas and focusing exclusively on federal venues) when multiple states considered and enacted bans on gay marriage. Such a dramatic shift in the political environment essentially forced the organization to broaden its tactical repertoire. The third proposition captures this dynamic.

Proposition #3: Most advocacy organizations will search for alternative decision venues and/or policy arenas when external political opportunities significantly change. Groups predisposed to act in ways consistent with the static model will need a greater external shock than groups predisposed to act in ways consistent with the dynamic model.

As a whole, we should expect more venue-shopping in systems with multiple venues and arenas. Regardless of the proclivities of particular advocacy organizations, multiple venues lead to an aggregate increase in the level of venue-shopping in a system. Venue-shopping should also be more prevalent in systems with shared authority over policy issues (as in the US federal system). Fragmented authority over decision-making allows advocacy organizations to advance their claims in any number of venues. As E. E. Schattschneider (1960: 10) remarked some time ago about the US federal system, "[o]ne of the most remarkable developments in recent American politics is the extent to which the federal, state, and local governments have become involved in doing the same kinds of things in large areas of public policy, so that it is possible for contestants to move freely from one level of government to another in an attempt to find the level at which they might try most advantageously to get what they want." By contrast, if an issue is firmly under the jurisdiction of just one decision venue, advocacy organizations have little choice but to target that venue. If unsuccessful, they will have to use "outsider" strategies in policy arenas such as the media.

In short, opportunities to venue-shop vary in different political systems. Systems with multilevel governance structures offer opportunities to venue-shop vertically among different levels of government. The rise of regional governance structures, such as the European Union, gives advocacy groups additional avenues along which to pursue their policy claims when national governments either cannot address their grievances (because of a lack of jurisdiction), or will not (because of a lack of political will and capacity). Advocacy groups can also turn to international arenas when national governments are unresponsive. Even if these international arenas do not have formal decision-making authority, they can provide groups with symbolic resources and allow them to advertise and publicize their grievances to a larger audience (see, for example, Pralle, 2003, 2006a).

Political opportunities for successful venue-shopping also shift in response to the actions of opposing advocacy organizations. Advocacy organizations who are the first to exploit a new decision venue or policy arena often enjoy a "honeymoon" period in which their opponents are caught off guard. Young (this volume) illustrates this in the case of the Natural Resources Defense Council, which enjoyed a heady period in its early years as it established the relatively new field of environmental litigation. A similar dynamic was at work when ASLF first exploited the courts to enforce the Clean Water Act. In general, as long as opponents are unorganized in a chosen decision venue or policy arena, an advocacy group can exploit the venue with little resistance from opponents. Put differently, a relatively "unoccupied" venue is generally attractive to advocacy organizations. If and when it becomes more crowded, particularly by a group's opponents, an advocacy group may search for another, less occupied venue. This can be stated in the form of a proposition:

Proposition #4: Advocacy organizations will be particularly attracted to unoccupied venues or arenas because of a lack of opposing interests who are organized in the venue and because of the possibility of filling a strategic "niche."

Policy subsystem context

Advocacy organizations not only work within a context defined by shifting political opportunities, but also work within a more or less defined interest group (or social movement) environment. How this environment is structured can impact the degree of venue-shopping by any particular group. A subsystem crowded with advocacy organizations focused on similar issues increases pressure on groups to find and maintain a unique organizational niche (Bosso, 2005). Over time, the subsystem may reach an equilibrium, whereby advocacy organizations adopt well-defined strategic roles. Knowledge about the "turfs" of different advocacy organizations will spread informally through the subsystem, resulting in few attempts to replicate the strategies of others. Stated as a proposition about venue-shopping, we have the following:

Proposition #5: Crowded subsystems lead to less venue-shopping by any one advocacy group, while less crowded subsystems encourage more venue-shopping by individual groups.

In crowded subsystems, policy battles are likely to be taking place in multiple venues and arenas, but this is a byproduct of the number of advocacy organizations in the subsystem. It is not necessarily due to the venue-shopping strategies of one or two groups. One of the virtues of a crowded interest group environment is that groups can specialize in particular decision venues and policy arenas. This specialization and fragmentation virtually guarantee that campaigns will be carried out in every decision venue that has jurisdiction over an issue, assuming access is granted and the issue is not kept off the agenda.

Conclusion

In the introduction to this volume, Prakash and Gugerty offer a way of understanding advocacy organizations that uses the analogy of a firm acting in a marketplace. Just as firms must choose markets in which to participate, advocacy organizations must choose policy venues and arenas as part of their overall strategy of policy reform. How do organizations go about the process of choosing and changing venues? Although a presumption of rationality is warranted, there is little reason to believe that all policy actors behave the same way. In other words, advocacy organizations will search for a venue that offers them the best chance of meeting their policy and organizational goals. But not all organizations are the same, and therefore, their calculations and patterns of venue-shopping are likely to differ.

I argue that different advocacy organizations will display different patterns of venue-shopping based in part on internal organizational beliefs and values, organizational resources, the preferences and expertise of leaders, and the nature of an organization's goals. Most advocacy organizations will respond to significant changes in external opportunities and constraints by shifting their strategies and tactics, and this may involve focusing on different policy venues and arenas. But smaller shifts in the political opportunity structure may not produce dramatic venue shifts if a group has a long-term view of policy change, works within a crowded interest group environment, and has considerable expertise in a particular venue or arena.

The institutional structure of a political system affects opportunities for venue-shopping, and may shape the interest group environment more generally. The fragmentation of power in the US political system across different branches and levels of government creates many potential niches within which interest groups can organize. In addition to distinguishing themselves by issues (or by positions on issues), interest groups can differentiate themselves by adopting unique strategies and this may include targeting particular venues or arenas. Therefore, we can expect systems with multiple venues and arenas to have a more varied and crowded interest group environment than systems with fewer venues and arenas. Similarly, in issue areas where decision-making authority is fragmented and overlapping, we should expect multiple interest groups. The rise of interest group politics in America, then, may be due in part to the existence and opening up of multiple policy venues and arenas, in addition to the more typical factors cited for this growth, including the expansion of government and the relative decline of political parties (see Loomis and Cigler, 2002).

The sheer number and variety of advocacy organizations creates a situation in which conflict is being carried out in multiple decision venues and policy arenas. Under these conditions, there is greater potential for policy change. Of course, venue-shopping does not always lead to substantive policy change. In other words, not all venue-shopping strategies are successful, as illustrated in the case of the Partnership for Onondaga Creek. Lack of success can be due to a number of factors: some targets may refuse to take up an issue; other venues might assert jurisdiction but decide in a way consistent with competing venues; still others may issue decisions favorable to the advocacy group, only to have their decision overturned in another venue. In short, while advocacy organizations have some control over where to shop their issues, they have less control over whether it will lead to substantive policy change.

The collective action framework adopted in this volume helps to make sense of advocacy organizations' strategies generally and venue-shopping in particular. A collective action perspective assumes that advocacy organizations are acting rationally to achieve goals in a competitive environment. To survive and prosper, they must find ways to distinguish themselves from other organizations that may compete with them for prestige, members, resources, and the like. As such, advocacy organizations may target particular strategic niches and policy venues to distinguish themselves from others. While helpful in understanding advocacy group strategy, the collective action model would benefit from a more nuanced view of the environments in which organizations operate and the different types of organizations engaged in advocacy. Not all organizations behave similarly when faced with a set of choices, because responses will be shaped by the particular history, mission, identity, and leadership of the organization.

References

Atlantic States Legal Foundation. n.d. A Brief History of ASLF. www.aslf.org/ASLF/index.html.

Baumgartner, F. R. and B. D. Jones. 1993. *Agendas and Instability in American Politics*. University of Chicago Press.

Bosso, C. 1987. *Pesticides and Politics: The Life-Cycle of a Public Issue*. University of Pittsburgh Press.

2005. *Environment, Inc.* Lawrence: University Press of Kansas.

Burnett, M. and C. Davis. 2002. Getting Out the Cut: Politics and National Forest Timber Harvests, 1960–1995. *Administration and Society*, 34(2): 202–228.

Cobb, R. and C. Elder. 1983. *Participation in American Politics: The Dynamics of Agenda-Building*. Baltimore: Johns Hopkins University Press.

Dudley, G. and J. Richardson. 1998. Arenas without Rules and the Policy Change Process: Outsider Groups and British Roads Policy. *Political Studies*, 46: 727–747.

Engel, S. 2007. Organizational Identity as a Constraint on Strategic Action. *Studies in American Political Development*, 21(Spring): 66–91.

Environmental Protection Agency. 2006. "Environmental Justice in the News" for the Week Ending September 29, 2006 (memorandum). www.epa.gov/compliance/resources/newsletters/ej/ejnews/ejnews-sept29–2006.pdf.

Gais, T. L. and J. L. Walker. 1991. Pathways to Influence in American Politics. In J. L. Walker (ed.), *Mobilizing Interest Groups in America*. Ann Arbor: University of Michigan Press.

Galanter, M. 1974. Why the Haves Come Out Ahead: Speculations on the Limits of Legal Change. *Law and Society Review*, 9(1): 95–160.

Godwin, M. and J. Schroedel. 2000. Policy Diffusion and Strategies for Promoting Policy Change: Evidence from California Local Gun Control Ordinances. *Policy Studies Journal*, 28(4): 760–776.

Gray, V. and D. Lowery. 1996. A Niche Theory of Interest Representation. *Journal of Politics*, 58: 91–111.

Hansen, K. and D. Krejci. 2000. Rethinking Neoinstitutional Interaction: Municipal Arena-specific Strategies and the Base Closure Process. *Administration and Society*, **32**(2): 166–182.

Hoberg, G. 1997. From Localism to Legalism: The Transformation of Federal Forest Policy. In C. Davis (ed.), *Western Public Lands and Environmental Politics*. Boulder, CO: Westview Press.

Johnson, T. 2004. EPA to Investigate Midland Sewer Plant. *Daily Orange*, September 24.

King, D. C. 1994. The Nature of Congressional Committee Jurisdictions. *American Political Science Review*, **88** (1): 48–62.

Kingdon, J. 1984. *Agendas, Alternatives, and Public Policies*. Boston: Little, Brown.

Kollman, K. 1998. *Outside Lobbying: Public Opinion and Interest Group Strategies*. Princeton University Press.

Lane, A. n.d. It's Not Over Yet: An Update on the Midland Avenue Sewage Plant Controversy. www.peacecouncil.net/pnl/03/723/NotOver.htm.

Loomis, B. A. and A. J. Cigler. 2002. The Changing Nature of Interest Group Politics. In A. J. Cigler and B. A. Loomis, *Interest Group Politics*, 6th edn. Washington, DC: CQ Press.

Mariani, J. 2008. Armory Sewage Plant Scrapped; County Executive Mahoney Concludes Alternatives Technologies Can Do the Job. *The Post-Standard* (Syracuse, NY), May 3.

Miller, L. 2007. The Representational Biases of Federalism: Scope and Bias in the Political Process, Revisited. *Perspective on Politics*, **5**(2): 305–321.

Perreault, M. n.d. A Better Solution in the Works?: An Update on the Midland Avenue Sewage Treatment Plant. www.peacecouncil.net/pnl/02/708/708 MidlandAve.htm.

Pralle, S. 2003. Venue Shopping, Political Strategy, and Policy Change: The Internationalization of Canadian Forest Policy. *Journal of Public Policy*, **23** (3): 233–260.

    2006a. *Branching Out, Digging In: Environmental Advocacy and Agenda Setting*. Washington, DC: Georgetown University Press.

    2006b. The Mouse that Roared: Agenda-Setting in Canadian Pesticides Politics. *Policy Studies Journal*, **34**(2): 171–194.

Sabatier, P. and H. Jenkins Smith 1999. The Advocacy Coalition Framework: An Assessment. In P. Sabatier (ed.), *Theories of the Policy Process*. Boulder, CO: Westview Press.

Sabatier, P. and H. Jenkins-Smith (eds.). 1993. *Policy Change and Learning: An Advocacy Coalition Approach*. Boulder, CO: Westview Press.

Schattschneider, E. E. 1960. *The Semisovereign People: A Realist's View of Democracy in America*. New York: Holt, Rinehart, and Winston.

Shipan, C. and C. Volden. 2006. Bottom-Up Federalism: The Diffusion of Antismoking Policies from U.S. Cities to States. *American Journal of Political Science*, **50**(4): 825–843.

Timmermans, A. 2001. Arenas as Institutional Sites for Policymaking: Patterns and Effects in Comparative Perspective. *Journal of Comparative Policy Analysis: Research and Practice*, **3**: 311–337.

Wenner, L. 1982. *The Environmental Decade in Court*. Bloomington: Indiana University Press.

Part 3

International advocacy and market structures

8 The political economy of transnational action among international NGOs

Alexander Cooley and James Ron

The central premise of this volume is that a collective action approach based on a firm analogy can help both scholars and practitioners understand how non-governmental organizations (NGOs) interact with their organizational environment and make strategic choices. In doing so, the book seeks to challenge the dominant view (or perhaps complement it, as Risse [this volume] suggests) that NGOs are primarily driven by their common moral purpose and commitment to norms (Wapner, 1995; Finnemore, 1996; Keck and Sikkink, 1998; Boli and Thomas, 1999; Clark, 2001). While not denying that normative considerations play an important role in influencing NGO tactics and strategy, this volume seeks to reveal how structural forces and organizational pressures also guide the choices of international NGOs (INGOs), making their behavior akin to that of firms in the marketplace. In other words, instead of normative considerations dominating their decisions about advocacy strategy and tactics, the collective action approach suggests that instrumental concerns such as the desire to please multiple donors who control the budget strings play an important role in explaining INGO behavior. As a result, the normative gloss recedes in importance and INGOs can no longer be clearly distinguished from their instrumental counterparts that function in the economic marketplace

This chapter examines transnational humanitarian action in the Democratic Republic of Congo and Bosnia.[1] It highlights how organizational insecurity, competitive pressures, and fiscal uncertainty shape the choices of INGOs, and how these pressures can be traced to the institutional and structural context in which these groups function. This chapter

This chapter draws on Cooley and Ron (2002) and is reprinted by permission of MIT Press. The original Cooley and Ron article was one of the early investigations of the material incentives facing NGOs. Though the article was not written from the collective action perspective, many of its insights dovetail with those developed by this volume's editors and contributors.

[1] For space considerations, the original case of Western technical assistance providers promoting economic reforms in Kyrgyzstan has been omitted from this version.

demonstrates how powerful institutional imperatives can subvert INGO efforts, prolong inappropriate aid projects, or promote destructive competition among well-meaning transnational actors. Attempts by INGOs to reconcile material pressures with normative motivations often produce outcomes dramatically at odds with liberal expectations.

Echoing some of the themes outlined by Bob (this volume), we argue that many aspects of INGO behavior can be explained by materialist analysis and an examination of the incentives and constraints produced by the transnational sector's institutional environment. The pressures generated by these institutional constraints can dominate normative or principled intentions. We advance two theoretical propositions. First, the growing number of INGOs within a given transnational sector increases uncertainty, competition, and insecurity for all organizations in that sector. This proposition disputes the liberal view that INGO proliferation is, in and of itself, evidence of a robust global civil society. Second, we suggest that the marketization of many INGO activities – particularly the use of competitive tenders and renewable contracting – generates incentives that produce dysfunctional project outcomes. This claim disputes the popular assumption that market-based institutions in the transnational sector increase INGO efficiency and effectiveness.

While we recognize that INGOs exhibit firm-like behaviors, we do not *per se* criticize their normative agendas or moral character. Our position has always been more moderate than what is outlined by Bob (this volume). Rather we suggest that dysfunctional organizational behavior is likely to be a rational response to systematic and predictable institutional pressures. In many cases, uncooperative local actors or project targets will take advantage of the transnational sector's perverse incentives to further their own opportunistic agendas. Of course, this raises the question whether firms can also be considered as moral actors that behave badly because of the structural pressures they face. This is a difficult question to answer primarily because it is difficult in non-experimental settings to understand *ex ante* the real (as opposed to stated) preferences of actors; in many ways, preferences tend to be inferred from behavior. We do not enter this debate here. Our key argument is that even actors that are considered (correctly or incorrectly) to be guided by moral concerns, tend to display strategic and instrumental behaviors in ways that undermine the normative bases of their emergence. Of course, one might be concerned as to why such actors do not display moral resilience and keep their instrumental impulses in check. Indeed, some INGOs may resist material pressures, either because of idiosyncratic funding patterns, unique organizational cultures, or remarkable leaders or coalitions. Others may even define themselves in opposition to the mainstream, condemning their rivals' "marketized" or "corporate" mentalities. These are certainly important issues and future work can focus on understanding the organizational DNA of resilient moral actors. For the purpose of this chapter, we are concerned as to how the imperatives of organizational survival and budgetary needs lead INGOs to display firm-like behaviors.

We focus on the incentives and institutional outcomes generated by contractual relations, incomplete information, transaction costs, and property rights (Williamson, 1985; Hodgson, 1988; Eggertsson, 1990; North, 1990). By applying these concepts to the environment in which contemporary transnational actors operate, we identify sources of organizational insecurity and explain patterns of behavior that liberal theories of transnationalism either fail to acknowledge or cannot address conceptually. INGOs compete to raise money and secure contracts. These contracts, moreover, are often performance-based, renewable, and short-term, creating counterproductive incentives and acute principal–agent problems. Opportunism and dysfunctional outcomes are particularly rife when groups seek control over the same project, a phenomenon known as the "multiple-principals problem." Indeed, we find that INGOs respond to contractual incentives and organizational pressures much like firms do in markets.

To illustrate our argument, we examine two cases of transnational assistance to uncover hidden behavioral imperatives. Our first case shows how inter-INGO competition in Goma, Democratic Republic of Congo (formerly Zaire), undercut the collective action necessary to protest misuse of refugee aid. This case draws on thirty-five discussions with staffers from Refugee Help, a respected nonprofit organization with a budget in the tens of millions of dollars (Ron, 1999). The second case draws upon events in wartime Bosnia, showing how inter-INGO competition empowered local military commanders seeking to resist international POW protection efforts. Here, we make use of some hundred interviews with members of the International Committee of the Red Cross (ICRC), the UN, INGOs, and Bosnian military officers (Ron, 1996).

Although two qualitative cases cannot provide a definitive test of our claims, they fulfill important criteria of social inquiry and suggest a global trend. The cases are drawn from different geographic regions, allowing us to control for local cultural factors, identity-based action, and other potential regional idiosyncrasies. In addition, the cases involve different sectors of the transnational world: humanitarian aid/refugee relief and POW monitoring. Controlling for geographical setting and issue area we observe dynamics consistent with a political economy approach.[2]

A "civil" global society? Organizational density and marketization

The notion that growth in the transnational sector heralds a more benign global civil society is fast achieving doctrinal status (Matthews, 1997; Keck and Sikkink, 1998). Liberal scholars and Western aid donors view two key trends in transnational activity – increasing organizational density and marketization – as important contributions to a global civil society. Because they assume that transnational behavior is shaped chiefly by liberal norms, they believe that the more INGOs exist, the better. Moreover, marketization of aid funding, through the creation of competitive project tenders, is supposed to boost efficiency. Competition cuts waste and curbs corruption, and allows new INGOs to become transnational players. We question the optimism embedded in both propositions, suggesting that more is not always better and that marketization can produce dysfunctional incentives and results.

There is little doubt that the transnational world is increasingly dense. Between 1960 and 1996, for example, the number of INGOs grew from 1,000 to 5,500 (Simmons, 1998). This growth was particularly dramatic in the transnational aid sector, as private aid agencies expanded their operations by 150 percent from 1985 to 1995, affecting the lives of 250 million people worldwide (Charlton and May, 1995). In 1992 the total amount of assistance to the developing world channeled through INGOs was $8 billion, representing 13 percent of all development assistance (Simmons, 1998: 87). War-related relief in particular is growing rapidly. In 1989 the US Agency for International Development (USAID) spent $297 million on humanitarian relief, a figure that rose to $1.2 billion four years later, in large part because of the relief effort in Bosnia (Natsios, 1995). Increasing organizational density is also evident from the number of INGOs operating near or within zones of armed conflict. In 1980, for example, there were thirty-seven foreign relief agencies in a major Cambodian refugee camp along the Thai border. By 1995, more than 200 INGOs were present in Goma and in 1996, 240 INGOs were active in

[2] The technical assistance providers in Kyrgyzstan, presented in the original version of this chapter, were usually for-profit corporations that had received project contracts from USAID and other international donors. Hence, we view our argument as equally applicable to both for-profit and not-for-profit entities.

Bosnia (Smillie, 1998: 42),[3] requiring some thirty coordination meetings per week.[4] In our interviews, most professional aid officials expressed concern with this trend, viewing it as an indication of the relief market's low barriers to entry.

The explosion in INGO numbers stems in part from shifts in donor strategies, which increasingly rely on private transnational groups as contractors and intermediaries (Berrios, 2000). USAID, for example, disburses 25–30 percent of its budget through private groups, as do the governments of Sweden, Switzerland, Norway, and the European Union (EU) (Smillie, 1997: 564). In 2000, the UN High Commission for Refugees (UNHCR) budget was $1 billion, most of which was disbursed through competitive INGO contracts (Rekacewicz, 2001). "Willy nilly," Simmons (1998: 87) notes, "the UN and nation-states are depending more on NGOs to get things done." This increased reliance on competitive contract tenders has stimulated further INGO growth, because as the numbers of tenders increase, so do contractors' ranks.

Although some transnational sectors have assumed oligopolistic qualities, the increase in tenders has boosted overall INGO numbers for several reasons. First, there are often low barriers to entry in the humanitarian market, which has no binding set of regulatory agencies or rules (a point also made by Bob, this volume). Moreover, because many donors are governments, they tend to give preference to INGOs from their own countries, spurring greater growth. Thus, for example, major aid groups such as Save the Children are often divided into multiple and independent national branches. Specific countries also have greater connections to conflicts for historical reasons. For instance, Portuguese aid groups are particularly active in Angola, a former colony. Finally, the individual country offices of INGOs continue to press for financial self-sufficiency. Thus each country branch of a single NGO behaves as an autonomous entity, and these subunits may actually vie for the same contracts.

The growing reliance on INGOs and the marketization of transnationalism is propelled by searing critiques of project failures, demands for accountability by domestic politicians, and broad neo-liberal agendas (Barber, 1997; Maren, 1997; Uvin, 1998). Western, Japanese, and other aid donors are increasingly issuing short-term, renewable contracts for discrete aid projects, requiring aid contractors to bid competitively and demonstrate concrete results (Smillie, 1997). As one study of Bosnian assistance noted, for example, "virtually all donor grant mechanisms had a time frame of one year or less. Some were for six months or even three"

[3] And interviews with Refugee Help officials, August–November 1998.
[4] Interview with ICRC Head of Office, Sarajevo, April 12, 1996.

(Smillie and Todorovic, 2001: 31). Donors, moreover, seek to fund projects, not administrative overhead, hoping that this will push INGO contractors to rationalize procedures, demonstrate effectiveness, and slash overhead. They view marketization as a way to curb waste, improve professionalism, and enhance project implementation (Charlton and May, 1995; Berrios, 2000). Marketization can also generate support within donor countries by reassuring skeptical legislators that foreign assistance is being spent responsibly and efficiently.

Western technical assistance efforts in Eastern Europe and the former socialist states constitute an increasingly lucrative, crowded, and marketized transnational sector. Cumulative technical assistance from the EU to the former Soviet states totaled $2.804 billion in 1991 to 1996; US assistance from 1992 to 1997 totaled $10.967 billion (Lubin, 1997: 351). Most of these disbursements funded projects implemented by well-known for-profit multinationals. In 1995 alone, contracts worth $476 million were awarded to just four corporations – Arthur Anderson, Booz Allen and Hamilton, Chemonics, and KPMG/Peat Marwick – for economic restructuring efforts (Lubin, 1997: 351). Indeed, the annual value of technical assistance and INGO projects to many post-Soviet states exceeds that of financial assistance from established multilateral lenders such as the International Monetary Fund (IMF) (Cooley, 2000: 38).

INGO insiders are increasingly concerned by this growth of actors and marketization. A UN-commissioned study notes that coordination efforts among war-relief INGOs are being systematically undermined by the growing number of humanitarian groups vying for contracts (Reindorp and Wiles, 2001). "Competitiveness," the report states, is "built into the system" of war-related aid, while competition within the UN relief system, according to one senior UN official, is even fiercer than in the private sector. The results have been deeply corrosive (Reindorp and Wiles, 2001).

Organizational environments, contracting and NGO incentives

When an organization's survival depends on strategic choices in a market environment characterized by uncertainty, its interests will be shaped, often unintentionally, by material incentives. We assume that INGOs behave similarly to other organizations, internalizing the values, goals, and methods of their institutional environment through imitation and isomorphism (March and Olsen, 1989; Scott 1997). The more nonprofit groups attempt to secure and maintain contracts under market-generated

pressures, the more they will copy the structures, interests, and procedures of their for-profit counterparts (Powell and DiMaggio, 1991).

The influence of material incentives is further bolstered by the organizational structures of aid INGOs emulating private-sector models. INGOs
are in the business of implementing programs. Most large nonprofit
groups have developed elaborate structures for handling public relations,
fundraising, internal audits and accounting, human resources, and the
like. Transnational organizations are embedded in market-based institutions created by contracts between donors and INGO contractors, or
between contractors and recipients. Donors typically seek the effective
implementation of their projects; contractors are tacitly preoccupied with
organizational survival. In unstable or competitive markets, aid contractors cannot take their survival as a given. Securing new contracts – or
renewing existing ones – is the best way to remain solvent (Korten, 1996:
102). In this respect, the dependence of major US relief groups on short-
term, renewable government contracts is notable. In 1995, for instance,
US government contracts constituted 62 percent of CARE-USA's total
revenue and 54 percent for Save the Children-USA (Smillie, 1998: 43). In
turn, principal–agent problems, competitive contract tenders, and the
presence of multiple principals exacerbate INGO insecurity and create
organizational imperatives promoting self-interested action, inter-INGO
competition, and poor project implementation.

Principal–agent problems

Short-term contracting can lead to acute agency problems. Relations
between donors, contractors, and recipients can be modeled as a double
set of "principal–agent" problems wherein the donor is a "principal" and
contractors are "agents." At the lower half of the hierarchy, the contractor
functions as the principal and the aid recipient is the agent (Moe, 1984).
As in all relations of authority, an agent's fulfillment of a principal's
directives cannot be taken for granted (Pratt and Zeckhauser, 1985;
Eisenardt, 1989), and donor-principals face the problems of hidden
action and information (Miller, 1992). Because contractor-agents often
have *de facto* control over a project's resources, they will try and guide the
project so that it promotes their own goals, which may or may not be
identical to those of the donor (Sappington, 1991). If the project is not
going according to the donor's plan, contractors or recipients – or possibly
both – may conceal, withhold, or distort information harmful to their
interests (North, 1990). More importantly, most projects are renewed
after an initial evaluation, giving contractor-agents little incentive to
report failing or inappropriate projects. If contractor-agents were to be

entirely truthful about implementation problems, they might hurt their chances of contract renewal and threaten their own organizational survival.

Relations between contractors and project recipients are also characterized by agency problems. It is more difficult, however, to *a priori* impute a project recipient's preferences than it is those of the contractor. Recipients may genuinely welcome all project support and use aid resources for the purposes for which they were intended. On the other hand, without adequate monitoring, recipients may appropriate the contractor's resources for opportunistic gain. One of our key hypotheses is that when faced with pressure to renew existing contracts, aid contractors will be reluctant to report recipients' opportunistic behavior unless donors can credibly guarantee that they will not terminate or reduce funding for the project. Two other institutional features can exacerbate these agency problems: competitive bidding and multiple principals.

Competitive bidding

The competitive nature of short-term contracts acts as a powerful institutional constraint on International Organization (IO) and INGO contractors. Donors initiate projects with a semipublic tender, which contractors then bid on. In war-related relief, three- to six-month contracts are the norm, with contractors constantly facing threats of layoffs, cutbacks, and capacity reductions. Contractors incur significant start-up costs to service a new contract – hiring staff, renting offices, and leasing new equipment – and can recoup their expenses only by securing additional contracts. Because alternative contractors threaten to appropriate projects, INGOs are under constant pressure to renew, extend, or win new contracts, regardless of the project's overall utility. Some INGO headquarters order their country offices to become financially self-sufficient, exacerbating the competitive dynamic. Securing new funding is an ever-expanding part of the INGO's function, pushing other concerns – such as ethics, project efficacy, or self-criticism – to the margins.

The multiple-principals problem

A final institutional constraint arises when multiple donors or contractors compete for the same project. If IOs and INGOs were members of a purely normatively driven and robust global civil society, we might expect them to cooperate, pool resources, and share information. There are good theoretical reasons, however, to believe that the opposite may occur because of the multiple-principals problem. The more contractors there are, the more each organization's position within the market seems insecure (Spiller and Urbiztondo, 1994). As a result, some organizations may seek to undermine competitors, conceal information, and act unilaterally. Rather than burden- and cost-sharing, this generates project duplication, waste, incompatible goals, and collective inefficiencies (Tirole, 1994; Aghion and Tirole, 1997). In addition, competing multiple contractors often dilute the coherence of their collective project goals, advice, and strategies.

The presence of multiple contractors also increases recipients' ability to play contractors and donors off against one another. Recipients can use cross-cutting advice and strategies offered by multiple principals to pick and choose among the project elements they most like, disregarding projects that are more disruptive. This is especially likely when recipients seek concessions or payoffs from one or more principals and can threaten to withdraw their cooperation as a bargaining tactic.

Calls for INGO coordination are ubiquitous in the humanitarian aid literature, prompting periodic creation of new UN coordination studies and agencies (Natsios, 1995; Reindorp and Wiles, 2001). Recurring coordination problems, however, are not caused solely by poor communication, lack of professionalism, or a dearth of coordinating bodies. They are also – and perhaps chiefly – produced by a crowded and highly competitive aid market in which multiple organizations compete for contracts from the same donors. Inter-organizational discord is a predictable outcome of existing material incentives.

In sum, our analysis highlights the political economy of relations among transnational actors. Agency problems, competitive contracts, and multiple principals generate incentives promoting self-interested behavior, intense competition, and poor project implementation. Our cases illustrate these claims in practice.

Competitive bidding and refugee relief in Goma

Competition and an over-abundance of organizations helped cause a myriad of problems during refugee relief operations around Goma, a town in the Democratic Republic of Congo, formerly known as Zaire. From 1994 to 1996, representatives from over 200 relief organizations traveled to Goma to secure UN contracts seeking to aid desperate Rwandan refugees. Contrary to the "more is better" hypothesis, however, the presence of multiple international aid groups did not produce optimal outcomes. In particular, competitive contract bidding created powerful disincentives for Refugee Help, a respected private Western relief organization, to strongly protest aid diversion by Hutu militants and suspected war criminals. Refugee Help's reluctance in this respect is particularly striking, given its stated commitment to a deeply ethical view of global affairs.

Humanitarian aid in Goma

In the summer of 1994, 1.5 million Rwandans of ethnic Hutu origin fled to Tanzania and eastern Zaire.[5] In April, extremist Hutu groups had launched a deadly campaign of genocide against ethnic Tutsis, but a reversal of military fortunes pushed Hutu soldiers and civilians alike into exile. NGOs, including Refugee Help, moved quickly to provide refugee relief in four major Zairean and Tanzanian camp complexes, often working on relief contracts provided by the United Nations High Commission for Refugees (Millwood, 1996). UNHCR representatives extended dozens of tenders for short-term contracts dealing with food distribution, camp administration, airport off-loading, transportation, warehousing, and medical and sanitation services.

Conditions were particularly atrocious in and around Goma, where a series of camps housed 800,000 ill and malnourished refugees, making it one of the largest-ever concentrations of human misery (Fainaru, 1994). As a result of the genocide and mass civilian flight, Goma attracted unprecedented press and Western and international donor interest. Two hundred NGOs made their way to Goma in 1994 and 1995, competing for over $1 billion in relief-related contracts, making the Goma relief operation one of the highest profile and best-funded relief operations in history (Millwood, 1996). Established NGOs specializing in general camp administration and food distribution were joined by dozens of intermediate and smaller groups specializing in niche activities such as public health education, sanitation, firewood provision, community development, psychological counseling, and unaccompanied child protection.

Goma's hyper-competitive relief market   The combination of vast sums of donor money, short-term contracts, and an over-abundance of NGOs created an unstable and competitive environment for Refugee Help and others. NGOs constantly renegotiated old contracts whose due dates were fast approaching, while competitors kept lobbying the UNHCR for new contracts. "It's perhaps embarrassing to admit," one mid-level Refugee Help manager recalled, "but much of the discussion

---

[5] Prunier (1997). For broader discussions of war and refugees, see Dowty and Loescher (1996), Posen (1996), and Weiner (1996).

between headquarters and the field focused on contracts: securing them, maintaining them, and increasing them. The pressure was on: 'Get more contracts!'"[6] When headquarters staff visited the field, another manager recalled, "[t]hey mostly asked about contracts. How many did we have? When were they up? What were the chances that they would be renewed? Were there any competitors?"[7] "Contract fever" was in the air, and most of the international relief groups found themselves slipping into a deeply competitive frame of mind.

Refugee Help was by no means the only Goma-based NGO to react this way. As one journalist noted after a 1995 visit, Goma had become a "three-ring circus of financial self-interest, political abuse and incompetence" where aid had become "big, big money," and any NGO "worth its salt ... recognized that it had to be in Rwanda." As a result, he said, aid INGOs "parachuted" by the hundreds into Goma, creating "chaos and madness" (Vidal, 1995: T2). Another Western reporter described Goma as an "aid agency supermarket" in which aid groups "blare[d] out their names and logos like soft drink manufacturers," plastering everything from water pumps to T-shirts with advertisements. Competition was fierce, he wrote, and aid groups were desperate to be involved in the Goma relief so that they could bolster their fundraising capacities back home (Dowden, 1994: 11).[8]

There is no doubt that Refugee Help and other like-minded groups sincerely wanted to provide relief to needy refugees. The human needs were tremendous, and the NGOs were able to do much good. Normative considerations aside, however, Refugee Help's material stakes were also high; at the peak of the crisis, some 13 percent of Refugee Help's European headquarters costs were funded by Goma-related administrative recovery. No major organization concerned about self-preservation could risk losing such an important source of funding, and Refugee Help was no different. In addition, a major presence in Goma created a foothold for future work in the country and allowed for the possible expansion of Refugee Help's global capacities. This latter consideration was particularly important; if Refugee Help could secure more contracts in Goma, it could then deepen its reservoir of trained staff, purchase relief hardware (such as trucks and radios), and expand its stocks of emergency material, allowing it to respond quickly to emergencies elsewhere. Typically, major relief contracts were secured only after an NGO first demonstrated a

---

[6] Interview in North America with former senior Refugee Help staffer, October 1, 1998. Precise interview locations and NGO informant names have been withheld to protect anonymity.
[7] Telephone interview with former Refugee Help camp manager, October 8, 1998.
[8] See also Luttwak (1999: 43).

significant field presence. Refugee Help's long-term prospects, therefore, depended on its ability to use current contracts to boost capacity for future operations. Goma, in other words, was important both for the enormity of the suffering Refugee Help could alleviate, and for its boost to Refugee Help's competitiveness in the global relief market.

Aid diversion and ethical dilemmas

Although relief groups were saving lives in Goma, their efforts soon drew harsh criticism from Western human rights groups and the new Rwandan government (Omar, 1995; Barber, 1997; Prunier, 1997; Gourevitch, 1999). Hutu armed forces responsible for the genocide had regrouped near Goma, recruiting among the refugees, importing weapons and organizing military training. Soon the number of armed Hutu militants swelled to more than 50,000 (Human Rights Watch/Arms Project, 1995). Over time, the refugee camps became *de facto* safe havens for Hutu fighters, some of whom were suspected war criminals. They also came to serve as rear bases for cross-border guerrilla operations against Tutsi civilians and the Tutsi-led Rwandan government. The fighters diverted some relief items for sale on the open market and used the camp population as a source of political legitimacy. Critics increasingly accused the UNHCR and its aid contractors of indirectly fueling the conflict and unwittingly aiding Hutu war criminals (Block, 1994: 14; Jelinek, 1994: A18; McGreal, 1994: 11; Prunier, 1997; Gourevitch, 1999). As a relatively important component of Goma's international relief machinery, Refugee Help found itself implicated in an acute ethical dilemma.

Weak protest and collective action

Given the competitive nature of Goma's INGO environment, Refugee Help headquarters was reluctant to encourage self-critical analysis or publicly to protest aid diversions. Refugee Help managers who fended off competitors, renewed UNHCR contracts, and ensured smooth delivery systems were valued for their work. Those interested in exploring the potentially unethical by-products of Refugee Help's relief activities, however, received little encouragement. "Nobody told me to stop looking into that kind of thing," one former Refugee Help emergency manager said, "but I was never asked to work on it either."[9] Competition created incentives for contract renewal and growth, not self-reflection or protest.

---

[9] Interview in North America with former senior Refugee Help staffer, October 1, 1998.

In the camps, NGO staffers were frustrated with the UNHCR and Zairean government's refusal to crack down on Hutu militants. Although there was little the UNHCR could do without Zairean cooperation or a UN-supplied military force, its representatives might have launched a stronger and more public advocacy effort. Specifically, UNHCR representatives might have pressed the issue with greater public vigor in the media, the UN Security Council, and among interested publics. The UNHCR, however, was eager to ensure a smooth, problem-free relief operation and was not keen to do anything that might jeopardize its contracts, or undermine broader international support for the Goma aid effort. A vigorous and public UNHCR protest against Hutu militants living in the refugee camps would have reduced international support for relief efforts, and might have transformed Goma into an unmanageable, even dangerous, quagmire. The UNHCR thus quietly lobbied the UN Security Council, but dared not raise its voice too loudly. As a result, Hutu militants continued to use the camps for their own purposes.

Although many Refugee Help staffers recognized the ethical dilemmas involved in the Goma aid effort, the organization as a whole made few systematic efforts to address the problem. Refugee Help never convened an internal conference or debate on the issue, and never wrote an internal position paper probing the dilemma. When asked, relief officials attributed this in part to the frantic pace of work, including Goma's prevailing "contract fever," concern about losing aid contracts, and fear of inspiring a violent reaction by Hutu extremists.

Even if it had launched an introspective effort, Refugee Help might have still chosen to continue in Goma, as it was helping thousands of refugees. Were it not for Goma's highly competitive environment, however, Refugee Help might have taken steps to address the urgent ethical concerns. In addition to conducting an internal analysis, the group might have tried to push the UNHCR or Western powers into a more publicly principled stand. Given the multitude of potential NGO competitors already in Goma, however, Refugee Help staffers felt they had to exercise caution. After all, if Refugee Help earned a reputation as a loud-mouthed troublemaker, the UNHCR might push it aside and award lucrative relief contracts to less vocal aid groups. This was especially true given the eagerness of other aid contractors in Goma to offer similar relief services at similar or lower cost.

Competition among international relief groups also undercut the potential for Refugee Help-led collective action. For example, Refugee Help might have tried to organize a protest coalition with other groups, threatening to temporarily cease food distributions if the Zairean government or international agencies did not drive the militias out. Given inter-NGO competition, however, Refugee Help could not be sure that other relief groups would join in. Some might have agreed to protest, but others might not have, preferring instead to take over Refugee Help's contracts. In fact, during a security crisis in one of the Goma camps, another Western relief group did signal its willingness to immediately take over Refugee Help's contract if the latter so much as temporarily ceased aid distribution.

Finally, competition and the ready presence of rival NGOs made Refugee Help feel powerless. Given that many other groups were able and willing to assume Refugee Help's aid contracts, what difference would it make if the group withdrew in protest? Refugee Help was not irreplaceable, and it therefore had little bargaining power. As one staffer opined, "[n]o one would have paid any attention if we left. They would have just carried on without us."[10] Given the presence of multiple competitors, withdrawal – the ultimate act of protest by a high-profile relief organization – seemed an empty gesture.

Comparing today's multitude of relief NGOs to previous eras, one expert notes a decline in NGOs' ability to resist Goma-like problems of aid diversion: "Competition for turf and difficulties of coordination ... make [today's] humanitarian actors easy targets for political actors seeking access to the scarce resources they control" (MacFarlane, 2000: 45). When there were only a few aid providers in a war zone, NGOs could vigorously protest recipient opportunism. Today, NGOs are more cautious, fearing they might be pushed aside by rival groups.

Organizational survival was a particularly pressing concern for NGOs situated in Goma's competitive and uncertain environment. Individual Refugee Help officials realized Goma's ethical dilemmas, but the organization kept its eyes firmly fixed on securing and renewing contracts. Had competitive pressures not been so heavy, Refugee Help might have publicly protested, vigorously lobbied, openly organized, and even threatened to withdraw.

Not all NGOs allowed themselves to be caught up in Goma's "contract fever," including the Belgian chapter of Médecins sans Frontières (MSF), which resolved to avoid competition and forgo Goma-related revenue, refusing to bid on new Goma contracts and replacing its relief operations with an advocacy campaign pushing for limits on the Hutu militant camp presence (Frohardt, Paul, and Minear, 2000). According to MSF's secretary-general, "food represents power, and camp leaders [in Goma] who control its distribution divert considerable quantities towards war

---

[10] Interview in North America with senior Refugee Help staffer, August 25, 1998.

preparations," as well as "skim off a percentage of the wages earned by the thousands of refugees employed by relief agencies."[11] The majority of aid groups, however, chose to stay on. Indeed, MSF's experience is the exception that proves the rule: it was able to protest aid abuse only by opting out of the Goma contract system altogether. As long as relief groups remained embedded in Goma's competitive humanitarian market, institutional pressures forced them to tone down their criticism. These dynamics were not unique to Goma, but are present in other war zones where donor interest attracts multiple relief groups.

In Afghanistan, for example, a similarly competitive NGO environment evolved in the town of Herat, when Taliban forces banned women from schools in 1996. Development and relief NGOs were unable to develop a common response, largely because of inter-NGO competition. Two leading aid groups suspended their education programs in the area, but the Taliban were not deterred, according to journalist Ahmed Rashid, because they realized that "other UN agencies were not prepared to take a stand against them on the gender issue," and because IOs and INGOs in Herat could not mount a sustained negotiating effort. "As each UN agency tried to cut its own deal with the Taliban," Rashid writes, "the UN compromised its principles, while Taliban restrictions on women only escalated" (Rashid, 2001: 113). As had been true in Goma, intra-NGO competition hindered collective protest and empowered local armed forces.

More broadly, the Goma case highlights the role of material struggles within the transnational world, rather than the harmonious and liberalizing civil society of globalization theory. What is striking, however, is that as a result of institutional conditions, nonprofit humanitarian groups were pushed to behave like their for-profit counterparts in the technical assistance sector.

Multiple principals and Bosnia's POWs

Competition also created uncertainty among IOs and INGOs in the former Yugoslavia, and again empowered uncooperative local recipients. Instead of technical assistance or refugee care, however, this case involves the promotion of international humanitarian law, with specific reference to the protection of POWs.

The International Committee of the Red Cross (ICRC) is an international non-governmental organization chartered in Switzerland with a

---

[11] MSF Secretary-General Alain Destexhe, quoted in Bishop (1995: 13).

legal mandate through the Geneva Convention to visit prisoners, organize relief operations, and undertake humanitarian activities in situations of armed conflict. From 1992 to 1995 the ICRC saw its position as the lead international guarantor of POW rights eroded by competition from UN forces and European Community monitors, both of which sought to protect Bosnian POWs. The existence of these multiple principals unduly empowered Bosnian Serb, Croat, and Muslim military commanders, helping them to evade international prisoner monitoring by playing the three international groups off against one another. Strictly speaking, there was less of a monetized "market" in Bosnia than in Goma, where all relief operations were generated through competitive contract tenders. With the exception of the ICRC, IOs did not receive funds explicitly for prisoner-of-war visitation, although their funding overall was tied to their usefulness and productivity. This, in turn, required that they demonstrate engagement with key humanitarian issues, including prisoner protection.

POW monitoring in Bosnia

The ICRC's lead role in prisoner monitoring was established by the Fourth Geneva Convention, which entrusted the Swiss group with responsibility for implementation of international humanitarian law (Forsythe, 1977). The convention stipulates that warring parties must permit ICRC delegates to register and privately interview all war prisoners and to transmit messages from them to their families. Private, one-on-one prisoner interviews and prisoner tracking help to protect prisoners from abuse, disappearance, or murder (International Committee of the Red Cross, 1997). If ICRC delegates learn of abusive conditions during their interviews, they are obligated to confide their findings to prison commanders, local authorities, and senior state officials.[12]

ICRC delegates collect information on prison commanders, evaluating their compliance with the Fourth Geneva Convention. The ICRC's relationship with warring states is highly legalistic, including the signing of an agreement granting the organization the right to visit prisons in accordance with convention and internal ICRC guidelines. Because the ICRC cannot certify compliance with the Geneva Convention without physically inspecting prisons, access is required.

When fighting began in Croatia during the summer of 1991, the ICRC was recognized by combatants, IOs, and Western powers as the sole agency responsible for safeguarding war prisoner rights. To ensure its leading role,

---

[12] In extreme cases, the ICRC may break confidentiality.

the ICRC signed an agreement with Croatian republican authorities, the Yugoslav federal army, Bosnian republican authorities, and other combatants. Although the ICRC did not gain access to all Bosnian prisons, it initially faced no rivals in the monitoring business. Other IOs and NGOs engaged in humanitarian relief work, but none dealt with POWs.

When the fighting in Bosnia began in 1992, however, the UN Protection Force (UNPROFOR) initially sent to protect aid convoys, gradually began to conduct their own inspections of POW camps.[13] The UN soldiers were stationed throughout the Bosnian Croat and Muslim enclaves and were aware of intense international concern for Bosnian POWs, especially following reports of Bosnian Serb prison camp atrocities (Gutman, 1993). UNPROFOR officers were eager to ensure that similar abuses did not occur in their zones of responsibility and hoped to show skeptical donors that they were effective protectors of POWs. After being heavily criticized for not blocking Bosnian ethnic cleansing early on, UN officers were eager to show journalists, Western publics, donor governments, and other significant audiences that they could protect Bosnia's war victims (Rieff, 1995). The agency's normative agenda was thus joined by concern for its image and survival.

A second international organization, the European Community Monitoring Mission (ECMM), was also increasingly keen to protect POWs. The ECMM was an observer mission funded by the European Community, with a vague mission to monitor and reduce violence in the former Yugoslavia. Like its UN counterpart, the ECMM was searching for high-visibility opportunities to prevent human rights abuses. The ICRC had a clear mandate under the Geneva Convention, and UNPROFOR was in Bosnia because of a UN Security Council resolution. The ECMM, by contrast, had been sent there only on the European Community's say so, and thus had less international legal backing. Originally designed by European mediators seeking to monitor long-failed ceasefires, the ECMM was verging on irrelevance. Continued fighting in Bosnia and elsewhere made its work virtually irrelevant, while UNPROFOR's overwhelming presence threatened to marginalize it. POW camp inspections, the ECMM hoped, might justify its existence, enhance its credibility with donors, and secure future funding.

Theorists of global civil society would expect multiple international monitors with similar principled beliefs to cooperate and enhance Bosnian prisoner welfare. Our model, however, suggests the opposite: more

---

[13] The UN Peace Forces were sent to Croatia in 1991 and became known as UNPROFOR in 1992. In 1995 the contingent was split into UNCRO (UN Confidence Restoration Operation) for Croatia and UNPROFOR for Bosnia.

organizations would create multiple-principals problems, empowering local military commanders to subvert external monitoring. This is ultimately what happened.

Before the UN and ECMM interventions, Bosnian military commanders had relied exclusively on the ICRC for certification of their Geneva Convention compliance. ICRC certification, however, was often burdensome to POW prison commanders, as its inspection procedures required unimpeded access to all prison areas and detainees, and private, one-on-one interviews with prisoners, allowing ICRC representatives to obtain accurate information from persons who might otherwise fear to speak out. ICRC delegates were also trained to conduct thorough evaluations of prisoners' mental and physical condition. The art of ICRC prison inspection had been developed over decades, and was closely monitored by internal supervisors.

The UN and ECMM inspectors, by contrast, were poorly trained, rendering their efforts far less effective. Neither organization provided specialized prison inspection training, and neither regarded prison visits as a core function. UN and ECMM staffers typically did not insist on full access and confidential interviews, and thus could not guarantee that the information they received was accurate or that prisoners would not suffer retaliation. More important, the UN and ECMM did not register the prisoners they interviewed, and thus could not track detainees as they were released or transferred. As a result, the UN and ECMM could not know if a prisoner was killed or tortured for speaking freely. Prisoners meeting with the ICRC, conversely, were registered and tracked until their release, upon which they were reinterviewed about their experiences.

The presence of multiple international monitors threatened the welfare of POWs by empowering POW prison commanders to resist proper inspections. Prison authorities preferred the UN and ECMM visits to those of the ICRC, because the latter were more intrusive. Openness to international monitoring was a public relations gain, but UN or ECMM visits were quicker, simpler, and less likely to provoke difficult questions about the fate of individual prisoners, or the conditions in which POWs were held. With three organizations eager to act as principals for the international community, Bosnian commanders, as agents, could pick and choose.

The three-way competition for prison inspections also helped Bosnian commanders to play one IO off against another. When ICRC representatives demanded access to a POW camp, commanders often balked, saying that they had already been visited by the UN or ECMM. Indeed some prison commanders made that argument even if the UN or ECMM had not visited the prison. In the chaos of war and with high turnover rates among international aid personnel, the "prior visitation" argument was plausible.

All three international groups identified themselves to Bosnian commanders as international community representatives seeking to promote humanitarian law. Publicly, all three had normative and complementary agendas. Their organizational environment and interests, however, made cooperation difficult. Here, more organizations did not generate higher rates of prisoner welfare, and competitive pressures did not enhance the efficiency of POW monitoring. Instead of leading to greater POW protection, the multiplicity of concerned transnational organizations empowered prison authorities seeking to evade the requirements of international humanitarian law.

The competitive aid market in Bosnia was not restricted to POW monitoring, however, and INGO competition in Bosnia created other dysfunctions following the 1995 Dayton peace accords. According to one source, local humanitarian NGOs were "quick to fall into competition with each other, vying for donor attention and funding," chasing whatever new donor funds and priorities emerged in a desperate "search for security and employment." Although many Bosnian groups originally were concerned with helping war victims overcome psychological trauma, they shifted their attention to reconstruction and public infrastructure following the reordering of international donor priorities. "Because funding was drying up in one programming area, NGOs, in order to survive, were being drawn to new areas where they had no special expertise and little interest" (Smillie and Todarovic, 2001: 28–31). Contrary to the expectations of liberal globalization theorists, the transnational market for aid in Bosnia led to opportunism and poor project implementation, despite the normative inclinations of local NGO staffers.

Conclusion

Scholars need to rethink their approach to the emerging world of transnational action and advocacy. To date, most theorists have seen transnational groups as harbingers of a new, liberal, and robust civil society, but our theory and case studies suggest that this view may be overly optimistic. The evidence we have compiled suggests that scholars should also analyze the transnational world with tools drawn from the economics of institutions and collective action perspectives. We should recognize the powerful, if often unacknowledged, role of material incentives, competitive struggles, and tacit collusion with uncooperative government officials or local militias. Given the structure of today's transnational world, organizations may find financial considerations more pressing than liberal norms. In short, the firm analogy may have useful explanatory power.

There is no doubt that many of today's INGOs are motivated by normative agendas. Insecurity and competition, however, often pushes them to behave in rational and rent-seeking ways. As scholars of institutional isomorphism have long suspected, organizational environments have powerfully homogenizing effects on their constituent units (Ritzer, 2000). When placed in competitive, market-like settings, nonprofit groups are likely to behave like their for-profit counterparts. Consequently, there should be little disagreement over whether our approach is ontologically appropriate, given that the transnational actors in question are responding to actual market incentives. Donors, INGO contractors, and recipients behave in manners consistent with agency theory precisely because they have entered into contractual relations and, consequently, agents have different preferences from their principals. Complicating matters, preferences among multiple principal are also likely to differ.

The transnational sector has opened new channels for political access and action, but its dynamics are often inconsistent with the views of scholars who argue that the growing number of INGOs will create a liberal and normatively driven transnational civil society. In fact, organizational density and marketization pose a formidable challenge to the consolidation of such a transnational civil society. More is not always better, tenders do not always promote efficiency, and competition does not solely reduce waste. As the volume and intensity of transnationalism grows, scholars should pay as much attention to the tacit material relations among transnational actors as they do to their nominal liberal agendas.

It is likely that different conflicts create different types of humanitarian market, and that different markets will lead to variations in organizational behavior. In some cases, conflicts may take place near or within strong states capable of creating barriers to entry, limiting the penetration of transnational actors, and reducing inter-organizational competition. Elsewhere, competition could be reduced by declining donor interest or tacit donor agreements to divide the aid market. In still other cases, a single donor or aid contractor may dominate the aid market for historical or political reasons, crowding rivals out and creating a more stable transnational hierarchy. Although our analysis is likely to hold true at the most general level, there will be important regional and sectoral variations in transnational markets.

Our analysis highlights structural contradictions within the transnational world, rather than the dispositions or morality of specific transnational actors. Opportunism may be a rational response to institutional configurations of material interests, not an inherent characteristic of individual INGOs. This is an important finding for a field marred by accusations of immorality and corruption. Although we do not ignore individual organizational responsibility, we believe that many problems within the transnational sector, including aid diversion and poor project implementation, are institutionally conditioned.

Our analysis suggests that a large amount of assistance does not guarantee project effectiveness or provide NGOs with the freedom to address their normative concerns or mission, especially in uncertain and chaotic post-conflict environments. Providing NGOs with the opportunity to follow more cause- or mission-driven strategies may require changes in the institutional structure of donor funding. Once established, international NGOs are organizations like any other actor seeking to cope with structural pressures for survival. To survive in a competitive world, they must justify their existence to donors, secure new contracts, and fend off competitors. Under specific institutional conditions, these imperatives will lead them to function like instrumental actors; such conditions are becoming increasingly pervasive especially in the humanitarian aid sector. In the 1990s, scholars established the importance of transnational networks and organizations for global politics; our contribution, as is the focus of the rest of this volume, is an attempt to turn our attention to the material incentives shaping their actions.

References

Aghion, P. and J. Tirole. 1997. Formal and Real Authority in Organizations. *Journal of Political Economy*, **105**(1): 1–29.

Barber, B. 1997. Feeding Refugees, or War? The Dilemma of Humanitarian Aid. *Foreign Affairs*, **76**(4): 8–14.

Berrios, R. 2000. *Contracting for Development: The Role of For-Profit Contractors in U.S. Foreign Development Assistance.* Westport, CT: Praeger.

Bishop, P. 1995. Aid Workers Pull Out of Refugee Camps. *Daily Telegraph*, February 14.

Block, R. 1994. Wolves Lie Down with the Lambs: Killers Are on the Loose among the Refugee Camps in Zaire. *Independent*, July 24.

Boli, J. and G. M. Thomas. 1999. INGOs and the Organization of World Culture. In J. Boli and G. M. Thomas (eds.), *Constructing World Culture International Nongovernmental Organizations Since 1875.* Stanford University Press.

Charlton, R. and R. May. 1995. NGOs, Politics, Projects, and Probity: A Policy Implementation Perspective. *Third World Quarterly*, **16**(2): 237–255.

Cooley, A. 2000. International Aid to the Former Soviet States: Agent of Reform or Guardian of the Status Quo? *Problems of Post-Communism*, **47**(4): 34–44.

Cooley, A. and J. Ron. 2002. The NGO Scramble: Organizational Insecurity and the Political Economy of Transnational Action. *International Security*, **27**(1): 5–39.

Dowden, R. 1994. Battle of Logos and T-Shirts Rages in Refugee Camps: Aid Agencies Scramble for Cash. *Independent*, September 4.

Dowty, A. and G. Loescher. 1996. Refugee Flows as Grounds for International Action. *International Security*, 21(1): 43–71.

Eggertsson, T. 1990 *Economic Behavior and Institutions*. Cambridge University Press.

Eisenardt, K. M. 1989. Agency Theory: An Assessment and Review. *Academy of Management Review*, 14(1): 57–74.

Fainaru, S. 1994. When Death Becomes Casual: Defying Solutions, Rwandan Tragedy Overwhelms the Senses. *Boston Globe*, July 31.

Finnemore, M. 1996. *National Interests in International Society*. Ithaca, NY: Cornell University Press.

Forsythe, D. P. 1977. *Humanitarian Politics: The International Committee of the Red Cross*. Baltimore: Johns Hopkins University Press.

Frohardt, M., D. Paul and L. Minear. 2000. *Protecting Human Rights: The Challenge to Humanitarian Organizations*. Providence, RI: War and Humanitarianism Project, Brown University.

Gourevitch, P. 1999. *We Wish to Inform You That Tomorrow We Will Be Killed with Our Families: Stories from Rwanda.* New York: Picador.

Gutman, R. 1993. *Witness to Genocide*. New York: Macmillan.

Hodgson, G. M. Economics and Institutions: A Manifesto for a Modern Institutional Economics. Philadelphia, University of Pennsylvania Press.

Human Rights Watch/Arms Project. 1995. *Rearming with Impunity: International Support for the Perpetrators of the Rwandan Genocide*. New York: Human Rights Watch.

International Committee of the Red Cross. 1997. *ICRC Action on Behalf of Prisoners*. Geneva: ICRC.

Jelinek, P. 1994. Foreign Aid Fattens Exiled Hutu Regime: Agencies Aghast as Rwandans Plot Return to Power. *Toronto Star*, December 4.

Keck, M. E. and K. Sikkink. 1998. *Activists beyond Borders: Advocacy Networks in International Politics*. Ithaca, NY: Cornell University Press.

Korten, D. C. 1996. *Getting to the Twenty-First Century*. West Hartford, CT: Kumarian.

Lubin, N. 1997. U.S. Assistance to the Newly Independent States: When Good Things Come in Smaller Packages. In K. Dawisha (ed.), *The International Dimension of Post-Communist Transitions in Russia and the New States of Eurasia*. Armonk, NY: M. E. Sharpe.

Luttwak, E. N. 1999. Give War a Chance. *Foreign Affairs*, 78(4): 36–44.

MacFarlane, N. 2000. *Politics and Humanitarian Action*. Providence, RI: War and Humanitarianism Project, Brown University.

March, J. G. and J. P. Olsen. 1989. *Rediscovering Institutions: The Organizational Basis of Politics*. New York: Free Press.

Maren, M. 1997. *The Road to Hell: The Ravaging Effects of Foreign Aid and International Charity*. New York: Free Press.

Mathews, J. T. 1997. Power Shift. *Foreign Affairs*, 76(1): 50–66.

McGreal, C. 1994. Hutu Extremist Holds UN and Refugees to Ransom. *Guardian*, December 5.

Millwood, D. (ed.). 1996. *The International Response to Conflict and Genocide: Lessons from the Rwanda Experience.* Copenhagen: Steering Committee of the Joint Evaluation of Emergency Assistance to Rwanda.

Moe, T. M. 1984. The New Economics of Organization. *American Journal of Political Science,* 28(4): 739–777.

Natsios, A. S. 1995. NGOs and the UN System in Complex Humanitarian Emergencies: Conflict or Cooperation. *Third World Quarterly,* 16(3): 405–419.

North, D. O. 1990. *Institutions, Institutional Change, and Economic Performance.* Cambridge University Press.

Omar, R. 1995. *Death, Despair, and Defiance.* London: African Rights.

Posen, B. R. 1996. Military Responses to Refugee Disasters. *International Security,* 21(1): 72–111.

Powell, W. W. and P. J. DiMaggio (eds.). 1991. *The New Institutionalism in Organizational Analysis.* University of Chicago Press.

Pratt, J. W. and R. J. Zeckhauser. 1985. *Principals and Agents: The Structure of Business.* Boston: Harvard Business School Press.

Prunier, G. 1997. *The Rwandan Crisis: History of a Genocide.* New York: Columbia University Press.

Rashid, A. 2001. *Taliban: Militant Islam, Oil, and Fundamentalism in Central Asia.* New Haven, CT: Yale University Press.

Reindorp, N. and P. Wiles. 2001. *Humanitarian Coordination: Lessons from Recent Field Experience.* London: Overseas Development Institute.

Rekacewicz, P. 2001. How the Burden of the World's Refugees Falls on the South. *Le Monde Diplomatique* (English version), April: 8–9.

Rieff, D. 1995. *Slaughterhouse: Bosnia and the Failure of the West.* New York: Simon & Schuster.

Ritzer, G. 2000. *The MacDonaldization of Society.* Newbury Park, CA: Pine Forge Press.

Ron, J. 1996. *Compete or Collaborate? The ICRC and Other Protection-Related Agencies in the Former Yugoslavia.* Geneva: ICRC.

1999. *Human Rights vs. Humanitarian Relief in the Goma Refugee Camps.* Refugee Help.

Sappington, D. 1991. Incentives in Principal–Agent Relationships. *Journal of Economic Perspectives,* 5(2): 45–66.

Scott, R. W. 1997. *Organizations: Rational, Natural, and Open Systems.* New York: Prentice Hall.

Simmons, P. J. 1998. Learning to Live with NGOs. *Foreign Policy,* 112: 82–96.

Smillie, I. 1997. NGOs and Development Assistance: A Change in Mind-Set? *Third World Quarterly,* 18(3): 563–578.

1998. *Relief and Development: The Search for Synergy.* Providence, RI: War and Humanitarianism Project, Brown University.

Smillie, I. and G. Todorovic. 2001. Reconstructing Bosnia, Constructing Civil Society. In I. Smillie (ed.), *Patronage or Partnership: Local Capacity Building in Humanitarian Crises.* Bloomfield, CT: Kumarian.

Spiller, P. and S. Urbiztondo. 1994. Political Appointees vs. Career Civil Servants: A Multiple Principals Theory of Political Bureaucracies. *European Journal of Political Economy,* 10(3): 465–497.

Tirole, J. 1994. The Internal Organization of Government. *Oxford Economic Papers*, **46**(1): 1–29.

Uvin, P. 1998. *Aiding Violence: The Development Enterprise in Rwanda*. West Hartford, CT: Kumarian.

Vidal, J. 1995. Blood Money. *Guardian*, April 5.

Wapner, P. 1995. Politics without Borders: Environmental Activism and World Civic Politics. *World Politics*, **47**: 311–340.

Weiner, M. 1996. Bad Neighbors, Bad Neighborhoods: An Inquiry into the Causes of Refugee Flows. *International Security*, **21**(1): 5–42.

Williamson, O. 1985. *The Economic Institutions of Capitalism: Firms, Markets, and Relational Contracting*. New York: Free Press.

9 Advocacy organizations, networks, and the firm analogy

Jesse D. Lecy, George E. Mitchell, and Hans Peter Schmitz

Transnational non-governmental organizations (TNGOs)[1] in general, and advocacy groups in particular, have gained considerable visibility and influence in global affairs. Since its creation in 1961, Amnesty International has become an authority on human rights issues around the world. Oxfam, Greenpeace, and Doctors Without Borders have gained a similar status on global issues related to development, the environment, and humanitarian relief, respectively. As these organizations have become significant players in global affairs, scholars across a variety of academic fields have begun to analyze the power of transnational advocacy organizations and their networks (Keck and Sikkink, 1998). The majority of early studies in the academic field of international relations viewed advocacy organizations as altruistic actors seeking to advance universally accepted principles. More recent scholarship responding to the principled advocacy literature has argued that TNGOs are better understood as interest-driven actors motivated primarily by the imperative of organizational survival in a competitive environment (Cooley and Ron, 2002; Bob, 2005; Ron, Ramos, and Rodgers, 2005).

In this chapter, we take a different approach to the study of advocacy organizations by inquiring into the nature of transnational advocacy itself as well as its organization as a collective endeavor at both the level of individual organizations and the level of networks. To answer questions

The authors are listed in alphabetical order; equal authorship is implied. This research was supported by National Science Foundation Grant No. SES-0527679 (Agents of Change: Transnational NGOs as Agents of Change: Toward Understanding Their Governance, Leadership, and Effectiveness) and the Moynihan Institute of Global Affairs at Syracuse University. For comments and suggestions, we thank our entire research team, the anonymous reviewers, the editors Aseem Prakash and Mary Kay Gugerty, and the other contributors to this volume.

[1] "Transnational" and "NGO" have become conventional terms widely used in the academic literature, although activists frequently reject those terms and prefer "international" and "civil society organization." For the purpose of this chapter, we will use the term "advocacy organization" to distinguish this subset of transnational activism from more service-oriented organizations (e.g. CARE and World Vision).

about the role of advocacy in contemporary transnational activism, we rely on evidence collected in a large-scale study based on 152 interviews with leaders of transnational non-governmental organizations registered in the United States.[2]

This chapter engages the issue of "international advocacy and market structures" and explores how TNGO leaders define advocacy and understand the role of collaborations in advancing their goals. Understanding how leaders perceive of their advocacy efforts as well as take part in collaborations as part of transnational networks provides a fresh look, illuminating the organizational and strategic choices within the TNGO sector.[3] By providing insights into how TNGO leaders perceive the advantages and challenges of cross-sectoral coalition-building, we complement Maryann Barakso's contribution and its focus on how brand identity may shape the likelihood of individual organizations entering into partnerships and coalitions. We also agree with McGee Young's concern for how advocacy groups innovate as a result of facing competition from other groups. We add to their insights by providing a detailed account of how TNGO leaders' perceptions about the boundaries of their organizations change as they discuss the role that networks and partnerships play in advancing shared goals.

It is useful to separate the question of how advocacy organizations emerge from questions about their subsequent growth and survival as well as choices of strategies. The first question asks how and why advocacy organizations are initially formed, and, indeed, a collective action perspective provides compelling insights into many of the obstacles associated with organizational creation (Johnson and Prakash, 2007). In this chapter, we take the existence of advocacy organizations for granted and ask in what ways the firm analogy can help us better understand their behavior once formed. We explore this question with regard to how advocacy groups define their goals and activities and the ways they pursue partnerships in efforts to further their objectives.

This chapter is organized as follows. The next section provides a brief overview of the interview study and its methodology. Subsequently, we present two main empirical sections. The first of these examines the extent of instrumental and principled reasoning among TNGO leaders and further explores the empirical and analytical bases for applying the firm

---

[2] A number of earlier large-N studies have focused primarily on TNGOs in the environmental and human rights areas (Smith, Pagnucco, and Lopez, 1998; Rohrschneider and Dalton, 2002; Dalton, Recchia, and Rohrschneider, 2003).

[3] A similar logic is expressed when Michael Barnett and Martha Finnemore argue with regard to inter-governmental organizations (IOs) that "we can better understand what IOs *do* if we better understand what IOs *are*" (Barnett and Finnemore, 2004: 9).

perspective specifically to advocacy organizations. Our data support the view presented in the introductory chapter to this volume that advocacy organizations are driven by both a principled regard for mission accomplishment and a highly salient concern for organizational growth and survival. Rejecting the dichotomous view prevalent in the literature, we hold that TNGOs, including advocacy organizations, are dynamically constrained impact-maximizers (Mitchell and Schmitz, 2009). In this view, financial concerns represent a significant *constraint*, rather than a competing *goal* with regard to the principles embodied in the overall mission of an organization. Most scholarship subscribing to purely principled or self-interested views fails to take into account the long-term behavior of organizations continuously balancing both concerns.

Beyond a discussion of the general motives of TNGOs, we also investigated a basic premise of this volume by searching for a subset of TNGOs in the sample that could accurately be described as advocacy organizations. Using cluster analysis, we found that such a distinct group exists. However, the analysis also discovered a significant difference between advocacy and public education organizations that has implications for the collective action problem. Additionally, advocacy organizations represent a relatively small proportion of TNGOs and most organizations employ highly heterodox strategies including "rights-based approaches" in which advocacy is combined with a range of other methods. If there is indeed a particular subset of TNGOs for which the use of the firm analogy is particularly appropriate, it is conventional service delivery, not advocacy, organizations. Taken together, these results question the applicability of the firm analogy specifically to advocacy organizations and suggest that the relevant scope conditions should be clearly enumerated and justified. Building on this analysis of the TNGO sector, we then turn to questions of how advocacy is produced in networks and other collaborative arrangements.

The second main section discusses how TNGO leaders understand the benefits and challenges of collaboration in partnerships and coalitions. As an empirical matter, advocacy groups regularly form networks to increase their collective leverage, organizing in an alternative form to bounded hierarchies in a market context. While such networks are certainly not free of conflicts and power inequalities mimicking hierarchical relationships (Keck and Sikkink, 1998: 16; Jordan and Van Tuijl, 2000; Bob, 2005), we find evidence that advocacy organizations regularly form non-hierarchical relationships as a core component of their strategies. We recognize that such coalitions do not emerge naturally, based on shared principles alone, and acknowledge that specific opportunities and challenges influence the likelihood of their formation and maintenance. The ubiquitous nature of these networks leads to the question of organizational boundaries in a collective action perspective. We show that TNGO activities are often better understood when the level of analysis is shifted from the organization to the networks they form. We draw upon the literature of the theory of the firm, including transaction costs and asset specificity, to examine the behavior of TNGOs in choosing partnerships and forming coalitions. We also find that advocacy organizations have significant latitude in demonstrating to donors that their efforts are effective, which can be usefully understood within a principal–agent framework. Advocacy organizations usually specialize in highly segmented markets, attracting donors interested in their specific "products" (e.g. anti-slavery, biodiversity, etc.). To the extent that advocacy markets are naturally segmented, competitive pressures are mitigated.

The transnational NGO study

Our researchers interviewed leaders from a sample of 152 transnational NGOs drawn from a population of 299 US-registered international not-for-profits rated by Charity Navigator (www.charitynavigator.org) in 2004/05. The Charity Navigator database was chosen because it provides financial efficiency and financial capacity ratings for each organization, which we used to construct a stratified sample. The population was delimited in order to capture only those organizations widely considered to be TNGOs. The interviews were recorded, transcribed, and coded to enable statistical analysis.[4]

Our approach privileges leadership perspectives. This choice was deliberate and addresses a gap in the existing literature on advocacy groups, which rarely explores how organizational characteristics are linked to strategic choices and outcomes. While our interview data reflect respondents' subjective understandings, we took a number of measures to enhance candor. First, interviewees were assured that their responses would be kept strictly confidential. Second, the team members conducting the interviews assessed the candor of respondents in their debriefing notes written shortly after the interviews; these notes suggest high levels of candor. Also, most respondents exceeded their original time commitments during the actual interviews, indicating a sincere interest in the results of this study. Third, our interview transcripts contain many lengthy and forthright discussions of highly sensitive issues, indicating prima-facie

---

[4] Information about the project, including the codebook, the interview protocol, and a detailed description of the research design and implementation is available on the Transnational NGO Initiative's website (www.maxwell.syr.edu/moynihan_tngo.aspx).

candor. We also organized numerous follow-up workshops with TNGO leaders, which centered on the more sensitive issues related to TNGO governance and accountability. We found in these conversations that organizations face different challenges depending on their size and main activities, but we also found remarkable consistency with regard to what TNGO leaders perceive to be key financial and operational challenges. Finally, the majority of the questions in the protocol do not lend themselves to overt manipulation because they solicit information (e.g. how frequently do you communicate with field offices?) or simply probed leaders' understandings of concepts such as collaboration, accountability, effectiveness, and leadership. Whenever we asked leaders to assess the performance of their own organizations, their answers clustered toward the high end of the range of scores we offered. However, the results presented here are based on responses to questions for which leaders had little incentive to foster false perceptions of their own organizations or the sector overall.

TNGOs and advocacy

This section examines the empirical basis underlying the focus on advocacy organizations and explores how leaders of TNGOs define their goals and strategies to include advocacy. While many transnational groups engage in some form of advocacy, they do so with different emphases and objectives. The TNGO literature tends to generalize from the principled character of advocacy networks and views advocacy in terms of pursuing policy change. Our interviews offer a more complex picture of advocacy organizations. TNGOs vary in the extent to which they employ advocacy techniques and many eschew the label advocacy in favor of less loaded terms, especially public education. Meanwhile many traditional service delivery organizations in the relief and development sector have recently expanded their advocacy efforts and have become much more open to collaborations and partnerships designed to create social and political change that complement their development efforts.

Relief and development TNGOs are increasingly "going global" (Lindenberg and Bryant, 2001) and the expansion of advocacy strategies among such groups signals a decreasing emphasis on service delivery. Many global advocacy campaigns of the past decade (e.g., landmines, small arms, child soldiers, etc.) have not only featured the prominent participation of development and humanitarian organizations, but have also signaled a widespread adoption of the rights-based approach to development (Uvin, 2004) across international institutions and transnational NGOs. The adoption of rights-based approaches to development entails an explicit development of advocacy strategies, previously not necessarily part of needs-based or participatory development strategies. Instead of service delivery, development groups are now paying more attention to empowering local communities to make rights-based claims toward their own governments in areas of education, healthcare, or other public services. Transnational NGOs no longer simply augment under-provided government services, but actively facilitate accountability relationships between populations and governments.

Within this context of a growing role of advocacy strategies across TNGO sectors, the next two subsections confront some of the conventional wisdom on advocacy groups prevalent in the literature. We find that the current literature tends to reduce TNGO behavior to either principled or instrumentalist motives, providing little insight into the complex decisions TNGOs continuously confront. Based on the responses from TNGO leaders, we find that there are several non-trivial differences that distinguish organizations previously subsumed under the advocacy label. We believe that organizations primarily focused on public education (as a form of advocacy) may be facing different pressures than organizations primarily seeking to change public policy through lobbying efforts. Our results show not only significant diversity within the advocacy sector, but also confirm the view that the diffusion of "rights-based approaches" (Nelson and Dorsey, 2007; Hickey and Mitlin, 2009) among development and relief organizations has undermined the service/advocacy distinction.

The focus on advocacy groups

The literature on transnational activism emerging in the 1990s within the international relations discipline addressed a simple puzzle about the increasing prominence of non-governmental organizations generally: how can groups lacking significant material and military resources shape global governance and domestic social and political change? The answer to this question relied upon showing how NGOs[5] acquired unique resources of power while their counterparts lost control relative to those emerging non-state actors. In this view, power is derived from the claim to represent universal principles (e.g. human rights or environmental protection), rather than particular interests. As states increasingly proclaim to

---

[5] The term "NGO" (non-governmental organization) remains contested among scholars (Martens, 2002; Willetts, 2002) and is frequently rejected by leaders of civil society organizations. These reservations are primarily based on the state-centric view expressed in the term non-governmental.

support universal values, activists find a rhetorical opening to push for the diffusion and implementation of global norms. Increasingly porous borders, the decline of conventional sovereignty, and the spread of communication technologies enable advocacy groups to level the playing field.

The so-called principled view is expressed by Keck and Sikkink (1998: 35): "What distinguishes principled activists of the kind we discuss in this volume is the intensely self-conscious and self-reflective nature of their normative awareness." Central to this idea was the existence of a "world culture" (Meyer *et al.*, 1997; Boli and Thomas, 1999) which represents an ideational space separate from parochial state interests. During the 1990s, the emergence of the constructivist viewpoint within the IR literature enabled scholars to move beyond earlier attempts to theorize about transnational relations, which saw those groups primarily as agents of increased state interdependence (Keohane and Nye, 1971). The transnationalism of the 1970s never succeeded in creating a sustained research agenda because it remained limited to a material understanding of world affairs. Transnational activists succeed in their norms-based mobilizations because they can shame norm violators, recruit like-minded allies, build transnational coalitions, and ultimately persuade others to follow collectively shared understandings of appropriate behavior. Many studies sharing this view then proceeded to describe the expansion of the transnational non-governmental sector as a sign of an emerging "global civil society" and to view each new organization as further proof of the growing strength of underlying norms (Anheier, Glasius, and Kaldor, 2004; Salamon and Sokolowski, 2004).

More recent scholarship on transnational activism has challenged the principled view of non-governmental actors and advanced a more traditional material and interest-based explanation for the emergence and expansion of the sector (Cooley and Ron, 2002). In this view, transnational activism is not *replacing* a world of material nation-states with a principled global civil society, but is most likely *reproducing* the domestic power of non-state actors and the global inequalities of the state system (Rohrschneider and Dalton, 2002: 511). Transnational activism is driven by market forces which are likely to reproduce the existing power differentials between the North and South (Bob, 2005). Advocacy organizations such as Amnesty International or Human Rights Watch do not pick their targets primarily on the basis of the greatest violation of human rights principles, but instead are driven by a need for mass media exposure and for securing increased funding (Ron, Ramos, and Rodgers, 2005). Organizations more oriented toward traditional service delivery find themselves in an increasingly competitive environment as they seek out contracts and donor resources. As a result, the growth of the transnational non-governmental sector is interpreted not as a sign of the growing strength of global norms, but as a free-market scramble of self-interested TNGOs vying for attention in an economic environment of limited donor funds.

Until recently, we lacked systematic, cross-sectoral studies that could help us evaluate the validity of this dichotomous perspective. The field has remained largely driven by case studies and in-depth analyses of specific campaigns that have attracted the attention of scholars because of their success and media prominence. Such examples include the landmines campaign (Price, 1998), the establishment of the International Criminal Court (Glasius, 2002; Spees, 2003), the conflict diamond issue (Tamm, 2004; Le Billon, 2006), the role of transnational networks in humanitarian relief (Cooley and Ron, 2002) and the promotion of human rights and environmental concerns on the global, national, or local level (Wapner, 1995; Keck and Sikkink, 1998; Risse, Ropp, and Sikkink, 1999). But case studies tell us little about the larger population of organizations or what position advocacy organizations hold in relation to other types of NGOs.[6]

What do TNGOs actually do?

The concept of advocacy as a transnational practice remains poorly defined and understood and consequently what constitutes and distinguishes an advocacy organization is also a largely neglected topic in the literature. Our interviews reveal a more nuanced understanding of advocacy than commonly found in the literature. A first observation from our qualitative evidence indicates that interviewees are generally reluctant to use the term "advocacy" and prefer to use terms such as "research" and "public education." This can partly be explained by legal requirements associated with not-for-profit status under US Internal Revenue Service (IRS) regulations. Under section 501(c)(3) an organization with tax-exempt status cannot "participate in, or intervene in (including the publishing or distributing of statements) any political campaign on behalf of (or in opposition to) any candidate for public office." While interview responses indicate that this legal requirement has some salience in privileging references to public education, it cannot account for the observed heterogeneity among most organizations with respect to their goals and strategies. Transnational NGOs are not only focusing much of their attention abroad and are therefore less likely to run afoul of the American tax code, but the law also explicitly allows not-for-profits to

---

[6] See note 2 for exceptions to this dominance of case studies in the field.

take positions on any public policy issue as long as they do not favor or oppose a specific candidate running for office. While the legal context defines the basic perimeters of permissible advocacy strategies, other factors related to the external environments of TNGOs (variation in principals or the contexts in which they operate) as well as their internal characteristics, shape the choice of program activities beyond what scholars label "policy advocacy."

Second, our study finds that it is important to analytically distinguish between TNGOs, advocacy organizations, and public education organizations. Theorizing about heterogeneous classes of goal-directed actors, such as TNGOs or advocacy organizations, is a difficult task because it is hard to identify a single non-trivial characteristic (such as budget maximization or average-cost minimization) that all TNGOs share in common. Because model fit is generally improved with narrower scope conditions, many scholars concentrate on particular subsets of TNGOs rather than on TNGOs writ large. The majority of TNGO studies thus focus on a single sector (e.g. human rights, environmental protection) or even a single organization or campaign. Implicit in this kind of analysis is the assumption that differences among various types of NGOs and sectors exist. One of the more common ways of dividing up the nongovernmental sector is by goals and activities, i.e. service delivery vs. advocacy, which also appears to serve as a means for defining the boundaries of some academic subdisciplines in this area. Cooley and Ron, for example, focus mainly on service delivery NGOs. While international relations scholars tend to focus exclusively on the role of a small number of prominent transnational advocacy groups, development studies frequently focus on very different types of (transnational) NGO seeking to improve the livelihoods of the poor in the global South.[7] If we assume that this strategy of breaking down the field of NGO studies is a useful intermediate step for improving model fit, then we can develop more accurate theories of TNGOs by considering their more homogeneous constituent subgroups separately. A theory of the firm or collective action approach to understanding TNGOs, in other words, may be a better match for some types of TNGO than for others. To better judge the empirical basis for this implicit scope condition, we explored the structure of our sample with hierarchical cluster analysis and found that a distinct

---

[7] These differences are also reflected in the primary publication venues. IR scholars will write about advocacy organizations (or "global civil society") in *International Organization*, *World Politics*, or *International Studies Quarterly*, while journals such *World Development* or *Development and Change* serve as outlets for authors interested in the non-governmental development service sector.

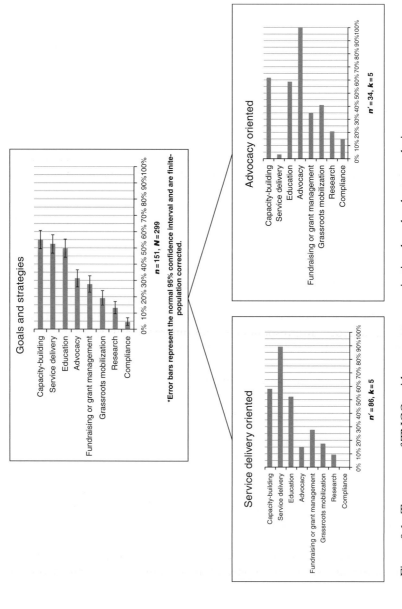

Figure 9.1. Taxonomy of TNGOs with respect to organizational goals: cluster analysis.

advocacy subset does indeed emerge. We find some evidence that the traditional distinction between service delivery and advocacy organizations is justifiable, although it is increasingly challenged by the widespread adoption of rights-based frameworks among development organizations. However, although the traditional distinction finds some (temporary) empirical support, it fails to capture widespread heterogeneity within the most important classes of organization.

The TNGO study enables us to examine the taxonomic problem directly. The interview protocol contained an open-ended question asking TNGO leaders: "What is it that your organization is trying to accomplish?" Respondents answered in their own words and their responses were organized into nine emergent response categories. The categories were public education, advocacy, grassroots mobilization, compliance monitoring, service delivery, research, capacity-building, fundraising or grant management and other. Since the collective action perspective posits that firms are goal-directed actors, we wanted to explore what organizational goals actually prevail among TNGOs and to assess the appropriateness of focusing on a single subset – advocacy organizations – as if they were a distinct and coherent subgroup.

We performed hierarchical agglomerative cluster analysis on the interviewees' responses to search for substructures in the data. The algorithm iteratively combines organizations into increasingly large groups based on a similarity measure. Respondents with similar answers are combined into the same group and respondents with different answers are placed into different groups. Clustering in this context generates a taxonomy of TNGOs in which we would expect a significantly large and distinct subgroup of organizations to emerge specializing in advocacy. We did not know how many groups would emerge from the data, so we evaluated conventional stopping rule statistics to identify the optimal number of groups and visually inspected the dendrograms and group-level statistics to ensure that the results were clear and meaningful. Once the optimal number of groups was determined, it was possible to examine the characteristics of the organizations within each of the groups. We found that advocacy organizations did emerge as a distinct subset of the TNGO sample, but that the overall taxonomy is much more complex than is commonly assumed, raising questions concerning the implicit scope conditions for the framework presented in this book.

The number of groups that produces the cleanest taxonomy is five, of which the largest two are of interest here.[8] Figure 9.1 is intended to be

---

[8] The other three groups are characterized as public education oriented ($n = 11$), capacity-building oriented ($n = 13$), and null ($n = 7$). They are excluded for convenience of display.

read from the top down. Overall, capacity-building, service delivery, and public education are the most prevalent organizational goals and strategies among US-registered TNGOs. Advocacy is significantly less pervasive. When the sample of organizations is disaggregated, two main groups emerge, the larger of which contains organizations oriented toward service delivery. TNGOs in this group are primarily engaged in service delivery, capacity-building, and education. The smaller group that emerges contains organizations oriented toward advocacy. TNGOs in this group are engaged in advocacy, followed more distantly by capacity-building and education. Leaders' responses suggest that service delivery organizations rarely engage in advocacy and that advocacy organizations almost never engage in service delivery. Several interesting findings follow from these results.

First, advocacy organizations themselves appear to be divided on the question of whether they are actually doing advocacy or public education. The top graph in the figure shows that leaders overall are more likely to report public education as a goal or strategy than they are to mention advocacy. Not shown in the figure is another group of eleven organizations classified as education-oriented. The existence of this education-oriented group suggests that many respondents preferred the term education instead of advocacy, not merely in conjunction with it. This can be partly attributed to respondents' sensitivity to US laws that restrict not-for-profits from certain types of political activity. However, there may also be a more substantive distinction to be made between organizations that lobby institutions on the one hand and engage in strategic communications directed at the public on the other. It is not clear whether the collective action perspective, or firm analogy, would apply equally to both types of organization. In terms of obtaining funding, for example, advocacy organizations may have more concentrated constituencies seeking more specific policy changes and exercising greater influence as principals. Public education organizations, by contrast, may have more diffused constituencies (including funders) as they focus instead on influencing public discourses in a more general manner. Both types of organization produce goods and services that are ideational in nature and which exhibit different economic characteristics than do material goods and services. Ideational outputs are essentially public goods: they are costly to produce, free to reproduce, and non-excludable, and the benefits cannot be reliably captured by individual organizations – except perhaps through vigorous branding efforts connected with fundraising. To the extent that advocacy or public education organizations specialize in the production and diffusion of ideas, we would expect coalitions and networks to be more efficient organizational forms than traditional, more clearly circumscribed firms.

Second, the organizations in the largest group of TNGOs are not primarily engaged in advocacy. The majority of TNGO leaders reported capacity-building, service delivery, and public education as their core organizational goals, which is consistent with the increasingly popular "rights-based approach" in the transnational development sector. In other words, for most TNGOs advocacy is only one component within a multifaceted constellation of goals and strategies, and not even the most prominent one. Insofar as this largest group of TNGOs is more likely to produce material goods and services that are costly to reproduce, excludable and saleable, it seems logical to suppose that service delivery organizations – rather than advocacy organizations – more closely resemble bounded firms, which are able to capture some of the benefits of their activities for their members, thus solving the collective action problem.

Whether the arguments presented in this volume refer to advocacy organizations, public education organizations, both, or NGOs generally is not obvious without a more detailed explication of why advocacy organizations should be singled out as being particularly amenable to the collective action perspective, or firm analogy.

Production functions, theories of the firm, and organizational boundaries

Amnesty International USA recently opened an online store offering T-shirts with the AI logo under the signature line reading "Fighting Bad Guys Since 1961" ($17.95–19.95). Many consumer items can now be had with the AI logo, including (for $720) a "Fender Amnesty International Music for Human Rights Acoustic Guitar." Only a decade ago, such a marketing effort would have been frowned upon by many inside and outside of this venerable transnational human rights organization. The brand "Amnesty International" now sells and it can be used in partnerships with for-profit organizations (such as the Fender Corporation) to attract consumers to certain products as well as principled causes. Critics would say that AI has "gone corporate" and may see this as further vindication of the appropriateness of a firm analogy. In this section, we discuss in what ways the creation of goods or services is similar to or different from what advocacy organizations produce. In what ways is the creation of non-tangibles like public discourse or legitimacy different from services or goods?

The introduction to this volume emphasizes that "a careful appreciation of the similarities and differences between NGOs and firms can help scholars to employ insights from theories of firms to explore the organization and functioning of advocacy organizations and inform knotty management and policy concerns about accountability, evaluation, and governance" (Prakash and Gugerty, this volume). The appeal of this lens is self-evident: the theory of the firm provides a coherent framework that can be adapted to advocacy organizations in order to generate insights about their behavior. In order for this research agenda to be effective, scholars should develop non-traditional ways of thinking about firm activity, transactions, assets, and boundary issues specific to transnational advocacy groups. Specifically, we argue here that boundaries of advocacy organizations are protected in order to maintain brand identity and revenue models distinct to the individual firms. But in studying the production of social change, the network is the more appropriate unit of analysis.

Norm production

What exactly do advocacy organizations do? In the most generic sense firms combine capital, labor, and technology to produce economic output in the form of products or services. One can argue similarly that advocacy organizations combine norms, information, strategies, mass communication channels, and coalitions to produce a consensus about social issues, to influence policy or implementation, or to change behaviors. Advocacy groups primarily rely on communicative power – the ability to persuade or influence key decision-makers or the general public. In a for-profit marketplace a transaction occurs between two individuals or firms. In the marketplace for ideas, participants exchange competing ideas in public in ways similar to a transaction. In this way, the primary activity of an advocacy group is to produce, or reproduce, norms shaping the public sphere or campaigns targeting institutional and policy change. They challenge the status quo through ideas, persuasion, education, and lobbying.

Add to this another layer of complexity: norm production as an industry is difficult to commodify, so NGOs often resort to carefully managing their brand since it is a key factor for their funding strategies (see Barakso, this volume). Name recognition translates to legitimacy in the eyes of donors and membership fees from individuals. Such legitimacy translates into income through the commodification of the brand, such as Amnesty International's symbol of a candle behind barbed wire. The larger and better-known an organization is, the more opportunities will arise to market its brand. In 2003, the Nature Conservancy, for example, received $100,000 from S. C. Johnson & Sons to use their logo in its ads. Although we can say generally that (most) advocacy groups (re-)produce principles and can profit materially from building a brand around those ideas, we find that larger and more prominent groups are much more likely to enjoy such direct material gains.

We also find that advocacy groups are more likely to share success as members of transnational networks that soften the boundaries of individual organizations. While service delivery organizations primarily deliver material resources (e.g. food aid, micro-credit, shelter) or tangible services (e.g. cleft palate surgeries, potable water) and the outcome can be easily traced to their activities, advocacy groups frequently join in large networks sharing tasks of lobbying governmental officials and educating the public. In the case of service delivery, a per-unit cost-minimization scheme may be a very useful way of understanding behavior or creating benchmarks for donors. In the case of advocacy organizations, the emphasis is less on securing a contract by demonstrating cost minimization in direct competition with others. Instead, the focus is on impact maximization driven by the participation of a large number of like-minded activist organizations contributing their diverse resources to a common cause.

While we know that advocacy groups are engaged in advancing principles, we have not yet developed compelling ways of characterizing these activities in a collective action framework. If one accepts norm production or campaign production as the primary activity of advocacy organizations then it is not clear whether the organization or the network should be the appropriate unit of analysis. The next section discusses in what ways economic theories can explain the permeability of organizational boundaries.

Organizational emergence and boundary

From a superficial reading of the theory-of-the-firm perspective, networking by an NGO is somewhat paradoxical. While it makes intuitive sense to create internal hierarchies which facilitate hiring, training, and fundraising, advocacy NGOs also build and maintain resource-intensive external networks with many of their natural competitors. Why would the advocacy organization create distinct boundaries between itself and the market of ideas and then proceed to blur those boundaries by entering into partnerships with governments, corporations, and other NGOs? The answer emerging from our study focuses primarily on the benefits which accrue from partnering with others or from building short-term coalitions during specific campaigns (see Figure 9.2). This observation raises the question of the appropriate level of analysis. We suggest that the researcher focus on the advocacy networks instead of the NGO itself.

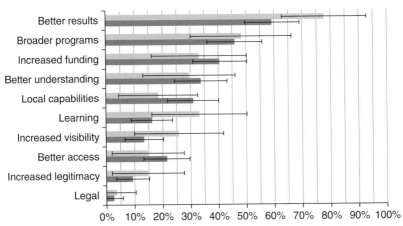

Error bars represent the normal 95% confidence interval and are finite-population corrected.

Advocacy-oriented, *n* = 27 Service-oriented, *n* = 74

Figure 9.2. Transaction costs and organizational boundaries: benefits of collaboration.

Individual advocacy organizations rarely act alone to further their agendas. They play a crucial role in bringing together a collection of individuals, giving norms a voice, aligning interests and strategies, developing campaigns, and creating an emotional link between membership/staff and the mandate. Advocacy organizations have strong incentives to enter networks and partnerships in order to utilize shaming strategies, exchange information and resources, amplify their voice, or extend their reach in the large-scale mobilization of public opinion.

In this section we address the question of organizational emergence using two classic perspectives from the theory of the firm: transaction costs (Coase) and asset specificity (Williamson). Both perspectives are explored in order to make the argument that the network, not the organization, is the appropriate level of analysis in studies of advocacy organizations. Organizational boundaries can be understood through the necessity to commodify a brand in order to generate revenue, but studies that desire to understand efficiency or effectiveness considerations in the norm production process need to utilize network-level perspectives.

Coase's (1937) lynchpin article on the theory of the firm explores the question of why firms exist in the first place. He surmises that transaction costs such as price discovery and the enforcement of contracts are the friction in the commercial machinery. These costs are minimized by trading market mechanisms for the direction of an entrepreneur within the confines of an organization. Employees give up certain freedoms and accept high task specialization in order to perform more efficiently than they would alone in the marketplace. According to Coase, "a firm will tend to expand until the costs of organizing an extra transaction within the firm becomes equal to the costs of carrying out the same transaction by means of an exchange in the open market or the costs of organizing in another firm" (Coase, 1937: 395). In this way, a theory of organizational emergence develops. If economic activity can be made more efficient (and thus profitable) by hierarchical organization, then collective action via incorporation ensues. When no gains are possible, transactions take place within a marketplace.

NGOs prove to be a more difficult case. Advocacy organization allows individual activists to specialize in areas of fundraising, research, and community-organizing, for example, and thus many people working together can be more efficient than their working alone. But these organizations also engage in resource- and time-intensive relationships with other organizations with which they may compete for funding. These activities create transaction costs. Members of a network must first identify a common set of issues shared by all parties. Then members must agree upon guiding principles for action and outline strategies that they believe will lead to desired outcomes. Finally, plans must be devised, delegated, and resourced in order to achieve the stated goals of the campaign or network. Coordination and conflict resolution occur in every step of this process. If the firm is a meaningful boundary for advocacy organizations, then why would they undertake these costly activities? Coase's transaction cost theory of the firm does not adequately explain the empirical behavior of advocacy organizations.

Williamson's modern synthesis of the theory of the firm offers a more nuanced examination of organizational boundaries. He predicts that high asset specificity leads to strong boundaries, whereas low asset specificity results in more open-market transactions between firms. Asset specificity arises when a technology or product is developed that is central to a firm's operation and is expensive to develop. If this asset is created through a contractual partnership then the firm is vulnerable to the partner seeking rents or colluding with the competition. As a result, highly specific assets are generally developed within an organization. Asset specificity can affect the complexity of organizations in an industry and their propensity to collaborate (Williamson, 1986).

Asset specificity within the industry of advocacy can be understood as contacts, knowledge, advocacy approaches, or expertise that gives one NGO a comparative advantage over others. In practice there is little evidence that advocacy organizations seek to develop idiosyncratic assets or achieve comparative advantage. Instead, market segmentation offers a more plausible explanation of revenue models. All environmental organizations market themselves to environmentally minded members, for example, but some organizations market themselves to those who wish to preserve wilderness areas (Sierra Club) and others market to those who care about the preservation of species (World Wildlife Fund). The technologies of these two organizations are interchangeable, though, so organizational boundaries are driven by the need for a clear brand signal, not the protection of assets.

The low asset specificity of advocacy NGOs leads to an important prediction about their behavior. Increasing competition for resources will not lead to a reduction in partnerships since partnerships are not a threat to comparative advantage. We argue that the organizational boundary is useful for understanding the NGO revenue model – organizations need to build and maintain individual brands so that they can attract members, secure grants, and win contracts – but the boundaries do not adequately capture the productive activities of these NGOs. Advocacy work is better understood at the level of the network since it is largely through networks that advocacy organizations achieve their goals. Thus a collective action approach to the study of NGOs necessitates two levels of analysis – sustainability of individual firms studied at the organizational level, and the effectiveness of campaigns at the network level.

This proposition received empirical support from the TNGO project results. Partnerships and networks are considered essential to achieving outcomes. As the leader of one large TNGO explained, "there are huge benefits [of partnerships]. It's about making the issues heard rather than having a single voice; it's about building popular momentum... around issues that otherwise would not have traction." When asked about the benefits of collaboration, the most common response was that it leads to better results, a view shared by almost 80 percent of the advocacy organization leaders interviewed. The leaders also emphasized that networks lead to better understanding of issues, broader programs, more funding, and learning (see Figure 9.2).

Partnerships are important, but they are not cheap. The resources allocated to building and maintaining these relationships are sizable, and thus the decision to create or enter networks is an important organizational process. Further analysis of the data is likely to yield additional insights into which types of organization are more likely to prefer going it alone, working loosely with others, or building closer partnerships. We know that service-driven organizations bidding for a contract to deliver certain goods to a given region will have incentives to partner with local organizations. This insight is confirmed in Figure 9.2, where service

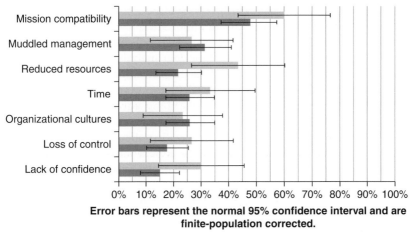

Error bars represent the normal 95% confidence interval and are finite-population corrected.

▨ Advocacy-oriented, $n=30$ ■ Service-oriented, $n=73$

Figure 9.3. Obstacles to collaboration.

organizations name better access and local capabilities more frequently when asked about the benefits of collaboration.

Similar differences emerge with regard to the data on "obstacles to collaboration" (Figure 9.3). Advocacy groups much more frequently name "loss of control" and "incompatibility of missions" as disincentives to collaboration. While service delivery groups are more likely to find themselves in short-term contractual situations where the goals are externally imposed, advocacy groups are more concerned about maintaining autonomy.

Conclusions

Interviews with leaders of 152 US-registered TNGOs active across multiple sectors of transnational activism provide unique insights into the meaning of advocacy in everyday practices and the significance of collaborations and partnerships in shaping the boundaries of organizations and the nature of collective action. In this chapter we explored how a collective action perspective is likely to advance our understanding of advocacy organizations and their behavior. We agree with the claim articulated in this volume that advocacy organizations are not exclusively principled *or* self-interested and assert, based on evidence from our study, that TNGOs can be understood as dynamically constrained impact-maximizers.

Our research confirms that advocacy groups do represent a small but distinct and coherent subset of TNGOs. However, for the overwhelming majority of TNGOs advocacy only represents one component of a diverse menu of goals and activities, raising important questions about the justification for a focus on not-for-profit organizations that specifically undertake advocacy as a primary activity. Our data analysis challenges the focus on the "advocacy" sector and identifies theoretically relevant distinctions among advocacy organizations, public education organizations, and TNGOs generally. TNGO leaders describing advocacy-like goals and strategies as public education may face different incentives than those pursuing lobbying strategies aimed at specific policy change. These findings challenge the scope conditions for the applicability of the firm analogy because it is likely that different types of advocacy NGO may face different incentives from different stakeholders.

We explored the emergence of organizational boundaries through transaction costs and asset specificity considerations as key concepts and found some evidence which sets advocacy groups apart from service delivery or profit-making enterprises. We observed from our interviews that advocacy organizations operate more as nodes in unbounded social networks than as bounded institutions with clear hierarchies and hard distinctions between the domestic and the external environment. In practice, our interview respondents systematically blurred the lines between their own organization's activities and those of other actors within their networks. On paper, advocacy organizations may appear to the outside world as bounded hierarchical organizations with official headquarters, professionalized staff, and unique objectives. However, our study reveals that this formality is sometimes just sustained for tax and legal purposes and is less relevant when describing organizational activity. More work is needed to understand the calculus of partnership undertaken by each organization when determining whether to enter partnerships and with whom.

While one could view advocacy organizations as a relatively small subgroup of TNGOs writ large, we are only beginning to understand the value of the firm analogy in explaining the behavior of activists, organizations, and networks engaging in collective action with respect to advocacy. Our data suggest that advocacy NGOs exhibit many similarities to firms in dealing with organizational survival and competition for funding. But as communicative actors nested in dense social networks, advocacy groups have developed ways of organizing that defy conventional notions of bounded firms operating in markets. Advocacy organizations generate results by entering into networks integrated by shared norms and understandings, which suggest alternative organizational impetuses to those normally thought to motivate firms.

We find in the interviews that advocacy is a multilayered and heterogeneous concept. Leaders of advocacy groups engage in very different types of activity designed to change policies and behavior. In addition, most advocacy groups pursue their goals in collaborative ways and routinely build transnational networks to enhance their voices. The types of collaboration we identify fall into two major categories – partnerships and networks. While the academic literature tends to generalize across all networking activities, we find that leaders themselves distinguish between partnerships, understood as more formalized efforts at pooling resources for project implementation, and networks, defined as more loosely connected coalitions focused on information exchange. Both networks and partnerships offer TNGOs opportunities to overcome collective action problems and force scholars to take networks and other collaborative arrangements seriously when deciding on the proper level of analysis.

Three current developments point toward future directions in research and may have significant long-term effects on the activities of organizations engaged in advocacy. First, growth among TNGOs and other not-for-profits is not evenly distributed and the gap between the wealthiest and the least wealthy organizations is increasing. We expect that differences in size will become more pronounced and wonder whether a wealth gap could undermine possibilities for collective action at the network level. Second, the landscape for acquiring funding for organizations is diversifying and offers new challenges as well as opportunities. All TNGOs are facing greater scrutiny from individual and institutional donors seeking a measurable return on their investments. Additionally, not-for-profit rating agencies represent a new force in the sector, and their evaluative practices create incentives for organizations to satisfy relatively narrow financial efficiency criteria (Schmitz and Mitchell, 2009). At the same time, most TNGOs are acutely aware of the need to become more accountable to those they are claiming to help (Ebrahim and Weisband, 2007). Third, the shift toward multifaceted rights-based approaches among development-oriented organizations creates opportunities for new collaborations across sectoral divides, but also challenges traditional mandates and requires knowledge on how to effectively manage complex relationships within networks and across borders. Balancing the needs and demands of an increasing number of widely dispersed stakeholders represents a key challenge to the TNGO sector.

References

Anheier, H. K., M. Glasius, and M. H. Kaldor. 2004. *Global Civil Society 2004/5*. London: Sage.
Barnett, M. and M. Finnemore. 2004. *Rules for the World. International Organizations in Global Politics*. Ithaca, NY: Cornell University Press.

Bob, C. 2005. *The Marketing of Rebellion: Insurgents, Media, and International Activism*. Cambridge University Press.

Boli, J. and G. M. Thomas (eds.). 1999. *Constructing World Culture. International Non-Governmental Organizations since 1875*. Stanford University Press.

Coase, R. 1937. The Nature of the Firm. *Economica*, 4: 386–405.

Cooley, A. and J. Ron. 2002. The NGO Scramble: Organizational Insecurity and the Political Economy of Transnational Action. *International Security*, 27: 5–39.

Dalton, R. J., S. Recchia, and R. Rohrschneider. 2003. The Environmental Movement and the Modes of Political Action. *Comparative Political Studies*, 36: 743–771.

Ebrahim, A. and E. Weisband (eds.). 2007. *Global Accountabilities. Participation, Pluralism, and Public Ethics*. Cambridge University Press.

Glasius, M. 2002. Expertise in the Cause of Justice. Global Civil Society Influence on the Statute for an International Criminal Court. In M. Glasius, M. Kaldor, and H. Anheier (eds.), *Global Civil Society 2002*. Oxford University Press.

Hickey, S. and D. Mitlin (eds.). 2009. *Rights-Based Approaches to Development. Exploring the Potential and Pitfalls*. Sterling, VA: Kumarian Press.

Johnson, E. and A. Prakash. 2007. NGO Research Program: A Collective Action Perspective. *Policy Sciences*, 40: 221–240.

Jordan, L. and P. Van Tuijl. 2000. Political Responsibility in Transnational NGO Advocacy. *World Development*, 28: 2051–2065.

Keck, M. E. and K. Sikkink. 1998. *Activists Beyond Borders. Advocacy Networks in International Politics*. Ithaca, NY: Cornell University Press.

Keohane, R. O. and J. S. Nye (eds.). 1971. *Transnational Relations and World Politics*. Cambridge, MA: Harvard University Press.

Le Billon, P. 2006. Fatal Transactions: Conflict Diamonds and the (Anti) Terrorist Consumer. *Antipode*, 38: 778–801.

Lindenberg, M. and C. Bryant. 2001. *Going Global. Transforming Relief and Development NGOs*. Bloomfield, CT: Kumarian Press.

Martens, K. 2002. Mission Impossible. Defining Nongovernmental Organizations. *Voluntas. International Journal of Voluntary and Nonprofit Organizations*, 13: 271–285.

Meyer, J. W., J. Boli, G. M. Thomas, and F. O. Ramirez. 1997. World Society and the Nation-State. *American Journal of Sociology*, 103: 144–181.

Mitchell, G. E. and H. P. Schmitz. 2009. The Strategic Pursuit of Impact: A Cross-Sectoral Analysis of Transnational NGOs. Moynihan Institute of Global Affairs, Syracuse, NY.

Nelson, P. J. and E. Dorsey. 2007. New Rights Advocacy in a Global Public Domain. *European Journal of International Relations*, 13: 187–216.

Price, R. 1998. Reversing the Gun Sights: Transnational Civil Society Targets Land Mines. *International Organization*, 52: 613–644.

Risse, T., S. C. Ropp, and K. Sikkink (eds.). 1999. *The Power of Human Rights. International Norms and Domestic Change*. Cambridge University Press.

Rohrschneider, R. and R. J. Dalton. 2002. A Global Network? Transnational Cooperation among Environmental Groups. *Journal of Politics*, 64: 510–533.

Ron, J., H. Ramos, and K. Rodgers. 2005. Transnational Information Politics. NGO Human Rights Reporting, 1986–2000. *International Studies Quarterly*, **49**: 557–587.

Salamon, L. M. and S. W. Sokolowski. 2004. *Global Civil Society. Dimensions of the Nonprofit Sector*. Bloomfield, CT: Kumarian Press.

Schmitz, H. P. and G. Mitchell. 2009. Bracing for Impact. *Monday Developments*, **27**: 20–22.

Smith, J., R. Pagnucco, and G. A. Lopez. 1998. Globalizing Human Rights: The Work of Transnational Human Rights NGOs in the 1990s. *Human Rights Quarterly*, **20**: 377–412.

Spees, P. 2003. Women's Advocacy in the Creation of the International Criminal Court: Changing the Landscapes of Justice and Power. *Signs: Journal of Women in Culture and Society*, **28**: 1233–1254.

Tamm, I. J. 2004. Dangerous Appetites. Human Rights Activism and Conflict Commodities. *Human Rights Quarterly*, **26**: 687–704.

Uvin, P. 2004. *Human Rights and Development*. Bloomfield, CT: Kumarian Press.

Wapner, P. 1995. Politics Beyond the State: Environmental Activism and World Civic Politics. *World Politics*, **47**: 311–340.

Willetts, P. 2002. What is a Non-Governmental Organization? In UNESCO (ed.), *Encyclopedia of Life Support Systems: Encyclopedia of Institutional and Infrastructural Resources*. Oxford: Eolss Publishers.

Williamson, O. E. 1986. *The Economic Institutions of Capitalism*. New York: Free Press.

10 Shaping civic advocacy: international and domestic policies toward Russia's NGO sector

Sarah L. Henderson

In the past few decades, advocacy organizations have grown in number and variety in virtually every region of the world, creating what some have termed a "global associational revolution"; a development, they argue, which may match the significance of the rise of the nation-state in the late nineteenth and early twentieth centuries (Salamon, Sokolowski, and List, 2003). This expansion has been mirrored by an increased scholarly interest in understanding more clearly what has contributed to the emergence, structure, and impact of this sector. In particular, a collective action approach, which assumes that advocacy NGOs, like firms, can be viewed as instrumental actors pursuing policy goals in policy markets (Prakash and Gugerty, this volume), highlights the ways in which institutional context, at both the domestic and international levels, can affect the supply and demand for advocacy. Domestic factors, such as the legal environment, levels of organizational capacity, financial viability, and infrastructural support, as well as larger socio-economic and political contexts can stimulate or dampen domestic demand for advocacy organizations, as well as raise or lower the costs of advocacy provision. In particular, as Bloodgood (this volume) notes, governments can dramatically shape the costs of advocacy, through the passage of a wide array of permissive and/or constricting regulations, the establishment of policy machinery that grants access to advocacy organizations, and the provision of funding. In addition, the international context has also become an important variable; since the 1980s, bilateral and multilateral development agencies, as well as various private foundations, have become actively involved in providing technical and financial assistance to advocacy organizations in primarily developing and democratizing regions of the world, in the hopes of strengthening the nonprofit sector, and by extension, civil society, and often, ultimately, democracy. These actors have also had a substantial impact on the supply and demand of advocacy by privileging (through funding and other forms of technical assistance) some advocacy themes over others and supporting advocacy organizations that may not have survived on domestic demand alone. In sum, governments and international donors both act as critical advocacy NGO principals in that they both provide resources for and impose costs on actors in the advocacy industry.

Advocacy sectors arising out of the ashes of communist systems in Eastern Europe and the former Soviet Union were faced with particular collective action challenges. Despite the international euphoria over the sudden collapse of authoritarian regimes, citizens and governments alike, in addition to addressing economic and political transitions, faced a significant social transition as well, and often in an unfriendly and hostile socio-economic environment. Except for cases such as Poland, most societies had little experience with the concept or practice of organizing independently of the state, and social norms and patterns of association were still heavily influenced by the communist past. As a result, there was little domestic demand for organized advocacy; as a region, the postcommunist bloc in the 1990s had the lowest levels of independent organization among democratizing countries (Howard, 2002). And governments were often overwhelmed by the task of drafting and bolstering the regulatory framework to support and encourage not only a nonprofit sector (which was often not a top priority) but an institutional democracy and market economy as well. Meanwhile, the international context had also shifted significantly; inspired by the romantic image of "people power" in Eastern Europe, bilateral and multilateral donors dramatically stepped up levels of funding and technical assistance for fledgling advocacy organizations, often focusing on Western-style advocacy organizations that worked on human rights, women's rights, and other issues they considered central to democracy-building. In the postcommunist context, given that many of these societies had little previous experience with anti-state advocacy, international donors were often "purchasing" the demand as well as providing the supply of advocacy. As a result, the impact of donors on the emergence and shape of advocacy sectors was particularly marked.

This chapter looks at the emergence of the advocacy sector in one of the most critical postcommunist cases, Russia, and asks how the institutional context at the domestic and international levels impacts the supply of and demand for advocacy NGOs. During the Yeltsin era (1991–1999), the domestic government did relatively little to either facilitate or impede NGO development, while foreign donors at the international level often provided the key material and social supports for advocacy organizations. In contrast, during the Putin presidency (1999–2008), the administration implemented a variety of policies that have the potential to dramatically reshape the advocacy sector. Stating a desire to directly involve Russia's citizens in Russia's regeneration, the Putin administration has among other things, created a federal-level Public Chamber to advise the Duma on social issues, increased domestic funding for non-governmental organizations, and urged businesses to give to "appropriate" charitable causes. This has been combined with hostility toward Western donors and their efforts to promote the development of a nonprofit sector (and indirectly, democracy) in Russia. Prompted in part by concerns that Western aid had facilitated democratizing "color revolutions" in the neighboring countries of Georgia, Ukraine, and Kyrgyzstan, President Putin pushed for the passage of new legislation in 2006 governing NGO registration and state oversight. The international reaction to these changes has been overwhelmingly negative; as one critic has argued, these policies are "virtually strangling" NGOs, and by extension, democracy in Russia (Proskuryakova, 2005). In this interpretation, these policies toward NGOs are part of a larger effort to stifle all opposition to the state in an effort to regain some of the political centralization, power, and prestige of the days of the former Soviet Union. In addition, they are part of a broader backlash against the perceived interference of foreign actors on Russia's "sovereign affairs," and represent an organized campaign to counteract the influence of external, pro-democratization forces.

Yet, drawing from interviews and survey data collected from NGOs in eight cities in five regions from 2002 to 2004[1] as well as primary documents from Russian NGOs and government bodies, this chapter argues that the Putin policies have had a significant impact on NGOs, but often in unexpected and unusual ways. It argues that the administration does not seek to eradicate the demand for, and supply of, advocacy NGOs; rather, it is presenting an "import substitution" model of development for the third sector by providing domestic institutional incentives to replace the role of international donors in impacting supply and demand for advocacy.[2] Further, the state, rather than seeking to stamp out all advocacy NGOs in general, has designed a system to favor the supply of NGOs that work on issues that align with the national interest.[3] Finally, despite

---

[1] Regions covered are Central Russia (Moscow), Southern Russia (Rostov and Krasnodar), Urals (Ekaterinburg), Siberia (Irkutsk and Novosibirsk) and the Russian Far East (Novosibirsk and Yuzhno-Sakhalinsk). In addition, the author draws from interviews with NGO activists, local government officials, and USAID officials resulting from her participation as the civil society expert for the assessment of USAID's Democracy Program (ARD, 2005) as well as her authorship of the Russia section of the United States Agency for International Development's work on the 2004 NGO Sustainability Index for Central and Eastern Europe and Eurasia (USAID, 2005).

[2] The author would like to thank the editors, Aseem Prakash and Mary Kay Gugerty, for pointing out the parallels with import substitution industrialization strategies.

[3] One reviewer maintained that in the Russian case, advocacy organizations are not analogous to firms because, in the reviewer's view, firms with government connections are considered trustworthy while advocacy organizations, particularly those interested in social justice issues, that have government connections are not seen as trustworthy, or doing their jobs.

the concerns that an all-powerful state has the ability to dampen the supply and demand of advocacy, the Russian case indicates that the increased legislative and policy infrastructure has created an increased role for advocacy NGOs, particularly at the regional level. While the government holds the upper hand, the situation is not as dire as pundits predict. More broadly, the Russian case tells us how states, particularly in newly democratizing countries with little previous experience of anti-statist advocacy politics, shape the costs of organization, by lowering and/or erecting legal and financial barriers to activism.

NGO emergence

What factors facilitate the emergence of NGO sectors, and advocacy organizations? What is the role of the state in facilitating, impeding, or shaping the incentives and costs of organizing? The answers to these questions are complicated by the fact that two threads of scholarship tend to give competing, and sometimes contradictory, answers. While civil society literature tends to focus on organizations' abilities to counter state power, the NGO literature tends to be much more pragmatic, focusing on NGOs' legal autonomy but simultaneously recognizing the significance of their partnership activities with the state. These two views create particular problems for interpreting the development of the non-profit sector in Russia.

On the one hand, civil society refers to the space of "uncoerced human association and also the set of relational networks ... that fill this space" (Walzer, 1992: 89). This focus on the autonomous nature of civil society emphasizes the space's separation from the state. And in practice, the collapse of communism revived the interest in civil society as an anti-statist project, in that it served as a critical bulwark against over-encroaching state power. At the same time, however, the state is actively involved in terms of institutionalizing the space through laws, regulatory frameworks defining the space as well as citizens' rights to maneuver within it. As Cohen and Arato argue, "both independent action and institutionalization are necessary for the reproduction of civil society" (Cohen and

However, the author and editors argue that this distinction does not hold up under closer inspection. As argued later in this chapter, in most countries, advocacy organizations receive a substantial portion of their funding from the government; yet, the reliance on government funding does not necessarily impact their trustworthiness. Further, there are many examples of firms that have connections with government that are not seen as trustworthy (in the United States Blackwater and Haliburton are examples). The larger point of this chapter is that governments play a large and understudied role in shaping the costs of advocacy, and that previous analysis of the Russian case has tended to look at government policy as shutting down rather than setting the costs of different types of activism.

Arato, 1992: ix). And as Michael Walzer points out, the state "fixes the boundary conditions and the basic rules of all associational activity." He continues: "Civil society requires political agency. And the state is an indispensable agent – even if the associational networks also, always, resist the organizing principles of state bureaucrats" (Walzer, 1992: 104).

In practice, the rise of the nonprofit sector in the post-World War II era has complicated the already complex theoretical relationship between the state and civil society, for governments have become critical players in influencing both the supply of and demand for advocacy NGOs. As Bloodgood (this volume) explains, governments rarely (if ever) serve as neutral actors that respond to advocacy pressures; rather, they can raise or lower the costs of organization and operation. Legislation often stipulates conditions for NGO registration, operation, and dissolution. Further, states can potentially encourage the growth of the nonprofit sector by passing laws, which, for example, grant NGOs tax exemptions, or provide tax deductions for corporate and individual giving to nonprofits. Legislation regulating NGO earned income and the possibility of competing for government contracts and procurements are other ways in which states can impact the shape of the nonprofit sector.

In addition, governments (often in response to citizen mobilization) have added what is known as "policy machinery," or formal and informal systematic links between policymakers and organized segments of the public. Often, these mechanisms take the form of government bodies, such as commissions and/or panels devoted to promoting particular interests, such as women's rights, human rights, environmental rights, etc. The establishment of this machinery has often been seen as a critical development for advocacy groups seeking to gain access to and influence on the state (Stetson and Mazur, 1995). Thus, NGOs assist and seek to influence governments in other ways, by providing input on initiatives, commenting on legislation, drafting legislation, or providing other forms of expertise. As Bloodgood (this volume) notes, the degree to which the presence of this policy machinery is symbolic as opposed to real often depends on how much governments need the information, expertise, services, or even resources from NGOs as well as the degree to which NGOs may need access, information, or material resources from the state. This relationship may be asymmetric, depending on the degree to which each side needs something from the other and the relative capacity of each. Further, the nature of the relationship depends on the comparative advantages of both the government and the NGOs, as well as the complementarity of both sets of players' goals.

Further, the expansion of the welfare state, and states' efforts to offload some of their responsibilities onto NGOs has meant that NGOs now wear many different hats in their relationships with states. With regard to social service provision, they have become critical partners, implementing programs, often with state funding. This source of income for NGOs is significant; worldwide, while fees are the largest source of support for NGO sectors (53 percent), governments provide 35 percent of NGO funding, while the private sector, in the form of philanthropy, provides a mere 12 percent (Salamon, Sokolowski, and List, 2003). Strong state support tends to facilitate NGO emergence; a comparative study of NGO sectors found a positive relationship between the monetary level of support for nonprofit organizations and the size of the nonprofit sector. All of these trends certainly complicate the theoretical concept of civil society's autonomy from the state. This trend has also complicated the actual relationships between organizations and the state, in terms of how they organize, how they are funded, and how they interact with their constituencies and the state. In sum, while many of the various strands of literature addressing advocacy organizations stress their roles as a counterweight to the state (expressed primarily through protest), in reality, advocacy sectors effectively counter and balance the state by also working with it, and cooperation is as much a part of effective state–society relations as is confrontation.

Finally, international actors working to promote advocacy organizations abroad and transnational advocacy also define the incentives and costs for advocacy organization and, ultimately, impact the supply and demand for advocacy. In particular, donors, through the provision of moral support, technical assistance, and financial funding to advocacy organizations, can provide critical support to domestic NGOs that work in hostile political, economic, and social environments, thus counteracting some of the domestic impediments to advocacy provision. Keck and Sikkink maintain that international support can help advocacy organizations impact policy by providing further pressure on recalcitrant domestic governments (Keck and Sikkink, 1998). Yet, others have questioned how the supply of additional resources and assistance from abroad (often according to the funding themes donors are willing to support) will impact what used to be perceived as primarily a process driven by domestic levels of demand. Marina Ottaway characterizes donor programs as "supply driven" in that donors define the parameters of the programs and advocacy organizations respond to them (Ottaway, 2000). This creates perverse incentives, Clifford Bob maintains; advocacy groups respond to the supply of funds from abroad by drifting from their domestic constituencies that they claim to represent. Given the often more generous terms of foreign funding, these groups have few incentives to expand their domestic support base. Often taking on new projects unrelated to their former missions, they ultimately undermine their long-term sustainability (Bob, 2002). The result is a sector that advocates on the behalf of largely silent constituents. The outcome is the development of vertical relationships between domestic advocacy groups and their international patrons, often at the expense of domestic needs (Henderson, 2003). In sum, while states are still the critical players in terms of setting up the institutional and regulatory framework for NGOs, international donors have increasingly played a supporting role in shaping advocacy, and often in unexpected and not always positive ways.

As mentioned previously, advocacy sectors in postcommunist countries faced particularly severe challenges. Apathetic (or exhausted) citizens had little time to participate in (and thus demand) advocacy. Governments had to quickly establish the legal parameters defining and supporting a sector, while also completely restructuring the political and economic systems. At the international level, many donors hoped to export patterns of civic associationism to areas of the world that had little domestic preconditions for independent civic activism, and funded a variety of projects that provided technical and financial assistance to thousands of newly formed NGOs.

This task was particularly difficult in Russia, where Soviet patterns of associationism were inculcated the longest, where support for the transition to democratic governance and free-market economics by both the population and elites was uneven, and where the logistics of Russia's political, economic, and social transitions were perhaps most severe. And, as the decade of the 1990s wore on, it seemed as if Russia was caught in a "gray zone" between democratic transition and consolidation, until under President Putin it began to move toward increasingly autocratic tendencies. In this context, how does the Russian state shape the costs of organizing, the financial structure and membership of organizations, determine access to the state, and impact advocacy strategies? The following sections compare and contrast how domestic institutions and international actors provided resources for and imposed costs on advocacy actors during the Yeltsin (1991–1999) and Putin (1999–2008) presidencies. While the Yeltsin era demonstrated a relatively indifferent policy stance toward NGOs, leaving early development efforts in the hands of international players, President Putin established a much more vigilant state, designing policies to lessen the impact of foreign donors and increase support from the state for advocacy groups working on issues that align with national interests.

Yeltsin's Russia: NGOs' first decade

The advocacy sector during the Yeltsin era emerged from less than ideal domestic conditions, although the international context was relatively conducive to advocacy NGO formation. In the first decade following the collapse of the USSR, Russia's continued financial crisis ensured that NGOs faced a relatively hostile socio-economic environment and struggled to find enough social and economic capital to survive. While the Yeltsin administration did not attempt to impede the nonprofit sector, or citizen activism more generally, it also implemented relatively few policy initiatives to encourage it. Nor were there many formal mechanisms or channels of communication between the federal government and society, and those that existed were infrequently used. The nonprofit sector that emerged in the first decade of the post-Soviet era was weak, fragmented, and poorly connected with political elites and with the populations it claimed to represent. Of the organizations that did operate, many were either holdovers from the Soviet era, or heavily dependent on Western aid and support for their survival.

In the first decade of postcommunist Russia, Russia's third sector grew from a ragtag collection of forty or so informal organizations to more than 450,000 formally registered organizations as of early 2001, although, as we shall see, this figure is somewhat deceptive (USAID, 2002). Many NGOs formed in response to the economic exigencies of the 1990s, trying to fill in the gaps created by a collapsed state. In the first nine years of reform, gross domestic product (GDP) declined by 45 percent. The majority of the population watched their standard of living fall precipitously, while a small, wealthy elite benefited enormously from a flawed privatization process. As a result, the economic meltdown provided an initial impetus for organization, and as many as 70 percent of NGOs were involved in some type of social service provision in an effort to cover the social responsibilities of a quickly retreating state (Alexeeva, interview, October 7, 2002). Many of these organizations were originally state-supported Soviet-era groups, representing strata such as the disabled, pensioners, and veterans, for example, and were continuing their work as legally independent entities. Leaders of organizations perceived themselves as concerned with preserving quantity of life, rather than furthering quality-of-life issues. NGO activists explicitly perceived themselves as advocates involved in "rights protection" rather than the Western-style advocacy rhetoric of human rights. Western-styled advocacy NGOs, that is organizations that attempted to shape the public agenda, public opinion and/or legislation, were virtually non-existent. Organizations that self-identified as involved in advocacy often had learned the word (which was transliterated into Russian) as a result of exposure to Western technical or financial assistance (Henderson, 2003).

Yet, while the economic climate of the 1990s provided the impetus for organization and issue focus, it simultaneously kept groups from developing a stable presence. There was a large gap between the statistical presence of NGOs and the substantive reality of their operations; a much smaller percentage of groups carried out their activities on a regular basis. Rather, they operated sporadically when time and money permitted. Groups were often weak and fragmented, or consisted of a membership of one (Nikitin, 2001). Outside of the major metropolitan areas, NGOs were thinly stretched across vast swathes of territory, and there were enormous differences in levels of NGO development between and within Russia's regions (Sevortian and Barchukova, 2002).

Further, there were few incentives to encourage a professionalized staff to fill the NGOs. Citizens rarely chose the nonprofit sector for a career; one very optimistic estimate placed the number of people involved in the nonprofit sector at about 1 percent of the country's adult population (Oslon, 2001). In addition, the lack of university programs in nonprofit management made it difficult for NGOs to consistently recruit talented students to a profession in the nonprofit sector (Borovikh, interview, Fall 2002). Further, the terminology of nonprofits was unfamiliar to many Russians, who often could not understand the difference between a nonprofit organization and an organization that was not making a profit.

This situation was further exacerbated by the lack of legislation creating a friendlier environment for NGO emergence. The Russian Constitution of 1993 granted all of the rights that one associates with fostering a civil society – freedom of speech, assembly, press, etc. A small collection of legislation pertaining to nonprofits would soon follow in 1995 and 1996, with the passage of the law "On Public Associations" (1995), the law "On Charitable Activity and Charitable Institutions" (1995), and the law "On Noncommercial Organizations" (1996). However, the legislation was confusing, and poorly articulated. No single system for registration existed, and NGOs could register, depending on the territory and scope of their operations, at the local and/or regional departments and agencies or through the Russian Federation Department of Justice. As a result, the amount of required paperwork (which even then was quite substantial) differed, as did the cost of registering. One aspect that was relatively uniform was the lack of regulation of the sector; while the federal law required public associations to submit an annual report to the Department of Justice, the Department did not have any legal basis to penalize NGOs or the staff to enforce regulations. In 1999, with no clear idea how many NGOs were operating at which level (federal, regional, or local), the Department issued a decree requiring all NGOs to reregister in the hope of finding out how many organizations had dissolved in the previous years. Thus, while there was a legal framework defining NGO rights and activities, it was complex, poorly communicated, and inconsistently implemented across the regions (Henderson, 2003).

Nor did the Duma follow up with further legislation that is commonly used in other countries to support a third sector, such as the provision of tax breaks for individuals or businesses engaged in charitable activities. Businesses could donate up to 3 percent of their profits, but businesspeople were often hesitant to admit to making a profit, and thus incite state interest in their taxable revenues. Even if the citizenry had money and time to give, there were no legal incentives to stimulate activism, checkbook or otherwise.

Many NGOs also lacked a visible constituency. Organizations were small, insular, and wary of outreach to the public. In turn, citizens were ambivalent about joining organizations. While citizens deserted their former Soviet-era organizations, they did not immediately run out and join new ones. Russia's rate of associationism in the 1990s, at 0.65 organizations per person, was low, even for postcommunist countries, which, as a bloc, had the lowest rates of organization among democratizing countries (Howard, 2002). Most citizens had neither the time, the money, nor the inclination to devote to organizations, either as workers, volunteers, or donors. Many viewed NGOs with hostility, mistrust, or, at best, indifference (Howard, 2002; Henderson, 2003). This distrust was no doubt magnified by a series of scandals involving legally registered nonprofit organizations the 1990s. For example, in the period 1992–1995, the National Foundation for Sports became the biggest importer of alcoholic beverages in Russia, providing for 80 percent of imports (Dokuchaev, 1997). In addition, the financial pyramid "MMM," which absconded with millions of people's savings, called people's investments "charitable donations." This was problematic; without domestic sources of support (financial as well as moral), NGOs struggled to sustain themselves, not only in terms of financial resources, but in human resources as well. In addition, however, the lack of a visible constituency made it difficult for NGOs to be taken seriously by government administrations at the local, regional, and national levels.

This was compounded by the lack of machinery to allow NGOs access to influencing government policy. There were few formal mechanisms of communication between NGOs and government. NGOs could attempt to establish relations at the federal level with the administrative offices, but it often depended on NGO initiative and personal connections. The experience of establishing an administrative bureaucracy on human rights is instructive. The 1993 Constitution created the office of Ombudsman, a national representative for human rights, to be elected by the legislature, although it could not come into being until the passage of federal legislation defining the parameters of the office. Russia's accession to the Council of Europe in 1996 meant that it needed to enact legislation securing the office. Thus, in May 1996, Yeltsin issued a decree "On the Russian President's Human Rights Commission," establishing the composition and mandate of the body, and in December, after three years of efforts, the legislature passed a law creating an Ombudsman's office, although the Duma could not agree on an ombudsman by absolute majority until May 1998 (Saari, 2009). Thus, throughout much of the Yeltsin administration, mechanisms, even if they existed on paper, often did not materialize, or materialized much later than originally planned.

There were more formal channels of communication at the regional and local levels, although the channels were rarely used. Most regional and city governments had an administrative department whose job was to communicate with social actors, often defined as media, political parties, and/or social organizations (the most commonly used Russian term to refer to NGOs). In addition, some of the developments that were to become more formalized under the Putin regime originated in the Yeltsin era. For example, in 1994, the Yeltsin administration had encouraged regional governors to set up Public Chambers (Obschestvennaya Palatas), where representatives of registered social organizations could participate in the review of legislation pending before the regional Duma and offer recommendations for further revision (Petro, 2001). Regional governors responded to these urgings differently; cities such as Novgorod the Great, for example, already had such an institution, while other regions ignored the suggestion. Overall, however, NGOs had difficulty gaining access to government at the federal level, and gaining access at the regional or local level proved the exception rather than the rule. Finally, the lack of any kind of stable party system also made it difficult for NGOs to influence state policy. A large percentage of the representatives of the Duma in initial elections had no party affiliation. NGOs complained that this party instability made it difficult to establish relationships with politicians; there was no guarantee that aligning with a party would create greater access, since few parties survived from election to election, and independent candidates were not bound by clear ideological preferences or policy positions with which NGOs could reliably align. What little influence NGOs gained was through making personal connections, for there were few incentives to work with parties.

As a result, bilateral and multilateral donors, as well as a host of international organizations and foundations, were often the only forces working actively to promote a nonprofit sector. While USAID was the most visible actor promoting a nonprofit sector, the agency was not alone; the European Union, the United Kingdom, Canada, and Scandinavian countries also sponsored civil society programs through their development agencies. They were joined by international agencies such as the

United Nations and the World Bank, and by foundations such as George Soros' Open Society Institute, the Ford Foundation, the MacArthur Foundation, and the C. S. Mott Foundation.

Donors such as USAID tended to move through phases of funding strategies designed, in part, to create a new, rather than support a pre-existing, nonprofit sector. This was, in part, because independent organ-ization was not legalized until the early 1990s; thus, there was no preexisting sector to work with, although, certainly, groups had begun to appear in the era of Gorbachev. In addition, Soviet-era groups, which were now legally independent and thus technically part of a nonprofit sector, were judged to be too "Soviet" in mentality, approach, and activity to merit Western aid, which was directed toward groups that reflected, even if only in rhetorical statements, a new, democratic, pro-Western sentiment. And groups that adapted Westernized NGO rhetoric also sought out international donors in the face of public apathy. Thus, in the early to mid 1990s, USAID sponsored several partnership programs, which joined Russian organizations with Western counterparts in order to transfer knowledge and skills from experienced Western NGOs to infant Russian ones. Other programs focused on providing training and techni-cal assistance to NGOs on such topics as registration, social marketing, budgeting, etc. USAID then worked to expand beyond the major metro-politan areas, where the larger NGOs were located, by sponsoring small grants competitions to distribute money to smaller organizations scat-tered all around Russia. Starting in the mid 1990s, USAID began to focus more intensively on funding networking projects, and on supporting resource centers in order to spread knowledge and expertise to regional NGOs located far from Moscow.[4] Many of these centers evolved into civil-society development organizations, and focused on facilitating gov-ernment interaction or community activism, rather than simply providing services to regional NGOs. At the end of the Yeltsin era, USAID, in addition to its work with NGOs, moved toward stimulating citizen acti-vism in the hope of fostering the emergence of a civic culture as well as building social capital.[5] The approach to developing grassroots activism

---

[4] These efforts to strengthen regional development evolved into the Pro-NGO Program, which linked over twenty resource centers in four regions in an effort to further institution-alize NGO development in the far corners of Russia. In addition, a separate project run by ISAR in the Russian Far East also linked NGOs across a broad expanse of territory.

[5] The second Civic Initiatives Program, located in the Russian Far East, as well as Pro-NGO-funded grant competitions, marked the shift away from a solely NGO focus to one with a broader definition of civic participation. Programs such as "You the People," as well as the Community Service School Program, further moved USAID away from the nar-rower NGO approach.

was, in many ways, top-down; build a few large NGOs from the start, then hope they spread and multiply from the center outward.

The combination of weak domestic support for a nonprofit sector and Western and Westernized support created a strange mix of voluntary organization. On the one hand, international assistance was invaluable in terms of helping to create a weak nonprofit sector where none had existed ten years previously. These efforts created an entirely new vocabulary for activists as well as a new way of visualizing and creating linkages with the state, political society, other actors on the civic sector, and the private citizen. Concepts such as advocacy and government transparency, the idea of women's rights as human rights, and even terms such as NGO all entered the discourse within the small NGO community. It was not as if Russians could not grasp the ideas behind the terms; however, foreign donors helped teach the specific language of advocacy, even if the translations were figuratively and literally quite awkward. (For example, there is no real Russian word for advocacy; activists simply transliterate it into Russian.) However, donors' emphasis on "Western" NGOs that promoted issues such as human rights and women's equality often meant that they were working with a relatively narrow and unrepresentative group of NGOs. For example, the majority of "human rights" organizations were Soviet-era groups that worked to protect the rights of vulnerable groups, such as the disabled, the developmentally delayed, or the elderly; yet, to donors, supporting human rights meant supporting a small group of activists dedicated to exposing the crimes of the Soviet system and the weaknesses of the new Russian one. Further, donors' efforts to supply funding for projects which they wanted to see, rather than responding to domestic NGO demand, often created a civic sector heavily reliant on Western funding and divorced from the Russian clientele it claimed to represent (Sperling, 1999; Mendelson and Glenn, 2002; Henderson, 2003). Issues such as combating domestic violence and establishing safe houses for abused women were well supported by donors such as USAID and the Ford Foundation during the 1990s, but had difficulty finding resonance among a Russian public caught up in an economic and social transition of unparalleled magnitude.

In sum, the domestic environment for NGOs under the Yeltsin administration can best be described as one of benign neglect. While the economic conditions provided the stimulus for organization, a lack of legal regulation and policy machinery, as well as a pervasive culture of apathy, meant that NGOs struggled for survival. Western aid was the predominant player in terms of encouraging Western-style versions of a third sector; however, in the absence of amenable domestic conditions, the impact was limited, and at times, subversive. These conditions were to change significantly under the Putin administration.

The Putin presidency

Since Vladimir Putin's accession to the presidency on December 31, 1999, many have argued that although Russia still adheres to the institutional forms of democracy (elections and the codification of civil rights and liberties in the Constitution), nonetheless, the actual democratic content has eroded considerably, if not vanished completely (McFaul and Stoner-Weiss, 2008). Relatively uncompetitive presidential and legislative elections, a quiescent legislature, neutered political opposition, and a centralized federal structure reconfigured to give the President increased powers of appointment to formerly elected positions are all attempts to channel and recentralize political power to a level unprecedented since the collapse of the USSR. Other critical supports that have traditionally strengthened democratic systems, such as independent media, have been eroded substantially, and the arrest and imprisonment of Mikhail Khodorkovsky, Russia's richest oligarch and also a Kremlin opponent, indicated that Russia would be governed by the selective use of rule by law, rather than rule of law.

Reflecting the centralizing trends in the design of institutionalized politics, President Putin has established a much more directed approach toward citizen activism. If the Yeltsin administration presided over a negligent state *vis-à-vis* civil society, President Putin has established a vigilant state. The creation of the Public Chamber, the reconfiguration of the Presidential Council on Civil Society Institutions and Human Rights, expansion of the human rights ombudsman's office, increased government funds for NGOs, legislation allowing for social service subcontracting, as well as the Law on Local Self-Governance all establish or further delineate formal mechanisms of communication and financial support between the state and society. Further, the Duma passed additional legislation regulating the nonprofit sector. These changes at the federal level have led to the replication of these efforts throughout Russia's eighty-nine territorial units at the regional level. At the federal level, these changes have been met with dismay among academics and policy practitioners interested in promoting democratic development in Russia (Stoner-Weiss, 2007; USAID, 2007). Yet, these changes, rather than eradicating the space for autonomous citizen activism, reshape that space, and often in interesting and unexpected ways. Legislation governing NGO organization and registration, state support and funding for NGOs, and the establishment of formal channels for citizen input, in and of themselves, are not unusual in advanced industrialized (and stable democratic) societies (Salamon, Sokolowski, and List, 2003); thus, the question lies in the design and implementation of these policies within a weakly democratic state rather than necessarily the presence or absence of them. The following sections discuss how the Putin administration has approached advocacy NGOs, and how these policy preferences translate into the supply of advocacy in Russia.

Unlike Yeltsin, President Putin has talked quite extensively about NGOs and, more broadly, civil society in a variety of speeches. Putin's overall statements reflect, like other areas of his political vision, a different view of civil society and democracy, in which he wants to join Europe while maintaining commitment to Russian cultural values and traditions of centralized power and paternalism. Certainly there is a tension between these two. Putin's vision of civic activism, for example, is one in which "people, participating in civil society, will regard as of primary importance not so much the idea of freedom, not so much the idea of interests, as the idea of service to a certain common cause" (quoted in Evans, 2005). In his view, civic groups can create unity and overcome distrust among social groups and serve as a force to pull together the nation in agreement on the main strategic tasks facing the country. The value of various actors within civil society is in their abilities to serve as potential helpmates and midwives to the state. Putin's vision is one that emphasizes patriotism rather than political protest as a mobilizing theme. Thus, in speeches since 1999, he has simultaneously bemoaned the underdevelopment of civil society and the inability of various organs of the state to effectively communicate and collaborate with it.

This interest in harnessing Russia's social organizations that work primarily on improving the direct quality of people's lives has been coupled with a suspicion of those Russian organizations that work on larger democracy-themed issues that have found support from the myriad Western organizations and foundations promoting civil society and democracy in Russia. Putin addressed this issue in his State of the Union address of May 2003; some NGOs, he maintained, were primarily concerned with obtaining financial resources from abroad, or served "dubious group and commercial interests." As a result, he argued, these civic groups do not serve the real interests of the people, in contrast to the thousands of organizations on the ground which continue their work unnoticed. This contrast between the "fake" nonprofit sector, which is motivated solely by money and career aspirations, and the "real" nonprofit sector, toiling away out of patriotic concern for the fate of the country, was reinforced in a meeting with the Kremlin-friendly youth group Nashi. Putin declared that "[w]e need a civil society, but it must be permeated by patriotism, concern for one's country, and should do things not for money but from the heart, eager to put right those problems that we indeed have and do this, I repeat, not for money but as the heart dictates" (BBC Monitoring, 2006). This suspicion of Western donors soon turned to hostility as a result of the color revolutions in the neighboring countries of Georgia, Ukraine, and Kyrgyzstan in

2003–2005. In each country, massive protests, in reaction to disputed elections, led to the resignation or overthrow of the previous, more authoritarian leadership. Western-funded pro-democracy NGOs often led the opposition forces, and were widely credited with playing a pivotal role in pushing for a more democratic (and pro-Western) electoral outcome. Suspicion of Western donor motivation in Russia soon turned to hostility against Western interference in Russia's informal "sphere of influence" as well as Russia's "sovereign affairs."

As a result, President Putin launched substantive policy changes, which reflect an "import substitution" model of advocacy development. NGO policies embody a nationalist approach to reducing foreign dependency through the "local" production of advocacy, which is driven by an active and interventionist state. For example, President Putin has steadily increased and formalized corporatist mechanisms of communication between NGOs and the state. Putin revived the Yeltsin-era idea of Public Chambers as a way to facilitate state–society collaboration, although this time at the federal level. In 2001, the Kremlin organized the Civic Forum, a conference that brought together 5,000 civic activists from across Russia and key government personnel. This was the first time that government officials and NGO representatives from throughout Russia met to discuss various pressing social issues in an effort to create more channels of communication and a potential for greater NGO–state cooperation. In November 2004, the government unveiled legislation to create a Public Chamber at the federal level in order that "citizens' initiatives could be presented and discussed" (BBC Monitoring, 2004). This legislation was subsequently passed and came into effect on July 1, 2005. The key function of the Chamber is to submit recommendations to members of the Duma about domestic policy and proposed legislation, and to request investigations into potential breaches of the law as well as request information from, and monitor, state agencies (Evans, 2006). The members of the Chamber also serve on one of eighteen commissions that examine bills or provide advice and expertise to the Duma on a variety of pressing issues, such as public control over the activities of law enforcement and reforming the judicial system, communications, information policy and freedom of expression in the media, culture, healthcare, environmental policy, and so on (Obschestvennaya Palata, 2008).

Reflecting the centralizing trends of Putin's other reforms, membership is driven from the top down; the President designates one-third of the membership, and those appointed members will, in turn, appoint another third of the members. The two-thirds then will pick the final third nominated by regional social groups. This federal-level Public Chamber has been replicated in most of Russia's eighty-nine territorial units.

In addition, in 2002, the President reconfigured the existing Commission on Human Rights to create the Presidential Council on Civil Society Institutions and Human Rights, with thirty-three members drawn from human rights and broad-based social organizations as well as individuals from other institutions of civil society (www.sovetpamfilova.ru). While some feared that this was an attempt to dilute the human rights element of the committee, the administration pointed out that it already had the equivalent of a human rights commissioner (and resulting policy machinery) with the office of the Human Rights Ombudsman (which as of 2007 was fielding 48,235 complaints) (Commissioner for Human Rights, 2008).

Finally, in 2003, the Duma adopted legislation which, though not specifically directed at NGOs, will potentially impact on their activities. The Federal Law on Local Self-Governance, which further delineates the division of legal and financial authority between federal and regional power structures and local government, took effect (Shipov, 2003). Over one-third of the regions began to put the legislation into practice in 2006, and full implementation was slated for the beginning of 2009. In particular, chapters 3–6 of the law provide avenues for citizen participation on issues of "local significance" such as the formation and execution of municipal budgets, the provision of utilities and other government services, and on housing reform and city planning. It allows for local referenda sponsored by citizens where the outcome is binding, and establishes mechanisms to recall deputies or other elected officials of local self-government (Rossiiskaya Federatsiya, 2004). While still largely untapped, this legislation provides additional formal opportunities not just for NGOs, but for citizens more broadly, to organize around and mobilize around particular interests.

The federal government has also provided financial support for NGOs, in part to counter Western assistance. In 2006, the federal government authorized the Chamber to distribute 500 million roubles ($15 million) to NGOs in a grant competition. The following year, the amount was more than doubled to 1.25 billion roubles ($50 million) to fund grant competitions in projects related to youth, health, civil society, and socially disadvantaged groups, to education, culture, and art, and to support social-related research. In 2008, the number was raised again to 1.5 billion roubles (roughly $70 million), and the expected sum for 2009 was 2 billion roubles.[6] While the first grant competition was organized by the Public

---

[6] In 2008, the most money was budgeted towards education, art, and cultural initiatives (320 million roubles), followed by youth initiatives (250 million roubles), health (230 million roubles), protection of socially disadvantaged groups (200 million roubles), and social research (100 million roubles). The number of applications has increased; in 2006, the Civic Chamber awarded 1,054 grants out of 3,500 applications, and in 2007 1,225 projects were funded out of 4,200 applications.

Chamber and the Presidential Representatives of the federal districts, the following two competitions were run by the Public Chamber, which then contracted the work out to six NGOs (Obschestvennaya Palata, 2008).

In addition, Putin has instructed business leaders to become more socially responsible, and declared 2006 the year of philanthropy to encourage businesses to support the government's four national projects – improving Russians' healthcare, housing, agriculture, and education. This social responsibility has its limits; it has not encouraged the philanthropy of Khodorkovky's Open Russia Foundation (modeled after George Soros' Open Society Institutes), which promoted the much more explicit political goal of developing civil liberties. In March 2006, it froze the bank accounts of that Foundation. Nonetheless, the development of Russian philanthropy has also been bolstered by the passage of Federal Law No. 275 "On Endowments," which lays out the conditions under which endowments may be established and operated.

Finally, and perhaps most controversially, in 2006, the Duma passed legislation that increased the regulatory framework within which NGOs operate. This law amended four existing laws that governed the nonprofit sector. It introduced several new requirements for public associations, non-commercial organizations, and foreign NGOs. The new requirements restrict who may form an organization in the Russian Federation, expand the reasons for which registration may be denied, and increase the supervisory powers of the state (Bourjaily, 2006). Of particular concern is the stipulation that foreign NGOs may be denied registration if their "goals and objectives ... create a threat to the sovereignty, political independence, territorial integrity, national unity, unique character, cultural heritage and national interests of the Russian Federation." Further, foreign NGOs can be barred from transferring funds or other resources to recipients for purposes of "protecting the basis of the Constitutional system, morality, health, rights and lawful interests of other persons, and with the aim of defending the country and the state security." Finally, the law increases the number of documents that the government can request from organizations, and allows the government to send a representative to an organization's meetings and other events. In sum, the law expanded the grounds upon which an organization can be denied registration and deepened government supervisory powers over both domestic and foreign NGOs. Thus, some maintain, while previous legislation, though confusing, unclear, and poorly drafted, and not particularly proactive, was guided by the principles of information, the current legislation is inspired by the principle of permission (www.sovetpamfilova.ru). In other words, the government now has the ability to more selectively pick and choose who can operate and under what conditions.

What has been the impact of the Putin administration's policies on NGO development? The external reaction has been primarily negative. As Celeste Wallander noted in her testimony before the US Commission on Security and Cooperation in Europe, "civil society organizations can operate only if their activities and objectives are non-political. The Kremlin has created onerous requirements for NGOs seeking foreign funding, and most Russian NGOs subsist on donations from Kremlin approved businesses, or from the government's NGO monitor, the Civic Forum" (Wallander, 2008). Certainly, high-profile examples, such as the government closure of the Soros Foundation-supported European University for violating fire safety regulations, indicate a similar "rule by law" tactic, originally used on businessman Mikhail Khodorkovsky, to rein in other potentially wayward oligarchs. Yet, this blanket prognosis overlooks many of the complexities of NGO development in Russia; nor does it fully reflect what NGOs themselves are experiencing on the ground. While it is important not to overstate the gains of a relatively weak sector in the context of a weak, and weakly democratic, state, nonetheless, at the federal level, the design and implementation of actual policy machinery has provided NGOs with increased visibility and institutionalized access to policymakers. Second, the impact has been particularly significant for NGOs in the regions. Further, the impact has diverged in interesting and unexpected ways; federal envoys, regional governors, and mayors have interpreted the changes at the federal level in differing ways, leading to an increased role for NGOs in policymaking, advocacy, and service provision in some regions, as well as potential increased cooptation in others. Finally, the predicted annihilation of the sector has not occurred; in fact, a significant percentage of NGOs have not complied with the law, nor has the federal registration service pursued noncompliance. Rather than confirming President Putin's legacy as the consolidator of an all-powerful state, the experience of NGOs indicates that there are numerous interests at work in shaping the civic space, and the variation in advocacy paths indicates a lack of monolithic state control, rather than an excess of it. Local, regional, and federal elites all have different agendas, as do the NGOs that choose to try to leverage the increased points of access in the system. While the state plays an important role in shaping civic activism in Russia, the larger challenge facing Russian NGOs is an apathetic public and a weak advocacy sector, rather than an all-powerful state.

One of the most significant developments that NGO leaders themselves noted about state–society relations, at a workshop to compile the Russia section of USAID's *2004 NGO Sustainability Index* (USAID, 2005), was the importance of the Civic Forum and the (at the time) proposed Public

Chamber in reestablishing languishing formal mechanisms of communication as well as creating new policy machinery. During the Yeltsin era, NGOs had to rely on personal contacts to wrest an audience with the appropriate vested interests. For example, Charities Aid Foundation Russia noted how the Civic Forum granted their lawyers access to the Working Group of the Ministry of Finance, giving them more routine ways to push for improved taxation benefits, as well as to the Department of Labour and Social Development to discuss writing federal legislation regulating the provision of social services (Avrorina, interview, June 4, 2004). For ANNA (Association of Crisis Centers for Women "Stop Violence") it also improved spotty access to the Committee of Women and Children, and their abilities to give input to the drafting of legislation on domestic violence (Abubikirova and Reshtova, interview, June 3, 2008). For Oleg Zykov of NAN (No to Alcoholism and Drug Addiction), it helped formalize the years of work he had put into fostering personal connections with Ella Pamfilova (Head of the Commission of Human Rights), and encouraged the hope that more formal representative bodies of communication could be developed (Zykov, interview, June 4, 2004). Particularly for NGOs working in the regions, the organization of the Civic Forum, and the efforts to establish Public Chambers signaled to regional governors and mayors that they were to be included in the political dialogue. Further, this machinery, whatever the intent, has also given the sector the institutional space to advocate on policies, either within the seventeen subcommittees or within the advisory councils attached to nine ministries and fourteen agencies. While there are limitations on this – we do not yet know what the nature of this input is, or how effective it is – this has at least granted a sector access to policymaking where previously it had none (Petrov and Lipman, interview, June 4, 2004).

Thus, while we do not know what impact the Public Chamber is having on policy, nonetheless it is functioning as a means for civil society actors and NGOs to weigh in publicly on policy. One of its first actions was to oppose the registration law. While we do not know what impact it had on the final product, we do know that when legislation was first introduced governing NGO reregistration, the first version of the law was much more punitive. Proposed draft amendments to the tax code (which eventually failed) imposed registration requirements on all types of grant, which would have further complicated the work of foreign donors and recipient NGOs.

But the biggest impact of Putin's reforms has been in Russia's regions, and points to the organization not of an all-powerful state, but of a relatively weak state, where governors still have enormous latitude to interpret Kremlin policy as they see fit. These changes at the federal level filtered down in different ways to the regions, for regional governors and mayors interpreted President Putin's interest in civil society in remarkably different ways. Politically moderate or progressive figures took this as a sign to either initiate dialogue with or deepen preexisting relationships with NGOs, develop channels for policy input, or design relatively open, government-funded grant competitions. Other regions interpreted these moves as opportunities to coopt civic actors and direct their activities. Still other regions became mired in conflict between a reformist political figure at one level (e.g. the governor) and a conservative intransigent at another (e.g. the mayor). Nearly all NGOs interviewed in eight cities in five of Russia's *okrugs* argued that the Civic Forum and Public Chamber signaled to local and regional leaders, many of whom had previously ignored them, that they now needed to work with them in some capacity. For many NGOs, this provided a political opening for them to develop more regular avenues of communication.

Thus, in many regions, Putin's policies *vis-à-vis* NGOs at the federal level created the stimulus for the creation of similar policy machinery at the regional level, and it revitalized previously underutilized government offices whose job was to liaise with public organizations. It also prodded regional and local governments to create mechanisms by which NGOs could compete for funding, as well as to experiment with contracting out social services.

In particular, progressive presidential envoys, governors, and/or mayors interpreted Putin's remarks as a green light to attempt to stimulate citizen activism from above by passing regional and local legislation – in the absence of federal legislation – to allow NGOs to implement social policy. This was particularly evident in the Volga district, where, envoy Sergei Kirienko interpreted Putin's call to foster economic and social development and combat corruption as a need to establish better connections with the citizenry and NGOs (Nelson and Kuzes, 2003). This has manifested itself in a variety of ways: the creation and use of mechanisms to relay citizen and NGO concerns; the effort to create grant competitions which draw on government, business, and private funds; and the effort to further regional legislation allowing for social service contracting by NGOs. Thus, for example, Tatarstan (a republic within the Volga district) established a Public Chamber to encourage public hearings and civic involvement in questions of broad concern. In addition, a public office and telephone hotline were also established so that citizens could communicate issues and concerns directly, to "not only help individual citizens defend their rights ... but ... to reveal and systematize common problems in the operation of the state bureaucracy." As another federal inspector commented, "[p]eople still don't believe they are capable of solving their own problems. But state power and strong public organizations have to help show society that times have changed" (Nelson and Kuzes, 2003: 515). Similarly, in Samara, the organization Povolzhe was able to use the impetus created by President Putin to formalize communication with the regional government by establishing formal round-tables composed of NGO and government leaders to cooperate on social policy (Pestrikova, interviews, June 18 and November 21, 2004). Further, Kirienko was one of the first envoys to provide government funding through grant competitions to NGOs, as well as organize a yearly Civic Forum conference for NGOs in the region (Malitskaya, interview, November 15, 2004).

In other regions, governors and mayors interpreted the creation of the Civic Forum and Chamber as a potential way to coopt NGOs. Thus, some NGOs, in places such as Rostov or Krasnodar, which had hoped that the changes at the federal level indicated that they might now be taken more seriously by local and regional administrations, were bitterly disappointed to see the administrations use the opportunity to allot money to NGOs, but behind closed doors (Chernishova, interview, September 28, 2002; Rostov Community Foundation, interview, June 15, 2004). Similarly, in Vladivostok, the Moscow Civic Forum served as a highlight for NGOs interested in breaking into working with regional governments; they were sadly disappointed to find that the regional government wanted to work only with selected NGOs.

In other areas, such as Irkutsk, the city government and NGOs had tentatively started a dialogue, and had begun to hammer out relatively transparent policies to distribute funds to NGOs in a competition. This was a learning curve for both sides: the government was disappointed that NGOs had not accomplished more with the small sums they were given (grants were approximately $1,000 each), and NGOs were frustrated that the administration wanted them to accomplish miracles with small pots of money that often could not cover salary costs (Tvorogova, interview, June 8, 2004; Vasiliev, interview, June 8, 2004). Further, NGO activists were frustrated that for the previous two years, NGOs were invited to participate in judging grant applications; however, in the recent competition, they were invited only to give feedback but not allowed to participate in the final decision.

In sum, NGO activists, while wary of the intent and meaning of changes at the federal level, were nonetheless cognizant that this provided a political window for many of them that had not existed previously. For many NGOs, after spending the 1990s fighting for access to government administrators, the new opportunities offered by Putin's changes meant they had to walk the fine line between cooperation and cooptation, but that this was an improvement from standing on the sidelines, watching policy being made without their input. In their eyes, administrations were unsure whether they wanted to build civil society rather than work with the "real" one that existed; yet, they all admitted that they had had increased interaction, and thus potential impact, on the administration and its policies.

However, one of the largest concerns has been regarding the impact of the 2006 NGO law, which was greeted with such dismay. Critics of the legislation feared it would be used selectively to close NGOs critical of the Kremlin, or that the Federal Registration Service would close a few high-profile organizations to encourage remaining organizations to censor themselves. It is hard to measure the impact of the law, given that so many organizations are "dead souls"; they exist on paper but they have ceased to function. Thus, it is unclear how many organizations are being shut down simply because they no longer exist. However, a December 2007 survey of NGOs in twenty of Russia's regions, designed to measure the impact of the new requirements on NGOs, found that the majority of NGOs have not complied with the new regulations. According to the Federal Registration Service (FRS), only 32 percent of NGOs had submitted the required paperwork. As of the time of the report, the FRS has yet to apply involuntary liquidation to NGOs that have failed to submit reports (and the FRS has extended the deadline for submitting paperwork yet again). Nor did NGOs report any penalties for lack of submission. Nonetheless, as of the end of 2007, the biggest cost to them of the legislation, according to Russian NGOs themselves, was time spent in filling out the papers. Neither survey respondents nor focus group participants felt that the law had been disproportionately applied against human rights or advocacy groups. Instead, respondents felt that all groups were suffering equally from the demands of new paperwork and confusion over ambiguity of the requirements. Perhaps because of the fears of the selective use of rule of law, human rights organizations are more likely to have filed their paperwork than other NGOs (International Center for Not-for-Profit Law, 2007). One interesting impact of the legislation has been the increase of foreign funds to Russian NGOs to support projects that monitor the implementation of the law; the Center in Support of Civic Initiatives in Siberia is currently managing three grants to monitor the reregistration process.

Conclusion

Governments make the rules within which NGOs operate; they set the formal and informal costs for organization. Whether it is through rhetoric, drafting and redrafting legal frameworks, establishing formal channels providing access to advocacy organizations, or providing funding, governments can provide incentives and place constraints on the emergence and shape of advocacy sectors. The conventional wisdom regarding President Putin's policy agenda toward NGOs is that he is trying to crush the sector by erecting too many barriers and imposing too many costs for most, if not all, advocacy organizations. Although Putin himself has dismissed charges that the state wished to coopt opposition, noting that "civil society cannot be established at the state's initiative, at the state's will, much less in accordance with the state's plans" (Putin, 2001), he has also demonstrated a remarkable talent, as some have noted, of talking like a democrat and walking like an autocrat. Yet, this chapter maintains that the administration's strategy is a bit more complex. It has designed a complex of policies to encourage and select for NGOs that are likely to support, not so much the Kremlin, as has been argued, but the national projects that the Kremlin has deemed compelling and important. These policies have been designed to reward "good" behavior for NGOs whose advocacy originates out of performing valuable social services that have the potential to improve the social and economic well-being of the population. Legislative policy also provides enough stipulations that the administration now has the capability of punishing (if it so chooses), or at least deterring, NGOs that pursue advocacy on issues related to political rights and liberties. In other words, the government, rather than being anti-advocacy, is trying to select the advocacy that it prefers to see. However, particularly in the Russian context, where there is little preexisting tradition of independent advocacy, particularly of the anti-state variant, the federal administration has, by far, the comparative advantage. And given that Russia is a federalist system, the policy changes initiated from Moscow have been interpreted in varying ways across Russia's regions, sometimes in ways that were more favorable to NGOs than originally intended by the federal authorities.

Thus, the largest problem facing NGOs today is not potential capture and cooptation by an all-powerful state, but the inability to captivate the average Russian citizen, who still remains suspicious and leery of organizational activity. Part of this is due to the fact that after nearly two decades of independent organization, Russians still know relatively little about the sector. When asked in October 2007 if they had heard anything or knew anything about the activities of NGOs or social organizations in their region, about 55 percent of the population knew nothing – a figure about 7 percent higher than when asked in 2001 (Obschestvennaya Palata, 2007). But ignorance about the sector is only part of the problem; a larger issue is that citizens do not like what they do know about the sector. The 2008 Edelman Trust Barometer reported that in Russia, when asked on a scale of 1–9, "How much do you trust each institution to do what's right?" only 29 percent of respondents answered in the range 6–9, behind government (38 percent) and business (42 percent). This was in marked contrast to Western Europe, where NGOs came in as the most trusted institutions in all countries surveyed except Sweden and the Netherlands (where, nonetheless, 59 percent of respondents answered in the 6–9 range) (Edelman, 2008).

Russia is in the strange position of having a nonprofit sector organizing on behalf of a society that has shown less interest in organizing itself. Few organizations have developed mass constituencies. Other issues that have mobilized the population (such as government attempts to overhaul Russia's outdated pension system) have not turned into formal organizations. Certainly, Russia does not lack potential issues and problems around which advocacy organizations could emerge. Through the 1990s and the first decade of the twenty-first century, foreign donors stepped in to supply financial and technical assistance, as well as funding areas that they were willing to support. In contrast, much of the Putin administration has been about countering the Western supply of what they deem Russians should demand with its own supply of themes and projects. On top of this, they have supplied various mechanisms by which NGOs can choose to operate. But what is still missing is the basic demand at the citizen level for organizational representation.

This chapter, like Bloodgood's (this volume) contribution, highlights the ways in which government administrations shape the costs of advocacy. In the case of Russia, President Putin regulated the formation and operation of advocacy NGOs not in order to strangle the entire sector, as some charge, but to encourage the supply of some types of advocacy and deter the formation of others. The administration has done this by using its power to write legislation to raise the entry costs for NGOs, to increase access to policymaking for some advocacy themes but not others, and to provide financial and moral support for causes that align with state interests. Thus, in some ways, collaboration between NGOs and government has increased, resulting in increased influence for some advocacy organizations.

Only time will tell whether Putin's NGO development strategy of "import substitution" will run a similar course to economic development strategies of import substitution industrialization in Latin American countries from the 1950s to the 1980s; we now know that in the Latin American case, initial decades of growth were ultimately not sustainable, and also incurred significant economic and social costs. While Putin's import substitution model of civic development has created some short-term gains for some NGOs, the long-term costs imposed by increased regulation could decrease the range of perspectives and issues appearing on policy agendas, particularly if they do not match those of the Kremlin.

Regardless of the long-term impact, the policies of the Putin administration point to the significant role that governments can play in setting the short-term costs for advocacy, particularly in countries where domestic civic impulses are underdeveloped and weak.

References

BOOKS, ARTICLES, ETC.

ARD, Inc. 2005. *Democracy Assessment: Political Process, Local Governance, and Civil Society*. Washington, DC.

BBC Monitoring. 2004. Full Text of Putin's State of the Nation Address to Russian Parliament. May 26.

——— 2006. Putin Meets Youth Activists. Channel One TV, May 19.

Bob, C. 2002. The Merchants of Morality. *Foreign Policy*, March/April: 36–45.

Bourjaily, N. 2006. Some Issues Related to Russia's New NGO Law. *International Journal of Not-for-Profit Law*, 8(3): 4–5.

Cohen, J. L. and A. Arato. 1992. *Civil Society and Political Theory*. Cambridge, MA: MIT Press.

Commissioner for Human Rights in the Russian Federation. 2008. Annual Report of the Commissioner for Human Rights in the Russian Federation for the year 2007. Moscow.

Dokuchaev, D. 1997. Fond Sporta – Natsionalny, a Prinadlezhit Edinitsam. *Izvestiya*, June 5.

Edelman. 2008. The 2008 Edelman Trust Barometer.

Evans, A. 2005. Ideological Roots of Putin's Monocentrism. Paper presented at the American Association for the Advancement of Slavic Studies Annual Convention, Salt Lake City, UT, November 3–6.

——— 2006. The Public Chamber in Action: Representation or Coordination? Paper presented at the American Association for the Advancement of Slavic Studies Annual Convention, Washington, DC, November 16–19.

Henderson, S. L. 2003. *Building Democracy in Contemporary Russia: Western Support for Grassroots Organizations*. Ithaca, NY: Cornell University Press.

Howard, M. M. 2002. The Weakness of Postcommunist Civil Society. *Journal of Democracy*, 13(1): 157–169.

International Center for Not-for-Profit Law. 2007. Analysis of the Impact of Recent Regulatory Reforms on Non-commercial Organizations and Public Associations in Russia. [Washington, DC].

Keck, M. and K. Sikkink. 1998. *Activists Beyond Borders: Advocacy Networks in International Politics*. Ithaca, NY: Cornell University Press.

McFaul, M. and K. Stoner-Weiss. 2008. The Myth of the Authoritarian Model: How Putin's Crackdowns Hold Russia Back. *Foreign Affairs*, 87(1): 68–84.

Mendelson, S. E. and J. K. Glenn (eds.). 2002. *The Power and Limits of NGOs: A Critical Look at Building Democracy in Eastern Europe and Eurasia*. New York: Columbia University Press.

Nelson, L. D. and I. Y. Kuzes. 2003. Political and Economic Coordination in Russia's Federal District Reform: A Study of Four Regions. *Europe–Asia Studies*, 55(4): 507–520.

Nikitin, A. 2001. Talk given at the Center for International and Strategic Studies, Washington, DC, December 13.

Obschestvennaya Palata [Public Chamber]. 2007. Doklad o Sostoyanii grazhdanskovo obschestva v rossiiskoi Federatsii 2007.

    2008. Struktura Palati: Kommissii 2008 god. www.oprf.ru/ru/structure/commis sions2008/.

    2008 Konkursi NKO 2008: Press reliz dlya SMI po konkursu "NKO 2008." www.orpf.ru/678/679/680/.

Oslon, A. 2001. *Pogovorim o Grazhdanskom Obschestve*. Moscow: Fond Obschestvennoye mneniye.

Ottaway, M. 2000. *Funding Virtue: Civil Society Aid and Democracy Promotion*. Washington, DC: Carnegie Endowment for International Peace.

Petro, N. N. 2001. Creating Social Capital in Russia: The Novgorod Model. *World Development*, 29(2): 229–244.

Proskuryakova, L. K. 2005. Russian Civil Society Will Find it Harder to Breathe. *YaleGlobal*, December 8. www.yaleglobal.yale.edu/display.article?id=6607.

Putin, V. 2001. Vladimir Putin: States are Judged by the Level of Individual Liberty. Excerpts from President Vladimir Putin's Speech at the Civil Forum. *Vremya Novosti*, November 22.

Rossiiskaya Federatsiya. 2004. Federal'ny Zakon ob obschestvennoi palate possiiskoi federatsii. November 10.

Saari, S. 2009. *Promoting Democracy and Human Rights in Russia*. New York: Routledge.

Salamon, L. M., S. W. Sokolowski, and R. List. 2003. *Global Civil Society: An Overview*. Baltimore: Johns Hopkins University Center for Civil Society Studies.

Sevortian, A. and N. Barchukova. 2002. *Nekommercheskii Sektor I Vlast' v Regionakh Rossii*. Moscow: Charities Aid Foundation.

Shipov, V. 2003. Perspectives in the Development of Local Self-Governance. In *Local Self-Government and Civic Engagement in Rural Russia*. New York: World Bank.

Sperling, V. 1999. *Organizing Women in Contemporary Russia: Engendering Transition*. Cambridge University Press.

Stetson, D. M. and A. Mazur (eds.). 1995. *Comparative State Feminism*. Thousand Oaks, CA: Sage.

Stoner-Weiss, K. 2007. Russia. In *Countries at the Crossroads 2007*. Washington, DC: Freedom House.

USAID (United States Agency for International Development). 2002. *The 2001 NGO Sustainability Index for Central and Eastern Europe and Eurasia*. Washington, DC: USAID.

    2005. *The 2004 NGO Sustainability Index for Central and Eastern Europe and Eurasia*. Washington, DC: USAID.

    2007. *The 2006 NGO Sustainability Index for Central and Eastern Europe and Eurasia*. Washington, DC: USAID.

Wallander, C. A. 2008. Russian Power and Interests at the Next Stage in US–Russian Relations. Testimony before the US Commission on Security and Cooperation in Europe, United States Congress, May 8.

Walzer, M. 1992. The Civil Society Argument. In C. Mouffe (ed.), *Dimensions of Radical Democracy: Pluralism, Citizenship, Community.* New York: Verso.

INTERVIEWS

N. Abubikirova and M. Reshtova, Association of Crisis Centers for Women, Moscow, June 3, 2008.

O. Alexeeva, Director, Charities Aid Foundation, Moscow, October 7, 2002.

L. Avrorina, Charities Aid Foundation, Moscow, June 4, 2004.

A. Borovikh, Moscow, Fall 2002.

S. Chernishova, Southern Russia Resource Center, Krasnodar, September 28, 2002.

E. Ershova, President, Women's Consortium, Moscow, Summer 1998.

E. Malitskaya, Siberian Center in Support of Civic Initiatives, November 15, 2004.

V. Pestrikova, Polvolzhe, June 18, 2004; November 21, 2004.

N. Petrov and M. Lipman, Carnegie Endowment for International Peace, Moscow, June 4, 2004.

Rostov Community Foundation, June 15 , 2004.

E. Tvorogova, Rebirth of the Land of Siberia, Irkutsk, June 8, 2004.

A. I. Vasiliev, Head of the Committee of Relations with Society, oblast' administration, June 8, 2004.

O. Zykov, No to Alcoholism and Drug Addiction, June 4, 2004.

Part 4

Toward a new research program

11 Rethinking advocacy organizations? A critical comment

Thomas Risse

Over the past fifteen to twenty years, the study of transnational advocacy networks, of NGOs, and other such groups has blossomed. While the original focus was mostly on the policy effects and consequences of such groups (do they matter?), more recent work has started treating them as ordinary organizations emphasizing their internal organizational structures, their material and immaterial resources, and their strategies from a variety of perspectives. This volume is part and parcel of this scholarly effort. It attempts to outline a "new agenda for the study of advocacy organizations" (Prakash and Gugerty, Chapter 1) by treating them analogously to firms and using a collective action perspective to get a fuller understanding of their emergence and structure as well as their tactics and strategies. In doing so, the authors try to move away from and criticize a perspective which sees advocacy groups as primarily motivated by principled beliefs (e.g. Keck and Sikkink, 1998). One of the authors calls this the "moral theory" of advocacy groups (Bob, Chapter 5) and points to some alleged anomalies of such a theory. The editors of this volume view "advocacy NGOs as special types of firms which function in policy markets" (Prakash and Gugerty, Chapter 1).

It speaks to the editors' intellectual honesty and rigor that they have asked me to provide a critical comment to their endeavor from somebody who has tried to contribute to the original advocacy network literature (e.g. Risse, Ropp, and Sikkink, 1999). I am happy to offer my reading of the volume's findings in the following. First, I argue that the collective action perspective complements the original advocacy network literature in important ways, but does not challenge it. Second, I find that the collective action perspective on advocacy organizations indeed sheds some new light on old questions. However, most of it is consistent with claims put forward by the earlier literature. Third, I suggest that one should not overdo the firms analogy with regard to NGOs, since some fundamental differences remain which a constitutive analysis demonstrates. The findings of this volume actually confirm rather than challenge this view. Finally, I turn the analogy around and ask what we can learn if we treat firms as norm entrepreneurs.

This chapter begins with a short intellectual history of the advocacy network literature in order to pinpoint its main theoretical and empirical concerns.

From regimes to norms: the intellectual origins of the advocacy network approach

This volume uses the firm analogy and a collective action perspective resulting from it to shed new light on the emergence, organizational developments, and strategies of advocacy organizations. Interestingly enough, it was precisely the limits of this analogy and the resulting rational choice approach that triggered the original work on transnational advocacy coalitions during the mid 1990s. At the time, however, the international relations literature treated states as firms, not NGOs. During the 1980s, a powerful theoretical alternative to the realist paradigm in international relations emerged to explain international cooperation among states. This perspective used institutional economics including transaction cost economics (e.g. Coase, 1960; North, 1986) to explain the emergence of international regimes and institutions (e.g. Krasner, 1983; Keohane, 1984; Oye, 1986). Neo-liberal institutionalism, as it was called later, treated states analogously to firms and demonstrated under what conditions egoistic utility-maximizing states are likely to cooperate "under anarchy" in order to reach their objectives. Rational choice institutionalism was firmly established in the field by the end of the 1980s (e.g. Keohane, 1989).

By the late 1980s, neo-liberal institutionalism was again challenged by what was later called social constructivism – on both theoretical and empirical grounds. The theoretical challenge concerned what Friedrich Kratochwil and John Ruggie called the inherently intersubjective quality of international institutions as arrangements consisting of norms, rules, and decision-making procedures (Kratochwil and Ruggie, 1986). From this perspective, norms were understood as "collective expectations about appropriate behavior on the basis of a given identity" (Jepperson, Wendt, and Katzenstein, 1996: 54). It was hard to see how one could talk about institutional norms without taking their intersubjectiveness into account ("collective expectations about appropriate behavior"). This criticism of rational choice institutionalism then gave rise to a more sociological study of international institutions (e.g. Kratochwil, 1989; Katzenstein, 1996; March and Olsen, 1998).

But there were also empirical challenges to neo-liberal institutionalism. While this approach was able to explain the emergence of regimes governing the global economy and partly international security, it was hard to see why egoistic and utility-maximizing states would be prepared to constrain their own domestic rule and authority through international human rights regimes and the like. Resulting from these empirical as well as theoretical anomalies, scholars started paying increasing attention to those actors who were actually doing the norms promotion in international society. These scholars also started abandoning the overly state-centric view of international relations and began focusing on transnational actors (e.g. Sikkink, 1993; Risse-Kappen, 1995b; Smith, Chatfield, and Pagnucco, 1997; Boli and Thomas, 1999). This was the origin of a literature focusing on transnational advocacy coalitions as norm entrepreneurs.

It might be helpful in this context to quote the famous Keck and Sikkink definition of advocacy networks in full:

Transnational advocacy network includes those relevant actors working inter-nationally on an issue, who are bound together by shared values, a common discourse, and dense exchanges of information and services ... What is novel in these networks is the ability of nontraditional international actors to mobilize information strategically to help create new issues and categories and to persuade, pressure, and gain leverage over much more powerful organizations and govern-ments. (Keck and Sikkink, 1998: 2)

Several points are noteworthy in this definition and demonstrate that the original approach to advocacy organizations is not far away from the purpose of this volume.

First, constitutive features of advocacy networks are shared values, a common discourse, and a dense exchange of information and services. It is the "shared values" part that has led some scholars to the misleading claim that the earlier literature on NGOs has taken a normative stance on advocacy organizations (e.g. Clifford Bob's characterization of this liter-ature as "moral theory" in Chapter 5 is simply wrong, unfortunately). While the focus on advocacy networks certainly has normative implica-tions (see Price, 2008), the perspective is strictly analytical and has been all along.

Second, "shared values" does not necessarily imply altruistic motiva-tions as some authors in this volume seem to suggest. Advocacy networks usually share a concern for universally accepted values or the global common good and, thus, pursue what they perceive as the public interest. But they normally are not charity organizations. Collectively shared norms are different from individualistic "other help" preferences (see March and Olsen, 1998, on the logic of appropriateness). They might coincide, but not necessarily so. Labor unions that fight for workers' rights or womens' movements fighting for gender rights are doing advocacy work for their own interests, too (see the example in Prakash and Gugerty, Chapter 1).

Third and perhaps most important, transnational advocacy networks are described here as strategic actors ("mobilize information strategically"; "gain leverage over much more powerful organizations"). In other words, instrumental motivations and preferences are part and parcel of the definition. These networks want to change policies in their desired direction and, therefore, try to pick their strategies accordingly (see Young, Chapter 2, on the NRDC) and to adapt to the domestic institutional context in which they operate (see Bloodgood, Chapter 4; Barakso, Chapter 6; Pralle, Chapter 7). They also face severe collective action problems as this volume points out time and again. Their collective action problems might even be more severe than those of firms, since they are not primarily motivated by instrumental gains, but by shared values as a result of which the opportunities for free riding and for shirking are even greater (see Gill and Pfaff, Chapter 3, for the very instructive example of religious organizations and their strategies to deal with these problems). In other words, the authors of this volume by and large complement the earlier work on advocacy networks, since they focus in more detail on these collective action problems than the original scholarship did.

Fourth, as the editors point out (see Prakash and Gugerty, Chapter 1; Gugerty and Prakash, Chapter 12), the earlier literature on the subject focused more on the network characteristics of advocacy rather than on individual organizations. This volume, however, concentrates on these organizations as part of transnational networks. Once again, I see this as complementary to the original literature rather than a departure from it. Besides, the survey among US-based NGOs demonstrates that networking rather than strategic competition is an intrinsic part of the job description of these actors (Lecy, Mitchell, and Schmitz, Chapter 9).

Principled believers are no dummies

The central message that this volume drives home is that advocacy organizations pursue strategic goals and face severe collective action problems. This appears to be what the firm analogy is all about. But why should we be surprised? If you are a norms entrepreneur and want to change the world, why should this imply that you are not acting strategically? The volume demonstrates, therefore, that principled believers are no dummies.

To begin with, advocacy organizations tend to engage in those areas in which they have special expertise. If you are a group of smart Yale law students and you want to make a difference, you better use your legal skills to help the environment and specialize in litigation (see Young, Chapter 2, on the NRDC). As a result, one would expect a division of labor among advocacy groups and, to some extent, even competition among them (see Pralle, Chapter 7). As I see it, it is actually surprising that the volume does not show more examples of competition among advocacy groups given the necessity for product differentiation and division of labor.

Moreover, product differentiation is also a vital necessity given that the funding market for advocacy organizations is rather limited. There are only three funding sources available for NGOs: government money, foundation funds, and private donations. Each of these sources poses its own problems. State money might corrupt an organization's advocacy goals. The European Union (EU) is full of examples in which NGOs became dependent on euros from the European Commission, while, at the same time, their primary mission was to demand changes in EU policies. In some cases, this resulted in government-sponsored QUANGOs (quasi-non-governmental organizations). Foundation funds are problematic, since big foundations tend to change their policy priorities frequently, as a result of which NGOs have to adapt. In the case of Russia, NGO dependence on Western foundations led to perverse incentive structures since NGOs lost their local constituencies (see Henderson, Chapter 10). No wonder that the Putin regime could easily denounce these advocacy groups as "foreign organizations," a well-known strategy by autocratic regimes to counteract domestic opposition. Last not least, the market for private dollars or euros is limited. No wonder then that we observe "branding" and the development of core identities among advocacy groups, that Amnesty International now sells T-shirts and other products (see Barakso, Chapter 6), and that religious organizations develop sophisticated strategies to induce members to voluntarily contribute to the provision of public goods (see Gill and Pfaff, Chapter 3).

In addition, several chapters point to the domestic institutional and political constraints to which NGOs must adapt if they want to make a difference (e.g. Bloodgood, Chapter 4; Pralle, Chapter 9). This insight, while well taken, is not new at all. My own work on the subject matter of transnational relations argued in favor of a "domestic structure" approach to explain the differential impact of transnational actors on policy change (Risse-Kappen, 1995a, b). Social movement research has long advocated that movements face different "political opportunity structures" to which they must adjust if they want to further their goals (Kitschelt, 1986; Tarrow, 1996). Once again, NGOs and social movements pushing certain principled beliefs and norms are not stupid. As a result, they are expected to adapt and adjust to whatever the domestic environment is in which they operate. This concerns both institutional constraints, but also policy constraints. These constraints might explain Bob's (Chapter 5) finding that human rights NGOs often do not focus on the most serious violations of human rights, but on those on which they are most likely to achieve policy change in the respective target countries, both at home and abroad.[1]

Last but not least, and surprisingly, this volume actually overlooks that advocacy groups can be treated as strategic actors in one more respect, namely with regard to strategic constructions (see Finnemore and Sikkink, 1998, for details). Some chapters of this volume point to the use of strategic frames, but this issue is not investigated systematically, unfortunately. Norms are social constructions, of course, but promoting them necessitates the use of strategic framing. New norms, for example, need to resonate with given collective understandings, as a result of which advocacy groups tend to consciously make them compatible with existing norms of appropriate behavior. Gender rights have been advocated primarily within a larger human rights framework. The same holds true for the rights of indigenous peoples. Specific campaigns for human rights or environmental causes also use strategic constructions. Campaigns for biodiversity or for endangered species, for example, normally concentrate on "charismatic mega-fauna"[2] (elephants, rhinos, whales, cuddly harbor seals, etc.) rather than on some ugly spiders. In sum, strategic framing is part and parcel of the action repertoire of advocacy groups. It involves the deliberate use and active engagement of particular discourses in order to persuade a target audience to support policy changes.

NGOs are not firms: the limits of an analogy

This volume successfully uses the firm analogy to get at collective action problems which NGOs and other advocacy groups face in their effort to induce and promote policy changes. As argued above, in doing so, the authors complement rather than substitute the earlier literature on advocacy coalitions. However, one should not overdo the analogy. The social dynamics involving firms as compared to NGOs are still different. Here, I disagree with the claim advanced by the editors namely that "the distinction often made in the literature (Keck and Sikkink, 1998) between NGOs and

---

[1] There is one more reason for this finding which has little to do with a "market for human rights." It is very hard to come by reliable information in the most repressive regimes. Since the big advocacy groups such as Amnesty International and Human Rights Watch have reached the status of authoritative claimants to knowledge, they have very tough reporting standards. The "boomerang" effect theorized by Keck and Sikkink (Keck and Sikkink, 1998; see also Risse, Ropp, and Sikkink, 1999) often does not work with regard to the most oppressive regimes, simply because there are no domestic opposition groups on the ground to report the human rights violations in detail.

[2] I owe this expression to Ronald Jepperson.

firms – the former pursuing principled objectives and the latter pursuing instrumental objectives – is not valid" (Gugerty and Prakash, Chapter 12).

In my view, the distinction between the "for profit" and the "not for profit" sectors remains valid, even if this differentiation does not imply that only firms pursue instrumental goals or that NGOs are "selfless" actors. Profit-making is constitutive for firms which are neither charities nor public interest groups. Competition is an equally constitutive feature of markets. If firms fail in making money, they are out of business, at least in the long run. In contrast, NGOs or advocacy groups promote what they consider as the public interest, the common good, or particular social norms. Again, this is constitutive for them. If they fail in their primary tasks or if they are accused of making profits or if they compete too much over scarce public and private resources and funding, they are quickly in trouble, too. In many cases, they will be held legally accountable, but reputation loss is usually much worse and takes much longer to recover. I come back to this point below.

The example quoted in Prakash and Gugerty's introductory chapter is instructive in this regard. They argue that Amnesty International (AI) has a formal bureaucratic structure, similar to those of multidivisional firms. To prove their point, they discuss AI's job ads searching for an advisor on international organizations, a researcher on the Middle East and North Africa, and so on. What is interesting here is not – in my view – that a professional NGO seeks professionals and specialists to do various jobs. The interesting part is the pathetic salaries that AI appears to pay – in London, one of the most expensive cities in the world.[3] I submit that these are way below market salaries for the specialists that Amnesty tried to hire. I also submit that AI would probably not get away with this if it were a firm investing in North Africa and hiring a specialist with regional knowledge. It can probably pay low salaries because it is seeking professionals who are committed to the human rights cause and, therefore, are willing to work for less. Amnesty gets away with this precisely because it is not a firm.

But who controls these advocacy groups that proclaim to work for the common good? Who holds them accountable? Again, I submit that the "market for human rights" differs from the market for automobiles. The reputation of NGOs and, consequently, their power and influence on policy change stems from two sources, *moral authority and legitimacy*, on

---

[3] http://web.amnesty/jobs (accessed November 24, 2009) reveals salaries of a bit more than £37,000 for researcher positions, of up to £60,000 for an interim finance director, and almost $98,000 for the head of office position at the UN in New York. I seriously doubt that a major firm would be able to hire its chief financial officer or its top lobbyist in New York for these salaries.

the one hand, and the accepted claim to *authoritative knowledge*, on the other (see Risse, 2000, for the following). These two aspects – moral authority and knowledge – go together and cannot be separated. Moral authority is directly related to the claim by transnational advocacy groups that they represent the "public interest" or the "common good" rather than private interests. This is the most crucial condition for NGOs to play such a powerful role in the global discourse on human rights, the environment, and other causes. They can quickly lose their credibility if and when they become identified with some special economic or political interests, or if they are caught wasting private or public donations.

In such cases, the markets for NGOs react immediately, as the example of UNICEF's German branch documents. In 2008, UNICEF Germany was accused in the media of wasting money from private donors and engaging in very expensive schemes for fundraising. It then lost a label given by another NGO – some kind of rating agency evaluating advocacy groups and NGOs with regard to their fundraising activities and the way in which they use donations. The market reacted immediately, and UNICEF lost both public and private donations on a very large scale. Only when it completely reorganized its bureaucratic structure did UNICEF Germany manage to recover its market share of donations. The interesting point here is that an NGO lost on the market for private donations precisely because it was accused of acting like a firm, not an advocacy group.

Moral authority goes hand in hand with a widely accepted claim to knowledge. Today, Amnesty International, Human Rights Watch, and the Lawyers Committee for Human Rights *define* what constitutes a human rights violation. Other groups, INGOs, and even states might provide the information and disseminate it. But almost only if Amnesty, HRW, or the Lawyers Committee "approve" of this information as being correct, does this constitute a human rights violation in the eyes of the international community.

NGOs have to be extremely careful with regard to their authoritative claims to knowledge. If they are caught lying to the public, it takes them a long time to recover the reputational loss. Take the example of the Greenpeace campaign against Shell's Brent Spar oil platform in the North Sea in 1995 (see Wöbse, 2004). At the time, the Shell oil company and Greenpeace published divergent figures concerning the amount of poisonous oil deposits in the tanks of the platform. Of course, the public and the media initially believed Greenpeace as the norm-promoting underdog against the mighty oil company. After the campaign, it turned out, first, that Shell had been right all along, and that, second, Greenpeace had known the correct figures for quite some time and had lied to the public for some weeks. Even though Greenpeace later apologized, the reputational loss was enormous, as a result of which the NGO reorganized completely the way in which it conducted campaigns and gathered information. This example also documents that if NGOs behave like self-interested firms,[4] the markets for their products will punish them.

In sum, I do not suggest that advocacy groups do not have instrumental interests and that they do not pursue strategic goals (see above). But given the constitutive differences between NGOs, on the one hand, and firms, on the other, the markets in which they operate differ too.

Turning the analogy around: when firms become norm entrepreneurs

So far, I have made three claims with regard to the findings and arguments in this volume. First, while the original literature on transnational advocacy networks was heavily influenced by moderate social constructivism,[5] this scholarship by no means excluded treating NGOs as strategic actors pursuing instrumental goals among others. As a result, the approach chosen in this volume complements the original literature and does not present an alternative. Second, treating advocacy groups as firms and emphasizing collective action problems yields novel and interesting results, as the chapters in this volume document. Third, however, one should not exaggerate the "NGOs as firms" analogy. Constitutive analysis yields significant differences between the properties of firms and advocacy groups which also lead to different ways in which the respective "markets" of companies and NGOs operate.

In conclusion, I would like to turn the analogy around. What can we learn about firms if we treat them as advocacy groups and norm entrepreneurs (the following is inspired by Flohr et al., 2010)? The starting point for this reversed analogy is the observation that environmental and human rights norms have started to creep into the core business of many companies, particularly multinational corporations with a "brand name" to defend (see e.g. Prakash, 2000; Prakash and Potoski, 2006, 2007). What is now being called corporate social responsibility means in fact

---

[4] I am not suggesting that firms usually lie to the public about their products. But since self-interested behavior is constitutive for firms, we do not usually assume that they provide neutral and objective information about their products. This is precisely the difference from NGOs with an authoritative claim to knowledge coupled with moral authority.

[5] I understand "moderate social constructivism" as a meta-theoretical approach that differs from rational choice with regard to the mutual constitutiveness of agency and structure and other ontological issues, but accepts conventional approaches to knowledge generation in the social sciences. See, for example, Adler (1997, 2002).

that firms are increasingly obliged to integrate environmental and human rights norms into their production, management, and general business practices. In many cases, companies had been subjected to NGO campaigns including consumer boycotts (in the Brent Spar case mentioned above, Shell lost several million Deutschmarks within a few days at its German gas stations). They then started accepting human rights and environmental standards in similar ways as the "boomerang effect" or the human rights "spiral model" expected (Keck and Sikkink, 1998; Risse, Ropp, and Sikkink, 1999). Today, more and more companies have integrated these norms into their business practices including their risk management, even though their compliance records still vary enormously.

But how can firms then turn into norm entrepreneurs? Of course, the incorporation of environmental and human rights standards into their practices does not turn firms into charities. Their business is still doing business, as Milton Friedman's famous dictum suggested. However, companies increasingly realize that their markets are socially embedded and that their customers care about these issues. As footwear companies such as Nike learned the hard way, their American and European customers did not want to buy sneakers and running shoes produced with child labor in the Philippines. Moreover, more and more pension funds have started investing in companies that conform to certain social standards or are listed in various social indices such as the Dow Jones Sustainability Index. In other words, market mechanisms are used to induce companies into compliance with human rights and environmental norms.

As a result, reputational concerns about socially accepted behavior induce firms to take norms more seriously. Norm compliance can then turn into a strategic advantage in competitive markets. This is where companies transform into norm entrepreneurs. A study of South African firms has documented these mechanisms (Börzel *et al.*, 2010). Once again, there is nothing altruistic about this behavior. In fact, norm promotion becomes a matter of self-interest, since it pays off if a firm can set the industry standard with regard to environmental or human rights standards. Under particular circumstances, companies might actually promote rather than oppose higher regulatory standards, trying to turn norm compliance into a competitive advantage.

In the end, firms still remain firms, and NGOs remain advocacy groups. However, since neither of them are dummies, their social practices might actually converge to a larger extent than most scholars would have expected. This volume documents these effects with regard to NGOs from a rational choice perspective. A social constructivist account of firms becoming norm entrepreneurs has yet to be written.

References

Adler, E. 1997. Seizing the Middle Ground. Constructivism in World Politics. *European Journal of International Relations*, **3**(3): 319–363.

2002. Constructivism in International Relations. In W. Carlsnaes, B. Simmons, and T. Risse (eds.), *Handbook of International Relations*. London: Sage.

Boli, J. and G. M. Thomas (eds.). 1999. *Constructing World Culture. International Nongovernmental Organizations Since 1875*. Stanford University Press.

Börzel, T. A., A. Héritier, N. Kranz, and C. Thauer. 2010. Racing to the Top? The Regulatory Competition of Firms in Areas of Limited Statehood. In T. Risse (ed.), *Governing Without a State? Policies and Politics in Areas of Limited Statehood*. New York: Columbia University Press

Coase, R. H. 1960. The Problem of Social Cost. *Journal of Law and Economics*, **3**: 1–44.

Finnemore, M. and K. Sikkink. 1998. International Norm Dynamics and Political Change. *International Organization*, **52**(4): 887–917.

Flohr, A., L. Rieth, L. Schwindenhammer, S. Wolf, and K. Wolf. 2010. *The Role of Business in Global Governance*. Houndmills, Basingstoke: Palgrave Macmillan.

Jepperson, R., A. Wendt, and P. J. Katzenstein. 1996. Norms, Identity, and Culture in National Security. In P. J. Katzenstein (ed.), *The Culture of National Security: Norms and Identity in World Politics*. New York: Columbia University Press.

Katzenstein, P. J. (ed.). 1996. *The Culture of National Security. Norms and Identity in World Politics*. New York: Columbia University Press.

Keck, M. E. and K. Sikkink. 1998. *Activists Beyond Borders. Advocacy Networks in International Politics*. Ithaca, NY: Cornell University Press.

Keohane, R. O. 1984. *After Hegemony. Cooperation and Discord in the World Political Economy*. Princeton University Press.

1989. *International Institutions and State Power*. Boulder, CO: Westview Press.

Kitschelt, H. P. 1986. Political Opportunity Structures and Political Protest: Anti-Nuclear Movements in Four Democracies. *British Journal of Political Science*, **16**(1): 57–85.

Krasner, S. D. (ed.). 1983. *International Regimes*. Ithaca, NY: Cornell University Press.

Kratochwil, F. 1989. *Rules, Norms, and Decisions*. Cambridge University Press.

Kratochwil, F. and J. G. Ruggie. 1986. International Organization: A State of the Art on an Art of the State. *International Organization*, **40**(4): 753–775.

March, J. G. and J. P. Olsen. 1998. The Institutional Dynamics of International Political Orders. *International Organization*, **52**(4): 943–969.

North, D. C. 1986. The New Institutional Economics. *Journal of Institutional and Theoretical Economics*, **142**: 230–237.

Oye, K. A. (ed.). 1986. *Cooperation Under Anarchy*. Princeton University Press.

Prakash, A. 2000. *Greening the Firm: The Politics of Corporate Environmentalism*. Cambridge University Press.

Prakash, A. and M. Potoski. 2006. Racing to the Bottom? Trade, Environmental Governance, and ISO 14001. *American Journal of Political Science*, **50**(2): 350–364.

2007. Investing Up: FDI and the Cross-Country Diffusion of ISO 14001 Management Systems. *International Studies Quarterly*, **51**(3): 723–744.

Price, R. (ed.). 2008. *Moral Limit and Possibility in World Politics*. Cambridge University Press.

Risse, T. 2000. The Power of Norms versus the Norms of Power: Transnational Civil Society and Human Rights. In A. Florini (ed.), *The Third Force. The Rise of Transnational Civil Society*. Tokyo and Washington, DC: Japan Center for International Exchange and Carnegie Endowment for International Peace.

Risse, T., S. C. Ropp, and K. Sikkink (eds.). 1999. *The Power of Human Rights: International Norms and Domestic Change*. Cambridge University Press.

Risse-Kappen, T. 1995a. Bringing Transnational Relations Back In: Introduction. In T. Risse-Kappen (ed.), *Bringing Transnational Relations Back In: Non-state Actors, Domestic Structures and International Institutions*. Cambridge University Press.

(ed.) 1995b. *Bringing Transnational Relations Back In: Non-State Actors, Domestic Structures, and International Institutions*. Cambridge University Press.

Sikkink, K. 1993. Human Rights, Principled Issue Networks, and Sovereignty in Latin America. *International Organization*, **47**(3): 411–441.

Smith, J., C. Chatfield, and R. Pagnucco (eds.). 1997. *Transnational Social Movements and Global Politics: Solidarity Beyond the State*. Syracuse University Press.

Tarrow, S. 1996. States and Opportunities: The Political Structuring of Social Movements. In D. McAdam, J. D. Mc Carthy, and M. N. Zald (eds.), *Comparative Perspectives on Social Movements. Political Opportunities, Mobilizing Structures, and Cultural Framings*. Cambridge University Press.

Wöbse, A.-K. 2004. Die Brent Spar-Kampagne. Plattform für diverse Wahrheiten. In F. Uekötter and J. Hohensee (eds.), *Wird Kassandra heiser? Die Geschichte falscher Ökoalarme*. Wiesbaden: Franz Steiner Verlag.

12 Conclusions and future research: rethinking advocacy organizations

Mary Kay Gugerty and Aseem Prakash

This concluding chapter summarizes the key findings from the empirical chapters and identifies issues for future research. The scope of this volume is ambitious. Theoretically, we make the case that the collective action perspective presents an analytically novel and useful way to think about advocacy organizations. In doing so, we suggest that advocacy organizations and their networks, very much like firms, seek to fulfill both normative concerns and instrumental objectives, face challenges of collective action, and compete as well as collaborate with other advocacy actors that function in the same issue area. Empirically, we employ the collective action approach across a range of cases to study how advocacy organizations emerge, how they organize themselves, and how they choose their tactics.

Advocacy being a collective endeavor, we model advocacy NGOs as composite actors pursuing collective action toward potentially contested goals. While advocacy organizations are not profit-oriented, they systematically and rationally pursue policy goals, such as getting their preferred issues on public agendas, reforming policy, and shaping policy implementation. Importantly, some of them might pursue instrumental goals which create excludable benefits for their key constituents (Sell and Prakash, 2004). The empirical cases demonstrate the usefulness of the firm analogy to uncover and explain anomalies that the extant advocacy NGO literature has had difficulty in explaining, such as when and why advocacy groups do not collaborate, and why human rights organizations might choose to ignore the most egregious abuses and focus instead on lesser problems.

Our approach challenges the distinction often made in the literature (Keck and Sikkink, 1998) between NGOs and firms, the former pursuing principled objectives and the latter pursing instrumental objectives. Instead of providing analytical clarity to the study of advocacy, this distinction tends to assume that NGOs are "good" and "selfless" actors pursuing worthy causes. Thus NGO scholarship has tended to follow a template in which good NGOs motivated by normative concerns are able to discipline bad governments (or firms) motivated by instrumental concerns. Such normative biases tend to influence empirical enquiry as well. Consequently, the NGO scholarship tends to suffer from two types of selection bias: a focus on NGOs as the champions of "good" (liberal) causes, and concentration on successful cases of advocacy. Truncating the dependent variable to focus only on successful cases of advocacy hampers the efforts of scholars to explain when and why advocacy strategies work.[1] In contrast, the collective action perspective supports the study of advocacy on behalf of "good" as well as "bad" norms, and allows scholars to explain both failures and successes in advocacy efforts.

We hope that this volume will motivate scholars to carefully identify similarities and differences across (and within) various forms of collective action. While firms and NGOs share analytical similarities, the modes of collective action employed by each are likely to differ. Understanding why and when they diverge requires that scholars move beyond the clichéd slogans of principled versus instrumental actors; it requires careful theorizing and empirical testing. Recognizing the mixed motivations of all policy actors is an important first step in developing a systematic program to study the role of ideas *and* interests (as opposed to ideas *versus* interests) in politics. By so doing, we seek in this volume to bridge the constructivist–rationalist divide in the fields of international relations and comparative politics. Further, as echoed by Risse (Chapter 11), we hope this volume will provoke scholars to think how the study of advocacy NGOs can inform the study of firms; this is particularly important given the increased emphasis on corporate responsibility in recent years.

Key lessons

Agency matters: the role of entrepreneurs and strategy

The role of entrepreneurs and leaders in organizing collective action has been recognized by scholars interested in studying firms. While Coase (1937) and Williamson (1986) suggest that firms emerge in response to market failures, Barnard (1938) and Miller (1992) point to the important role of leaders and entrepreneurs in the emergence of a firm. Thus, an important finding in the literature is that market or institutional opportunities can motivate entrepreneurial activity, leading to the emergence of an advocacy organization (Risse also makes a similar point in

---

[1] The social movement literature has done a much better job because some scholars now employ the same theoretical constructs to systematically study counter movements which often propound illiberal objectives (Lo, 1982).

Chapter 11). Echoing Salisbury (1969), who points to the importance of entrepreneurs in the formation of interest groups, Chapter 2 by McGee Young on the emergence of the National Resources Defense Council (NRDC) suggests that the formation of advocacy organizations occurs when political entrepreneurs perceive a market for a given advocacy product that they can "sell" to willing buyers. In the case of the NRDC, political entrepreneurs had available a set of strategic repertoires in the form of litigation expertise and the Ford Foundation was a willing buyer. These entrepreneurs derived individual professional benefits (arguably, expressive benefits as well, à la Salisbury) from organizing collective action in pursuit of a public good. Thus, incentives for leadership and entrepreneurship are important factors explaining where, why, and how advocacy organizations get established. In addition, a key lesson that emerges from this chapter is that the institutional context and the distribution of resources – along with the skills and repertoires of leaders – shape strategy: litigation was a lower cost strategy in which NRDC entrepreneurs had a comparative advantage in an era in which public support for environmental activism was growing.

The role of leadership is also important in mitigating collective action issues in the context of religious groups. Gill and Pfaff (Chapter 3) highlight how accountability and responsibility deficits impact religious organizations' abilities to mobilize members, and how leadership is critical in mitigating these challenges. Given that the "products" created by religious groups tend to have the characteristics of credence goods (which are marked by severe information problems), the credibility of the group's messenger takes on central importance. Indeed, leaders need to exhibit behaviors and provide signals to assure their members that they can be trusted with donations and that they will not abuse the volunteer labor that they request. Thus many religions require costly actions on the part of leaders, including vows of chastity or poverty. Gill and Pfaff suggest that these ideological signals serve a strategic function as much as principled goals.

Advocacy organizations exert agency in the choice of strategy. While advocacy organizations are not dummies (Risse, Chapter 11), strategic concerns can and do trump normative or ideological considerations. How do advocacy organizations decide which issues to agitate on? Clifford Bob's chapter points out that if the "moral theory of advocacy" were to hold, international advocates should support causes primarily on the basis of the seriousness of the abuses. Echoing the criticisms of the revisionist school, Bob suggests that the moral theory fails to explain the disconnect between aggrieved groups' needs and international advocates' activism. He attributes this disconnect to several factors, including barriers to entering the human rights market that prevent the most deprived from participating. He suggests that advocacy organizations, as actors necessarily concerned with material survival (as well as political missions), pay attention to the costs of support and, all else equal, intervene first where these costs are lowest. On this count, he echoes the points made by Young (Chapter 2), Henderson (Chapter 10), and Bloodgood (Chapter 4) about the crucial role that the cost of advocacy plays in shaping organizational decisions about supply.

External structures and the choice of advocacy strategy

Institutions play an important role in shaping the costs and benefits of strategies advocacy organizations adopt. An important lesson is that instead of being "outsiders" acting against the current order or excluded by the political opportunity structure, NGOs are often the product of the political system and are sometimes key beneficiaries of the rules that govern the system. While the extant literature views states and international organizations primarily as the targets of advocacy organizations, Sarah Henderson (Chapter 10) emphasizes how states shape the supply of advocacy via the rules within which domestic and international advocacy organizations operate. She suggests that national regulations influence the costs of NGO organizing, the incentives available to attract members and financing, and available legal identities, in much the same way that such regulation affects the formation and structure of firms. Thus, government-supplied rules raise or lower barriers for the emergence of advocacy organizations. This is particularly true for Russia in the Putin era (from 1999) where the government has actively sought to reshape the advocacy sector, in contrast with the earlier Yeltsin era (1991–1999). Indeed, Henderson argues that the Putin administration is developing an "import substitution" model of advocacy whereby domestic institutions are designed to weaken the influence of foreign donors on the advocacy sector. This allows the state to create a context favoring advocacy work that aligns with the state's view of the national interest. The idea is to encourage "patriotic" firms which work alongside the state, instead of in opposition to it, as assumed in the adversarial model of advocacy. To the extent that the state controls important resources or authorizes NGO activity, organizations may have trouble resisting state pressure and sticking to core principles. Instead of looking at state versus civil society and claiming the autonomy of the civil society from the government (hence the term, non-governmental organizations), arguably scholars need to examine closely how the civil society is shaped by state policies.

The importance of the institutional context in shaping the supply of advocacy is further examined by Alexander Cooley and James Ron (Chapter 8). Examining the international humanitarian sector, they show how the marketization of the institutional context via the use of competitive tenders and renewable contracting by donors shapes the strategies of humanitarian organizations. The case studies of transnational humanitarian organizations operating in the Democratic Republic of Congo and Bosnia reveal how competition for limited donor funds leads humanitarian organizations to make choices which privilege the fiscal interests of the organization over the interests of intended beneficiaries. In this scenario, even if one assumes that advocacy groups are motivated by normative goals alone, the organizational DNA of a typical NGO is not strong enough to withstand constant pressure over time from the institutional context. Consequently, transnational humanitarian organizations tend to function like firms, responding to market opportunities in greater measure than ideological commitments. Gill and Pfaff (Chapter 3) also emphasize the corrupting influence of external institutions and point out that advocacy groups operating in "protected" markets that rely upon the government or foundations to meet their financial obligations invariably lose the organizational connection to the people that they need the most: the ones that believe in their mission.

The relevant institutional context within which advocacy organizations negotiate might operate at the international level (Cooley and Ron, Chapter 8), at the national level (Young, Chapter 2; Henderson, Chapter 10; Bloodgood, Chapter 4) or in specific venues within a country (Pralle, Chapter 7). The ways in which national regulations shape the supply of advocacy in a given policy market is examined by Elizabeth Bloodgood in Chapter 4. While Henderson examines the case of a newly democratizing country with little previous experience of anti-statist advocacy politics, Bloodgood examines how national regulations within the OECD countries shape the location decisions of international advocacy organizations. Taken together, these chapters emphasize the crucial role of *both* agency and structure in shaping advocacy. As in firms, entrepreneurs play a crucial role in incurring the start-up costs and establishing advocacy organizations. Their tasks are facilitated if national or institutional context provides the necessary resources for their activities. National-level regulations, in particular, are crucial because they can shape the costs of start-up and operations, restrict the domain of activity or fundraising, or even potentially cut off resources from the international context, as Henderson demonstrates. Ironically, an important implication is that the capacity of an advocacy organization to initiate a boomerang effect (Keck and Sikkink, 1998) might be contingent on the host government allowing any such advocacy organizations in the first place (Khagram, 2004).[2] A strong government not sympathetic to international influence can create sizable barriers for the working of advocacy networks.

Institutions are not given

There might be scope for advocacy organizations to choose the institutional context in which they function even within a given domain. While traditional literature focuses on how advocacy organizations may seek to skirt the national government and promote their cause abroad (Keck and Sikkink, 1998), venue-shopping may occur within a national context as well. Sarah Pralle (Chapter 7) suggests that, like firms, advocacy organizations make strategic choices about policy venues. Such decisions require organizations to undertake a careful market analysis in terms of opportunities and threats, market size, entry barriers, competitor profile, etc. In general, Pralle suggests that as rational actors, advocacy organizations are likely to search for venues that offer the greatest possibility of reaching their goals.

Pralle points to the limitations of extreme versions of the collective action perspective which might lead scholars to "black-box" advocacy groups,[3] assuming that groups will have undifferentiated responses to the same external stimuli. She identifies some conditions under which principles are likely to dominate instrumental incentives in the choice of advocacy venues. When organizations have a strong ideological orientation and feel pressure to occupy a certain policy niche, more instrumental venue-shopping behaviors may be blunted. But when organizations have high organizational capacity and are more pragmatist in nature, organizational identity will be less tied to particular strategy and more strategic venue-shopping behavior is likely to occur. Her chapter shows how the collective action approach will need to systematically incorporate organizational history, mission, identity, and leadership of the advocacy organization in order to make more systematic predictions about the choice of specific advocacy strategies and to illuminate when normative concerns might be more likely to prevail over pressures for more instrumental behavior.

---

[2] The importance of the "watchman" function of domestic governments comes out clearly in the context of international trade. Governments that allow international trade make themselves vulnerable to trade-induced pressures to reform labor laws (Greenhill, Mosley, and Prakash, 2009) or to environmental issues (Cao and Prakash, 2010). Such pressures are least effective in the case of North Korea and Myanmar where the governments control foreign trade, thereby leaving few opportunities for advocacy groups located abroad to influence their domestic practices, policies, and norms by trade pressures.

[3] Kenneth Waltz's (1979) "billiard ball" analogy falls in this category.

Participation in networks and coalitions

Alliances and networks are salient routes for organizing business operations as well as advocacy. By bringing together actors with converging preferences on some issues but diverging preferences on others, such organizational forms sometimes accentuate collective action issues. The focus on advocacy campaigns that predominates in the current literature tends to "black-box" the individual components of advocacy networks, obscuring whether these components systematically differ in their strategies or motivations for joining such advocacy networks. This is an important reason why collective action issues, which are partially predicated on varying preferences of the constituent units, have been less considered in the traditional advocacy literature.[4]

The volume presents two chapters examining advocacy organizations' participation in coalitions, both of which suggest that variation in organizational characteristics affect the propensity to engage in advocacy via alliances and networks. Lecy, Mitchell, and Schmitz (Chapter 9) explore how US-based transnational advocacy group leaders view the business of advocacy and how they understand the role of partnerships and collaborations in advancing their goals. The authors find that advocacy organizations are not exclusively principled or self-interested; like firms, they have mixed motives and employ a range of advocacy strategies. Indeed, Lecy, Mitchell, and Schmitz suggest that transnational advocacy organizations should be understood as maximizing agents, just like firms, but with advocacy impact, rather than profits, in their objective function. However, this chapter points as well to some limitations of employing the firm analogy. The authors suggest that, unlike firms with clear hierarchies, advocacy organization leaders tend not to make hard distinctions between internal and external actors (but see Carpenter, 2007).[5] Most of the NGOs in their sample that identify themselves as advocacy organizations claim to pursue their goals in collaborative ways and routinely build transnational networks to augment their voices. Advocacy strategies in multiproduct and service NGOs appear to be less collaborative. As the

---

[4] There is a widespread tendency to claim that advocacy actors work in networks which are "horizontal" (and therefore democratic) while firms and governments function as organized hierarchies (and therefore authoritarian). Network forms for organizations may or may not be horizontal. Even in ostensibly horizontal networks, actors controlling critical nodes can exercise disproportionate influence. Finally, it is empirically incorrect to claim that advocacy networks are horizontal; the literature on power asymmetries rooted in the dependence of Southern NGOs on Northern NGOs is a case in point.

[5] This assertion is empirically doubtful. The vast literature on networks, strategic alliances, commodity chains, and supply chains suggests that firms typically conduct some of their operations via networks, not as hierarchically organized entities.

authors note, understanding these choices requires better data on the internal organizational structure and decision-making, since advocacy organizations comprise a variety of types of organization, even within the transnational development NGO sector.

Barakso (Chapter 6) suggests another basis for understanding decisions about coalition participation. While she agrees with Lecy, Mitchell, and Schmitz (Chapter 9) regarding the propensity of advocacy actors to work through coalitions, she suggests an explanation rooted in the analysis of costs and benefits. Organizations with a diverse repertoire of advocacy tactics may find participation in coalitions less costly than organizations whose brand is predicated on a specific repertoire. Furthermore, she finds that advocacy actors remain alert to competitiveness concerns even when they decide to work alongside other advocates.

Organization maintenance and survival

All the empirical chapters presented in this volume highlight the imperatives of organizational survival with which advocacy actors must contend. The acquisition of material and reputational resources are critical to this objective. Anticipating donors' preferences and ensuring that the organization works in ways that cohere with these preferences becomes one way to ensure organizational survival, a point made by Cooley and Ron in Chapter 8. Advocacy organizations often exert influence in proportion to their numbers; organizations must therefore constantly pay attention to the need to mobilize recruits. This is also a constant concern, as Gill and Pfaff illustrate in Chapter 3, of religious organizations. Religious groups are interesting because they consciously seek to attract and retain members and to limit free riding and shirking. Gill and Pfaff illustrate how early Christians, Protestants in Latin America, and Muslims in the United States have all consciously used mobilization strategies designed to enhance organizational credibility and reward members through the provision of selective collective benefits. Secular advocacy groups face similar challenges; indeed, the notion of selective benefits introduced by Olson (1965) points to challenges in recruitment in the absence of excludable benefits of membership. Even religious groups are not immune from this challenge.

Another way to encourage organizational survival is to brand the advocacy "product." Maryann Barakso (Chapter 6) suggests that, like corporations, advocacy organizations develop distinctive brand identities as a means of differentiating themselves to internal and external audiences in a highly competitive market (a point also made by Pralle in Chapter 7). For both firms and advocacy organizations, branding facilitates the attraction and retention of investors and customers. Note that branding can take place via the attributes of the product (coffee rich in aroma) as well as the attributes of the process that created that product (such as fair trade coffee) (also see the discussion on the branding strategies of NRDC by Young in Chapter 2). Branding requires consistency in product and tactics. Barakso shows that advocacy organizations, in order to brand their distinctive advocacy processes, tend to adopt and maintain consistent tactics.

Future research

Several themes emerge from the empirical chapters regarding the limitations of the collective action approach in the study of advocacy organizations. This is useful because it helps us to identify the scope conditions of the argument our volume seeks to make. First, some neoclassical theories of the firm tend to "black-box" organizations, focusing on how the organizations respond to the incentives created by the external environment. While behavioral theories of the firm have paid attention to such internal factors (Cyert and March, 1963), the traditional advocacy literature, quite surprisingly, has followed the neoclassical template by ignoring organizational theory and organizational politics. As actors functioning in competitive, resource-scarce environments, both firms and advocacy organizations surely need to be sensitive to the external environment. However, the internal processes by which such signals are interpreted might differ across organizations (Prakash, 2000). Consequently, both firms and advocacy organizations functioning in similar institutional environments might adopt different strategies on account of their organization histories and the idiosyncrasies of their leaders. Thus, future studies on advocacy organizations, while drawing on "rational" theories of firms, should also engage with theories of organizational behavior and leadership that investigate how internal decisions are conceptualized and made. Indeed, like firms, advocacy organizations are complex actors with both instrumental and normative objectives. Their strategies are shaped by factors both internal and external to the organization (Child, 1972). Yet, instead of suggesting that everything matters, future research needs to pay close attention to the conditions under which one set of factors (external environment versus internal factors) is likely to serve as the dominant influence on organizational strategies.

The second theme pertains to the issue of accountability deficits (Gugerty and Prakash, 2010). Organizations that tend to rely on non-members (governments or foundations) for resources are less likely truly to represent the aspirations of their constituents. In some cases, this might eventually limit their effectiveness. Simply put, organizations that claim to be acting on behalf of the public must find ways actively to engage with the public, and draw resources from the public. Dependence on members for resources is an important way of ensuring that organizations have sustained incentives for such engagements, It follows that charitable foundations that fund advocacy might in the long run be hurting the actors they seek to support (but see Bartley, 2007). Similar issues have been raised in the context of foreign aid: excessive reliance on donor funding may cause governments to lose connection with their own citizens or NGOs to shift strategies away from their original constituency (Gugerty and Kremer, 2008). This issue of corporate governance needs to be investigated systematically in the context of advocacy organizations as well. In its current formulation, the collective choice approach tends to treat material resources as fungible and equivalent in influencing the choice of strategies. However, there may be systematic differences in how the source of resources shapes organizational strategies and ultimately advocacy efficacy. Advocacy scholars could probably take guidance from the "varieties of capitalism" literature in this regard. Reliance on members for resources, as opposed to outside foundations or funders, may create very different patterns of accountability that require a different set of strategies. Gill and Pfaff (Chapter 3) argue that such reliance on members creates stronger, more effective organizations, while Young (Chapter 2) demonstrates the advantages of a more insider strategy in emergent organizations. These differences may relate in part to the nature of the advocacy product produced.

To gain analytical clarity in this volume, we have subsumed a variety of organizations pursuing a range of objectives under the head of advocacy. Arguably, different sectors are structured differently, and this may systematically influence organizational emergence, structure, and strategy, as Lecy, Mitchell, and Schmitz note in Chapter 9. The collective choice perspective will need to pay more attention to the idiosyncrasies of different advocacy markets and how this shapes the incentive structures facing advocacy actors. One way, as Bob suggests in Chapter 5, is to look at competitive versus non-competitive markets. One might differentiate markets by types of product: excludable private and club goods versus non-excludable public goods. Arguably, the ability to mobilize resources from members might be higher when organizations advocate for excludable goods, although it is not clear how free riding is mitigated. More broadly, future work must systematically connect resource acquisition with choice of strategies.

This leads to the next set of issues pertaining to changes in the environment. As actors committed to organizational survival, firms and advocacy organizations can be expected to respond to institutional pressures. It is likely that (large) firms[6] possess greater resources than advocacy organizations, which they can use to anticipate changes in political, social, and economic environments, to seek to reverse them, and if unsuccessful, to carry out adaptations to those changes. Moreover firms' stakeholders may be less attached to the particular process by which production takes place, whereas advocacy organizations, as Barakso shows, often highlight their strategies as part of their product. Moreover, commitments made through participation in coalitions and networks may further limit options for adaptability. Given that advocacy organizations themselves differ greatly in size and in their embeddedness in networks, future research should exploit this variation to understand better how advocacy actors respond to and shape their environments.

Another critical distinction is that firms do not employ volunteers. As Risse points out (Chapter 11), the recruitment of volunteers or below-market-wage workers can be viewed as a distinctive feature of nonprofit organizations. Many advocacy organizations, including relatively high-profile groups, rely substantially on member volunteers and interns. Whereas firms can fire those who fail to adopt changes, or adopt new production technologies, advocacy organizations are often constrained in this respect. And to the extent that the particular strategies or brands of advocacy organizations play a role in recruiting workers or volunteers willing to work for below-market wages, advocacy organizations may be further constrained in changing these repertoires, a testable hypothesis that future work should consider.

The variation in the composition and structure of organizations engaged in advocacy provides an important opportunity for future research, as Lecy, Mitchell, and Schmitz (Chapter 9) illustrate. Some advocacy organizations are single-issue actors, while others subsume advocacy activities under a wide umbrella of activities and strategies. Does such diversification result in more or less scope to pursue ideological objectives? In many sectors NGOs that traditionally engaged largely in service delivery face greater pressure to engage in rights-based activity which is likely to increase the salience of advocacy for all organizations. At the same time, new financing strategies that include partnership with corporate entities for 'social entrepreneurship' and 'cause-based marketing' may create new pressures on advocacy strategies. Thus, the diversity of organizations engaged in advocacy is likely to grow.

---

[6] In reality, market economies are populated predominantly by small firms which typically do not have the resources for individual lobbying. Even in a developed economy such as the United States, 99 percent of all independent enterprises employ fewer than 500 people (http://economics.about.com/od/smallbigbusiness/a/us_business. htm, accessed November 10, 2009).

All of this suggests that future advocacy work in the collective action tradition should develop more explicit theories about how advocacy actors make decisions about internal structure and external strategy. The transaction cost version of the theory of firm, rooted in certain behavioral assumptions, tends to suggest that firms are hierarchically organized in response to market failures, in particular the inability to secure contractual agreements over a full range of inputs and resources (Williamson, 1986). More recent literature, however, highlights the important role of alliances and networks in business operations in which relationships are not governed by explicit contracts (Uzzi, 1996; Culpan, 2002; Sable and Zeitlin, 2004). This literature suggests that personal relationships and contacts among producers and suppliers help to structure production relationships, particularly in craft and project-based industries. Thus, firms both compete and cooperate with one another and may share resources, a curious phenomenon in light of the traditional view emphasizing competition over cooperation. Many firms are no longer organizations with clear boundaries, but a bundle of complex projects and interactions. In some industries, network ties have become so important that financial market analysts have begun to evaluate the quality of a firm's networks as part of their overall ratings strategy. Investigating the nature of specific ties, both formal and informal, among advocacy organizations engaged in collaborative relationships can help our understanding of how strategic decisions to collaborate are made. This would not only help to dispel overly limited notions about how firms operate but would also identify the conditions under which material interests or shared norms are more important in shaping collaborative strategies. We agree with Risse (Chapter 11) that scholars should examine not only how a study of firms informs the study of NGOs, but also how the study of NGOs informs the study of firms. We hope this collection will be viewed as an effort to build bridges between rationalist and constructivist scholars and aid the scholarly efforts to study collective actors – firms, NGOs, or governments – through a unified framework.

References

Barnard, C. 1938. *The Functions of an Executive*. Cambridge, MA: Harvard University Press.
Bartley, T. 2007. How Foundations Shape Social Movements. *Social Problems*, 54(3): 229–255.
Cao, X. and A. Prakash. 2010. Trade Competition and Domestic Pollution: A Panel Study, 1980–2003. *International Organization*, 64(3): 481–503.
Carpenter, C. 2007. Studying Issue (Non) Adoption in Transnational Advocacy Networks. *International Organization*, 61(3): 643–667.

Child, J. 1972. Organizational Structure, Environment, and Performance. *Sociology*, **6**: 1–22.

Culpan, R. 2002. *Global Business Alliances*. Westport, CT: Quorum Books.

Coase, R. 1937. The Nature of the Firm. *Economica*, **4**: 386–405.

Cyert, R. and J. March. 1963. *A Behavioral Theory of the Firm*, Englewood Cliffs, NJ: Prentice Hall.

Greenhill, B., L. Mosley, and A. Prakash. 2009. Trade and Labor Rights: A Panel Study, 1986-2002. *American Political Science Review*, **103**(4): 669–690.

Gugerty, M. and M. Kremer. 2008. Outside Funding and the Dynamics of Participation in Community Organizations. *American Journal of Political Science*, **52**(3): 585–602.

Gugerty, M. K. and A. Prakash. 2010. *Voluntary Regulations of NGOs and Nonprofits: An Accountability Club Framework*. Cambridge University Press.

Keck, M. and K. Sikkink. 1998. *Activists Beyond Borders*. Ithaca, NY: Cornell University Press.

Khagram, S. 2004. *Dams and Development*. Ithaca, NY: Cornell University Press.

Lo, C. 1982. Counter Movements and Conservative Movements in the Contemporary U.S. *Annual Review of Sociology*, **8**: 107–134.

Miller, G. 1992. *Managerial Dilemmas: Political Economy of Hierarchy*. Cambridge University Press.

Olson, M. 1965. *The Logic of Collective Action*. Cambridge, MA: Harvard University Press.

Prakash, A. 2000. *Greening the Firm*. Cambridge University Press.

Sable, C. and J. Zeitlin. 2004. Neither Modularity or Relational Contracting: Inter-Firm Collaboration in the New Economy. *Enterprise and Society*, **5**(3): 388–403.

Salisbury, R. 1969. An Exchange Theory of Interest Groups. *Midwest Journal of Political Science*, **13**(1): 1–32.

Sell, S. and A. Prakash. 2004. Using Ideas Strategically. *International Studies Quarterly*, **48**(1): 143–175.

Uzzi, B. 1996. The Sources and Consequences of Embeddedness for the Economic Performance of Firms: The Network Effect. *American Sociological Review*, **61**(4): 674–698.

Waltz, K. 1979. *Theory of International Politics*. New York: McGraw-Hill.

Williamson, O. 1986. *The Economic Institutions of Capitalism*. New York: Free Press.

Index

accountability, 11–19, 249, 289,
    297, 303
    enforcement of, 14
    external, 13
    multiple levels of, 13
Adams, John, 44, 48, 52
advocacy, definition, 1
advocacy organizations, 1–25, 33–34, 237,
    283–292, 306; *see also* international
    NGOs, non-governmental
    organizations, transnational NGOs
    access to the policymaking process, 94,
        191, 196, 256
    authority of, 39, 289, 290
    behaving like firms, 299
    benefits for constituents, 5; collective
        goods, 35, 36; excludable benefits, 5,
        38, 295; intangible, 34; material
        benefits, 5–6; partially excludable,
        38; purposive/expressive benefits,
        6; solidarity, 6
    boundaries of, 7–10
    choices of venue, 193, 198
    constituencies of, 5
    corporate governance of, 304
    donors' preferences, 258, 302
    emergence of, 4, 7–10, 20, 33, 34–37, 53,
        230, 297
    evaluation of, 7
    expertise in, 39, 191, 286
    as firms, 3, 229–249; motivations,
        6; strategies of, 6; *see also* firms
    funding, source and type of, 18
    future research on, 295–306
    human capital, 39
    ideological values and orientation, 192
    institutional and political constraints, 287
    institutional context of, 39, 91–127,
        298–300, 304
    instrumental concerns of, 4, 5, 7, 19, 230
    legal identities of, 91; types of, 109
    legitimacy of, 289

location decisions, 94, 299; access to the
    policymaking process, 94; and
    economic incentives, 94, 127; factors in
    96; political opportunities, 95; and
    regulation, 122, 123–127
motivation of, 286, 296, 301
and networks, 15, 17, 23, 243, 285,
    301–302; *see also* transnational
    advocacy networks
normative concerns of, 4, 7, 31, 295
"one-shotter" organizations, and venue-
    shopping, 195, 305
organization maintenance and survival, 7,
    31–55, 230, 258, 302–303
organizational development, 37–40, 52, 54
participation in coalitions, 163, 195,
    301–302
participation of members, 34
and patrons, 53
perceptions of, 155
policy goals, 178, 199, 200, 230, 295
power of, 151
principled beliefs of, 5, 19, 159, 194, 205,
    283, 286–292
professional staff, 34
relationships with governments, 96, 97
reputation, 289, 290, 291, 292, 302
resources of, 31, 95, 110, 157, 194, 297,
    303; sources of funds, 287, 303, 304
selection of issues, 15, 134, 138–139, 142,
    149, 192, 235
"stickiness" of internal practice, 160, 191
tactical orientation, 166, 167; analysis of,
    165–167, 172–173; and brand
    identities, 158–161, 164; diversity of,
    171; factors in, 162; insider versus
    outsider strategies, 158, 161–164, 166,
    169; and the organization's identity,
    157; and participation in coalitions,
    157, 164, 169–171; risk of changing,
    157; stability of, 157, 160–161,
    167–168, 171, 172

308